1001 CURIOUS THINGS

$35.

1001 CURIOUS THINGS

YE OLDE CURIOSITY SHOP AND NATIVE AMERICAN ART

KATE C. DUNCAN

UNIVERSITY OF WASHINGTON PRESS
SEATTLE AND LONDON

To my mother, who has patiently encouraged this book, and my father, who would have also enjoyed it.

This book was published with the assistance of the Getty Grant Program. Additional support was received from Ye Olde Curiosity Shop.

Printed in Hong Kong

Endsheets are an aerial shot of Seattle in 1924, with a handwritten note by Standley pointing to the "Colman Dock Tower." Photograph by the Pierson Photo Co.

Library of Congress Cataloging-in-Publication Data
Duncan, Kate C.
1001 curious things : Ye Olde Curiosity Shop and Native American art / Kate C. Duncan.
p. cm.
Includes bibliographical references and index.
ISBN 0-295-98010-9 (alk. paper)
1. Ethnological museums and collections—United States—History. 2. Standley, Joseph E.—Ethnological collections. 3. Ye Olde Curiosity Shop (Seattle, Wash.)—History. 4. Indian art—Collectors and collecting—Washington (State)—Seattle—History. 5. Indians of North America—Antiquities—Collectors and collecting—Washington (State)—Seattle—History. 6. Seattle (Wash.)—Antiquities. I. Title: One thousand one curious things. II. Title: One thousand and one curious things. III. Title.
GN36.U62 S439 2001
305.8'009797'772075—dc21 00-64824

The paper used in this publication is acid-free and recycled from 10 percent post-consumer and at least 50 percent pre-consumer waste. It meets the minimum requirements of American National Standard for Information Sciences–Permanence of Paper for Printed Library Materials, ANSI Z39.48-1984.

CONTENTS

Acknowledgments

THIS BOOK COULD NOT HAVE HAPPENED WITHOUT THE CHEERFUL assistance, encouragement, and patience of the family of Joseph E. Standley. I am especially indebted to Standley's grandson, Joe James, who opened shop records to me and cooperated in every way. He has answered innumerable questions and worked closely with me, dating photographs, piecing together chronologies, and recalling events in the shop's history. Other family members who have assisted are Joe's sister Emabelle Holt and her husband Richard, Joe's wife Janie, their son Andy and his wife Debbie (who now run Ye Olde Curiosity Shop), and their daughter Tammy (who runs the sister Waterfront Landmark shop).

For me, one of the pleasures of engaging in scholarship is the gracious generosity of my colleagues. In researching this book, almost every photograph, guest book notation, and story scribbled on a scrap of paper contained the seeds of a research project. The explication of those items I have chosen to work with could never have been accomplished without the generous assistance of many people. For their observations and information I am indebted to Jonathan Batkin, June Bedford, Burton Benedict, Margaret Blackman, Patty Blankenship, John Bockstoce, Dorothy Burnham, Edmund Carpenter, Douglas Cole, Bob DeArmond, Frederica deLaguna, Paul Dorpat, Kristen Griffin, Barbara Hail, Suzanne Currelly Hamilton, Ann Hedlund, Bill Holm, Kathleen Howard, Dale Idiens, Carol Ivory, Jan Steinbright Jackson, Nancy Jackson, Jean Low, Sally McClendon, Carmen McKillop, John McKillop, Mardonna McKillop, Brant Mackley, Frank Norris, Reggie Peterson, Mary Polhemus, Joyce Price, Dorothy Jean Ray, Helma Swan, Millie Tapscott, Art Thompson, Bob Turner, Jauvanta Young Walker, Alan Wardwell, Peter Welsh, Barbara Williams, Ida Williams, and Victoria Wyatt.

My thanks also go to the scores of museums and institutions in North

America and Europe that answered questionnaires regarding Ye Olde Curiosity Shop, and to the many curators and archivists who assisted with specific collections and information. The individuals, museums, and archives in Alaska include Steve Hendrickson, Alaska State Museum, Juneau; Kay Shelton, Alaska State Library and Archives, Juneau; Diane Brenner and Walter Van Horn, Anchorage Museum of History and Art; Peter Corey, Sheldon Jackson Museum, Sitka; staff of the University Archives, University of Alaska, Anchorage; staff of the Rasmuson Library, University of Alaska, Fairbanks; and Aldona Jonaitis and Molly Lee at the University of Alaska Museum, Fairbanks. In Washington special assistance came from Rebecca Andrews, John Putnam, and Robin Wright, Burke Museum of Natural History and Culture, Seattle; Mary Schlick and Colleen Schafroth, Maryhill Museum, Goldendale; Janine Bowchuk, Makah Cultural and Research Center, Neah Bay; Steven C. Brown and Pam McClusky, Seattle Art Museum; Elaine Miller, Washington State Historical Society Archives; Lynette Miller, Washington State History Museum, Tacoma. Archivist Carolyn Marr, Museum of History and Industry, Seattle, and the staff of the Manuscripts, Special Collections, and University Archives, University of Washington Libraries, deserve very special thanks for assistance beyond the call of duty.

Inquiries beyond the Pacific Northwest were far-flung. I wish to thank Jonathan King, British Museum, London; Anita Ellis, Cincinnati Art Museum, Ohio; Gerald Streit, Grotto of the Redemption, West Bend, Iowa; David Allen, Esther Filer, and Nicky Levell, Horniman Museum, London; staff of the Huntington Library, Pasadena, California; Jeanne Merritt, Montclair Art Museum, New Jersey; Anne Spenser, Newark Museum, New Jersey; Nancy Rosoff, New York Historical Society; Michael Wright, Old Capitol Museum, Jackson, Mississippi; Alena Calendar and Jayne Lambert, Palmer College of Chiropractic, Davenport, Iowa; Bill Mercer, Portland Art Museum, Oregon; Bryan Kwapil, Public Museum of Grand Rapids, Michigan; Elaine Ambrosia, Ripley Museum, San Francisco, and Edward Meyer, Ripley Entertainment, Orlando, Florida; Cynthia Altman, National Trust for Historical Preservation, Nelson A. Rockefeller bequest, Pontico Historical area, New York; Martha Black, Alan Hoover, Grant Keddie, and Peter McNair, Royal British Columbia Museum, Victoria; Ken Lister, Trudy Nicks, and Arnie Sletterbach, Royal Ontario Museum, Toronto; and at the Smithsonian Institution, Duane King, Mary Jane Lentz, and Ramiro Matos, National Museum of the American Indian, and Candace Greene and Jane Walsh, National Museum of Natural History.

Students in my graduate and undergraduate seminars have helped me explore ideas and have assisted with my research and shared their own. At

Arizona State University I wish to thank Cricket Appel, Lissa Howe, Tricia Loscher, Courtney Raymond, and members of the Museum Group in the Department of Anthropology. At the University of Washington I am indebted to Amy Lowell Adams, Graham Boettcher, Katie Bunn-Marcuse, Sylvia Ferrari, Mark Freeman, Dawn Glinsmann, Silvia Koros, Mary Lane, Dickson Preston, Deborah Swan, and Carolyn Swope.

I am ever grateful to many others for their assistance, hospitality, occasional research, suggestions, and moral support for this project. My deepest thanks to my family, Anne Corbin, Nancy Corbin, and Gavin Duncan; and to my friends Susan Aldworth, Erik Bilello, Albert Feldmann, Jan Steinbright Jackson and Paul Jackson, Larissa Karnitsky, Virginia Kobler, and Turid and Ron Senungetuk. If I have forgotten anyone, I apologize, and to all, I thank you heartily.

Paul Schwartz spent many hours making negatives and prints from the original photographs and records of Ye Olde Curiosity Shop. His able assistance and friendship have been essential to the book's success. The manuscript has also benefited from the observations of colleagues who have graciously read parts or all of it. For this my sincerest thanks to Jonathan Batkin, Albert Feldmann, Barbara Hail, Bill Holm, Simon Ottenberg, and Ellen Wheat. At the University of Washington Press I am most grateful to editor in chief Naomi Pascal, who championed this project from its infancy, and to managing editor Julidta Tarver, copy editor Amy Smith Bell, and designer Patrick Barber of Marquand Books for their expert work.

With deep gratitude I acknowledge the funding that has made this book possible. It was researched and written with the support of a Fellowship for University Teachers from the National Endowment for the Humanities, and with research and sabbatical funding from Arizona State University through the Office of the Vice President for Research, the College of Fine Arts, and the School of Art. The Getty Foundation Trust and Ye Olde Curiosity Shop assisted in production costs.

Finally, if in my research if I have overlooked any museums with important collections from Ye Olde Curiosity Shop, I apologize and would love to hear from you.

Chronology

1854	Joseph Edward (J. E.) Standley is born on February 24 in Steubenville, Ohio.
CA. 1876	Standley establishes his own store in Denver, Colorado.
LATE 1899	The Standley family moves to Seattle.
LATE 1899–NOVEMBER 1901	Standley's Free Museum and Curio opens, located on Second Avenue and Pike Street.
NOVEMBER 1901–JUNE 1904	The Curio (later Standley's Curio) is located at 82 W. Madison, opposite Seattle's Grand Hotel.
1907	Standley's son Edward joins the shop.
1912	Russell James (later Standley's son-in-law) joins the shop.
JUNE 1904–FEBRUARY 1916	Ye Olde Curiosity Shop and Indian Curio (changed to Ye Olde Curiosity Shop ca. 1907) is located at 813 Railroad Avenue, Colman Dock, Pier 52.
FEBRUARY 7, 1916–JANUARY 1, 1917	An interim shop opens at 809 Second Avenue (near Virginia Street), while Colman Dock is rebuilt.
JANUARY 8, 1917–JANUARY 1937	The shop reopens at 811 Railroad Avenue, Colman Dock, Pier 52; Standley places whale bones in an arch to frame the shop.
JUNE 1923	The shop moves one room south, with the same address. The whale bones in front are placed in a V-shape.
JANUARY–JUNE 1, 1937	An interim shop opens at 814 First Avenue, while Colman Dock is rebuilt. The whale bones are put in storage.
JUNE 4, 1937–MARCH 9, 1958	The shop reopens at 815 Alaskan Way, Colman Dock, Pier 52.
JULY 2, 1937	Standley is hit by a car while crossing Alaskan Way.
OCTOBER 25, 1940	Standley dies.
SEPTEMBER 2, 1945	Edward Standley dies.
FEBRUARY 1946	Standley's grandson, Joe James, joins the shop.
1952	Russell James retires from the shop.
1954	Russell James dies.
MARCH 12, 1959–JUNE 29, 1963	The shop moves to 801 Alaskan Way, Colman Dock, Pier 52.
JUNE 29, 1963–APRIL 10, 1988	The shop relocates to 601 Alaskan Way, Pier 51. Seattle architect Paul Thiry introduces the shop's longhouse design.
APRIL 10, 1988–PRESENT	The shop is located at 1001 Alaskan Way, Pier 54.

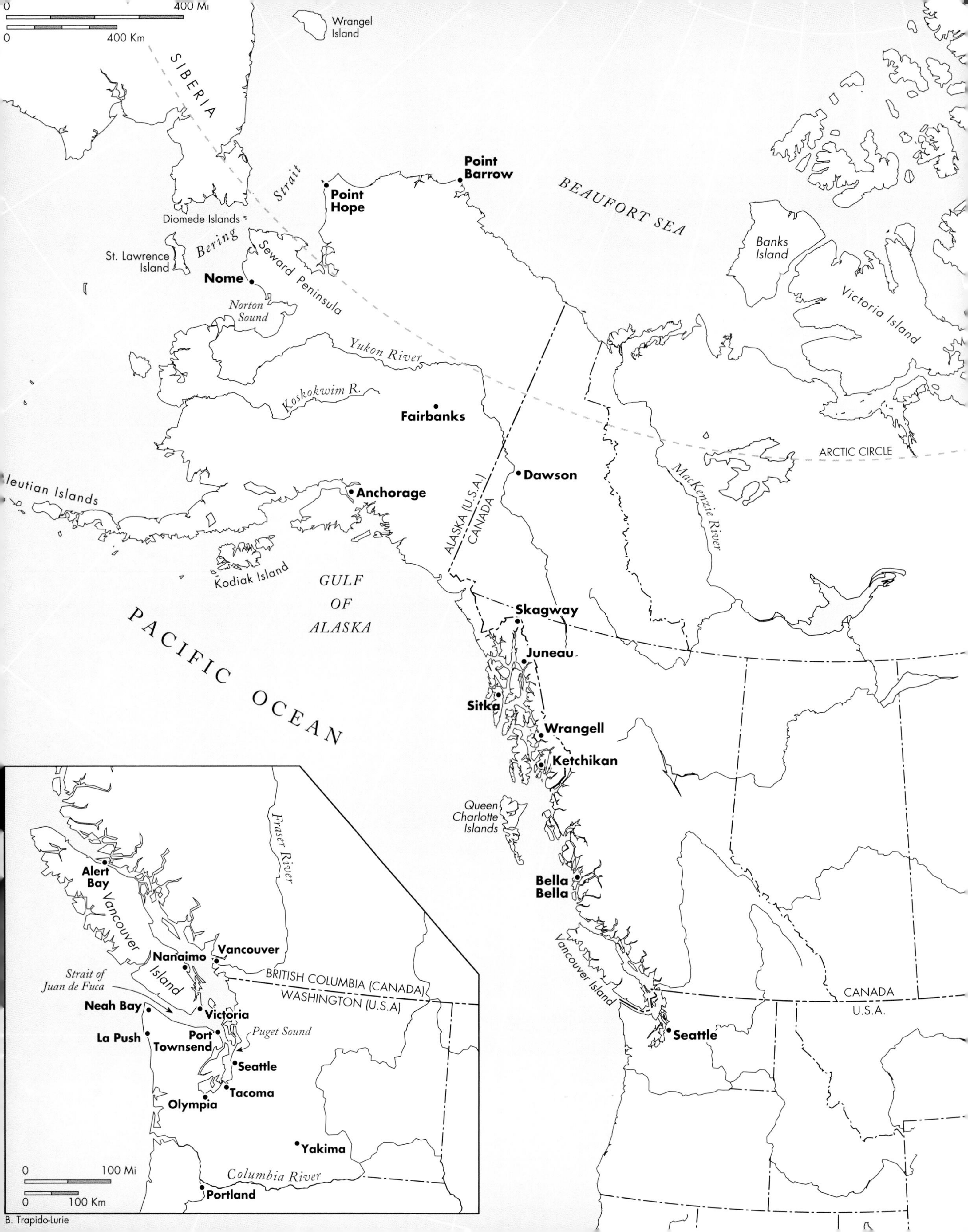

0
400 Mi
0
400 Km
Wrangel Island
SIBERIA
Bering Strait
Diomede Islands
St. Lawrence Island
Point Hope
Point Barrow
BEAUFORT SEA
Banks Island
Victoria Island
Nome
Seward Peninsula
Norton Sound
Yukon River
Koskokwim R.
Fairbanks
ARCTIC CIRCLE
Dawson
MacKenzie River
Aleutian Islands
Anchorage
ALASKA (U.S.A.)
CANADA
Kodiak Island
GULF OF ALASKA
PACIFIC OCEAN
Skagway
Juneau
Sitka
Wrangell
Ketchikan
Queen Charlotte Islands
Bella Bella
Vancouver Island
Seattle
CANADA
U.S.A.
Fraser River
Alert Bay
Vancouver Island
Vancouver
Nanaimo
Strait of Juan de Fuca
BRITISH COLUMBIA (CANADA)
WASHINGTON (U.S.A)
Neah Bay
Victoria
La Push
Port Townsend
Puget Sound
Seattle
Tacoma
Olympia
Yakima
Columbia River
Portland
0
100 Mi
0
100 Km
B. Trapido-Lurie

1001 CURIOUS THINGS

SEA SHELLS AND INDIAN BASKETS
IVORY CARVINGS
"YE OLDE CURIOSITY SHOP"
HISTORY OF TOTEM POLES
YE OLDE CURIOSITY SHOP
GRAPHIC ART OF THE ESKIMOS.

Prologue

Everything in the world is there, sardined
into Ye Olde Curiosity Shop. . . .
It's the world boiled down.
—*Seattle Post-Intelligencer*, June 1, 1927

THROUGHOUT THE TWENTIETH CENTURY A VISIT TO SEATTLE MANDATED A STOP in Ye Olde Curiosity Shop, where in the reassuring familiarity of a jumble of curios the inquisitive visitor could encounter the world of the unfamiliar and the exotic at a safe and comfortable distance. Voyeurism, longing, taste, and budget intersected at the shop, as tourists purchased thousands of mementos—miniature totem poles, baskets, moccasins, "Indian" bracelets, and "Eskimo" ivories. Museum representatives from across North America and Europe poked about and arranged for artifacts. For those who could not visit in person, there were catalogs that encouraged collecting as a hobby and investment.

In 1899, Joseph E. Standley opened what would become Ye Olde Curiosity Shop in a then rough coastal town: Seattle, Washington. It quickly became a hallmark tourist destination where one could purchase curios from across the globe and gaze in amazement at the rare, the exotic, the minuscule, the gigantic. Visitors were transported amid an overwhelming array of thousands of objects, the variety of which increased over the years. As Lawrence Weschler, who wrote about David Wilson's Museum of Jurassic Technology, might describe it, the shop seemed to capture and recalibrate "the astonishment of the world" in a single room.[1] Visitors could stroke the jaw of a whale or marvel at the entire Lord's Prayer written on the head of a pin. They could imagine arduous life in the Arctic, the mystery of totem poles in a misty Northwest Coast forest, or the terror of encountering head hunters in the jungles of Ecuador. There was even a mermaid. Blurring the boundaries between truth and fiction, education and amusement, Ye Olde Curiosity Shop provided indelible memories for millions of visitors and for many, mementos of the experience.

Although Native American objects vied for space with exotica from all corners of the globe, they quickly became the mainstay of the shop's identity and stock. Timing and location were critical. Positioned on the Seattle waterfront—just steps away from where whalers and traders, government personnel posted to the north, gold seekers, and even an occasional explorer docked—the shop welcomed them all. Of potential greater interest to some was the possibility of receiving quick cash from its proprietor for any Alaskan curiosities they had carried "outside."

Standley's shop soon became identified with the whale bones displayed in front and the "piles of old Eskimo relics" within. One could find Aleut grass baskets, ice-tanned moccasins, and recent ivory carving from arctic Alaska. There were Haida "jadeite" totem poles, Tlingit spruce root baskets and hair-seal moccasins, masks, paddles, and other curiosities from the Northwest Coast. Makah and Quileute women from the Olympic Peninsula brought baskets, canoeing up to the shop's back door after it had moved to Colman Dock, while Nuu-chah-nulth from British Columbia who lived nearby on the Duwamish Flats carved miniature totem poles by the thousands and full-size poles on commission. Trading companies supplied Indian curios from the Plains, the Southwest, and California. Goods available at every price level traversed boundaries of authenticity and imagination.

Located not far from its original waterfront site, Ye Olde Curiosity Shop celebrated its one-hundredth birthday in October 1999. During its century in existence the shop has played a tiny part in thousands of people's lives. Many who love it continue to return and to relish an enduring bond that dates from their childhood; others dismiss it as a tourist trap or relic of another age. There are new generations interested too. I confess to having once been a "dismisser." After moving to Seattle in the 1970s, I stopped in the shop occasionally, usually when someone came to town and wanted to see that bizarre place they had been told not to miss. As an art historian trained in the classic arts of the Northwest Coast, I did not take the shop seriously. I was surprised, then, while on a research trip in 1993, by a chance question from a colleague at the Royal Ontario Museum. Did I know Ye Olde Curiosity Shop? A part of the museum's Northwest Coast collection had come from there.

On returning to Seattle, I took a new interest in the shop and discovered that nearly a century after its founding, it was still in the Standley family, run by Standley's grandson Joe James and Joe's son, Andy James. After expressing surprise that the shop's early records could be of significant interest, the James family generously agreed to let me work with them. I found that the mass of early photographs, records, notes, and news clippings contained fragments of a complex, multifaceted story that combined essential information about the

YE OLDE
CURIOSITY SHOP.
THE KELLY PRINTING CO.
SEND A SOUVENIR
TO YOUR FRIENDS
Headquarters for Alaskan's and Globe Trotters on the
Water Front, COLMAN DOCK
SEATTLE, WASHINGTON, U. S. A.
J. E. STANDLEY, Sole Proprietor
My Shop
1907
EVERYBODY
WELCOME

Ye Olde Curiosity Shop brochure, ca. 1907, 6 in. × 9 in. when folded. These photographs, of the first Colman Dock shop, were probably taken soon after it opened in June 1904. It became proprietor Joseph E. Standley's habit to have each new shop professionally photographed soon after opening. The brochure highlights the shop's stock in a list foreshadowing the "1001 Curious Things" lists in future shop catalogs.

curio trade in the Pacific Northwest with little-remembered aspects of Seattle's history. I was soon drawn in with scores of questions. Just what was it that this shop provided its visitors that had caused it to become a legend at home and abroad? How had major museums become involved with it and why? Where did George G. Heye, Aleš Hrdlička, Robert L. Ripley, Queen Marie of Rumania, and dozens of other famous names recorded in the shop's guest book fit in? Had Ye Olde Curiosity Shop influenced public perceptions and expectations of the art and culture of the Native people of Alaska and the Northwest Coast and possibly the production of the art itself? My academic background and the abundance of information relating to that art seemed to be well matched.

An entire century of detailed and concrete data from one curio shop is rare. The wealth of specific information on the history and operation of Ye Olde Curiosity Shop between 1899 and 1940 is especially significant and forms the foundation for this book. The records examined include the shop's guest book, with forty years of prominent visitors' signatures and proprietor Standley's interspersed comments on events that intrigued him; address books of annotated supplier information; and illustrated brochures and catalogs with price

CURIO JOE, PROPRIETOR YE OLDE CURIOSITY SHOP SEATTLE

Postcard, 1913, Standley and polar bear rug.

lists. There are several hundred photographs, newspaper clippings, postcards, and specialized promotional cards and advertisements, as well as occasional correspondence and other memorabilia.[2] Through captivating, sometimes astonishing information and visuals, these early records document a complex and absorbing history. They trace the curio trade in Alaska and Northwest Coast Native art and artifacts through the first decades of the twentieth century and show that the shop played a pivotal role in an expanding regional tourist industry. The records convey society's general attitudes and Standley's personal fascinations with the unusual and the exotic, along with the constructed images of the greater region's indigenous people and their art that his shop fostered. They also sketch some of Seattle's history as viewed from the waterfront by an individual whose success was bound up with the city's primacy as a gateway and supplier to Alaska and a strategic port during wartime.

This book focuses on Ye Olde Curiosity Shop's first forty years. I have chosen 1940, the year of Standley's death, as its terminus for several reasons. The guiding personality behind the shop changed after Standley's death, and by 1940 it had essentially ceased to supply museum collections. The realities of World War II affected shop inventory, particularly imports from the Orient, as well as its operations and clientele. The shop has always nurtured the practice of wonder. With millions of American service personnel serving around the world during World War II, however, familiarity with different cultures and the mysteries of distant places became more the rule than the exception. By the 1940s the shop could no longer disarm in quite the way it had in earlier decades.

This history begins at the turn of the nineteenth century, at a critical juncture of time and place, when Standley first established his Seattle curio business. The book first traces Ye Olde Curiosity Shop's initial years, then considers its early sources for relics and handiwork from the Eskimos and Indians of Alaska and the Northwest Coast. One chapter deals with Standley and Seattle's 1909 Alaska-Yukon-Pacific Exposition; the next two detail collecting at the shop by major North American museums and private attractions. Following chapters examine Standley and his special involvement in Seattle as well as the shop's influence on the emergence of totem poles as a symbol for the Puget Sound region and the key role that Nuu-chah-nulth carvers living in Seattle played in the creation of tourist totem poles. The final chapters scrutinize the shop's catalogs and the goods and suppliers involved and sum up the shop's history after 1940.

My approach in this book is interdisciplinary, with debts to art history, history, and anthropology. Some chapters are structured chronologically, while others focus on particular aspects of shop operations or on Standley himself. All chapters deal with the multiple contexts within which the shop functioned. Because the history of Ye Olde Curiosity Shop is inextricably united with the unique history of Seattle, the book courses between the two, processing the shop's destiny within that of the city. The shop as a local institution and Standley's singular personality and showmanship were legendary and beloved by many. He was associated with a tireless boosterism of Seattle, and the shop—cited as one of the "Ten Wonders of Seattle" and featured in Ripley's "Believe it or Not!"® cartoon—became a place "not to be missed."

Many of the historical documents from the shop's first forty years, when Standley was at its helm, exist today only because he scrawled on them "save this"—and someone tossed the item into a box or a drawer each time the business moved. The shop's early history is also lodged in memory, not only that of living family members but also of Standley himself. During the final years of his long life, with the intention of writing a book, Standley jotted down notes about earlier events, sometimes more than once, on bits of paper, the backs of photographs, and in the shop's guest book. His memory also served as the basis for a number of news articles during the 1930s, which relate stories about the early days as Standley told them to reporters.

Historian Richard White has cautioned that memory and history must be respected but not confused, "that history is the enemy of memory," yet "there are regions of the past that only memory knows" and into which only memory can lead.[3] Standley's memories have guided much of this book, and wherever possible, I have tried to let him speak in his own voice. That voice is present in newspaper articles that quote him and in the small news clips that he initiated to keep the shop in the public eye. It is heard in his correspondence, in the text of shop catalogs, in the labels he hand-lettered for objects on display, and especially in his many notes. When quoting from this material, I have retained Standley's spelling and punctuation, although it is sometimes problematic.

I have also chosen to maintain the names Standley used for Northwest Coast tribes, noting the currently preferred alternative in parentheses the first time a tribe is named. Because he did not use the term Nootka, common at the time for Nootkan speakers from Vancouver Island (he instead called them Bella Bella, the name of yet another British Columbia tribe), I have used the now preferred name Nuu-chah-nulth. In Standley's time Eskimo was the term used for all of the Yup'ik- or Inupiaq-speaking people of Alaska, Canada, and Siberia. Although the name Inuit is used in Canada today and also by some Alaskan Inupiaq speakers, the language distinctions now commonly made cannot be distinguished in the shop's records, so I have maintained the name Eskimo.

The bulk of what Standley remembered over the years and thought worth relating in his notes centered mainly on what was exciting, adventurous, and unusual to him personally. White continues: "Memory, like history, is better thought of as plural rather than singular," and its stories must be interrogated and matched against each other.[4] Almost all of Standley's memories have held up to the process of historical interrogation, through interviews with his family and others associated with the shop and through cross-referencing information using newspapers and other sources.

Working outward from Standley's "memory" continually regrounds us in his world and time rather than in our own. The intention of this book is to present the multiple facets of that world rather than to try to interpret all that the recounted events may have meant to people then or mean to us today, more than a half-century later. There are a number of recent and important studies relevant to the information and concepts that surface throughout this book—many of them based in postmodern theory. This literature has been useful as I have worked with the records from Ye Olde Curiosity Shop. Although I have chosen to forgo here much of the postmodern rhetoric to keep this book accessible for a broad, nonspecialist audience, its influence will be recognized in observations throughout.[5] The study of curio shops is in its infancy, and much in this book is published here for the first time. I hope that this book may be useful to those sorting out similar material as well as to those wishing to further probe for meaning and implications.

I have thoroughly enjoyed working with the early records of Seattle's Ye Olde Curiosity Shop. The process has engaged me in rushes of discovery

similar to those that the shop's visitors have experienced over the years, introduced me to an ample amount of arcane information, and enticed me with bits of almost forgotten history of a city I have grown to love. Hoping to engage the reader in this experience of discovery, I have been generous in text and notes with minutia that has delighted me along the way. In addition to more serious matters, readers will discover in this book a Rookwood Pottery totem pole fireplace that once graced Seattle's New Washington Hotel, how to raise a one-ton whale bone from under water with nothing but rocks and logs, as well as information on artificial elk teeth, "man-eating" clams, the private amusement known as "A Little Bit O' Heaven," and much more.

Buying baskets on the street in Seattle, ca. 1905. Visitors to Seattle liked to barter for baskets from Indian women who sold them in front of Rhodes Department Store and other downtown businesses. This woman was selling trinket baskets from Neah Bay or La Push. Pemco Webster & Stevens Collection, 83.10.7929, Museum of History and Industry, Seattle.

An Indian friend in Alaska, an elder who knew I was writing about Ye Olde Curiosity Shop, took me aside a few months ago and said, "Can I ask you a question?" I agreed and he paused, then asked, "Is the mermaid real?" I paused and said, "Well . . . no." With a little embarrassment and a touch of sadness, he replied, "I've looked at that mermaid since I was a boy, and I *really* wanted it to be real." May the joy of new discoveries in this book temper such disappointments.

YE OLDE CURIOSITY SHOP
Jaw bones of a whale.
over 21ft. in length.
809
811
INDIAN RELICS
OLD
GOLD & SILVER
PURCHASES PACKED FREE FOR PARCEL POST
EVERYBODY WELCOME
CLAM SHELL
The most unique Shop in the World. On the Colman Dock Front. Seattle, U.S.A.
foot of Columbia St.
VISITORS ALWAYS WELCOME.

CHAPTER ONE

The Early Years of Ye Olde Curiosity Shop: "It Beats the 'Dickens'"

[Ye Olde Curiosity Shop is] the Mecca of the seeker after the extraordinary in curios.
—*The Grit,* October 25, 1925

IN EARLY JULY 1909 THE DISTINGUISHED BRITISH ANTHROPOLOGIST ALFRED CORT (A. C.) Haddon of Cambridge University strolled into Ye Olde Curiosity Shop on Colman Dock in Seattle. After his visit the shop's proprietor, Joseph Edward (J. E.) Standley, wrote excitedly in his Guest Book: "Dr Hadden visited the Shop and Bot big lot Indian and Eskimo curios to put in the museum at Haddon Hall. He was elated and yelled out I take my hat off to Mr. Standley's Unique Shop."[1] Haddon was energized by his visits to America and was known and appreciated for his enthusiasm and generosity of spirit. He obviously was a hit with Standley, although the shopkeeper was a bit confused about exactly who Haddon was: another enthusiastic Guest Book insert places him at Oxford. Although Standley had the spelling and affiliation confused—associating Haddon with the wrong university and with Haddon Hall, the celebrated estate of the Duke of Rutland in Derbyshire—there is no question that he was referring to the famous anthropologist A. C. Haddon.

Like many celebrities and scholars, Haddon was in town to take in Seattle's first world's fair, the Alaska-Yukon-Pacific Exposition (AYPE). An expert on the indigenous people of Malaysia, he was to lecture at the exposition on the evolution of culture around the Pacific Rim.[2] Haddon was also the advisory curator for the Horniman Free Museum on the outskirts of London, and in his travels he sometimes purchased artifacts to enhance the museum's exhibits.[3] It was probably Standley's diverse display in the Alaska building at the fair that suggested Ye Olde Curiosity Shop as a likely place for Haddon to find what he wanted.

In tune with anthropological theory of the day, Haddon planned for the exhibits at the Horniman to explain cultural evolution, to demonstrate "how the changing present had been

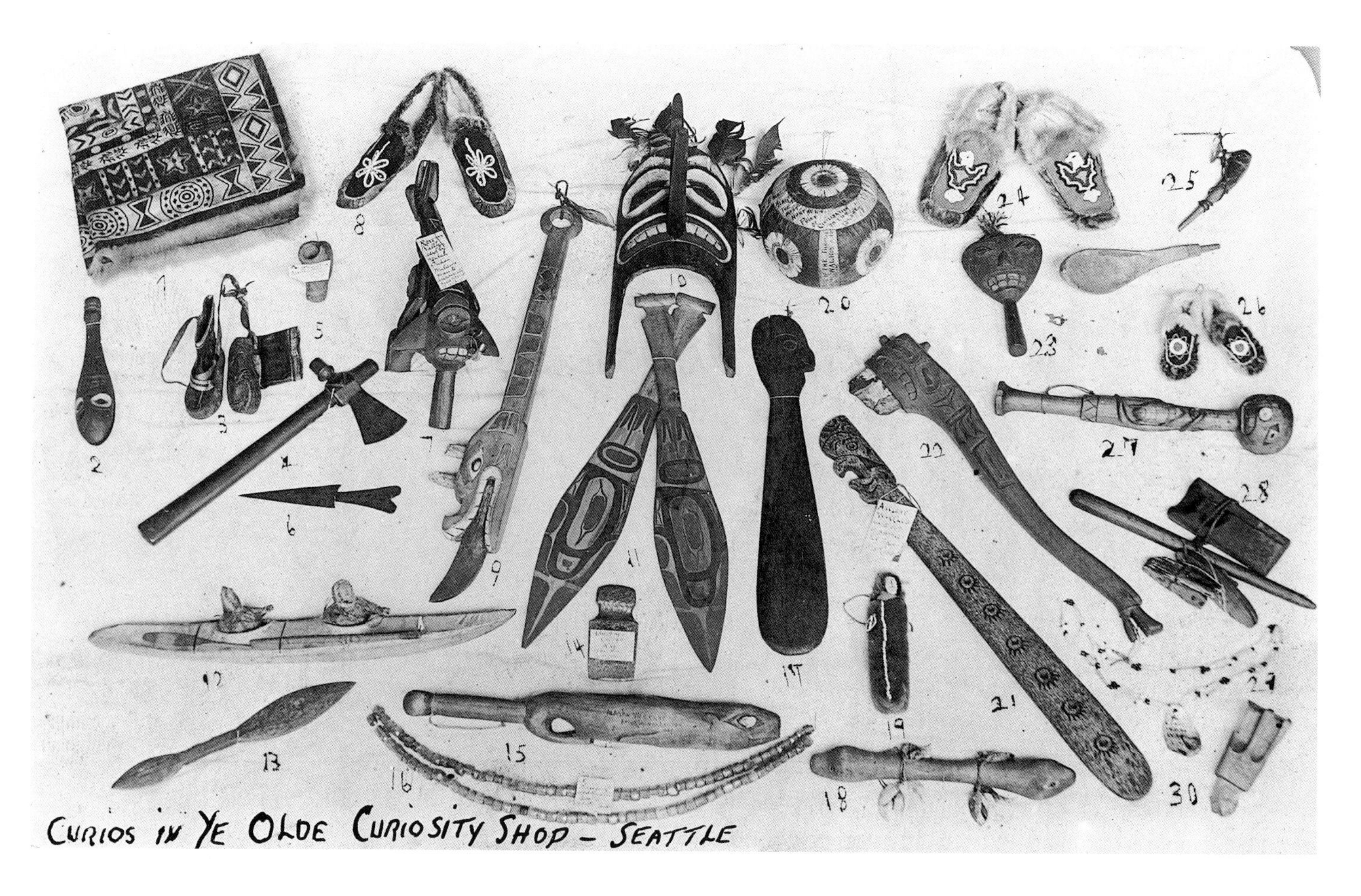

1.1. Postcard sold by Ye Olde Curiosity Shop during its early years. Almost all of the items pictured were made expressly for sale. Among the dozens of items that British anthropologist Alfred Cort (A. C.) Haddon purchased from the shop in 1909 for the Horniman Museum were for $4, no. 10, a "Raven mask"; and for $3.50 each, no. 15, a "carved seal knocker and salmon club" and no. 28, a "fire kindler of the Eskimo."

derived from the unstable past," and to "suggest the general line of advance in the arts, crafts, and ideas from the time of early man."[4] At the time indigenous people were viewed as illustrating an early stage of culture, and to represent the Native people of Alaska and the Northwest Coast, the museum would require examples of their tools and arts. By 1909 Standley's Curiosity Shop had established contacts with whaler-traders, government personnel, and others working in Alaska, and offered for sale thousands of such "relics" acquired from them.

Although Haddon did not have success convincing British universities to purchase Standley's Alaska exhibit, as he had hoped and suggested to Standley, he did buy from Standley 109 objects from Alaska, the Yukon, and the Northwest Coast for the Horniman Free Museum.[5] A mask, a wooden club, and a fire drill purchased on July 8, 1909, are among thirty curios that appear on one of the first postcards Standley put out to publicize his shop (fig. 1.1).[6] The drill was a typical old Eskimo one. The club, in the shape of a seal, was a recent tourist carving from the Northwest Coast, but Standley's interpretation was grander. To him it was an "Alaska war club and salmon knocker." As he typically did, Standley wrote his identification directly on the item.

The mask that Haddon purchased documents one of the ways in which Standley was already influencing the Northwest Coast art and artifacts that he sold. Identified as a Raven's head by the Horniman Museum, it is a copy of a mask collected by Johan Adrian Jacobsen in 1881 for the Royal Ethnographic Museum in Berlin.[7] At the time Standley could have known of the mask only through a line drawing in anthropologist Franz Boas's 1897 work, *The Social Organization and the Secret Societies of the Kwakiutl Indians,* of which he owned a copy (fig. 1.2). The mask Haddon purchased was a replication of the Berlin mask, most likely made by a Nuu-chah-nulth Seattle-area carver, after Standley had showed him illustrations in the Boas book. Haddon purchased another mask at this same time, which is likewise a copy from Boas, made under similar circumstances (fig. 1.3).[8]

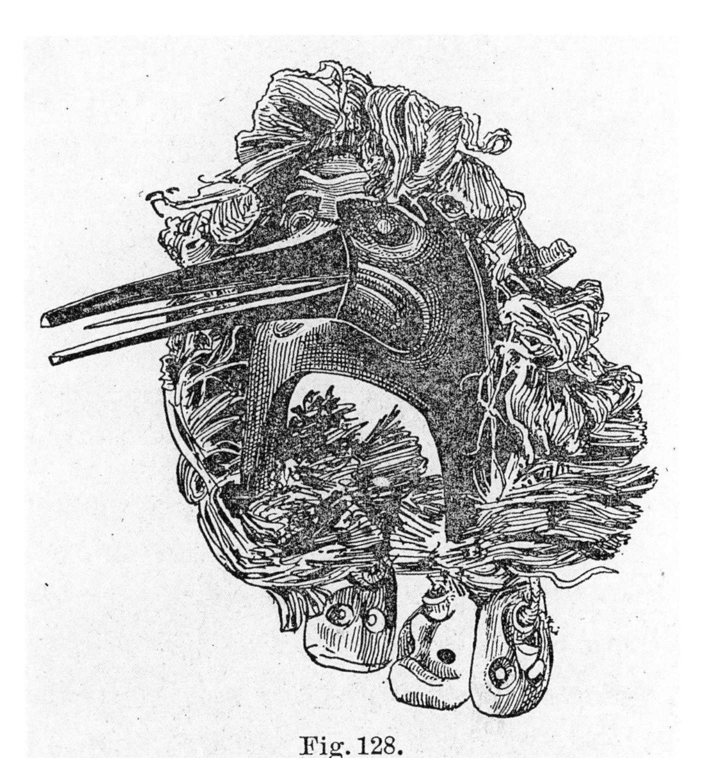

Fig. 128.
HEAD MASK OF NĀ'NAQAUALIL, REPRESENTING THE HŌ'XHOKᵘ
Length, 19 inches; black, white, red.
IV A, No. 1330, Royal Ethnographical Museum, Berlin. Collected by A. Jacobsen.

1.2. Drawing of a mask, in Franz Boas's *The Social Organization and the Secret Societies of the Kwakiutl Indians* (1897). With its cedar bark ruff and carved wooden skulls hanging below, the mask represents one of the cannibal bird helpers of Bakbakwalinooksiwey, the cannibal at the north end of the world, and was used in the Hamatsa initiation. The Raven mask pictured on Standley's postcard and purchased by A. C. Haddon was based on this drawing.

The encounter with Haddon, less than a decade after Standley's arrival in Seattle, demonstrates the reputation Ye Olde Curiosity Shop had established in only ten years. Haddon was just one of the many important visitors—politicians, scholars, entertainers, celebrities, and museum representatives—who poked about the shop and purchased items during the AYPE and in later years. There were thousands of ordinary tourists too. By 1909 the shop had developed a reputation for the variety and quality of its ethnographic artifacts; and, as the encounter with Haddon documents, Standley was even commissioning objects that despite their transcultural origins would be placed into both museums and homes as authentic and old.

The years after the exposition and between World Wars I and II would be busy, exciting, and profitable for Standley's shop. Eskimo items would continue to arrive from Alaska, Nuu-chah-nulth carvers living in Seattle would create thousands of totem poles for the shop, and Japanese and local manufacturing companies would supply carved ivory and silver jewelry of Indian and Eskimo design. During Standley's lifetime the shop would publish several brochures and at least nine catalogs that would expand its reach and reputation across the continent and beyond. At the same time Standley cultivated a personal reputation as an astute, if slightly eccentric, businessman, a regional

> I used to go down to the boats, when I was a boy, with a basket of things for them. That's how I got my first experience in trade. I didn't get off in time one day, and one of them took me up to Pittsburgh. So, while I was there, I saw the chance to buy some things cheap for the store.
>
> —Standley, Guest Book, p. 1

booster, and a passionate purveyor of curios. His enthusiasm for curios, especially Indian ones, dated back to his childhood.

An Early Passion for Trading

The 1860s were an exciting time to be the young son of a Steubenville, Ohio, grocer. Riverboats plying the Ohio River stopped to take on supplies at Steubenville, the sternwheelers tying up at the rock piers at the ends of the streets. On occasion President Abraham Lincoln came through town, as did other notable figures. Across the river there were ancient caves to explore and Indian petroglyphs to ponder. The young Standley never forgot how the entire area was dazzled when the first red circus wagons in the United States pulled into town with ringleader Dan Rice.[9]

J. E. Standley was born on February 24, 1854, seven years before the Civil War, to Casper and Sophia Standley. Casper and his brother George had left Württemberg, Germany, for the United States in the 1830s or 1840s to avoid conscription, changed their family name from Stüidly to Standley, and settled in Steubenville.[10] Standley was the youngest of six children. When his three older brothers went off to fight in the Civil War, it was left to Joe to assist in his father's butcher shop and business of supplying riverboats on the Ohio with fresh food and other items. Through this apprenticeship Standley became more and more experienced in shopkeeping. On a ride on a sternwheeler all the way to Pittsburgh, he noticed that city stores used shelves rather than piling things on the floor. When he put up shelving along the walls of his father's store, it became a local curiosity and people came from miles to see his innovation.[11]

1.3. A display in the Horniman Museum, picturing two masks that A. C. Haddon purchased from Standley. Like the Raven mask to its right, the large-mouthed mask was replicated from a drawing in Boas's 1897 work. Photograph courtesy Horniman Museum, London, image 1189. Undated.

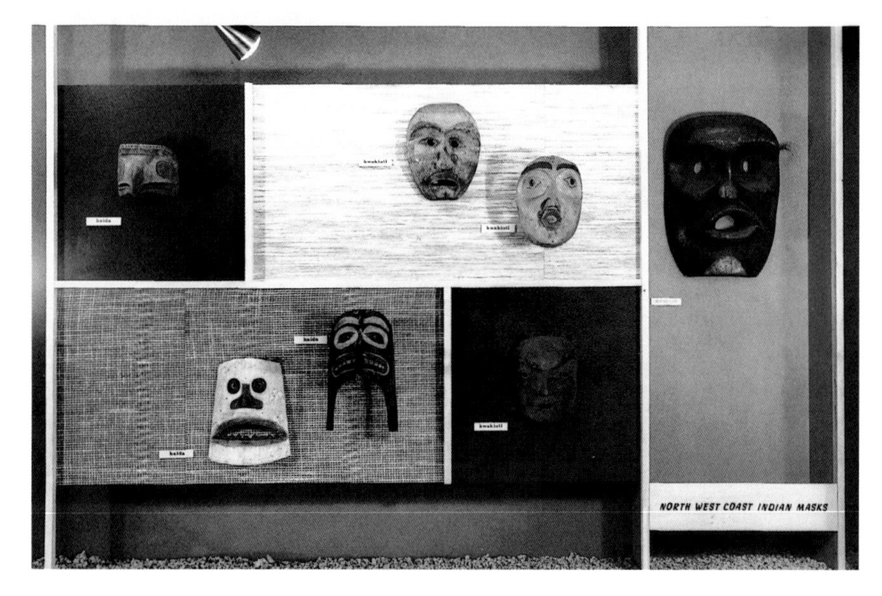

A single event during impressionable childhood years can exert great influence. For young Standley it was a schoolroom contest he won in the third grade for having the neatest desk and the nicest monogram. It was not the winning that was so important to him but the prize—a children's book on the wonders of nature as detailed by Alexander von Humboldt and other naturalists. As Standley explained later, "Since I read that book, I've thought about nothing else. I set about collecting things then."[12] His fascination with wonders and his enthusiasm for collecting grew along with his increasing experience in trade. Ultimately they directed his life's passion.

In 1875, at age twenty-one, Standley left Ohio and set out for the West. He may have gone as far as California before he settled on Denver as a promising place to establish a business. After clerking for just two days for Birk's Conforth Pioneer Grocer in 1876, Standley swore that he would never again work for anyone else but would "be my own Boss and start new on nothing."[13] And that he did, opening a tobacco and confectionery shop, then expanding into selling groceries and changing his location at least once during twenty-five years as a Denver merchant.[14]

Standley's business approach and acumen, his personality and singular sense of purpose, became firmly established during these years. Many of his activities in Denver foreshadowed the forty years he would later spend as a shopkeeper in Seattle. A lifelong fascination with the uncommon and a willingness to take risks, traits that would be vitally important to his Seattle enterprise, expressed themselves in his first Denver store. The J. E. Standley Old Reliable Grocery House carried tropical fruits and domestic and imported delicacies, along with a full line of groceries, ranch produce, milk, and cream. When no one else had the enterprise to do so, proprietor Standley would pay $10 a stem for exotic fruit such as bananas from Cuba. As would be the case later in Seattle, Standley was a staunch city booster of Denver. A card advertising his grocery advised: "If you want to build up the town you live in patronize your home manufactories and Colorado packers. . . . I make a speciality of Denver made products, and ask a share of your patronage." As a public service he devoted the back of the card to "Sights Around Denver, the Queen City of the Plains one mile above the sea" with forty-five lines of minuscule text listing more than a hundred local points of pride.[15]

Standley's childhood interest in Indians and famous personalities continued in Denver. His notes recall Ute Indians camped in front of J. P. Lowers gun store, where they had come to buy supplies for the big winter hunt, and stories about Colorado governor John L. Routte, Kit Carson, and Buffalo Bill Cody, who sometimes headquartered at the Alvord Hotel, just above Standley's grocery during the 1870s.[16] His desire to share with others his passion for intriguing and unusual things also became established in Denver. As he explained, "I started putting curios on the counter for decoration and people began to buy them. So I got more and more curios."[17] It was later said that as Standley tacked up items he thought would interest his customers, the collection of curiosities began to overwhelm the groceries. At the time it was common for those selling curios in "Indian country" to also handle groceries and dry goods to assure a steady income, but in Standley's case selling groceries allowed him to branch into curios, some of which were probably obtained in barter from Indians in exchange for food and supplies. When Standley left Denver for Seattle in 1899, he took several crates of curios with him. There is no record of what these contained, but photographs of his first waterfront shop in Seattle include examples of Plains, Southwestern, and Woodlands Indian arts that probably had come with him from Denver.

Standley ornamented his Denver home in ways that also foreshadowed the later Seattle years. In 1877 when he built a fence out front, he used roots and limbs to spell out "J E STANDLEY." In the side yard he created a conical structure using large seashells, petrified wood, and cactus, parts of which traveled with him to Seattle and were eventually installed in a similar fashion in the side yard of his West Seattle home known as Totem Place.[18]

Seattle, the Gateway to Alaska

In 1899 doctors in Denver advised Standley that for the sake of his wife Isabelle's health, the family should move to a lower altitude. He first considered La Jolla, California, but a sea captain friend pointed out that the potential for acquiring curios would be far greater in Seattle, which in the wake of the Klondike and Nome gold rushes of the late 1890s had become known across the country as "the gateway to Alaska." That fall, at age forty-five, Standley packed up his small but beloved collection of curios and headed to Seattle with his wife and four children. There he decided to make what had been a hobby his occupation.

The Standleys probably arrived in Seattle by train, catching their first good glimpse of the young city as they approached the passenger station on Railroad Avenue between Marion and Columbia Streets in what is now downtown Seattle. Against a looming backdrop of enormous old-growth evergreens, the small bustling town tumbled down to a boardwalk edging a magnificent Puget Sound. For several blocks above the busy waterfront, pedestrians, horse-drawn delivery carts, and a trolley line moved with purpose along wide streets faced with the solid, forward-looking structures of new hotels and business buildings. Many of these were constructed of stone in sturdy Romanesque revival style to echo the elegance of such substantial urban centers as Chicago and Philadelphia. It is not known on which day in October the Standleys arrived, but if it was after October 18, they would have seen not far from the station a curious sculpture reflecting just how different their new home would be from Denver. On that day the Seattle Chamber of Commerce erected, in the heart of the city, a sixty-foot-tall totem pole taken from Alaska. Known as the Seattle Totem Pole, this carving became an important image to Standley,

1.4. In October 1899 the Seattle Totem Pole was installed at First Avenue and Yesler Street, amid downtown's progressive new buildings. For businesses and the public it would become a symbol for Seattle. University of Washington Libraries, neg. UW 8571.

who would reinforce its significance as a public symbol for Seattle through the shop he would soon open (fig. 1.4). South of the passenger station, during the fall hop-picking season in the Puyallup and Yakima Valleys, hundreds of Indians from La Push, Neah Bay, Vancouver Island, and elsewhere gathered at a canoe camp on the flats of the Duwamish River (fig. 1.5).

In 1899 Seattle was not quite fifty years old. The town's first settlers, the Denny party, had landed in late 1851 at Alki Point in West Seattle, not far from where Standley would later build his family home. Historian Roger Sale has credited pioneer Arthur Denny—his vision, strong sense of duty, and dedication to encouraging other early settlers—as a major force in the city's destiny.[19] Denny and others realized that for Seattle to become a city, rather than a company town existing primarily to support the exploitation of such natural resources as timber, it needed economic independence and diversity—and the ability to offer potential settlers a wealth of opportunity. City founders set about creating such a cultural climate, and by the time the Standleys arrived, the community had become established as a port and had its own small railroad. Local manufacture provided much of what its population needed and commerce was thriving. Denny had dreamed of Seattle as the capital of the

1.5. During hop-picking season hundreds of Indians gathered in canoe camps on the Duwamish Flats. University of Washington Libraries, negs. UW 698, 680.

Washington Territory and even platted out a Capitol Hill district. In 1861, however, he and others wisely chose instead to house the territorial university, a move that further enriched the young city's economic promise.

The 1880s and early 1890s were boom periods: Seattle's population of about 3,500 in 1880 increased twelvefold during the 1890s, then settled into a measured and rooted growth and doubled to more than 80,000 by 1900. After the disastrous fire of June 1889 that destroyed its downtown, Seattle's movers and shakers had resolutely engaged in rebuilding, to create a "modern and permanent city" of brick and stone rather than wood. Despite its pretensions, Seattle was still a rough and wide open town, where prostitution and gambling were tolerated as long as they operated south of Yesler Way in the so-called Skid Road area.[20] It would be a difficult adjustment for Standley's wife, who missed the culture of Denver.

> Those were exciting and interesting days. There was a big Indian settlement on the tide flats just this side of Spokane street. During the hop picking season scores of war canoes would bring hundreds of natives and their families from all over the Sound and British Columbia. They had sails made of cedar bark. After the season there would be much ceremonial dancing and feasting. The whites sold them liquor and there would be bloody battles.
>
> —Standley, *Seattle Star*, 1936

When the Standleys arrived in Seattle, the town that was fast becoming a city was energetic and intent on its own destiny, one securely linked with Alaska. It was still bristling with the excitement of the Alaskan gold fever from which it had profited handsomely. Almost as soon as the ship Portland had arrived on the waterfront in July 1897 with a ton of Klondike gold, the brilliant public relations campaign of city booster Erastus Brainerd had convinced the world that Seattle was the preferred gateway to Alaska, helping to engineer a codependency between the city and the territory from which Seattle had richly benefited. As outfitters for the thousands of gold seekers on their way North,

Seattle city merchants had reaped $25 million in trade in just eight months.[21] After the U.S. Assay Office was moved to Seattle in 1898, a portion of the millions of dollars in gold that passed into the city also stayed.

Seattle's economic diversity, its location, and its increasing transportation connections created a climate ripe for the sort of business that Standley would establish. The city was solid and booming. Transport to and from Alaska was well established and men traveling there could bring out thousands of Native relics to pass on for quick cash. The extension of James J. Hill's Great Northern Railroad to Seattle in 1893 had established a link with rail transport across North America. Battleships moving in and out of Elliott Bay during the Spanish American War had generated a new awareness of the Pacific Rim. Goods and customers for the shop that Standley would establish could now travel back and forth with ease—across the United States, to Alaska, to the Orient. Russian brass, Chinese cloisonné, and an enormous variety of seashells were now easy to import. Rail connections to the southwestern United States meant that curio dealers and suppliers could conveniently ship not only armadillo shell baskets and Mexican jumping beans, but also the Navajo rugs, Pueblo pottery, and Indian jewelry that were already established as staples of the Southwestern Indian tourist trade. Increased efficiency in transportation also meant that sailors and tourists, as well as local residents, furnished a ready audience for a vicarious experience with the exotic that the shop would provide. A shop of curiosities offering something for everyone could thrive in a city such as Seattle.

J. E. Standley's First Seattle Shop and the Guest Book

After he settled his family in their new home, Standley opened a small store at Second Avenue and Pike Street. Little is known about it except that during the first three days of business Standley took in a total of twenty-five cents. He wanted to be near the waterfront, and sometime during November 1901 the shop relocated to the foot of Madison Street, below First Avenue and opposite the Rainier Grand Hotel. With the help of Chad George, a local Indian silversmith, Standley constructed a small shop from wood, tin sheets, and a secondhand storefront. He called it The Curio (and later Curiosity Shop and Indian Curio) and dangled relics in front to lure in passersby. The earliest photograph of this shop (fig. 1.6), taken soon after it opened, indicates that at this time Standley's stock of items from the Natives of Alaska and the Northwest Coast was small. The Southwestern baskets, Navajo rug, cow horns, and elk horn chair in front of the shop attest that he was somewhat dependent on what he had brought from Denver. So far, in Washington he had been able to acquire a few baskets; and from Alaska, several Tlingit baskets and a little Tlingit

1.6. Standley's first shop, The Curio, near the waterfront, at 82 Madison Street. Here, as in later photographs of his shops, Standley arranged relics out front that were usually kept inside. He wrote on the back of this photo at two different times. In an earlier firm hand: "This is the House that Joe Built, it was on foot of Madison st where The National Grocery Co are now about 1901. I helped build the shak out of 2d hand material. JES. Old Chad George the Indian Silversmith sits in the middle of the Junk Pile." Later, in the shakier hand of his final years, Standley added, "Take Note no Totem Poles to be had when."

beadwork. There were none of the totem poles that would later become the mainstay of Ye Olde Curiosity Shop's image.

A believer in the value of pictures as well as objects, and lacking additional Alaskan merchandise to display, Standley promptly devised another way to attract the interest of passersby and to announce his commitment to Alaskan curiosities. Timing was on his side, for he could draw on three almost brand-new annual reports of the Bureau of American Ethnology of the Smithsonian Institution, the most respected anthropological source in the nation. Franz Boas's *The Social Organization and the Secret Societies of the Kwakiutl Indians* (1897), Walter J. Hoffman's *The Graphic Art of the Eskimos* (1897), and Edward W. Nelson's *The Eskimo About Bering Strait* (1899) all included photographs and drawings. Standley cut pictures from each work and combined them in a large framed collage featuring Northwest Coast and Eskimo artifacts and people (fig. 1.7). In photographs of the Madison Street shop the photomontage can be seen at the far left. In subsequent shops it was moved inside; a century later it is still on display. Because the montage did not identify the sources of the photographs, its implied legitimization of the shop's collections would have been understood entirely by only the very few who recognized the photographs. For others the images suggested that what could

1.7. Framed montage of photographs and drawings that Standley hung in front of his Madison Street shop about 1901. Cut primarily from Franz Boas's *The Social Organization and the Secret Societies of the Kwakiutl Indians* and Walter J. Hoffman's *The Graphic Art of the Eskimos,* the illustrations captured the attention of passersby and suggested that there were similar items inside.

be found in the shop was an extension of what the photos pictured. In a sense that became so, for local carvers soon began copying items in these and other pictures that Standley showed them.

Standley was a self-educated man. He liked to read and kept a few books on natural history and ethnology that related to shop merchandise. Warren K. Moorehead, the author of *Stone Ornaments Used by American Indians in the United States and Canada,* scholar-collector George T. Emmons, and probably others gave Standley books, perhaps to help educate him. But he especially depended on newspaper articles and the stories credentialed visitors related, and he sometimes accepted fanciful explanations as fact. In most of the books Standley owned (including the now lost *Encyclopaedia Britannica* kept at the family home), he wrote on the end pages and frontispieces and pasted related postcards, photographs, and clippings on blank pages. Each of these randomly compiled books-plus-additions became for him research files of a sort.

Standley's most influential source, however, was his uncut copy of Boas's 1897 book on the Kwakiutl Indians. With Standley as mediator, the book exerted influence of a type that Boas could not have possibly imagined. In Standley's mind and hands this study of one central coastal tribe represented the entire Northwest Coast, and it was thus a convenient source for images and ideas. The most lasting effect resulted from his showing the book to local non-Kwakiutl carvers and encouraging them to replicate some of the items pictured, thereby acting as agent to new hybrid styles that would become significant in the development of Northwest Coast tourist art. Standley also loaned the Boas book to planners for the 1909 Alaska-Yukon-Pacific Exposition (AYPE) and to the committee designing floats and costumes for Seattle's first Potlatch Carnival in 1911, the precursor of today's summer celebration known as Seafair. The book had been so well used that the carnival committee returned it to Standley rebound. The totem poles and other figures that were copied introduced yet a different version of "hybridity" and reinforced the idea of the totem pole as associated with Seattle. In both cases the Boas illustrations became a foundation for an amalgam of visual representations that to the general public came to represent Northwest Coast indigenous art.

Standley quickly made the acquaintance of old Alaska hand L. L. Bales, lately returned from the Seward Peninsula, and bought from him old Eskimo tools and recently carved ivory that Bales had carried "outside." As it became known that the shop would eagerly take in whatever curiosities came out of the North, other Alaskans came forth—whaler-traders, personnel from U.S. revenue cutters (the precursors of today's Coast Guard), and Alaskans retiring to the Puget Sound region. In Standley's shop the old Eskimo tools and pieces of ivory were piled into bins through which visitors could rummage. A later photograph of the 1901 Madison Street shop pictures Bales and some of the other people on whom the shop depended during its first years (fig. 1.8).

In 1900 Standley started using a tall ledger as a guest book, an important but curious document that has proved invaluable in the study of Ye Olde Curiosity Shop. Embedded in the book's signatures and in Standley's notes about memorable Seattle events lies a history of the city as seen from the waterfront, through the eyes of a man fascinated by the unusual, captivated by celebrity, and always aware of the direct impact of visitors on the success of his business. Simple penciled signatures and addresses on the earliest pages of the Guest Book record visitors from across the country and suggest that initially almost everyone was invited to sign the book. As the shop became known as a be-sure-to-see attraction, however, the emphasis moved toward including only the signatures of famous or especially interesting people. Joe James, Standley's grandson who ran the shop from the late 1940s until the mid-1990s, remembers that Standley would get to talking to someone and if he felt that person was significant enough, would ask him or her to sign the Guest Book. Guests

1.8. A second and later photograph of the shop at 82 Madison Street, at this time called Ye Olde Curiosity Shop Indian Curio. On a copy of this photograph Standley wrote, "This was my first shop 14 × 16 foot, foot of Madison st. near the famous Bismark Saloon & Cafe. L. L. Bales and Mrs. J. E. Standley Chad George making indian silver Ear-rings & Braceletts. J. E. S. with straw Hat next to Post. Indian Painter Wood totem carver. showcase on wall was full Alaska Indian & Eskimo things. Covered at night."

Standley leans against a light pole, wearing a straw hat, his trademark during his early years in Seattle. Two seated Indian men hold carving and engraving tools. The younger man on the left may be Sam Williams, who carved for the shop until mid-century. A paddle and bow are arranged over his feet and a beaded octopus bag sits at his chest. On the right sits silversmith Chad George, who has been posed with a Chilkat blanket tucked over his knees and snowshoes at his feet. Standley's wife Isabelle stands next to L. L. Bales.

would see the names of other well-known visitors there and be flattered to have been asked. At the end of the day Standley sometimes annotated signatures with specific information about the guests: what they had purchased and occasionally, using a private letter code, the amount they had spent. He also added the names of important people who had visited the shop but had not signed the book.

In the years just before Standley died in 1940, he continued to have visitors sign the Guest Book, but he also used it and scraps of paper as a place to record his own memories in preparation for one day writing a book (fig. 1.9). By his final years the early signatures and addresses meant little, and on a number of pages he simply erased the names as best he could and wrote over them in dark ink, recalling events that lodged vivid in his mind in multiple locations in the book. Sometimes he grouped anecdotes about a particular topic, such as the names of steamers that had sunk nearby or had run into Colman Dock over the years.[22] Standley was also an avid newspaper reader and often in the evening clipped out articles that interested him. Short ones about celebrities who had visited the shop were sometimes pasted into the Guest Book next to the signatures. Other articles were saved or inserted into the family encyclopedia. An avid correspondent, when Standley read about something he thought would interest a friend, he clipped and mailed off the article.

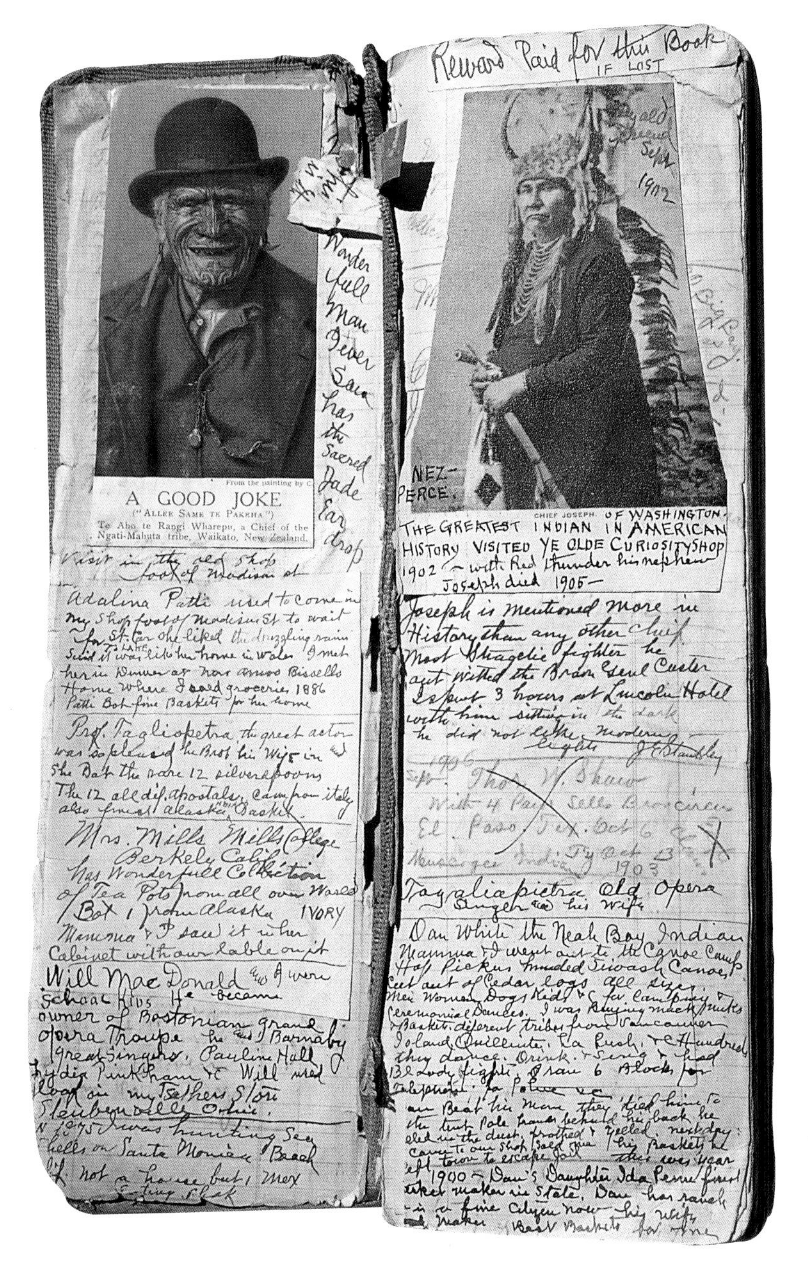
Reward Paid for this Book
IF LOST
A GOOD JOKE
("ALLER SAME TE PAKEHA")
Te Aho te Rangi Wharepu, a Chief of the Ngati-Mahuta tribe, Waikato, New Zealand.
NEZ-PERCE.
CHIEF JOSEPH OF WASHINGTON.
THE GREATEST INDIAN IN AMERICAN HISTORY VISITED YE OLDE CURIOSITY SHOP 1902 — with Red Thunder his nephew
Joseph died 1905—

1.9. Ye Olde Curiosity Shop's Guest Book includes signatures of visitors, pasted-in postcards and news clippings, and names of visitors and anecdotes that Standley jotted down.

The Turn-of-the-Century Curio Trade and Seattle's Visiting Indians

Getting established in Seattle required hard work, but Ye Olde Curiosity Shop's early years were exciting for Standley as he carved out a niche for his business. Indian relics and seashells were especially important to the stock, but there were also coins, souvenir spoons, rare marine specimens, and other items. Small shops stuffed with goods were the norm at the time, but there was no one else in town who could challenge Standley's variety of uncommon objects and merchandise. Marketing curios in the American West combined both retail and entertainment. Some shops, including Standley's, were called "free museums."[23] Ye Olde Curiosity Shop quickly became a place that word-of-mouth referrals made hard to ignore, a must-see for visitors and a favorite of local residents who liked to wander among the clutter to look for treasures. In later years the shop would draw in the curious to stare at a mermaid, shrunken heads, and a mummy, and to ponder whether such items were actually real. Standley enthusiastically welcomed everyone. In 1902 he began listing the shop in *Polk's Seattle City Directory.*

At the turn of the century the term curio was shorthand for "curiosity" and still meant something unknown, exotic, and rare. Historical Seattle city directories indicate the local curio shop activity, listed under the owners' names and/or under the category "Curios." Entries between 1890 and 1910 show an increasing trade in Asian curios but little activity in American Indian ones.[24] Only the Arctic Trading Company, a short-lived venture recorded as selling Indian relics and curios in 1897, is listed.[25] In 1901 three businesses are recorded in the city directory, each run by a woman. The Klondike and Nome gold rushes had increased both the availability of Alaskan goods and the public's interest in them. At the same time basket collecting was in vogue, especially among women in the West. In the well-appointed home, Indian baskets were considered integral to an artful display known as the "Indian corner." Shops

> Mamma & I went out to the Canoe Camp. Hop pickers, hundred Siwash canoes cut out of cedar logs. All sizes. Men, Women, Dogs, Kids etc. for Camping and Ceremonial Dances. I was Buying muckmuks [bowls] & baskets, different tribes from Vancouver Island, Quilliute, La Push, etc. Hundreds, they dance, drink & sing.
>
> —Standley, Guest Book, p. 2

along the West Coast and in Alaska sold thousands of baskets from Alaskan, Californian, and Southwestern tribes; they were purchased directly from Alaskan Indians in such communities as Sitka, a major stop on steamboat cruises up the Inside Passage. Although they were generally viewed as quaint products of Indian domesticity, these baskets were also much admired for their beauty, craftsmanship, and utility.

In Seattle, baskets from the Tlingit in Southeast Alaska, from Puget Sound tribes, and from the Makah of the Olympic Peninsula were the most available. Running a business of selling baskets and other curios, especially out of the home, was an acceptable occupation for a gentlewoman, perhaps a widow who needed to support herself. The three businesses registered in Seattle's city directory in 1901 met varying fates. Henrietta Hamilton's Basket Rooms appears to have lasted but a year, and Mrs. Marion Pearsall's business only through 1904, but Mrs. Emma M. Rhodes's "curios and Indian baskets" continued for more than a decade. In 1905 she and Fred B. Kendall joined as business partners, and the E. M. Rhodes Company moved into Seattle's new Arctic Building. In about 1914 the business failed.[26]

Competition with Ye Olde Curiosity Shop in selling baskets was not of great concern to Standley. His shop carried a variety of baskets, but they were merely part of a large inventory. Photographs indicate that baskets were most important to Standley during the earliest years when they were popular, relatively inexpensive, and most available. At that time Makah and Quileute women from Neah Bay and La Push (identified by Standley as Mora, the nearby non-Indian community) brought baskets in when they traveled to Puget Sound, and sources in several Southeast Alaska communities wholesaled Tlingit baskets as well.

Indians living in Seattle were important from the beginning in supplying the shop. Soon after Standley arrived, he visited the Indian settlement on the tide flats just north of Spokane Street and established connections there. In the fall there were large numbers of Indians who stayed at the camp on their way to the hop fields. At other times the population varied, with some Indians living there year-round and others part-time. Many came and went, visiting friends, trading fish, and selling handicrafts in town.

Standley was fascinated by Indian and Eskimo people, and he wrote often about them in his notes of information to be included in his future book. His observations are brief, usually anecdotal, and objective. Critical remarks and words such as dirty and savage, common in accounts of Native people of

1.10 a, b. Postcards of Chief Seattle and his daughter Princess Angeline were among the most popular sold in Seattle for decades. When Standley was running out of color Chief Seattle postcards, he stuck a shop label on one and had it photographed and printed in black and white. He carried several different Princess Angeline cards, including this one, which he had made exclusively for sale in his shop. Photograph 1.10b, c. 1910, courtesy University of Washington Libraries.

the time, are extremely rare in his notes. Using his nickname, "Daddy Standley," a news reporter commented: "'Daddy' likes the Indians and their objects of art, and doesn't care who knows it."[27] He was especially tickled to meet particularly accomplished Natives, but he seems to have accepted everyone as they were. Standley enjoyed talking with Indians and Eskimos, but there was a cordial distance. There is record of Isabelle Standley entertaining a group of Eskimo women for tea at the Standley home, Totem Place, when the trader L. L. Bales brought them to visit, but for the most part friendship was played out in the context of the shop rather than in social settings.

The text on Standley's information card on the "History of Chief Seattle and Princess Angeline, Seattle"—which relates their assistance in warning Seattle settlers about an Indian raid—reflects a major contradiction in Standley's seemingly tolerant view (fig. 1.10a, b): "In 1856 she creep thro' big woods, tell white man, bad Indians cum mountains, kill all white faces. Say her father . . . come in two sleeps. . . . U.S. gunboat Decatur heap shoot in woods." Although this text is said to have been related by the chief's grandson, known as Moses, the history is presented in fractured English cut through with generic clichés typical of non-Indian mimicry of Indians speaking English, so much so that its authorship is in doubt, although the events narrated do approximate the truth. Standley may have composed the text himself, however, seeing the language as entertaining rather than the derogatory ethnic stereotyping that it was.

With the most varied and visible Indian collection in the city, Ye Olde Curiosity Shop became a stop for visiting Indians and Eskimos, as it remains today. Standley wrote about some of them in his Guest Book and sometimes included a postcard or photograph of the more famous Natives. Cheyenne Chief Mad Wolf left his card while in Seattle for the AYPE. Lakota Chief Red Cloud was there in about 1913 with his son Jack and Mr. DeRhodes, an Indian trader from Chadron, Nebraska. Standley's most vivid memory was of Chief Joseph, about whom he wrote: "The greatest Indian in America visited Ye Olde Curiosity Shop 1902 with Red Thunder his nephew." That evening Standley sat with Joseph for three hours in the dark at the Lincoln Hotel because the elderly Nez Perce chief did not like modern lights. Over the years performing Indians and Indian heroes would stop by the shop—tenor Chief War Eagle (known as War Cloud in his earlier years), the Sioux actress Princess White Cloud, the Navajo prizefighter Joe Cortez, and Dan Sittcelahchy from British Columbia, who saved the captain and crew of the U.S. schooner Puritan in 1896. Standley purchased special articles that belonged to such well-known Indians as Chief Seattle and Miss Columbia, who was born at the Chicago Columbian Exposition in 1893.

The Colman Dock Waterfront Shops

In June 1904 the row of Madison Street shacks in which Standley's business had stood was torn down, and he moved to the Colman Ferry Dock on Pier 52 (fig. 1.11). At first Standley added "Ye Olde" to the "Curiosity Shop and Indian Curio" on his sign, but he soon shortened the name to Ye Olde Curiosity Shop—an allusion to the shop Charles Dickens described in his 1841 book. The reference was familiar to the public and Standley advertised that his shop actually "beat the Dickens."[28] The new shop sat among several other storefronts facing Railroad Avenue, on the entrance side of the dock, "built upon piles, where an 18-foot tide swishes under the floor and steamers brush noses on the rear window sills of the shop."[29] Along its sides the small steamboats of the Mosquito Fleet landed passengers, cargo, and mail. It was an excellent location, actually on the waterfront, where there was always pedestrian traffic.

A 1905 article in the *Seattle Post-Intelligencer* captured the area's ambiance and history.[30] There had been great growth in the ten years since the land south of Jackson Street had been under water and coal bunkers stood at the foot of King Street. Among the factories, mills, foundries, and shops along Railroad Avenue, a visitor encountered a babel of tongues. Between Main and Jackson Streets, a colony of Jews who had recently fled Russia ran junk and

1.11. Railroad Avenue end of the Colman Ferry Dock, photographed June 1909 by Asahel Curtis. The broad entrance in the middle was for horse-drawn teams only. To its left were Plumb and Weber, cigar sellers, and Sunde and Erland, Co., sail makers and ship chandlers. To its right were the Sunset Boat Engine Company, the Morgan Oyster Company, Ye Olde Curiosity Shop (with a line of people looking at its wares), and Loggers Supply. Steamboats of the Mosquito Fleet stand alongside the one-story dock. Asahel Curtis Collection, #13542, Washington State Historical Society, Tacoma.

second-hand stores and old men sat in doorways reading the Talmud (although this was more likely the Psalms). Across the street the old side-wheel steamer *Idaho,* once engaged in smuggling, now operated as the emergency hospital. Just north, the Pacific Coast Steamship Company docks teamed with longshoremen and sailors sitting about whittling miniature ships and working out rope puzzles. Excursionists crowded the wharves that handled the steamers to West Seattle and across the Sound. Along the front of Colman Dock, sandwiched between wholesale commercial houses and fish markets, there was a bit of "concentrated interest"—Standley's little curio shop.

The shop was small, but bigger than the Madison Street one had been. There were now two large window areas flanking a double door, and upper paneled windows with diamond details at the top and bottom let in more light. The deep narrow interior was flanked on both sides with lengths of glass floor cases and wall shelves crammed with baskets, miniature totem poles, and other merchandise. Sea creatures, Indian drums, a reindeer sled, and a mermaid were suspended from the ceiling. The shop's crush of objects became an identifying aspect of its character. From the beginning, Standley shared the space with Charles T. Wernecke, an established dealer in raw furs, and would until 1916, when the rebuilding of Colman Dock required both of them relocate.[31]

The Colman Dock location was exciting because there was always activity relating to faraway places.[32] Officers from the U.S. revenue cutter *Perry* told

Standley about watching a volcanic eruption actually birth an island in 1906. Named Perry Island after its discoverers, it disappeared three years later.[33] In 1908, as Theodore Roosevelt's Great White Fleet circled the globe exhibiting U.S. naval power, thirteen ships sailed into the Seattle harbor. The following year, presidents, industrialists, scientists, and an array of other important visitors arrived for the Alaska-Yukon-Pacific Exposition, Seattle's first world's fair.

A dock location could also be precarious. A fire in 1908 spurred a major rebuilding and dramatic enlargement of Colman Dock, to seven times its previous length. The new waiting room at the Sound end was domed like a railway station and an Italianate clock tower now distinguished Colman Dock from more modest docks. Photographs from before and after the fire suggest that Standley's shop was not overly affected. A formal shop portrait taken in late 1908 or early 1909 shows the sign in front changed, but little else. Probably taken to use in advertising during the approaching AYPE, this photograph makes the shop appear especially large and impressive, through strategic placement of objects and a dramatic camera angle (fig. 1.12). The reference to Wernecke Fine Furs and Rugs above the door is obscured by a Chilkat blanket hung there for the occasion, and new and imposing acquisitions are displayed. The largest objects would not stay for long, however. The totem pole, nearly twelve feet tall, was related to a group of four poles that Standley had acquired for Seattle's private Ravenna Park as a special attraction during the exposition. He appears to have kept this pole, one of the original four, and had a copy of it made to complete the park's set. The Ravenna Park poles would influence other poles the shop would later commission.

Even more impressive than the totem pole was the shop's assortment of whalebones. The large scapula does not appear in earlier photographs, nor does the pair of enormous jawbones, which Standley identified as from a sulphur bottom whale (also called a blue whale) and at nineteen and a half feet in length, the largest on record. He was very proud of these bones and loaned them to Captain A. M. Baber for use in the Eskimo Village during the AYPE.[34] The photograph showing the whalebones in front of the shop was taken before the exposition opened in June, because after it closed in mid-October, Standley immediately loaned the bones to the University of Washington and had Baber deliver them there.[35] In late 1937, as he watched a rigger come to reinstall another pair of whalebones in front of his new shop, Standley described to a reporter how he had acquired the first bones with the help of Indians from Vancouver Island:

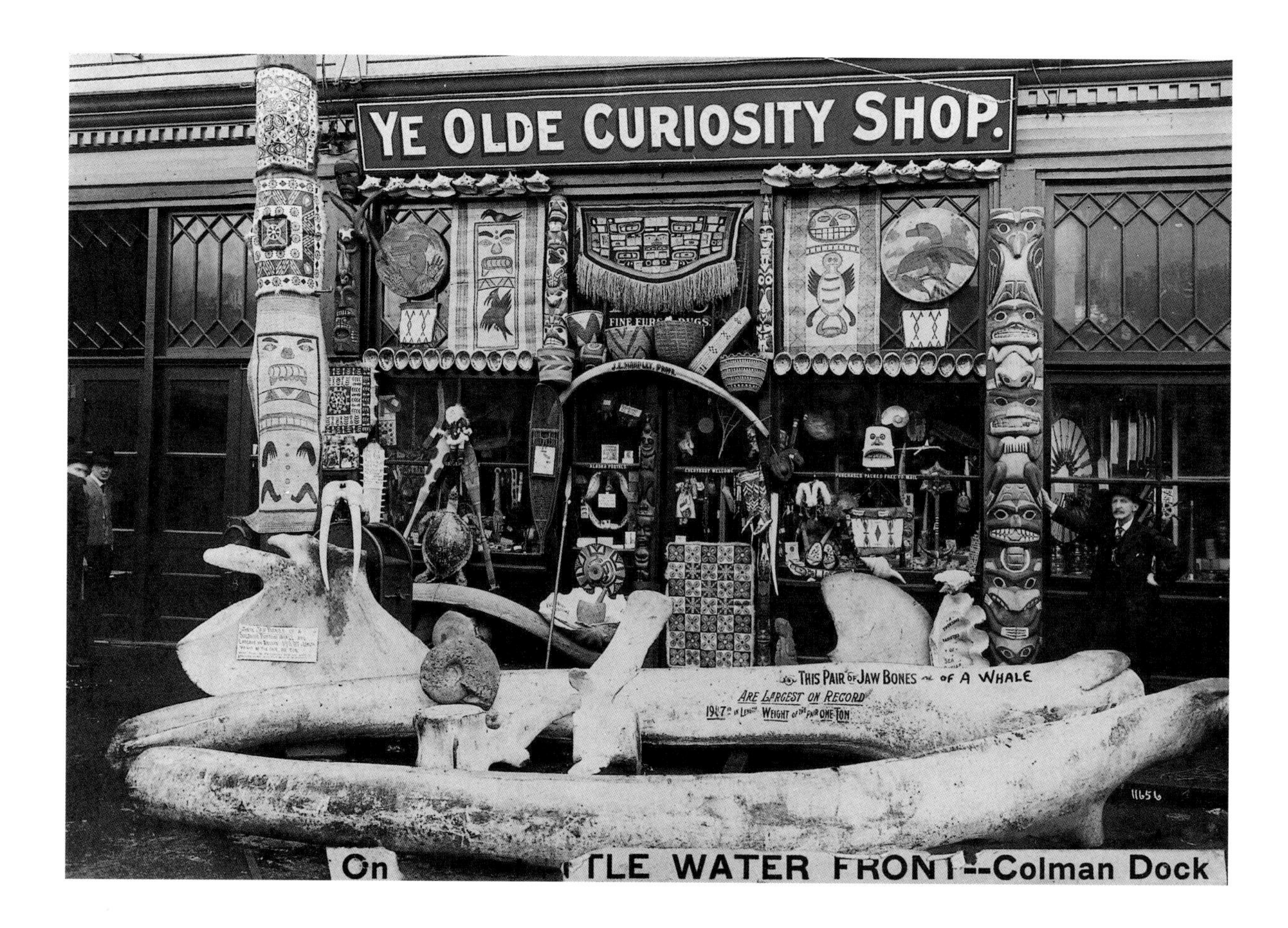
YE OLDE CURIOSITY SHOP.
THIS PAIR OF JAW BONES OF A WHALE
ARE LARGEST ON RECORD
WEIGHT of the PAIR ONE TON
On
TLE WATER FRONT--Colman Dock
11656

1.12. Ye Olde Curiosity Shop, 813 Railroad Avenue, Colman Dock, late 1908 or early 1909. Since the earlier photograph at this location, the shop had acquired impressive new stock, and Standley and the photographer worked to make the business appear as large and impressive as possible. The textiles tacked to the electric pole, the whale jawbones lying in the street, Standley leaning against a large totem pole, and the new horizontally oriented sign all contribute to this effect. The sign on the wedge-shaped whale scapula describes the whale jawbones displayed in front. Later in 1909 A. C. Haddon purchased the white large-mouthed mask to the right of the central doors for the Horniman Museum. Like the mask pictured earlier (see fig. 1.2), it was also replicated from a drawing in Boas's 1897 work. The shop's interior is pictured in chapter 2 of this book (see fig. 2.1).

> Those whalebones have been with me a long time. I found them in 1908, on a beach thirty miles north of Cape Race Light on Vancouver Island. One was in the water and the other was in the sand, half buried. I didn't know how to get them to Seattle. But finally I gave some Indians—they were King George Indians and they all liked to be called King George—five dollars to bring them to Seattle. They built a raft, put stones on it and sank it near one whalebone at low tide. They lifted the bone, which was lighter under water, up on the raft and then took the stones off. It rose right to the surface. They waited until high tide and got the other bone on the raft, and then they sailed the whole business to Seattle. I've had them [whalebones] ever since, over the doors of my shop.[36]

During Standley's lifetime the shop owned several sets of whale jawbones. Those he watched being reinstalled in 1937 were longer (21 feet) and thinner than the pair rafted to Seattle and posed in front of the shop in the 1908–9 photograph. The later jawbones may have come from the Akutan Whaling Station in Alaska, listed as a source in shop supplier books.

1.13. Behind Colman Dock, with the Mosquito Fleet of ferries alongside, sometime between 1908 and 1912. Indians would bring their canoes to the back of Logger's Supply and Standley's shop next door to trade when the ferries were not in. The Italianate tower that appears here was destroyed when the ocean liner *Alameda* crashed into it in 1912. Photographer unknown. Puget Sound Maritime Historical Society, Seattle, 5011-18, Museum of History and Industry, Seattle.

One night in April 1912 the steel-hulled ocean liner *Alameda* ran into Colman Dock and sliced through it, knocking the clock tower into Elliott Bay. The dock was long, however, and Railroad Avenue and Standley's shop were not affected (fig. 1.13). Two years later, in 1914, the adjacent Grand Trunk Dock burned. A West Seattle neighbor saw the fire across the water and notified Standley, who rushed to move the contents of his shop onto Railroad Avenue. Passersby volunteered their help and a few of them walked away with some of the items.

Ye Olde Curiosity Shop's fortune expanded with the city's. In 1906 the Standley family left downtown apartment living for a large new home across Elliott Bay in West Seattle.[37] As the Standley children grew older, they helped in the shop, as would their children and grandchildren. Over the years Standley's son Edward Venus Standley and several sons-in-law would join the store management. Paul Parker, who in 1900 married the eldest Standley daughter, Jessie, worked there for at least a decade. A 1907 shop brochure lists J. E. Standley as the shop proprietor, J. L. Charbneau as manager, and E. V. Standley as assistant manager. Jules Charbneau came to the shop in 1904, the day after he married Standley's second daughter, Caroline, and was employed there for several years before leaving for other business enterprises. Charbneau later became a collector of miniatures. Standley's son Edward, who had worked

In 19X The World Famous Ye Olde Curiosity Shop Estd 1899 upon the Waterfront of Seattle was Ordered out as Colman Dock was to be rebuilt. Daddy Standley the Propr. secured a 2d ave uptown Storeroom and the several truckloads of Missilaneous Curio Showcases, Shelveing etc had been placed OK in rear entrance. The last Load to go was several Alaska Indian Carved Wood Totem Poles from 10 to 20 feet in length. a snow storm has set in. The ther[mometer] was at 30 to 33 for several days. BUT when that Truck reached the alley On Columbia St. the huge truck began to slide and was hugging "Rippes" Cafe Walls, the 12 inch snow was 18 inches before Men with Blankets & Gunny sacks placed under the Tires struggling for 2 hours got [it] going.

Well after 40 hours the snow was 4 feet deep. Thousands of Clerks and their Bosses had to stay in Hotels as Every system was Paralized—in about a Week—"Fords" were the only thing that could climb over the Hillocks of snow that was shoveled off sidewalks. Roofs had caved in the Worst to Happen was that of the Great Catholic Cathedral whose metal Roof crashed down upon Empty Pews. Frederick Nelsons 2 story Building 2d ave had 50 men shoveling snow off into alley then city ordered a tunnel 15 ft deep to let water out.

—Standley, personal notes

in the shop as early as 1907, officially joined its management in 1915. Joe James's father, (Isaac) Russell James, joined the shop in 1912 and married Standley's youngest daughter, Ruby, in 1915.

The Colman Ferry Dock location was unparalleled for the number of commuters and tourists it brought to the store as the Mosquito Fleet of small commuter steamers buzzed back and forth, but there were some drawbacks. As modes of transportation changed through the century, the dock had to be reconstructed several times to adapt to them. By 1910, with the regrading of the hills adjacent to Seattle's downtown, the automobile became so viable that within a few years, in early 1916, the shop faced a move while the Railroad Avenue side was rebuilt with a ramp dedicated to automobiles and trucks. (Previously, motor vehicles had been carried on the freight floor.) Wernecke moved his fur business to the Grand Trunk Dock, while Standley leased an interim site on Second Avenue, near Virginia Street, and scheduled the move for February. What became known as the Big Snow of 1916 began just as Standley's large totem poles were being moved. The event was one of those that Standley wrote about on a scrap of paper, gathering memories for the book he planned to write one day. Transporting the totem poles was only part of the challenge of moving the shop. In addition to reassembling the stock on shelves and in cases, each item hanging from the ceiling had to be carefully taken down and painstakingly hung up in the new location.

Ye Olde Curiosity Shop operated out of its interim location at 809 Second Street for almost a year before it could return to Colman Dock. On January 8, 1917, when the shop opened again on the dock, now at 811 Railroad Avenue, the old upper windows with leaded-glass diamonds and the smaller front windows were gone, replaced by blocks of vertical windows above large single panes on either side of a central front door (fig. 1.14). Totem poles loosely replicating those that had been in Ravenna Park during the 1909 exposition flanked the shop's sides. At some point a set of whale jawbones was wired up to arch over the front to dramatically distinguish the business from others and to pique the curiosity of passersby.

Later photographs of the shop at the 811 Railroad Avenue location show an alteration, with the door now on the right and the whale jawbones forming a V-shape rather than an arch (fig. 1.15). The notation "moved to room south—better," dated June 1923 in Standley's account book, explains the change, necessitated by the need for better automobile access onto the dock. By this time there were twenty-three automobile ferries plying Puget Sound. The section to the right of the shop's central door was given up for an automobile exit from the dock, the door was maintained, and the shop was expanded south. The right-hand whalebone was moved to the left of the telephone pole, to which it was wired in the earlier photograph, to now create a V-shape (fig. 1.16). The new ascending automobile entrance ramp positioned to the left of the shop's new space, curved northwest a bit, narrowing the shop in the back. Both the earlier and this later version of the shop at 811 Railroad Avenue were used on postcard-sized booster cards that Standley gave out to visitors and included in his correspondence with museums.

1.14. After nearly a year in an interim location, while Colman Dock was rebuilt, Ye Olde Curiosity Shop reopened in January 1917 at 811 Railroad Avenue. Standley had acquired a new pair of especially long whale jawbones and wired them up to frame the entranceway. Inside, in the store's front section, cedar bark mats painted with Northwest Coast animal figures provided a backdrop for suspended sea creatures, while old currency papered the rear ceiling.

Seattle's Later Curio Trade and Northwest Tourism

During the second decade of the twentieth century a few other shops competed with Standley's. All shared in the business there was, during good times and bad, and although relations sometimes chafed a bit, competition was never cutthroat. Each shop had its own character, but none was like Ye Olde Curiosity Shop. The Hudson Bay Fur Company (which later took the name the Alaska Fur Company) and Mack's Totem Shop were the main players. The Hudson Bay Fur Company began in Seattle in the 1880s. It had been located in the Colman Building for well over a decade when Moritz Gutmann purchased the store about 1903. The primary business was tanned furs, fur coats, and rugs. During World War II it made parkas for U.S. military forces stationed in Alaska. As the shop began to acquire curios, especially ivories, from its fur buyer in Nome, Alaska, the company established "The Curio Department," located in an annex at the back of the store. The Hudson Bay Fur

1.15. Colman Dock, summer 1934. Ye Olde Curiosity Shop was forced to move one door south in June 1923 to allow for changes in the ferry entrance ramp. Standley extended the sign and windows to the south of the old door, moved the right-hand whale jawbone to the left of the other one, and kept a totem pole at the base of the V thus formed. Pemco Webster & Stevens Collection, 83.10.4483, Museum of History and Industry, Seattle.

Company began to list itself under "Curios" in the city directory in 1912.[38] It issued undated catalogs offering many of the same items that appeared in Ye Olde Curiosity Shop catalogs. In 1931, the year after Gutmann died, the shop moved to Fifth Avenue, where it continued to be run by his son Addis.

Seattle's Hudson Bay Fur Company was easily confused with the well-known Canadian business, the Hudson's Bay Company, which used a beaver as its logo. A suit filed in 1941 by the latter, "the oldest trading corporation in the world," to force a name change, was settled out of court. In 1943 Gutmann's business deleted the beaver from its advertising and purchased the name Alaska Fur Company from Herman Krupp, another Seattle fur and curio supplier who had used the name since 1917. Krupp sold off his fur interests and took the new name Oceanic Trading for his curio supply business. Gutmann's Alaska Fur Company closed out its curio unit over a period of several years in the 1940s and its remaining operations in the 1950s. Under both of his business names, Krupp ran a wholesale rather than a retail operation, which produced ivory and bone curios. Like many other shops in Seattle and Alaska, Standley's shop was one of its customers. Oceanic Trading closed in the late 1980s. In contrast to the atmosphere of Ye Olde Curiosity Shop, the demeanor and merchandise of Gutmann's Hudson Bay Fur Company were more dignified and upscale. Photographs of the store interior show spacious fur display rooms and well-ordered curio areas dedicated primarily to large groups of neatly arranged baskets, model totem poles, and carved ivory tusks.

Mack's Totem Shop was a late comer, smaller than Standley's shop or its competitors. Albert "Mack" McKillop opened the store in 1933 on the Marion Street walkover viaduct that connected the ferry terminal and First Avenue. He expanded the space in the mid-1930s and remodeled in the 1950s. McKillop was not the extrovert that Standley was, and he preferred to work undisturbed, carving cribbage boards and making jewelry from walrus teeth.[39] The Hudson

Bay Fur Company and Mack's Totem Shop purchased both large and model totem poles and carvings from the same local Nuu-chah-nulth carvers who produced items for Ye Olde Curiosity Shop, especially from Sam Williams and his son Wilson, but also from Jimmy Johns and other carvers. Other Seattle shops that carried Indian and Eskimo items included Berry's Arts and Crafts, located on the Marion Street viaduct, Mrs. Ferguson's Alaska Curio Shop on Second Avenue, and Dorothy's Gift Shop in the Olympic Hotel. Although many customers were locals, it was the tourists who kept Seattle curio shops in business.

1.16. Visitors Louise and Ann Boullin, photographed September 1, 1931, with "Daddy Standley" in front of the shop. The totem pole was carved by Nuu-chah-nulth carver Sam Williams, who lived much of his life in the Seattle area.

The early decades of the twentieth century were a time of burgeoning tourism, especially in the American Southwest, where the Fred Harvey Company managed a chain of hotels in New Mexico and Arizona in association with the Santa Fe Railway. The combination of railroad and company became the critical component in what has been called the "invention of the Southwest," the multifaceted creation of a regional identity based on its landscape and the Indian people who had lived there for centuries. Thousands of tourists came to the Southwest, to gaze at the mystic grandeur of its Grand Canyon and to observe the region's exotic Indians, especially the Pueblo in their ancient multistory dwellings. Traveling on the Santa Fe Railway and staying in Harvey hotels made the experience comfortable and safe. The well-mannered (as they were described at the time) Indians who waited to sell pottery as the train or touring cars arrived, and the company-operated curio shops in its hotels, encouraged the purchase of mementos of the trip. Pottery in styles that came to be associated with particular Pueblos meant that one might buy, perhaps directly from its maker, a Zuni bowl, an Acoma jar, "a Hopi," or "a San Ildefonso." Fine California Indian baskets and Navajo rugs were also important curio items. To a degree, the world of the Southwest Indians became one of fictive imagination, an essentialist myth that emphasized the Indian as naturally religious and artistic.[40]

Tourism in the Pacific Northwest operated differently. Trains could bring visitors there, but tourism campaigns rivaling the Fred Harvey operations in the Southwest were never orchestrated. From a tourist perspective, Puget Sound was more important as the point of departure for an Alaskan tour than as a destination in itself. Until World War II far more advertising was devoted to the Puget Sound region's commercial and agricultural advantages and the promotion of immigration to the area than to tourism. Tourist brochures early in the century focused on scenery and recreational opportunities and pictured Native people only occasionally. When included at all, male Indians were shown participating in this world, gazing in worshipful awe at Mount Rainier, "Nature's Cathedral," or traveling in canoes through scenic waters. There was an occasional young mother with her baby, but most Indian women pictured were elderly, participating in activities of a primitive past or selling their ancient arts. In one brochure an aged "burden bearer" pauses, bent from the wood she carries on her back; in another a woman sits "selling her baskets." Unlike the shyly smiling Indians in travel brochures for the Southwest, the few Indians in travel advertising for the Puget Sound area wore weary expressions of reserve and commercial blankets rather than picturesque Native dress. The implied message was that there were few Indians in this Pacific Coast paradise of evergreens and unlimited potential, that they were not to be considered an impediment, and that they would soon be gone.[41]

Indians in Alaska also lived amid awe-inspiring scenery, but they were viewed as much more picturesque, with their colorful Northwest Coast ceremonial clothing, totem poles, and curious associated customs. Steamer excursions up the Inside Passage to Alaska became established in the 1880s and the number increased each year. The Pacific Coast Steamship Company, the Alaska Steamship Company, and others offered organized tourist experiences similar to those available in the Southwest but limited in comparison.[42] Alaska tourism was economically insignificant until World War I provided a boost as travelers eschewed Europe for North America. The coordination of rail and steamship schedules in the 1920s offered further convenience.

Early tourist brochures focused on Alaska as primarily scenic and picturesque, usually emphasizing the land's natural mineral wealth. (The Yukon and Nome gold rushes were very much in the prospective traveler's mind.) Seeing Indians was not the major lure that it was in the Southwest, but Alaska Natives were regarded as providing a quaint attraction. Their curios—described in the brochure "Alaska Steamship Company, Copper River & Northwestern Ry [Railway]" (1917) as "weird totems, rich baskets, old carvings in ivory and slate, crude gropings toward art by a primitive race"—were readily available for purchase, directly from the maker or in curio shops. This brochure is curious also in its painted cover, an amalgam of borrowed images. Two Egyptianate birds (perhaps ravens?) border the top, while below, against a scenic Southeast Alaska fjord with a steamship waiting patiently in the distance, a fashionable woman traveler standing on a knoll bends benevolently toward a seated Native woman wearing a parka—and selling Hopi pottery! Tourist advertising brochures often borrowed images or text from each other, creating juxtapositions as bizarre as an Eskimo woman in Southeast Alaska selling Hopi pottery from Arizona. Such anomalies reflect a careless ignorance of distinctions among Native people that was common at the time. The combination of picturesque scenery, visitor, and Native selling handicraft had become a recognized convention in travel brochures featuring the American West, an accepted shorthand for an authentic experience. Thus, the specifics were less important, even interchangeable.[43]

A section from "Trip to Wonderful Alaska," published in 1905 by the Alaska Steamship Company, described the traveler's potential experience: "Wrangel is quite a totem pole town and the time spent here will be greatly enjoyed, visiting and inspecting and photographing these relics of Indian mythology and monuments of departed Indians; and in visiting the curio stores where miniature duplicates of the totem poles can be found." As alluring as cruising to Alaska sounded, however, many tourists came only as close as Seattle. For them, Ye Olde Curiosity Shop offered a vicarious experience through its thousands of Alaskan relics and the stories told by its entertaining proprietor. Visitors could see the whaling harpoons and dogsleds described in newspaper accounts, actually hold ancient ivory tools, examine totem poles (albeit souvenir ones) and fine woven baskets, and feel that they were actually experiencing Alaska—and even take away a bit of it too, by purchasing the same ivory cribbage boards, baskets, or moccasins they might have seen in Alaska. Along with its extensive inventory of recently made items for sale, Ye Olde Curiosity Shop was unlike other local shops in having an enormous collection of authentic old Arctic artifacts. When quantities of such material came into Seattle in the late 1890s and the first few years of the twentieth century, Standley had been handily positioned to gather them up for his shop.

Relics and Handiwork: Early Sources for Native Art and Artifacts

The floor, walls and ceiling are covered with Relics and Curiosities from the Primitive Races, who are fast disappearing from Bering Sea, Alaska, Puget Sound, as well as the natives of the South Seas. Here are Raw Furs and Rare Skins of the North, Rare Marine Specimens; also Indian Baskets, Moccasins and Curios of Eskimo and Coast Indians.

—Ye Olde Curiosity Shop brochure, 1907

IN THE TWO YEARS BEFORE JOSEPH E. STANDLEY OPENED HIS FIRST SHOP IN Seattle in 1899, the city had secured its place as the main point of embarkation and return for the thousands seeking gold in the Yukon and Alaska. Government personnel and traders working in the North came regularly into Seattle, and it was the established point of departure for travelers touring Alaska's scenic Inside Passage. With ships traveling to and from the Orient, local businesspeople were beginning to visualize their small city as the hub of an expanding Pacific Rim trade. There was also no serious curio shop competition at this time. Location and timing contributed initially to Ye Olde Curiosity Shop's success and later to the role it assumed and the influence it exerted (fig. 2.1).

Standley moved his shop as soon as possible onto the waterfront, on the Colman Ferry Dock, conveniently positioning himself to acquire a broad array of uncommon curios from Alaska, the Pacific, and the Orient, while assuring a constantly changing aggregate of potential customers—regional ferry users, the traffic related to Alaska, and increasingly, international travelers. The shop quickly established a reputation as an entertaining place that defied imagination—a "must see" for visitors to Seattle. Crammed with oddities and curiosities seldom seen elsewhere, it advertised itself not only as a business but as "a veritable free museum and most unique of its kind in existence." For many the shop in fact functioned as a museum.[1] Standley was outgoing and gregarious, enthusiastically intrigued by everything and everyone. When he died in 1940, he had lived with his daughter Ruby James and her family for twenty years; his grandson, Joe James, then sixteen years old, knew Standley well. James has characterized him as a curio lover first, an entertainer second, and a businessman third.

2.1. Interior of the Colman Dock shop with J. E. Standley, ca. 1912. In these early years natural history specimens dominated the layers of items hanging from the shop's ceiling. Baskets were a major part of the stock at the time. They and other merchandise that was offered in quantity were grouped, while other items were displayed randomly. For formal portraits such as this, Navajo rugs were arranged on the floor.

Standley loved to show people around the shop, telling the story behind a particular curio, explaining how he acquired it and how it worked, then sometimes becoming so excited about the object that he would refuse to sell it.

Those working in the North could bring into Ye Olde Curiosity Shop and readily convert to cash whatever ivory and Native manufactures they had managed to gather; they found in the shop's egalitarian proprietor an audience ever eager for stories about exciting adventures and uncommon experiences. The location was convenient, and everyone was welcome, which was not the case in all places of business at the time. This openness was both good business and a point of pride with Standley. In 1901 he announced "Everybody Welcome" on a giant clam shell that sat next to the entrance of the Madison Street shop, and later repeated this welcome above the door of his first Colman Dock shop. The short articles Standley wrote between 1905 and 1907 for the *Pacific Sportsman,* as well as the booster and promotion information cards he distributed, all announced this policy prominently. That Standley accepted and sincerely enjoyed people from all walks of life is reflected in the lack of critical tone in the scores of notes he made about events and people and in comments that journalists made about him.

Standley's decision to emphasize curios related to the Indians and Eskimos of the Northwest Coast and Alaska was an astute one—there was ready supply, and Seattle residents as well as visitors were greatly interested in such objects (fig. 2.2) Local newspapers gave ongoing coverage to the Territory of Alaska, and readers closely followed the tales of prospectors' successes and explorers' victories, tragedies of whalers stranded in the ice, and daring arctic rescues by revenue cutters. The papers also regularly reported on government and church-sponsored activities in Eskimo and Indian villages.

During the early years of the twentieth century, Eskimos visiting Seattle were often written up in local papers. Painted with a broad brush, they were generally depicted as friendly and good-humored. They wore beautiful fur parkas, and their admirable hunting skills allowed them to thrive in a climate whose harshness stretched the imagination. For a population made up essentially of pioneers—families who had founded Seattle, settlers who had come soon after, and others who had pitted themselves against the North in imagination if not in fact—the Eskimos embodied traits held dear. Seattle newspapers gave less attention to the Natives of the Northwest Coast, and when they did, the distinctions between tribes tended to be vague. Unlike the "cheerful" Eskimos, Northwest Coast Indians were considered by many to be secretive and inscrutable, and they erected totem poles with grotesque figures that had mysterious meanings. The rare old Eskimo and Northwest Coast objects exhibited in Standley's collection had a local as well as a tourist audience.

Alaskan Suppliers to Ye Olde Curiosity Shop

Standley's shop was strategically located to facilitate the acquisition of a multitude of objects made by Alaska Natives from traders who had direct contact with the Indians and Eskimos; in some cases the items had been secured in other ways, such as theft or the digging of archaeological deposits. Standley's Guest Book lists many of the whalers, whaler-traders, and revenue cutter captains who were essential to the shop's success by helping to supply it, and there were no doubt others. They brought thousands of natural history specimens, old hunting implements and tools, recently carved ivory tusks and miniatures, and other miscellaneous items out of Alaska. Within his first several years in

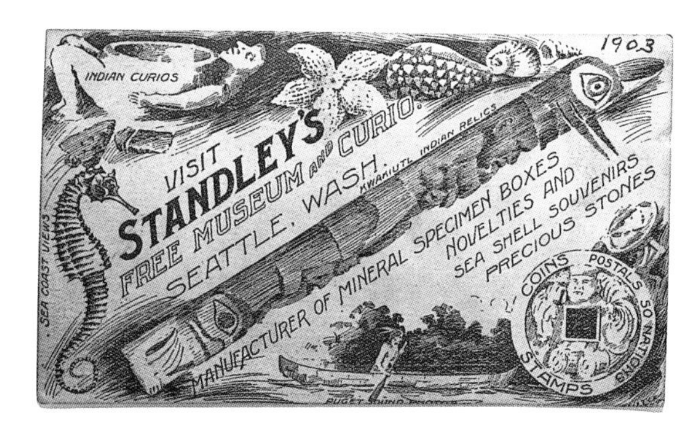

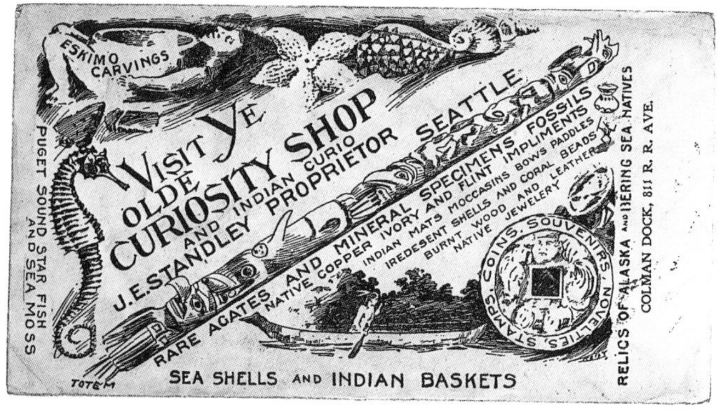

2.2. Three early shop advertisements, printed on envelopes or postcards, 1900–3 (upper), 1904–5 (middle), ca. 1907 (lower). All three picture the Seattle Totem Pole: on the earliest is a very loose version of the upper half and on the others the entire pole.

Seattle, Standley acquired more than two thousand Alaskan "relics," which he displayed at the Alaska Club beginning about 1904. A 1907 news article described these items as "probably the most comprehensive collection of Alaska Indian and Eskimo curios under one roof." In 1909 *The Westerner* magazine reported that the collection had been begun "by Mr. L. L. Bales, an Alaskan explorer, when he carried the mail to Nome in the early days" and added to by "Captain Tozier of the United States revenue cutter *Grant.*" The collection also included objects from "Capt Foster an Arctic navigator."[2]

In addition to Standley's connections with those working in and out of Alaska on commercial and government business, he established ties with individual Alaskan storekeepers such as Walter Waters in Wrangell and John Feusi in Douglas, who acted as middlemen in filling orders for moccasins and baskets. On occasion, Standley also bought directly from Alaskan or Canadian Natives visiting or living in Seattle. One special transaction was with Miss Columbia, the daughter of Captain J. Smith and his Labrador Eskimo wife. Miss Columbia's birth at the 1893 Chicago World Columbian Exposition at the time that Standley was actually there was heralded widely, as was her presentation as royalty at Seattle's 1909 Alaska-Yukon-Pacific Exposition (AYPE). Standley felt some connection with her and wrote variously in his Guest Book: "1st Eskimo child born in the US. Queen of A.Y.P.E. 1909, often came to my shop. A very pretty girl. Knew her well. I Bot her Bracelet and ivory beads 1918."[3]

The second photograph of the Madison Street store (see fig. 1.8) includes the man who had the greatest influence on Standley of any single person during the shop's earliest years. Alaska trader L. L. Bales established Ye Olde Curiosity Shop's Alaska collection with material collected on the Seward Peninsula and the Yukon and Kuskokwim Rivers. Standley met Bales, a writer with extensive Alaska experience, soon after moving to Seattle. Bales's stories about his experiences in the Far North captivated the shopkeeper, as did the relics Bales had brought out of Alaska. The two became staunch friends, and Bales spent a good deal of time at the shop.[4] Standley's jottings and Bales's

My Friend Lightner Bales was the Alaska Guide and Map Maker for the U. S. Govt when the Chilcat Pass Alaska Rail Road was being Built. He lived on the Kuskoqim River at Quick Silver Mines.

—Standley, personal notes and Guest Book

published articles hint of Bales's exciting life in Alaska, as do articles in Seattle and Alaskan newspapers.[5] None of these clarify exactly where, when, or how he gathered the arctic material that he sold Standley, however, but during his time in Alaska, Bales was a mail carrier to Nome, where he surely acquired some items. It is clear that he was a major and trusted source for both artifacts and information during the Curiosity Shop's first years, and he was influential in forming Standley's ideas about Alaska and Northwest Coast culture and art.

In the second photograph of Standley's Madison Street shop (see fig. 1.8), Bales appears to be middle-aged. Exactly when he first ventured to Alaska is unclear, but he appears to have already spent some time in the Arctic before the Nome gold rush of 1899, when he settled on the Seward Peninsula to mine and trade.[6] Standley liked to recount how his friend had carried mail by dog-sled and to recall bits of the stories Bales had told about his Alaska adventures.[7] Bales made his living in a variety of ways, as a mail carrier, a trapper, a hunting guide for wealthy clients, a freelance writer, and for a while, a miner. Between 1904 and 1907 both he and Standley published short articles on Alaska in the *Pacific Sportsman,* a magazine published in Seattle. Bales continued writing for the magazine after it became *Outdoor Life and Recreation* in 1908, but Standley did not. Bales's articles focused primarily on the habits of wildlife—birds, caribou, whales, grizzlies—and on big game hunting, fishing, and fur farming. He also wrote occasionally on Alaska's Native people.[8] Standley purchased the copyright to Bales's 1908 article on totem poles published in *Outdoor Life;* he drew from it over the years for random bits of information and misinformation about totem poles that he distributed to visitors on information cards. He also may have purchased the copyright to Bales's article "Illustrated Life among Alaskan Eskimo."[9] Bales spent so much time in Seattle that his home address was listed in the local city directory for five years between 1900 and 1913. His friendship with the Standleys was both a professional and a personal one. He was married at Totem Place, the Standley home, and his daughter Margaret became Standley's god-daughter.[10]

Whalers and Traders

By the late nineteenth century Alaskan Yup'iks and Inupiats, astute traders for centuries, had became accustomed to the *belunga* (foreigner) appetite for furs, ivory, and "good for nothing things," as they described their worn or cast-off tools and implements to ethnologist Edward William Nelson, who eagerly purchased these items in Bering Strait villages between 1877 and 1881. North of

Norton Sound, Inupiats had been trading with whalers since the 1850s. Daily contact increased as whaling ships began hiring Natives to work on them, especially during off-season commercial walrusing in the 1870s. In the 1880s families began to live aboard the ships, the women acting as seamstresses and the men working at hunting and dog driving when the ships wintered over in the ice.

Shore whaling commenced along the northern Alaska coast during the mid-1880s, when whalers dependent on a severely depleted bowhead fishery realized that to be successful, they must tap it in early spring as did Eskimo hunters. By late spring-early summer, as whaling ships were typically just beginning to move north of the Bering Strait, Native hunters had already been whaling for some time, approaching the migrating bowhead as soon as leads began to open in the pack ice in April. The answer was to establish shore whaling stations staffed with men ready to operate much as local hunters did and to employ the latter for their crews. After a whaling station opened at Point Barrow in 1884, others followed along the coast. Even when they took no whales, the men were on site to trade for the whalebone (baleen) from those whales the Natives killed. Shore whaling was increasingly successful through the 1890s, while baleen prices were high. The whalebone market softened in 1907, however, as fashion changed and women ceased to wear whalebone (baleen stiffened) corsets, and other materials replaced whale oil for use in illumination, lubrication, and manufacturing. By 1914 commercial whaling in Alaska had all but ceased.

With that decline, Point Barrow, Point Hope, and smaller whaling communities in North Alaska were thrown into economic hardship, and both the whalers and the Natives dependent on the industry had to increase other activities to make up for lost income. Some whalers expanded trading until it became their major occupation. Eskimo men could assure having something to offer the traders by accelerating their ivory carving and searching more for discarded artifacts (figs. 2.3, 2.4, 2.5).[11] Few dedicated whaling ships came into Seattle—most worked out of San Francisco—but as whalers turned to trading, Seattle became a port of call for provisioning. A number of whalers and whaler-traders also retired to the Puget Sound area. Whether active or retired, they all found that Ye Olde Curiosity Shop and a few other curio stores were eager for any Arctic items they wished to sell.

By the time Standley set up shop, there were many small schooners traveling and trading in the Arctic. His Guest Book includes the names of nineteen "Arctic navigators" who stopped into the shop. Most entries include a few annotations that make them men of legend. Some traders provided Standley with prehistoric and historic material; others made limited transactions or

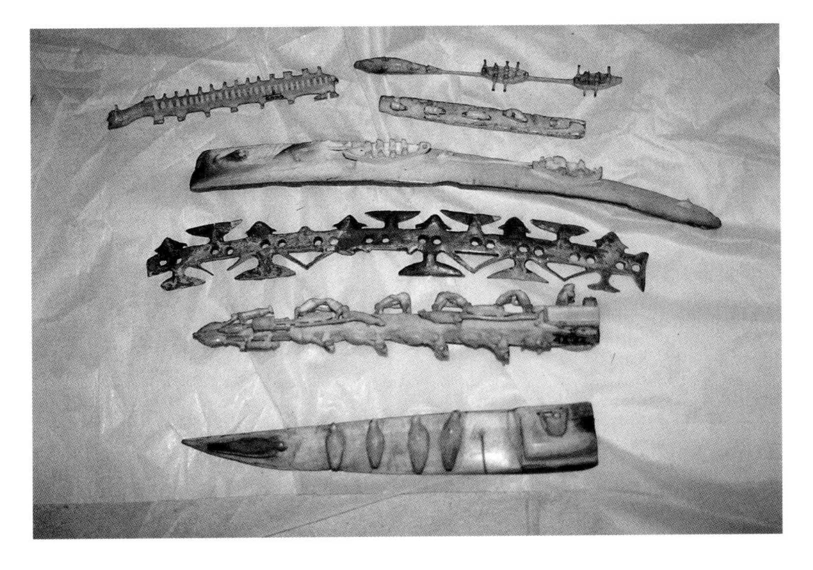

2.3. In the earlier years of market art, Inupiat and Yup'ik carvers often challenged themselves by creating complex arrangements of animals on tusks and carving delicate and fragile constructions. Ivory carvings, top to bottom: ice worm 5/6039; two umiaks pulling seal, 5/3161; ivory panel with seals, 5/6029; tusks with umiaks and animals, 5/3738; whale tails, 5/3152; tusk with wrestlers and animals, 5/4534; hunter and seals on tusk, 5/3739. National Museum of the American Indian, Smithsonian Institution, J. E. Standley Collection. Photograph by the author.

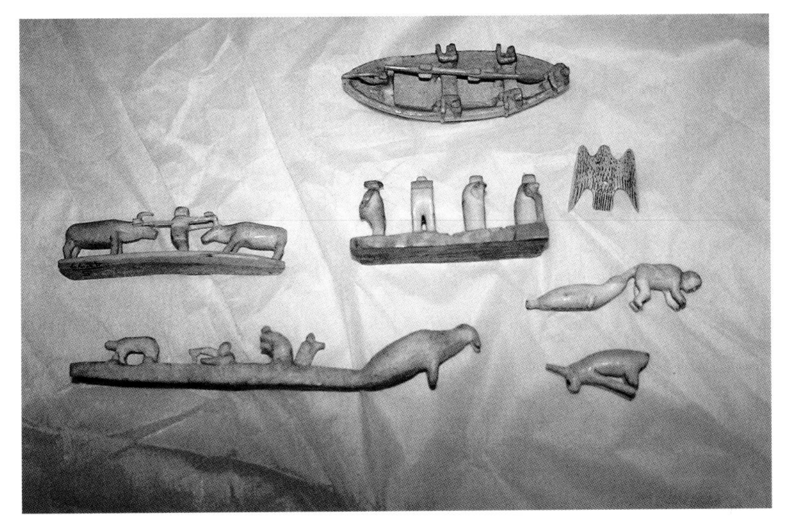

2.4. Ivory carvings made for sale, ca. 1900. Familiar animals and events were the subject of many carvings. Although museum records assign these and a wide range of other carvings in Standley's collection (including those in fig. 2.3) to Point Barrow, Alaska, they may have been made elsewhere, some likely in Siberia. Several of the figures appear to be the work of the same carver. Umiak with paddlers, 5/3132; man with two caribou, 5/4577; four human figures, 5/6035; bird, 5/4285; figures and seal on ice, 5/3323; man pulling seal, 5/6063; rabbit, 5/4745. National Museum of the American Indian, Smithsonian Institution, J. E. Standley Collection. Photograph by the author.

2.5. Hide ball. Standley romantically labeled this a "medicine ball" although there is no evidence that it was. Inupiat and Yup'ik women applied the skills they used in sewing and ornamenting hide clothing for their families to making items for sale. Anchorage Museum of History and Art, 83.53.9, from Ye Olde Curiosity Shop. Photograph by the author.

John Hackman came from Alaska with his boy & girl kids of Johns Eskimo wife. he caught a big sperm whale and made 20,000 dollars out of it. Came to Olympia Bot farm near Browns wonderfarm near Nisqually. I bot piles of old Eskimo Relics ivory & bone & wood and Mamma Standley and I used to visit him often.

—Standley, Guest Book, p. 10

merely visited the shop. There was H. W. Averill, "the Arctic Explorer & Eskimo curio gatherer for past 12 years for me," and Captain Patterson, "his Arctic Motor-boat and Mr. Blackwell gathered Eskimo Relics for us 1902. Lives at Santa Rosa Cal." A few men, like Captain Alfred H. Anderson ("the Banks Island whaler and explorer now at Gigg Harbor"), are mentioned in relation to only one or two important items. In the 1920s Standley accepted on consignment two large stone pieces, a stove and a lamp, that Anderson had brought from Banks Island and sold them to the Royal Ontario Museum.[12]

Some of these suppliers were merely acquaintances, but others, like "squawman" and shore whaler John Hackman, became Standley's friends. In 1889 Hackman and his brother-in-law set up a shore whaling station at Point Hope, Alaska, running it for several years before Hackman retired to the Puget Sound area.[13] Standley was always delighted to meet Natives who had successfully made their way in the world that he knew, and he spoke with admiration of Hackman's mixed-blood children, especially his daughter, "a fine woman and teaches school." He also admired Hackman's collection of Alaska artifacts, most from the Point Hope area. Both friendship and shrewdness may have motivated the short piece that Standley wrote about the collection in the *Pacific Sportsman,* exclaiming in enthusiasm and some contradiction: "Nowhere

2.6. Ivory pipe, East Cape, Siberia, ca. 1900. Standley wrote about this pipe in his 1906 article in *Pacific Sportsman:* "One beautiful pipe carved out of walrus tusk has many figures upon it and among the group are some gymnasts who are set in motion by the heat of the pipe bowl." Ivory, 9 5/8 in. long. Photograph courtesy National Museum of the American Indian, Smithsonian Institution, J. E. Standley Collection, 5/3320.

is there a finer collection of the relics of a primitive race . . . he has several thousand specimens of the rarest implements and utensils of every-day life of the present and ancient Eskimos."[14]

Traders working in Siberia also came into Seattle to provision and transact business.[15] Siberian items offered in the "1001 Curious Things" lists in some shop catalogs include baskets, Eskimo pipes from the Anadir River (fig. 2.6), and "mats made by Siberian Natives, Out of Bits of Skins Sewn in Designs."

Most important to the Standley's shop was Captain A. M. Baber, "the Arctic Trader [who] Brot the Eskimo Village from Cape Siberia to the A. Y. P. Exposition." Standley loaned Baber his large whale bones for the Eskimo Village entrance and, after the exposition closed, bought Baber's collection.[16] In his Guest Book, Standley recalled some of the names of the "Arctic navigators" in reference to their adventures or notoriety, rather than to curios they had brought in, although there may have been some. There was Captain James of the whaler *Morre William,* who founded the Walrus Club at Seattle's Rainier Club—"kiss the kassuke & drinks"—and Captain Anson, who, when his ship was captured by Russians, "seized the guards locked them up, and Brot back all to Nome."[17]

While Americans were thrilled to read of the adventures of explorers competing to reach the North and South Poles, Seattle residents were positioned to meet some of them. Standley was excited when anyone associated with the famous Norwegian explorer Roald Amundsen came into the shop. He talked with an officer who had been on Amundsen's ship *Maude* when it

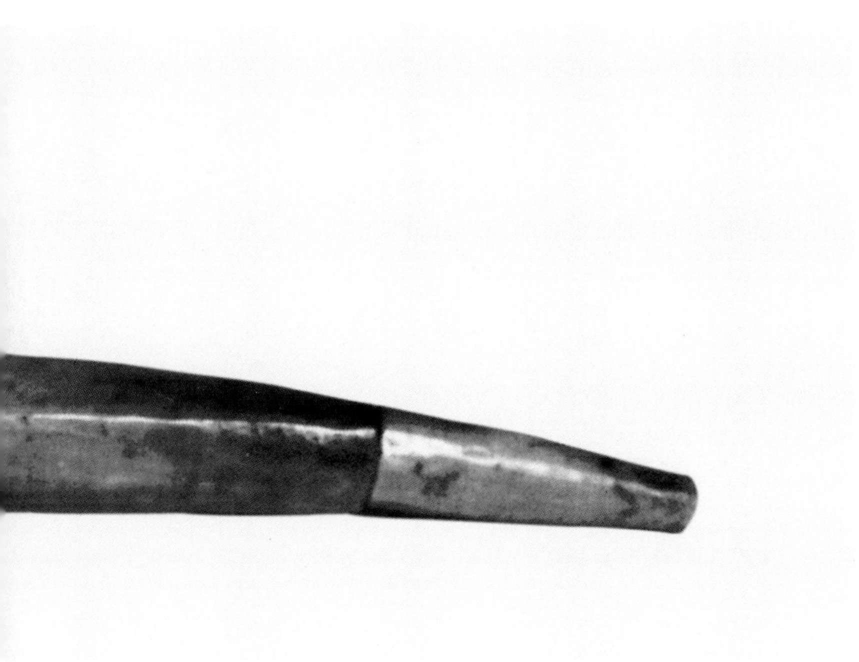

> Capt Amondsen the North Pole Navigator 1918 his Box Marked Horlick Malted Milk Sent from nome full of rare Eskimo old rare Ivory tools & Relics. I met Amonsen at his Picture lecture of Arctic scenes. he visited shop next day.
>
> —Standley, Guest Book, p. 31

wintered over twice between 1918 and 1920 while trying to make its way through the Northwest Passage. He also spoke with Captain O'Brien on whose ship *Victoria* Amundsen and his party traveled to Seattle in summer 1926, after the explorer's successful dirigible flight over the Polar Sea. Amundsen lectured while in Seattle in 1926, and it is most likely then that Standley heard and met him. Although another explorer, Vilhjálmur Stefánsson, was also sometimes in Seattle during these years, his name appears nowhere in Standley's notations.[18] Had Standley met Stefánsson, he would almost certainly have recorded it. Like others in the Pacific Northwest, he read about Stefánsson's adventures, and in memory Standley came to confuse him with explorer Amundsen, whom he actually had met. Several notes in his Guest Book about Amundsen actually regard incidents in Stefánsson's life that were given sensational news coverage. It was also surely Stefánsson, rather than Amundsen, who sent the Horlick Malted Milk box of curios from Nome in 1918. [19] Amundsen was caught in the ice in the eastern Arctic much of that year, while Stefánsson's diaries and papers were in Nome, waiting along with other items to be sent to him.

Captain Pedersen, the Arctic Navigator and Trader

Captain C. T. Pedersen, who brought a walrus embryo into Standley's shop, was the trader Standley wrote about most often in his Guest Book.[20] A Norwegian, Pedersen first came to the western Arctic in 1894 while still a teenager. He remained with the whaling steamer *Fearless* when it wintered east of Point Barrow and shortly became its storekeeper, beginning a forty-six-year career in the North. In 1914 he was hired by the H. Liebes Company of San Francisco to command the *Herman,* one of the last two large vessels engaged in whaling in the Bering Sea and the western Arctic. In 1920 Pedersen killed the last bowhead whale taken by an American commercial whaling ship.[21] The ship *Herman* also traded and resupplied the company's shore posts.

After leaving Liebes in 1923, Pedersen traded and supplied independent traders for some years under the name of the Northern Whaling & Trading Company, using first the ship *Nanuk* then the *Patterson.* Pedersen was held in the highest regard in both Norway and the United States for his skills as an ice pilot, his personal integrity, his fair prices, and the quality of his trade goods; his activities were regularly reported in Seattle newspapers. No wonder Standley admired him.

Pedersen and other traders documented their transactions in ledgers, recording items offered in trade and goods received in exchange, with the credit and debit in dollars canceling out each other. The *Patterson's* ledgers attest that in June 1932 at Little Diomede Island, "Jim" traded two pairs of waterproof boots, five hair-seal skins, and six long strings of mastodon beads; "John" brought ivory beads and billikens, a pair of short boots, and three pairs of slippers; while "Frances" produced two pairs of short water boots, one pair of hair-seal boots, ten and one-half pounds of ivory, and four paper knives. In families both husband and wife typically contributed their labor to the family's trade goods, the men by hunting and carving, the women by sewing. What was brought to trade in a given location in a given year was directly related to local circumstances and might vary from year to year. During the late 1920s and the 1930s, for example, raw furs, skin clothing (overwhelmingly skin boots), and a little raw and worked ivory were the major items that village Eskimos had to trade. Some villagers, especially old people, were dependent on what they could gather up in abandoned house sites and deposits. A few days' distance from Little Diomede Island, at Point Hope, several people brought in at least one "lot of junk"—Pedersen's nomenclature for old, worn miscellany. Among those trading was a Mrs. Jackie with "1 lot of junk, 1 lot old implements, 1 lot masks, etc. and a salmon."

Four years later, in June 1936, when the *Patterson* stopped at Point Hope, nearly fifty Natives came to trade, but each brought in only one or two items, usually a poke of muktuk (whale blubber), worth eight cents per pound, or a pair of deerskin boots (Pedersen paid $3 for short boots and $4 for long ones). No ivory and very few furs were offered in trade at this time.[22] As in previous years, what was bartered revealed recent circumstances. There had been successful whaling and after the distribution of the carcasses among the crews, as was customary, many had chosen to trade from their share of the muktuk (blubber). There was no walrus ivory, indicating that walrus had been scarce, but reindeer skins were plentiful. A reindeer industry had been introduced in 1908 to relieve starvation after later nineteenth-century commercial walrusing had decimated the herds on which the Point Hope community depended for food, and it had prospered.

This variation in local circumstances from year to year in Eskimo communities in turn defined what was available in the shops. Further analysis of Pedersen's trading ledgers will help to explain the mix of merchandise in Seattle and Alaska curio shops from the 1920s through the 1940s. Although Standley wrote about Pedersen often in the Guest Book, Ye Olde Curiosity Shop records list only H. Liebes Company specifically as a supplier of walrus teeth and ivory tusks; and for C. T. Pedersen the records simply note "ivory." Invoices in the Pedersen records do not include any to Ye Olde Curiosity Shop; however, there are several invoices to curio operations in Alaska and a Mr. Halford Lemke of

Relics off old Cutter U.S. Bear from Diomede & St. Lawrence Isl. Story of the Umiak. Sailors off Rev. Cutter old "Bear" needed Dough. Celebrated Sat. nite before sailing off. Dragged it to shop 7 pm. 1926

—Standley, Guest Book, pp. 20, 41, 75

Seattle.[23] They suggest that Pedersen is the most plausible supplier for the Alaskan-made ivory paper knives, napkin rings, pen holders, and strings of ivory beads that are offered in the shop's earliest catalogs (see chapter 8 of this volume), all listed in Pedersen's invoices to other shops. Pedersen also may have provided a part of the raw ivory that Standley's son Ed used to make pendants and other jewelry; items from his "lots" of old implements and "junk" were likely among the old tools and implements that Ye Olde Curiosity Shop offered.

U.S. Revenue Cutter Personnel

The precursors of today's U.S. Coast Guard, revenue cutter personnel were another source for Alaskan material. Roughly a decade after the purchase of Russian America in 1867, U.S. revenue cutters were stationed to Alaska to keep order along the thousands of miles of coast. Their major responsibility was to prevent the abuse of whiskey, especially its sale to Natives, by removing it from whaling and trading ships. Cutters also towed stranded ships, investigated shipwrecks, and assisted wreck survivors and the ill, bringing them to medical care when necessary. They carried mail, held court aboard ship, brought prisoners in for trial, and transported government officials and government-sponsored scientists, as well as missionaries, school teachers, and students, when needed. They also assisted the few settlers in Alaska trying to make a living at such enterprises as blue fox farming. Two cutters transported the reindeer brought from Siberia to establish reindeer herding in coastal Alaskan Eskimo villages. Many of the U.S. government's cutters operated out of Seattle.

It was accepted practice that revenue cutter officers barter with Natives. As with whaling and trading ships, when a cutter neared an Eskimo community, skin boats approached immediately to trade and their occupants were often invited aboard (fig. 2.7). Such trading encounters are described in the diaries kept by Mary Jane Healy, the wife of longtime revenue cutter captain Michael Healy, and their son Fred, when they accompanied the captain North in 1883 and 1884 on the *Thomas Corwin.* Mary Jane Healy's diaries from 1890 and 1891 while on the cutter *Bear* also describe trading. Although the diaries predate Ye Olde Curiosity Shop by several years, many of the pieces in Standley's early collection were acquired in the 1880s and 1890s, the period the Healy diaries describe. When speaking of Eskimos, both mother and son use the term Indians or occasionally Eskimo Indians, as was common in newspapers at the time.

The diaries reflect the writers' different interests. For example, Mary Jane Healy left the trading to the men. At the Diomedes in June 1883, on her first

2.7. Native boats alongside the revenue cutter *Bear*. Revenue cutter personnel traded with Natives in almost every community in which they stopped. When the umiaks came alongside, their occupants might be invited to come aboard to trade raw ivory, furs, and such curios as hunting implements and carved or engraved ivory. Photograph courtesy Michael Healy Papers, Album 131, #56. Huntington Library and Art Gallery, Pasadena, California.

trip, she was quite shy with the Native traders: "The Indians from both the Asia and American side visited us to sell their skins, bones [baleen], and I kept in the pilot house. I was quite a curiosity to them as I had glasses on." While anchored off Point Barrow, she offered visiting Eskimo women pins from her hair and needles. Interpreting both as ornaments, they put the pins in their ears and the needles in their noses. Seeing that Eskimo women wore gloves when dancing, she gave each woman a pair of her old gloves after several danced for her.[24] Her diary indicates that during her trip on the *Bear* in 1890, Mary Healy was far more comfortable. Dr. Sheldon Jackson was also aboard, collecting curios for his museum in Sitka, and Mrs. Healy had the company of Polly, a parrot who had a fur suit to wear on deck on cold days. At almost every stop there were "Indians selling their trinkets and fur," and she commented on the importance of trading to the Eskimos. In late June at St. Lawrence Island, "Indians came on board to see us and sell boots—this is their principal support." At Plover Bay "the Natives have come on board every day, the women sewing for the sailors, so we are indeed quite a bonanza to them for they are very poor in this place." A reciprocity had developed that assisted both sides, as cutters and other ships furthered Native economies by hiring Eskimo women to sew for their crews.[25]

Young Fred Healy was more interested than his mother in actually trading and in making a collection for himself. The officers aboard the *Thomas Corwin,* who "traded on their own account" for what they called bone (baleen), furs, curios, ivory, and even live animals, taught him about bartering. On June 14, 1883, "early in the morning we arrived at the Diomedes a lot of indians came aboard with skins and ivory to sell but the traders have been here and the indians do not want to sell any thing unless we pay high price for them." One man brought fox skins and was sent away after first trying to barter for the ship's spy glass, then for a box with forty pounds of powder and a bale of calico.[26] At one point as a joke a crew member hid the beads that the young Healy used for trading.

On June 17 there was success. According to Fred Healy's diary, "At two o'clock today a lot of Indians came aboard, I got two nice spears, a white fox skin and an indian fish-hook. Papa got two little reindeer skins. Father Healy [Fred's uncle] got a bidarchi & Mr. Story got a young white owl." As the trip progressed, he collected furs, bows, spears, a pipe, a *parkie,* and deerskin pants. When he went ashore on King Island, he came back with four spears, a half-dozen small canoes (model kayaks or umiaks), fishing tackle, and a dancing mask, while his father bought seventeen pairs of hair-seal boots for the crew.

Young Healy wanted some ivory, however, and wrote in his diary: "Papa and the officers are partners in all the ivory that they get and papa says he will try to save me a pair of walrus tusks out of his share for me." At Port Clarence (now Wainright) "when [the Indians] first came on board one of them gave a handsome pair of large walrus tusks and several pairs of little ones." Tusks were also offered at Cape Prince of Wales. He was probably unaware that walrus ivory was becoming scarce. By his 1883 trip, with the whale fishery severely depleted, commercial whalers had already hung on for almost two decades by taking walrus during the off-season and the animals were in steep decline. In 1881 on arriving at Saint Lawrence Island, the cutter *Thomas Corwin* had found that without the walrus on which they had depended, two-thirds of the population had starved the previous winter.[27]

Fred Healy's observations indicate that that which he traded for mirrored what the ship's officers were trading for—in addition to fox and bear skins, the ivory tusks, hunting gear (spears and bows), and occasional ivory curio like a pipe, were all items in the "male sphere." A large item like the umiak that the crew from the cutter *Bear* brought in one Saturday night in 1926 because they "needed dough" was unusual. The types of items that young Healy and the *Bear* crew traded for in the Bering Straits in the 1880s were the sorts of "relics" from the Diomedes and St. Lawrence Island that they later brought into Ye Olde Curiosity Shop. During the shop's first years even furs were of interest to

C. T. Wernecke, who ran a fur business in the back of the store until he moved from Colman Dock in 1916 (fig. 2.8). Men aboard the cutter *Bear* probably also sold the Curiosity Shop ivory beads they had made themselves. Bead making was one way to while away time during slack periods at sea. *Bear* personnel purchased walrus tusks from Natives, sawed them into cubes in the cutter's machine shop, rolled them in a rotating box, and drilled them. Curio shops were eager to buy the finished beads.[28]

In his Guest Book Standley wrote in several places about another revenue cutter captain, Dorr F. Tozier, from whom he acquired a part of his Arctic collection. In 1893 Tozier commanded the U.S. cutter *Grant* when it hauled from New York around Cape Horn to Puget Sound. During the next fourteen years the *Grant* became a common sight in the waters of the Sound, the Strait of Juan de Fuca, and the San Juan Islands, patrolling especially in the fight

2.8. Postcard, Standley with bear, tusks, and so on. This postcard of Standley romancing a polar bear rug was carried in the shop for years. When he sent a copy to C. T. Currelly at the Royal Ontario Museum in October 1917, he included the following prices: "Bear $100, 16 foot Kyak $85, Big Rugs $75 Each, the big Tusk with Jaw $300, Mans fur Parkee $15, Woman's fur Parkee on right of Picture $20." There is no record that the museum bought any of these.

against the smuggling of opium and illegal Chinese immigrants across the United States–Canada border. Tozier acquired his enormous Northwest Coast ethnographic collection at this time. During its service the *Grant* also made two trips to the Bering Sea, in 1895 and 1901 to carry out normal inspections, and in 1895 to oversee sealing operations. On these trips Tozier collected several thousand Eskimo and Northwest Coast ethnographic objects. Soon after the 1901 trip he sold most, if not all, of his Eskimo material to Standley, who added the ivories to others he had acquired, and to Grace Nicholson, a Pasadena, California, collector and dealer.[29] Both Standley's and Nicholson's Arctic collections would be displayed at the Alaska-Yukon-Pacific Exposition in 1909 and put up for sale afterward. None of Tozier's far more extensive Northwest Coast collections appears to have come to Ye Olde Curiosity Shop.

Suppliers from the Puget Sound Area, Washington, and Alaska

Baskets sold to tourists were a direct extension of long-established traditions in hundreds of Native communities. Some baskets were indistinguishable from those used by their makers; others were adapted in size, shape, or patterning to the preferences of non-Indian buyers. One of the earliest postcards that Standley sold pictures shelves of baskets inside Ye Olde Curiosity Shop (fig. 2.9). Makah baskets from the Olympic Peninsula and Tlingit ones from Alaska dominate, but there are also baskets from elsewhere in the Puget Sound region, the Aleutians, California, and even further afield. This photograph first appeared in shop catalogs in 1910 but was probably taken several years earlier, soon after the shop had moved to Colman Dock in summer 1904. The same shelves are also pictured in a shop interior view on the cover of the 1907 brochure (see p. 5).

When first arriving in Seattle at the end of the fall hop-picking season, Standley would have seen scores of Indians from the Puget Sound region, Vancouver Island, and as far north as Alaska who were in town on their way home from the harvesting or who lived on the nearby Duwamish Flats. Some of the women sold baskets on the streets. Word must have traveled quickly that Standley was interested in buying baskets, for the earliest known photograph of his shop (see fig. 1.6) pictures an assortment of mostly Puget Sound baskets set about in front. With the closure of Henrietta Hamilton's Basket Rooms in 1902 and Mrs. Marion Pearsall's basket business in 1905, it is quite possible that he had acquired some of their stock as well.

The rather fluid population on the Duwamish Flats included not only Duwamish but other Salish-speakers, and also Nootka (today called Nuu-chah-nulth) and Kwakiutl (Kwakwa̱ka̱'wakw) from Vancouver Island. These various Indian groups were all referred to as Siwash, a Chinook jargon term

INDIAN BASKETS IN YE OLD CURIOSITY SHOP SEATTLE

2.9. Basket shelf in Ye Olde Curiosity Shop, black and white postcard. One of the earliest postcards Standley sold in the shop, this image was also used in the first several catalogs.

that simply meant "Indian" at the time that Standley first came to Seattle (fig. 2.10). Derived from the French word *sauvage* (savage), the name Siwash is now quite offensive to Natives and non-Natives alike. During his early years Standley used the term for Salish speakers then dropped it. He called Nootka-speakers from Vancouver Island the Bella Bella and those from Neah Bay (the Makah) the Neah Bay Indians.[30]

Like most other Seattle curio dealers, Standley dealt directly with local Natives. His supplier address books—"See Where to Buy in Safe" and "Where to Buy"—list Indian basket makers, totem pole carvers, and distributors of baskets and totem poles by name. They usually provide an address and often include annotations. Several Indians, like Dan White and Sam Williams, became longtime friends of Standley. Although his supplier books also list several stores that supplied Puget Sound baskets, Standley preferred to purchase directly from the makers and their families when they came into Seattle. Indians living locally were sometimes waiting at the shop's door when he arrived in the morning. Others came in canoes and set their baskets out on the dock so he could place in each basket the amount he would pay. They preferred a transaction for each individual basket and did not want to sell in bulk as carvers of small totem poles often did.

2.10. Puget Sound Indians, color-enhanced postcard. Postcards with photographs of local Indians were always of interest to tourists. Most images, like this studio shot showing picturesque baskets and curios for sale, were posed. *Siwash* was the name commonly used at the time for Salish Indians.

The women listed in Standley's supplier books were overwhelmingly Makahs from Neah Bay and Quileutes from Mora or LaPush, on the Olympic Peninsula (fig. 2.11).[31] Theirs was a basketry tradition with at least a two-thousand-year history.[32] As settlers moved into the area, women making baskets for their own use found that they could earn a little money of their own and stretch family income by making some for sale. The looped bowl baskets and tiny, finely woven grass trinket baskets shown in Standley's postcard photograph were developed for the trade. As historian Douglas Cole and others have pointed out, "Natives entered the art and artifact market themselves, exploited it for their own uses and often welcomed the opportunities it offered."[33]

> In those days we had a back window that looked right over the bay. My grandfather said that you could see the Indians coming across the bay in their canoes with their wares and they'd come over to the back of the shop. The shop was right there on the Colman Ferry Dock...they'd bring all their things up and put them on the dock and he'd go out there with the money in his hands and he'd put a quarter on each basket, or a half or one dollar, or what ever it was, it wasn't too much in those early days.
>
> —Joe James

Over the years the shop also carried baskets from other Puget Sound tribes and Plateau tribes in Washington and Oregon. Yakama women often sent their daughters in with their goods. In Oregon, Orville Elliott, the agent on the Klamath Reservation, was a source for Klamath baskets, and W. T. Paul & Curios of Portland wholesaled Klickitat ones. Standley also advertised "west coast cedar bark hats" in his first catalog (1910) and even boasted a hat that had belonged to

Chief Seattle. Many of the baskets pictured on Standley's postcard (see fig. 2.9) are Tlingit spruce root baskets from Alaska, prized by collectors of the time. Flared, open-topped ones were more abundant than the knobbed-lid ones called rattle baskets. There is no record of traders bringing baskets out of Alaska for Standley. Instead, he appears to have depended on the Alaska-based suppliers, Walter Waters of Wrangell ("a fine fellow") and John Feusi of Douglas, a small community adjacent to Juneau.

> I Bot Chief's old cedar bark hat from moses the Dwarf Bowleg. Moses was Chief's nephew, free rider on all boats.
>
> —Standley, noted on Ye Olde Curiosity Shop information card, "History of Chief Seattle and Princess Angeline"

Representation of Alaska and Northwest Coast Natives in the Shop

Although Standley's personal interests guided the types of items that he wanted to offer, what was actually available to him determined what he displayed and sold. Availability and his notions about the origins and meanings of his collections in turn structured the framework through which Native American arts and cultures were represented and interpreted in his shop. Although early interior photographs included a few special curios arranged about, it is clear that from the beginning Standley staged a particular visual effect in his shop. Although such items as baskets, miniature totem poles, and ivories were displayed together, the whole of the shop was dominated visually by a sort of scrim composed of several hundred large and disparate natural history specimens and curios dangling from the ceiling and standing about. The incoherent contrasts transformed even the known into the curious and underscored the fact that objects were in themselves interesting. The visitor was thus drawn into a quest. The shop was a reflection of Standley's uneducated and undirected (but not unintelligent) examination of the world. Its invitation to wonder and speculate appealed to thousands over these years.

As was common in curio shops at this time, stereotypes dominated Ye Olde Curiosity Shop's Indian and Eskimo merchandise. Plains-type souvenir Indian dolls and bow-and-arrow sets represented both Plains Indians and Indians in general as they did in gift and curio stores across the continent. Totem poles were the primary icon for the Northwest Coast, although the shop also offered a few masks and other carvings, and for several decades, a respectable selection of Tlingit baskets. Totem poles were represented as a pan-coastal tradition, which they were not, and tribal distinctions among them were perplexingly confused, especially in regard to the hundreds of poles made locally. Northern and Southern coastal baskets were presented in mixed anonymity, both in the muddled explanation of basketry on the small basket information card the shop gave out and in its cramped display.

In the shop's early years the image of the Arctic tendered was more complex than that of the Northwest Coast, because Standley's Arctic collection was larger and more diverse. Like his Northwest Coast offerings, however, the Arctic collection also presented a fragmented "cultural construction of reality." The collection included a little of this and that—old tools and implements that were worn and to the average visitor looked crude and elementary, a few garments sewn skillfully from unusual and primitive materials, and engraved walrus tusks and cute toy-like carvings in ivory. There were also types of items that were staples of the souvenir trade across the continent, made from materials representative of the area. Ivory letter openers, napkin rings, and such were popular Alaska souvenirs. The shop's combination of old and new, made-for-use and made-for-sale items from the Arctic conveyed contradictory cultural images, but a questioning or integration of them was no more encouraged than it was of similar contradictions in the representation of Indians elsewhere on the continent. In the Southwest shy, picturesquely-garbed Pueblo women offered tourists quaint pottery at train stops and in the shops of the Fred Harvey Company. Although the pottery they sold was actually a hybrid art, adapted to the consumer's tastes and requirements, they and their pottery were represented as ancient and timeless. As did the sellers and buyers of Pueblo pottery, Standley wanted to believe that what he sold were the products of a shared communal tradition of anonymous makers still living in a past unaffected by historical change, despite the fact that most of the ivory carvings from Alaska that he offered were also hybrid arts made recently and expressly for sale.

Like the newspaper articles Standley eagerly read, his collection of arctic artifacts at the Alaska Club and in his shop allowed visitors a simple and comforting "experience" of the exotic Eskimos, based in the construct of a vanishing culture with primitive lifeways and noble traits, rather than in the complex realities of Arctic life at the time. The experience was one in which thousands would be able to participate when Seattle mounted its first world's fair, the Alaska-Yukon-Pacific Exposition in 1909, with Standley's Arctic collection and others on display.

2.11. (opposite) Women making baskets, probably at Neah Bay, early twentieth century. During this time Makah and Quileute basket makers from the Olympic Peninsula brought hundreds of trinket baskets to Seattle to sell. Photographer unknown. Burke Museum of Natural History and Culture, neg. 2.5A452.

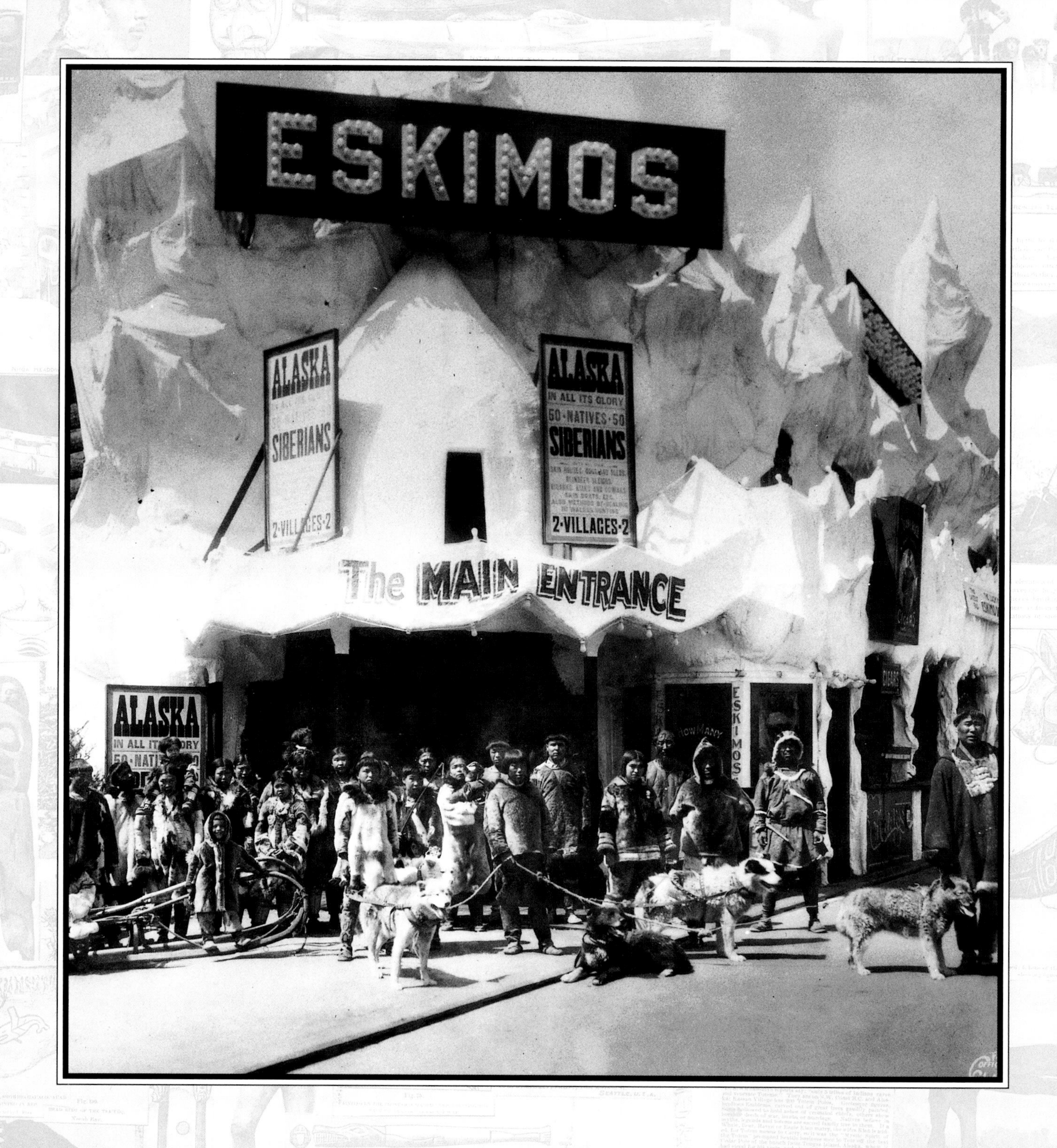

ESKIMOS
ALASKA
SIBERIANS
2·VILLAGES·2
ALASKA
IN ALL ITS GLORY
50·NATIVES·50
SIBERIANS
2·VILLAGES·2
The MAIN ENTRANCE
ALASKA
ESKIMOS
CIGARS

J. E. Standley and the Alaska-Yukon-Pacific Exposition

My Private Collection, 2253 Specimens of Alaska Curios, displayed at the Alaska-Yukon-Pacific Exposition, 1909, by the United States government, awarded the gold medal, was sold entire to Seattle Museum of Arts and Sciences.
—Ye Olde Curiosity Shop Catalog B, 1915

As GOLD RUSH EXCITEMENT COOLED IN THE NORTHWEST, BOTH SEATTLE AND Alaskan interests considered how to encourage continued economic development and exploitation of the territory. Much of this discussion took place in Seattle's Alaska Club, a sort of business exchange organized in the late 1890s to provide a place where those with Alaska interests could meet to discuss matters of mutual concern. In 1904, when the club moved into new quarters, it established a library and display area and requested that members contribute books, maps, photographs, and "new exhibits of every description." Joseph E. Standley, who appears to have been a club member, had by then amassed a large collection of Alaskan relics. Always a city booster, and aware that this opportunity would provide visibility for his shop, he decided to loan some of his collection for the club's informal museum.[1]

The Alaska Club benefited when its exhibits drew people in, and it publicized Standley's material in its 1906 *Almanac,* with a full page titled, "Alaska Exhibition of Curios Open to the Public." The text, no doubt provided by Standley himself, boasted, "Every part of Alaska has been represented and no modern curios are allowed in the collection." Elsewhere he wrote that in putting together the collection he had carefully avoided cribbage boards and "modern shop curios."[2] The objects were mostly Eskimo, and included such older used items as hunting and skin-processing tools, oil lamps, sinew ropes, and gut raincoats, but there was also a good deal of recent material made expressly for sale, in communities like Nome, Alaska, and to the traders and government personnel who visited remote arctic villages. As with many others in Seattle, Standley's knowledge about Alaska Natives was actually quite limited, and he held on to sentimental notions about a romantically remote arctic people, while leaving unexamined what today is so obvious, that the men from whom he obtained the objects in his collection had, by creating a market, influenced the collection itself. The ivory miniatures, engraved tusks, and pipes Standley acquired (as well as the cribbage boards he rejected) and many of the baskets and canoe and kayak models in his collection had been made recently for the curio trade.

When the Alaska Club moved in 1907 to the fifteenth floor of the Alaska Building, Standley's collection, which now included more than two thousand pieces, relocated along with the club. His collection remained there after the Alaska Club merged with the younger Arctic Club in 1908, taking on the name of the latter. The Arctic Club widened the earlier club's scope to include the Yukon Territory and the services were expanded. In addition to a library, exhibit area, and information bureau, the new club offered dining, billiards, and sleeping rooms for visitors from the North. In 1910 it boasted more than fifteen hundred members.[3]

An ongoing discussion among club members about how to generate more interest in Alaska's economic potential grew to encompass the Pacific Northwest and the Pacific Rim, and to envision Seattle as a major player. The 1904 Lewis and Clark Exposition in Portland, Oregon, had produced considerable development in western Oregon; surely Seattle could mount an even more successful fair. In June 1907 ground was broken for the Alaska-Yukon-Pacific Exposition (AYPE), Seattle's first World's Fair (fig. 3.1). Alaskans liked to point out that it was Godfrey Chelander, a former Alaskan, who originated the idea.

Collections for Seattle's First World's Fair

Unlike other World's Fairs, the AYPE would "not depend upon historical sentiment to arouse enthusiasm and interest" by celebrating an important historical event. Rather, it would acknowledge what such fairs were actually about and be a straightforward "international, industrial and commercial exposition," an opportunity to educate investors from the East about the economic and development potential of the Pacific Rim.[4] It would make clear that the state of Washington had passed the frontier stage of development and that Seattle was eager and prepared to be the hub of an economic boom. As if to demonstrate the strength and independence of the Northwest, the city itself would finance the fair through stock subscriptions, and without federal government loans. Buying a standard three shares, Standley joined the people of Seattle, who subscribed to $650,000 in AYPE stock in a single day.[5]

Alaskans also desired economic development and wanted to be sure that not only Seattle would reap the benefits of the AYPE. They were also concerned about how Alaska in general would be portrayed at the fair. The Ketchikan *Daily Miner* pointed out that since its purchase, Alaska had been

AUTHORIZED BIRDS EYE VIEW OF THE ALASKA-YUKON-PACIFIC EXPOSITION
SEATTLE, U.S.A. 1909
OPENS JUNE 1ST
CLOSES OCT. 16TH

3.1. The Alaska-Yukon-Pacific Exposition grounds, 1909. The Alaska Building, where Standley's and others' exhibits of Alaskan ethnology were housed, is shown here just behind the large dome of the Government Building. The Pay-streak amusement quarter with the Eskimo Village is positioned diagonally along the boulevard at the right. University of Washington Libraries, neg. UW 1378.

persistently misunderstood and underestimated, "represented in other fairs . . . as in current novels, by Esquimo [*sic*], dog sled, gambling camps and frontier life." The paper warned Seattle that to be successful, the exposition must adequately represent Alaska and the Yukon before the world by emphasizing their boundless forests, fisheries, mineral wealth, and agricultural possibilities with the most complete and up-to-date exhibits ever made.[6] It was also deemed important to have "the most comprehensive collection of relics and curios from the far north ever gathered for a world's fair," for these items also would support the exposition's purpose.[7]

For both scenic and practical reasons planners chose to locate "the most beautiful exposition ever held" on land that had been designated for the University of Washington's new campus. The gently rising site flanked by Lake Union and Lake Washington was stunning. Official ivory colored buildings in French Renaissance style would stand in elegance against "heaven-aspiring firs . . . and lakes of crystal water" in an architectural complex worthy of the imperial aspirations of the exposition's founders.[8] The young university would benefit from the AYPE construction because several buildings and other improvements to the site would revert to it, providing a ready-to-use campus after the exposition closed. Seattle itself would benefit economically, and local planners and businesses, expecting to be rewarded handsomely, prepared to entertain and minister to the thousands who would come.

Alaskans across the territory were pressed into service and responded with enthusiasm. In the exposition's Alaska Building territorial industries would exhibit their bounty and promise with pyramids of Alaskan ores, piles of enormous garden vegetables, and columns of canned salmon. Fox farming, whaling, and a fledgling timber industry would be explained. Steamship companies would emphasize the ease and comfort in which one could travel to the territory, and Alaskan railroad companies and the Road Commission would present their plans for expansion. The most impressive display—the one that would prove to be the most popular—would be an altar to the territory's most seductive lure: a secured glass case, within an iron cage, under a classic temple facade, for 1.25 million dollars worth of gold bars and nuggets.

Women's auxiliaries in a number of communities assembled progressive exhibits to demonstrate Alaska's educational and social progress and to dispel any notions of crudity and semibarbarism. The territory was indeed blessed with homes presided over by cultured women who appreciated literature, "womanly arts," and education—women who encouraged these civilizing influences among Alaska's Native people. Native handiwork would be featured in some of the exhibits; appropriately, it would be needlework, a symbol of domesticity and attention to the beauty and comfort of the home.

Ethnological Collections for the Fair

Ethnological exhibits had boasted such enormous success at earlier World's Fairs that they had become standard and imperative for such expositions.[9] Among the general public there was tremendous curiosity about the strange and picturesque habits and manufactures of people unlike themselves, but the exhibits served other purposes as well. World's fairs focused on the future and displayed the results of industrial technologies that would advance such a future. In dramatic contrast, exhibits about indigenous people showed simple (albeit carefully refined) tools and occupations, which were interpreted to represent the earlier phases of human development. While teaching the lessons of social Darwinism, such exhibits reinforced the central message of the expositions: that progress, technological growth, and exploitation of natural resources were virtues and inevitable. The exhibits also taught superiority of the viewers' more developed culture and reassured them in the premise of the exposition—the necessity of progress and the benefits of a benevolent colonialism.

After ethnology was designated as one of the seven principal divisions within the Alaska Building, Standley became involved.[10] AYPE organizers scrambled to put together the ethnological displays. Although the commissioner of the Alaska exhibits, J. C. McBride, had contracted men in Alaska to make collection for the Alaska Building, far more material was needed than what they could provide, and he had to draw on collections already assembled. In October 1908 he and others looked over Standley's exhibit at the Alaska Club and asked to borrow it, indicating interest in whatever else he could provide. Standley agreed to display his collection almost immediately.[11] It is not clear exactly what transpired, but five months later, with the opening just fourteen weeks away, the exposition that had advertised itself as "The Fair That Will Be Ready" found its Alaska Building exhibits "in terrible disarray." Standley was again suggested by exposition officials as a source for an ethnological exhibit, and again he agreed to assist.[12] Although the University of Washington housed a small collection of natural history and ethnological artifacts open to the public, at this time it was Ye Olde Curiosity Shop that functioned as Seattle's museum for such material. Standley's collections were drawn on in much the way that established museum collections would be in later years. In addition to loaning his Arctic and Northwest coast "relics" for the Alaska Building, Standley would also lend shells, corals, and marine curiosities from Puget Sound and the Pacific for the Washington State Building.[13]

The Alaska-Yukon-Pacific Exposition opened on June 1, 1909, with an attendance of 89,216 enthusiastic spectators, the first world's fair to be completed in every detail on its opening day. Seattle businesses closed so their employees could attend, and the Seattle Electric Company kept its 146 streetcars running all day to provide transportation. To keep the crowds coming, more than seventy-five conventions were scheduled to coordinate with the fair and railroads provided excursion packages. There were special rates from Chicago, for example, and the Santa Fe Railway advertised "Summer Excursion[s] to California and the North Pacific Coast," which traveled through the Southwest then up the West Coast to the AYPE.[14] Daily attendance averaged about twenty-seven thousand throughout the exposition's run. In later years Standley would tell reporters about how clean and free of crime the exposition had been and recall the immense number of visitors and the dignitaries who attended.

The Alaska Building, located just south of the U.S. Government Building, which anchored the main exhibit area, was one of the exposition's most important. Inside it, visitors could examine a broad array of Alaska Native manufactures displayed in cases by collector and loosely organized according to type (fig. 3.2). In addition to Standley's display, Lieutenant George T. Emmons lent approximately two thousand Northwest Coast ethnological objects that were "installed in nineteen double cases that took up considerable floorspace."[15] Grace Nicholson (the Pasadena, California, collector and basket dealer) displayed neatly arranged baskets on glass shelves and a group of Eskimo objects

An Exhibit of Alaskan Curios

More than Two Thousand Specimens Illustrating the Life of the Northern Aborigines

Cases in the Alaska Building at the A. Y. P. E. Containing the Valuable Assortment of Curios.

ONE of the features of the A. Y. P. Exposition which has attracted an unusual amount of interest is the private collection of Alaska curios owned by Mr. J. E. Standley of Seattle, and loaned to the United States Government for use in the Alaska Building at the Exposition in illustrating the history and tradition of ancient and modern Alaska. The collection comprises 2153 listed specimens, gathered from all the Indian tribes and Eskimo of Alaska. It represents articles used in their every-day life, in fishing, hunting, eating, games, sickness, dances, wars, witchcraft and amusements—the customs and traditions of a primitive race that is fast disappearing.

The collection was started by Mr. L. L. Bales, an Alaska explorer, when he carried the mail to Nome in early days. Hundreds of the rarest articles were brought out by him from the natives along the Yukon and Kuskokwim rivers, also from the Alaska Peninsula. Some of the curios were secured by Capt. Tozier of the United States revenue cutter "Grant," over twenty-five years ago; some from Capt. Foster, an Arctic navigator, thus forming a nucleus around which Mr. Standley has built, during the past decade or so, the most remarkable Alaska collection ever brought together.

The superiority of many of the curios is apparent. Baskets of early days were made with more perfect weave and design than at present, and only native-made dyes were used. Among the collection is a copper plate shield of great value and significance, made by hammering out a big, natural copper nugget upon which has been carved emblems totemic. This shield came from the Haidah tribe on Prince of Wales island; it is used only by the chiefs of the tribe.

The work in ivory is also both interesting and valuable. It consists of the tusks of the walrus, upon which records of aboriginal history are carved. The Eskimo had no language, therefore the great events in his life were recorded on these ivory tusks in a series of hieroglyphics. Hundreds of ancient tools are included in the collection, cut out of ivory, such as were used in fishing, hunting, fighting, in religious ceremonies, in the medicine men's practice, in games and amusements; in fact, as above stated, more than 2,000 items, ranging from the bones of prehistoric animals down to the finest imaginable hand work in ivory and copper, are included in the list.

The collection relates in concrete form the story of the rise of a race in prehistoric times and covers the period of its slow development down to the present. In no manner can the history of a tribe of people reaching across a long space of time be crowded into the space of a few hours, save by the study of such an assemblage.

The collection has attracted wide interest and universal praise. For four years it has formed, through the courtesy of its owner, the chief exhibit of the Alaska Club in Seattle, where its presence was highly valued. Dr. A. C. Haddon, of Christ College, Cambridge, England, considers it of such value that he is now attempting to finance the purchase of it among the educational institutions of his own country. The collection would form a valuable addition to the museum of any university or college; it likewise would represent a distinct conquest for the ambitious private collector. It is offered for sale by its owner, Mr. J. E. Standley of Seattle, and either Mr. Standley or the editor of this magazine, who has spent many hours of time in the absorbing study of its details, will be glad to furnish the interested reader with a carefully prepared catalogued list of the contents, together with any other desired information.

A Fascinating Group of Rare Specimens Contained in the Collection.

Coming from All Parts of the World, the Curios Hold an Unusual Interest.

3.2. Standley's collection was discussed in a September 1909 article in *The Westerner Magazine,* which made it known that Standley was hoping for a buyer. It is not clear how many of the Alaska Building cases pictured here were allotted to Standley. Special Collections Division, University of Washington Libraries, neg. 18376.

she had recently purchased from revenue cutter captain Dorr F. Tozier and other "ship captains on northern boats."[16] There were smaller collections from, among others, E. P. Pond of Winter and Pond Photographers, Juneau; George Kostromentinoff of Unalaska; and Rhodes & Co., a Seattle curio shop.[17] There were also exhibits assembled by community women's auxiliaries in Alaska. According to one official brochure, *The Exposition Beautiful,* these exhibits illustrated the successful work of Alaskan schools and churches among the Natives with "handiwork of the Indian chool-children [that] rivals the work of their little white brethren on the 'outside.'" It is unclear, however, which of the beadwork in exposition photographs is the work of school children.[18]

Photographs of the display cases in the Alaska Building show arrangements of Athapaskan Indian beadwork on hide, mostly decorative valences and pillow and table covers appropriate for the home.[19] It is unlikely that spectators knew that at this time Athapaskan beaders made these particular articles primarily for sale rather than for their own use. Such items represented a modest entrepreneurial response, probably encouraged by the women's auxiliaries, to the desire of gold rushers and others for a memento of their time in Alaska and the Klondike or perhaps a gift to take home to a wife or mother. Although produced for sale, these beaded valences and pillow and table covers do not appear to have been exported to curio dealers such as Standley, in Seattle or elsewhere. Unlike moccasins, to the buyer outside Alaska such objects were not considered typically "Indian" and were of limited interest.[20]

Standley's cases displayed approximately 1,240 relics from Alaska, most of them ethnological (figs. 3.3a, b). Eskimo work dominated, with several dozen Tlingit and Aleut pieces scattered throughout.[21] About 640 of the Eskimo pieces were ivory carvings and engraved tusks that had been made for the curio trade, but, as Standley had promised, there were no cribbage boards.[22] The material was organized neither by age, type, tribe, nor quality, and each case held a haphazard crush of ethnological objects along with a few pieces such as walrus tusks and whale teeth. Despite the lack of coherence and aesthetic, the size and variety of Standley's display were overwhelming. Perhaps for this reason, exposition officials awarded it a gold medal. There had been a plan for exhibitors to provide basic essential information on each piece

3.3 a, b. Two of Standley's display cases at the Alaska-Yukon-Pacific Exposition. Although the original plan was for exhibitors to provide information (name of object, tribe, use, etc.) to the commissioners so that labels could be made for all the objects shown, this does not seem to have been carried through. Standley's hand-written labels are similar to those he used in the shop. Most of the objects pictured were purchased in 1916 by George G. Heye for the Museum of the American Indian, Heye Foundation, in New York.

displayed to be used on labels that the exposition organizers would provide, but Standley appears to have installed his cases himself and printed his labels directly on the object or onto an accompanying card, his standard procedure.

In the Alaska Building, objects of Native manufacture were presented without context, grouped by type (baskets), broad culture area (Northwest Coast), use within a culture area (Arctic fishing implements, or, in Standley's cases, Alaska. There was little explanatory information. As was common in ethnographic displays in museums at the time, a culture was defined in terms of its objects rather than its social, ceremonial, or spiritual aspects, leaving the unfamiliar viewer to assume that there was little of the latter. Distinctions between different tribes, much less within them, were blurred if made at all. The spectator could exclaim over the skill of a maker, or puzzle over the strangeness of an tool, but the exposition's touted educational value was hampered by a lack of information on the "silent" objects in the Alaska Building. Visitors could, however, ask a few questions of Native ivory carvers, basket and blanket weavers, and metalsmiths (probably making silver bracelets) who worked in a small area registered to H. D. Kirmse of Skagway, Alaska. Allotted at the request of Commissioner McBride, the space provided a place to demonstrate and probably sell Alaskan tourist arts—gold nuggets and nugget jewelry, "carved ivory by the natives, souvenir spoons and forks, Alaskan Indian baskets, moccasins, and totems."[23] How much interest this "thoroughly live exhibit" garnered is not recorded.

The Alaska Building was not the only site at the AYPE where visitors could study North American Native peoples. Mandated by the U.S. Congress, the Smithsonian Institution provided "appropriate exhibits of an historical nature" for the U.S. Government Building.[24] Smithsonian-owned objects from the Northwest Coast and the Arctic were similar to those in the Alaska Building. Its other exhibits focused on the results of recent Bureau of American Ethnology archaeological study and collecting in the Southwest and California.[25] Curiously, the published description of the Canadian exhibit does not include any mention of the country's Native (First Nations) people.[26] Smithsonian exhibitions also included costumed "family group" dioramas and models of environments and cultural activities. As others have pointed out, it was but a small step from these to creating living exhibits in which people from exotic societies, housed in surroundings that simulated their native habitats, performed indigenous tasks and lived under the spectator's curious eye. Exposition organizers complained that the average visitor looked at the official exhibits briefly and mutely, then headed for the fair's amusement quarter, the Paystreak, where they found several "living exhibits."

3.4. Alaska-Yukon-Pacific Exposition designers appropriated images from both Alaska and the Orient, sometimes combining them. The pagoda roof of the imposing south entrance "of Japanese-Alaskan design" was supported by two pairs of totem poles, which, like the exposition seal were molded in plaster. The figures had been inspired by illustrations in Franz Boas's 1897 work on the Kwakiutl Indians. Photograph by Frank Nowell. University of Washington Libraries, neg. X1900.

Living Exhibits, the Paystreak, and Souvenirs

The "paystreak" was that sought-for streak of gold ore that signaled a placer miner's labor worthwhile. Accordingly, to many AYPE visitors, the amusement quarter known as the Paystreak signaled the respite that made the serious business of studying exhibits worthwhile. Its entrance, like the exposition's enormous south entrance gates, signaled that an uncommon and strangely mixed experience awaited. The dominating south entrance was "of Japanese-Alaskan design, consisting of totem poles supporting curved pagoda roofs" (fig. 3.4).[27] The Paystreak entrance, modest in comparison, featured a simple tile-roofed lintel supported by four totem poles.

After the city's appropriation of the Seattle Totem Pole as its novel public symbol a decade earlier, it was not surprising that Seattle city fathers chose totem poles to visually represent the Northwest at the fair. Unexpected as their use was to support pagoda roofs, the plaster and wood poles stacking several of a stock group of figures in various configurations were strikingly unusual. Standley's copy of Franz Boas's 1897 book, *The Social Organization and the Secret Societies of the Kwakiutl Indians,* again held an unexpected influence. The figures on the entrance poles were based on several of its illustrations.[28] The Paystreak totem poles were cheerfully painted; those at the south entrance were fitted with electric lightbulb eyes. A single street with amusements on either side, the Paystreak distilled Alaska and Hawaii as well as China, the Philippines, and other countries and territories into established clichés about cultural behavior. Hula dancers represented Hawaii, and the Near East was a place of exotic beauties in harem pants undulating suggestively in the attraction the Arabian Nights. The Nez Perce Indians wore fringed shirts and colorful feather headdresses, and the "primitive" Philippine Igorrotes wore almost nothing at all.[29] As in countless other displays before and after the AYPE, the complexities of cultures had evaporated into cheerful presentations of colorful folk costume and characteristic music and dance.[30] The public clearly preferred the distilled stereotypes of picturesque difference to the more serious concerns of the main exhibits in which indigenous people of Alaska, Hawaii, and the Philippines were represented as candidates for the benevolence of civilization, development, and resource exploitation.

The Paystreak included a Philippine Igorrote and a Siberian (also called Alaskan) Eskimo village. Both had been wildly popular at Portland's Lewis and Clark Exposition in 1904, and fair planners encouraged their organizer, Captain A. M. Baber, to bring them to Seattle. Standley left no comments on the Igorrote Village, although he clearly was aware of it. After the exposition closed, he bought shields, spears, baskets, and other items that had been made or used there. As might be expected, however, he was fascinated by the Eskimo Village. Standley loaned his collection of whale bones to Baber and visited the display whenever he liked. He wrote of the exchange: "Mr. Baber who Brot the Eskimo Village from East Cape Siberia to the A. Y. P. Exposition Borrowed my Big Jaw Bones of Whale, Big Ribs, Big Vertabraes Skull and Shoulder Blade for his entrance gate. he had the Families in their Native Igloos (Tents) made of Walrus hides. Men, Women, Dogs, Babies and Making curios out of ivory tusks of walrus. I had free access to the Village and learnt lots of their songs, native life & Customs, Dances etc."[31]

An Eskimo was an Eskimo and signs at the main entrance collapsed Siberia into Alaska, announcing: "Alaska in all its glory—50 Native Siberians" (fig. 3.5). The parka-clad occupants of the Eskimo Village, with its plaster frosted-log confection of a building, lived in huts constructed of walrus skins and furs, performed dances, sang songs, and demonstrated ivory carvings. They operated a "North Pole Express Train"—a dogsled that ran on wheels—and participated in canoe and kayak races, as well as a mock whaling contest using logs. A major portion of Standley's education on Eskimo culture was gleaned from his time observing the AYPE's Eskimo Village. In later years Standley recalled the "dandy letters" Baber wrote him, about taking his Igorrote and Eskimo Villages to Paris and London in 1911 and about his stay in Berlin with Carl Hagenbeck, the famous German animal trainer and

3.5. Most of the participants in A. M. Baber's Eskimo Village on the Paystreak at the Alaska-Yukon-Pacific Exposition, were Siberian. Ignorant and sensationalist advertising in the exposition's daily program described them as "strange People, Existing Only on the Limited Products of the Icy North, half Civilized in Their Nature, Knowing no God, Having no Laws, no Government, Unable to Read or Write, With no History of Their Antecedents." It also lauded their skills in marksmanship, canoeing, dancing, singing, and seal catching—all of which the participants demonstrated in continuous performance. Photograph by Frank Nowell, Special Collections Division, University of Washington Libraries, neg. X1766.

amateur ethnologist who imported animal exhibits and *Völkerschauen* (ethnographic displays of "natives") to Europe for educational and entertainment purposes. After Baber settled in Seattle, Standley bought his Siberian Eskimo collection.[32]

Items with images associated with Northwest Coast and Alaska Natives were popular souvenirs of the fair. One booth sold Totem Pole Lead Pencil souvenirs and another offered irregularly shaped hide pieces with Indians painted on them. The Grecian Lithographic Press demonstrated the ability of its machines by printing pictures of Indian maidens while the customer waited. Images based on the famous photographs by Asahel Curtis of Chief Si'aɬ (Seattle), for whom the city had been named, and his daughter Princess Angeline could be found on postcards (fig. 1.10) and on the handles of some "Seattle Spoons." The spoons were manufactured locally by Jos. [Joseph] Mayer & Bros., a metal stamping company, that ran a concession at the fair.[33] Since the gold rushes of the 1890s, Mayer Bros. had been producing a variety of spoons and jewelry that were especially appropriate to be sold at the exposition. The company's 1904 catalog pictured gold rush commemorative coffee spoons with nuggets soldered into gold pans on the handles, and bowls that often said Alaska or Yukon. Yet other spoon handles represented Seattle with "miniature reproductions of the Totem Pole brought from Ft. Wrangle, Alaska, by the P. I. business men's excursion, and which is now erected on Pioneer Square, Seattle."[34] The spoon bowls were plain, displayed the word "Seattle," or pictured Mount Rainier.

Chief Seattle, the Seattle Totem Pole, and Mount Rainier had already become major Seattle icons by the 1909 exposition. These three symbols—of "natural man," the primitive, and the mystical—had been appropriated by a community that at the very same time was transforming them. The local Indians had been all but eliminated; the totem pole, a meaningful symbol to some Northwest Coast tribes, had become a curious public attraction; and Mount Rainier had barely been saved from logging and development by its designation as a national park. Whether anyone considered the irony of this is not recorded. The mountain and the totem pole have remained popular symbols of Seattle on letterheads and advertisements throughout the twentieth century.

3.6. After the Alaska-Yukon-Pacific Exposition the fair's mascot, the billiken, became a popular souvenir carved in ivory. Ye Olde Curiosity Shop sold billikens for almost a century. Photograph by Steve Hendrickson. Sales Collection, 98-7-60, Alaska State Museum, Juneau.

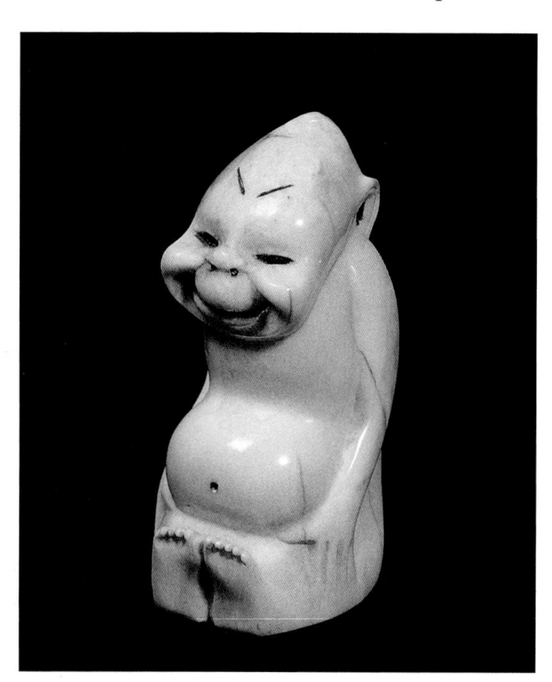

The 1909 date on a group of Mayer & Bros. stamping dyes used in making totem pole brooches and bracelets in silver almost assures that the company was also selling them at the AYPE. The jewelry replicated several Tlingit totem poles that had been made famous through the work of such photographers as Winter and Pond of Juneau, Alaska. An expanded variety of such jewelry would later be sold in Standley's Curiosity Shop catalogs, as would some of the souvenir spoons. The most sought-after AYPE souvenir was the billiken, a squat, naked figure with a big belly, a pointed head, slanted eyes, and a wide grin (fig. 3.6). At the time the billiken was not associated with Eskimo artisans, but it would come to be. Taken up by Eskimo carvers soon after the exposition, ivory billikens became a staple of Alaska and Seattle curio shops, among them Ye Olde Curiosity Shop, where thousands would be sold at the shop and through its catalogs.

Although Standley's 1907 shop brochure invites visitors to "meet us on the Pay Streak, Alaska-Yukon Fair, 1909," there is no evidence that he had a concession there or elsewhere on the exposition grounds.[35] Because so many visitors arrived on the Colman Ferry Dock where the shop was located, or the railroad station nearby, there was no need for one. Standley's listings and advertisements in exposition guides and his exhibition in the Alaska Building also brought the shop's treasures to the attention of visitors. The display in the Alaska Building brought more prestige and credibility than any concession could have.

> There are many other attractions, among which are six Totem Poles, representing the history, religion and legends of the Bella-Bella Indians; also Indian tepees and the aboriginal battleship or ancient Indian war canoe.
>
> —*Ravenna or Big Tree Park,* 1909

J. E. Standley, the AYPE, and Ravenna Park

Seattle had actively promoted its majestic scenery for some years; AYPE visitors would expect to experience it. For many visitors an afternoon amid the giant trees and mossy canyons of Ravenna Park would be the closest they would come to experiencing a natural wilderness. An opportunity to do this easily would be a valuable addition to the exposition, and the Reverend William W. Beck, who owned and operated Ravenna Park just seven blocks from the site, was in a position to provide it.[36] In 1889 Beck had purchased land along Lake Union that included a ravine area that had been designated Ravenna Park by earlier owners. He platted the town of Ravenna and built his home there, in which he ran a private women's college. He began developing the park—fencing it, bringing in exotic plants, and building a roofed picnic shelter and paths to a natural sulfur spring, christened the Wood Nymph Well. The park was easily accessible from downtown by trolley car after 1890 and had become a popular destination for Sunday outings.

Even in 1909, Ravenna Park was one of the few areas in Seattle still in its natural state. Descriptions of the park in advertising pamphlets are imbued with the rhetoric and expectation of psychological impact that had dominated travel literature for more than a century. Brochures published at the time of the AYPE promoted respite from the crowds within a "forest primeval . . . Seattle's only forest unshorn by axe . . . Ravenna Park, with its standing and fallen giant trees; moss and fern-clothed canyons." There were majestic rows of the state flower along Rhododendron Way and "nearly every plant known to Western Washington," but the trees—the giant firs three hundred to four hundred feet high and thirty to sixty feet in circumference—were the true marvels. City residents had named the largest ones in 1908—the President Teddy Roosevelt at forty-four feet in circumference, the Paderewski (named after the famous pianist), and the Robert E. Lee—and visitors were drawn to view them. Like such natural wonders as Niagara Falls, Yosemite, and the Grand Canyon, Ravenna Park offered a pilgrimage to the sublime, the contemplative, the spiritual, the terrifying. Among the ferns, moss, and virgin trees, a teepee, a wickiup, and an Indian canoe allowed study in their natural setting and totem poles invited an alternative type of "pleasurable terror." In addition, a teahouse offered refreshment. The pilgrimage to the park was a short and comfortable one, with trolley car service from the exposition every eight minutes at the cost of a quarter.[37]

Awe-inspiring natural forests had also been the promise of trips to Alaska since steamship companies began advertising excursions up the Inside Passage in the 1880s, and there was the added allure of totem poles in misty fjords. Although visitors to the AYPE would have seen the cast totem poles with lightbulb eyes at the fair's south entrance (fig. 3.4), encountering real poles standing in a forest would replicate an Alaskan experience more closely. It may have been at the suggestion of the university's Edmond Meany, who was helping Beck measure and identify his park's huge trees and other flora, that Beck decided to introduce an "Indian influence" in the park and install totem poles. Or it could have been Standley's idea. The origins of the teepee and the wickiup are not known, but Standley was the source for the totem poles and the Indian canoe.

Acquiring large totem poles was not a simple task, but Beck could turn to Standley, who by at least 1907 was advertising for sale poles of up to twenty feet tall and displayed several in front of his Colman Dock shop. In possibly his first experience in commissioning large totem poles, Standley arranged for a group of them to stand in Ravenna Park during the exposition. Photographs and information exist on five of what were six original Ravenna Park totem poles. The tallest was photographed in front of Seattle's *Post-Intelligencer* building while on its way to the park (fig. 3.7) and again for use on a post-card (fig. 3.8). The pole was a skinny forty-foot column rather crudely carved

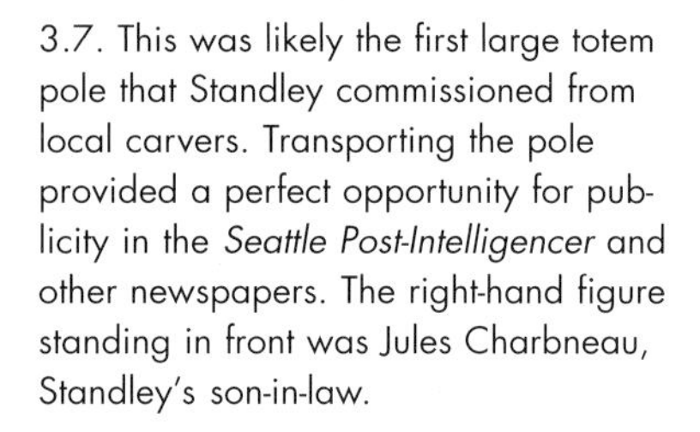
3.7. This was likely the first large totem pole that Standley commissioned from local carvers. Transporting the pole provided a perfect opportunity for publicity in the *Seattle Post-Intelligencer* and other newspapers. The right-hand figure standing in front was Jules Charbneau, Standley's son-in-law.

with figures loosely based on parts of the Seattle Totem Pole. This is the earliest pole known to have been commissioned by Standley from a carver living locally. He identified the carver as Siwash, the term he commonly used for Salish Indians. Standley also provided Beck with a composition titled "Tradition of the Whale, Eagle, Family of Kasaan, Alaska, East Coast of Prince of Wales Island" to explain the pole. The pole of course had nothing to do with Kasaan, a Kaigani Haida village, but if the same creatures were on both, Standley saw no reason not to use the story. Such careless and ignorant transfer of tribal and family-owned information associated with specific totem poles to other unrelated poles contributed to an increasingly muddled body of information on Northwest Coast art and customs that dominated public perceptions.

The four shorter totem poles, actually two pairs of very similar ones, installed together in Ravenna Park, are pictured on a small advertising brochure that Beck put out during the AYPE (fig. 3.9). The two poles with beavers at the bottom stand to the left and the two with frogs at the bottom to the right, each set into a niche cut into a living tree. One pole, the third from the left, is less skillfully carved, and painted with less precision and detail than the others. The four original poles are also pictured singly in the souvenir photograph booklet *Ravenna Park, Seattle* (fig. 3.10). In Standley's copy one of these photos has been cut out and the page taped back together. Other copies verify that the missing photograph pictured the totem pole on which Standley is leaning in the 1909 photograph of his first Colman Dock shop (see fig. 1.12). One can speculate that after the poles for Beck were carved, possibly even after they had been installed, Standley decided that he would like one of them in front of his shop during the AYPE. He then cut the photo of it from his copy of the *Ravenna Park, Seattle* booklet and gave it to a local carver for quick duplication.

BIG TREE PARK
One of the six Totem Poles in Ravenna Park, Seattle.
Seven blocks north from A.-Y.-P. Exposition Grounds.

3.8. Standley provided information on the back of this postcard of the totem pole standing in Ravenna Park: "Was carved out of 40 foot Cedar log, by Siwash Indian on sandspit. they were in barefeet in snow—Dec 1908. This is the 40 foot Cedar totem Pole I sold to W. W. Beck for Ravenna Park."

The origin of the four original poles remains unclear. Although Standley formally called them Tlingit, on one photo picturing two of them he wrote: "Made by the Bella Bella of Vancouver Island" (his name for Nuu-chah-nulth

ONLY SEVEN BLOCKS NORTH FROM A.-Y.-P. E. GROUNDS
Press of White Advertising Bureau Inc. Seattle
TO RAVENNA PARK EVERY 8
SOME OF THE TOTEM POLES AND BIG TREES AT RAVENNA PARK

3.9. A 1909 brochure advertising "Ravenna or Big Tree Park" pictured four totem poles set into niches cut into trees. Based on unidentified Alaskan poles, these were the work of Nuu-chah-nulth carvers from Vancouver Island who lived in Seattle. Standley erroneously called them Bella Bella. The second pole from the right is a copy of the one of the original four poles that Standley kept and displayed in front of his shop during the Alaska-Yukon-Pacific Exposition (see fig 1.12). The four poles from the park went to the Burke Museum in Seattle in 1913. Ethnology Archives, Burke Museum of Natural History and Culture, University of Washington, Seattle.

carvers from British Columbia living in the Seattle area). Carvers in both Alaska and British Columbia were producing large poles for sale at the time, and the Ravenna Park poles have more affinity with Tlingit and Kaigani Haida poles from Alaska than with the known poles that were later made for Standley by Nuu-chah-nulth carvers. Standley's use of the Kasaan story to explain the single tall pole he also acquired for Beck (see fig. 3.8) indicates that he had access to some sort of information on the Kaigani Haida of Old Kasaan on Prince of Wales Island in Alaska. The Ravenna Park poles do not correlate with photographs of poles at Old Kasaan, but there are some visual connections with individual figures on poles at Old Sukkwan village, another Kaigani Haida community.

The fanciful painting that obscures the interpretation of parts of some of the figures on the Ravenna Park poles suggests that their carvers may have been looking at black and white photographs in which they could see neither the figures nor the painted details very well.[38] One may argue that, unfamiliar with the exact identity of the figures on the modern poles in context of the stories they represented, as well as with the specifics of the Northern Northwest Coast formline system, the carvers interpreted what they saw, lensed through their own culture's limited tradition of poles. There are also stylistic relationships with several Nuu-chah-nulth poles photographed early in the twentieth century at Sarita, Barkley Sound. The Ravenna Park poles were hybrid, as would be thousands of other poles made for sale in Seattle, mixing several tribal styles. They were the work

> I brought the Big Siwash Indian canoe from Race Rocks Victoria for Mr. Beck. Largest hewn cedar log canoe known it held 40 warriors and was used as a ferry at Westminster B.C. also for years was engaged as a transport smugler. . . . There are flint arrow heads imbedded in the Wood of this famous old Relic.
>
> —Standley, note written on his copy of *Ravenna Park, Seattle*

Quotations

"SEATTLE SHOULD OWN RAVENNA."

"We believe it to be the opinion of almost every resident of Seattle who has ever visited Ravenna Park that it should become the property of the city. It is unique in its beauty and in its representative character. It stands as the survival of the older day; a relic of the ancient wood; a bit of this country as nature made it, set down amidst the changes through which advancing civilization has swept away remorselessly the picturesque sylvan retreats of the past. It cannot be duplicated. Once destroyed, it can never be reconstituted. It is ideal of its kind, and with every year of the future its novelty and wild beauty will become more impressive and more precious." "It will be the choicest possession, perhaps, of the city's future."—Editorials from the Post-Intelligencer.

By invitation of Colonel Blethen, Madame Eames visited Ravenna Park. In The Seattle Times of November 5th, 1905, is the following interview:

When asked what she most desired to see, Mme. Eames replied: "Your great trees. I want to compare them with the trees of Europe, where they make so much fuss over their giant trees."

"The party was taken at once to Ravenna Park and to the great trees so famous therein. When Mme. Eames beheld them she could scarcely contain herself, and cried out to her companions, consisting of her own immediate concert assistants: "Behold that tree! It is 44 feet in circumference twenty feet from the ground! Then look at that tree,—250 feet high, twice as high as the trees we rode one thousand miles in Europe to see last year! Behold what Uncle Sam produces in the State of Washington!" And then Madame compelled her party to follow her through the deep ravine and to the sulphur spring, pointing out all the time how grandly superior nature's parks were to those which man constructed."

"It is easily the most interesting spot in Seattle."—Argus.

"Ah, these Western forests! There is something in the beautiful, dim silence of the Western forests that is like holiness. One steps softly and bends his head as if expecting to hear a benediction sink earthward. For silent centuries on silent centuries the needles of the pine and of the fir have sifted down by day and by night, to carpet the

3.10. The twenty-page booklet of photographs, *Ravenna Park, Seattle* (1909), also pictured the four poles shown on the brochure. Each was paired with text extolling the Alaska-Yukon-Pacific Exposition and Ravenna Park, which park patrons encouraged the city to acquire.

of at least three carvers. In creating them, these men established an economic relationship with Ye Olde Curiosity Shop and tourists that is still critical to both Nuu-chah-nulth carvers and curio shops in Seattle.

Standley also arranged for the canoe in Ravenna Park. The notes he made about it and a card titled "Bella Bella Indian Reservation Canoe History," which he provided for the public, detailed a long and exciting history. According to the card, the "Hias Mammook Solleko Canim" (Chinook jargon for Big Fighting Cedar Canoe) was hewn in 1836 by the Kroquart on Vancouver Island. In 1857 the canoe was used in "a battle royal" with the Clallam, who captured it. Americans on San Juan Island then bought the canoe, rigged it as a schooner and used it as a passenger boat between San Juan and Victoria. After the treaty between Great Britain and the United States that concluded the Pig War, the canoe was used to smuggle Chinese laborers and opium across the Canadian border. When Standley purchased it in 1908 from Indian Henry, the canoe was being used for fishing. Henry arranged to have it sailed to Seattle with cedar bark sails.[39] Standley's story of the canoe is generally supported by history. Many large canoes were made on the west coast of Vancouver Island and various west coast tribes were warring with the Clallam about 1857 and in later years. That the Kyuquot (Standley's Kroquart) were one of those tribes is quite feasible. Indian Henry was probably Henry Charles of Becher Bay, Vancouver Island, and of Clallam ancestry.[40] It is very unlikely, however, that the canoe was as old as Standley suggested or that it was sailed with cedar bark sails; by 1908 cloth sails had been used for decades.

Even before the exposition, Beck had been hoping that Ravenna Park could become a part of the city park system. The Olmsted park plan commissioned by the city had recommended it, and souvenir booklets and local newspapers encouraged it. He had been unsuccessful in selling the park to the city in 1904, but its popularity during the exposition helped his cause, and Seattle purchased Ravenna Park in 1911. To the dismay of many, however, the giant trees were "quietly felled" over the next several years, and city engineers installed a new trunk sewer that destroyed the park's stream and its fish runs. The group of four totem poles and the canoe were saved when Mrs. Beck placed them on loan in the state museum at the University of Washington in 1913.[41] The poles were displayed in the corners of the "Tlingit Room" when the museum was located in the Washington State Building and on occasion later. They remain at the museum. The canoe, which sat outside, decayed and was discarded in 1940.[42] The pole that Standley had kept at the shop (see fig. 1.12) left Seattle some time after the exposition. In 1951 politician Nelson Rockefeller purchased it from a New York gallery and installed it on the lawn at his estate at Kykuit, New York; it was the only Native American sculpture in his collection (fig. 3.11).

The Exposition's Legacy and Collections for Sale

The AYPE closed on October 16, 1909, after nearly four million visitors had enjoyed it and spent $9 million while doing so. Thousands had been convinced of the Pacific Northwest's beauty and some, of its potential. Assessments in later years concluded that as an invitation for Eastern capital to come West and develop resources, the exposition failed. But the optimism and energy of Seattle's people succeeded in drawing settlers to the area, and the University of Washington had also benefited. Stockholders even realized a modest 4 percent dividend.[43] The exposition gave Ye Olde Curiosity Shop both the visibility and the financial boost it needed to become securely established and known across the country and abroad. Standley's Alaska Building exhibits provided his business important exposure and publicity, which he augmented with a quarter-page ad in *The A.-Y.-P. Exposition Official Guide.* The shop was also named in other exhibition publications in lists of places to see in Seattle.[44]

3.11. The totem pole that Standley displayed in front of his shop during the AYPE (see fig. 1.12) left Seattle soon after the exposition. It was eventually purchased by Nelson Rockefeller for his New York estate, Kykuit, where it remains on display in the summer. The pole combines a raven, frogs, dogfish, what is likely a bear with crest rings between his ears, and a beaver—creatures present on old poles from both the Tlingit and the Haida. Photograph by Charles Uht. National Trust for Historic Preservation, Nelson A. Rockefeller bequest, Pocantico Historical Area.

Through the AYPE's duration shop sales nearly doubled over those of the previous year, but over the long-term the validation and visibility the shop gained would be of even greater importance.

The choice of Standley's collection for exhibit at the AYPE, and the company in which it was displayed, lent it and the shop authority and legitimacy. Publications associated with the exposition emphasized that the displays in the Alaska Building were authentic and of scientific and educational interest. That Standley's display was shown alongside those of collectors who had been affirmed as knowledgeable, and with whom museums dealt, in turn suggested that Standley was also an authority. Lieutenant G. T. Emmons had sold items to the American Museum of Natural History, the Smithsonian

Institution, and the Field Museum. The Peabody Museum at Harvard had purchased from the dealer Grace Nicholson. As diverse and discordant as Standley's display was, knowledgeable observers recognized that much in it, especially the Eskimo material, was important and valuable. The average viewer was probably not as aware of the collection's unevenness, although a comparison of Standley's Northwest Coast pieces with Emmons's much more controlled collections nearby could have been instructive. Although what historian Douglas Cole has called "the scramble for Northwest Coast artifacts" by major museums was basically over by 1909, there were still some museums that were filling out their almost requisite ethnographic inventories. Their representatives, while visiting the fair, saw that among Standley's variegated clutter they could discover fine, well-priced material from the Northwest Coast, and especially from the Arctic, a region from which artifacts were not easily acquired. The exposure that the AYPE gave Ye Olde Curiosity Shop positioned it as a source for museum collecting.

Soon after the exposition's close, Standley formalized his earlier small brochure of 1907 into a multipage list titled "1001 Curious Things" and made it available to interested parties. How he distributed the brochure is not clear, but individuals and museums received it and following catalogs free of charge, and some parties placed orders from them. The shop's stock also benefited from the exposition, as objects from some of the displays and gift shops were disposed of locally rather than shipped back to their countries of origin. Whether Standley acquired Japanese or Chinese material is not recorded, although it is very likely that he did, but it is certain that he purchased from the Philippine Igorrote Village. Interior shop photographs picture shields and spears from the Philippines, and entries in some of the "1001 Curious Things" lists include an assortment of borongs, kreis, and other weapons as well as such items as "cute little hats" and woven baskets from the Philippines.

When the exposition was over, the contents of the Alaska Building exhibits that had been purchased through AYPE monies or were left behind were sent to the new museum at the University of Washington.[45] Several individual exhibitors looked for buyers. Nicholson's display was sold privately (and later went to the Montclair Art Museum in New Jersey). Emmons approached the young University of Washington. Expressing concern that "today there is not an Alaska collection west of Chicago," he argued that because "Seattle owes its growth largely to the development of Alaska . . . the coast should have at least one typical study of Alaska."[46] The Emmons collection eventually made its way to the university.

Standley also searched for a home for his collection. An article in *The Westerner,* published before the exposition closed, described the collection in terms of prevailing concepts of social Darwinism. It contained "2153 listed specimens from the Indian tribes and Eskimo of Alaska . . . [that] relate in concrete form the story of the rise of a race in prehistoric times and cover the period of its slow development down to the present." For the most part a notice of the collection's availability for sale, the article also noted with pride that "Haddon, of Christ College, Cambridge, England, considers it of such value that he is now attempting to finance the purchase of it among the educational institutions of his own country," but suggested that it would also "represent a distinct conquest for the ambitious private collector."[47] When no buyer stepped forth, Standley's collection returned to the Arctic Club. While in Seattle, Haddon had bought several dozen pieces for London's Horniman Museum, where he was advisory curator, but the Cambridge University purchase he suggested came to naught. However, plans among a group of local arts enthusiasts who had incorporated in 1906 as the Washington State Art Association were encouraging.

The association, which solicited its membership from the entire state as well as Alaska, had run a gallery in Seattle for several years. Even before the AYPE was over, the fair's success inspired association members to begin planning for a grand Washington State Museum of Arts and Sciences in Seattle. A pamphlet of information and endorsements sought to raise interest and funds.[48] The museum would sponsor exhibits, illustrated lectures, classes, and an art school "conducted along modern lines." Its three-thousand seat auditorium would be used by the Seattle Symphony. The *Seattle Post-Intelligencer* supported the idea and appealed to civic pride and competition, observing that "the public is awakening to the realization that it must keep abreast of other cities in matters of artistic and scientific and musical interest." A museum would provide "branches of popular education recognized as necessities in cities of even lesser size and importance."[49]

Money began to be raised and collections for the museum made public. There would be the bronzes, sculptures, and paintings that already belonged to the association and two large collections of Indian relics. One was Standley's Arctic collection; the other, of Northwest Coast artifacts, had come quite recently, in 1909. The association had purchased—some felt "rescued," from its rival city to the south—"the finest collection of Alaska Indian relics in the world," made by revenue cutter captain Dorr F. Tozier during his fourteen years as captain of the *Grant.* Tozier had removed his entire collection of Northwest Coast art and artifacts from his home in Port Townsend in 1900 and placed it on loan in the Tacoma Ferry Museum, home of the Washington State Historical Society. Seattle interests had eyed the collection for years. A 1904 newspaper article proclaimed that after having "lain in a great heap in the Tacoma

Museum," this "collection which can never be duplicated" would be worth twice the value "when properly cleaned, classified and exhibited."[50] Although Tacomans were outraged at an announcement on October 9, 1909, that the Washington State Art Association had purchased it, early on October 11 association members arrived from Seattle with sixty-two men and a steamer. Outwitting a pending injunction in part by locking the museum curator in his office, they took possession of the dock and moved an estimated sixty tons of Tozier relics to Seattle. Tozier had asked $40,000 for the collection, but had agreed to a sum of $24,500.[51] Even that price would prove impossible, however.

C. L. Berg, the association's director, called on Standley to help classify and put values on what was now proclaimed the Washington Art Gallery Collection of Ethnological Curios.[52] Berg also arranged to purchase Standley's Arctic collection from the AYPE. The 1910 pamphlet describing the association's proposed new museum followed a longer discussion of the Tozier acquisition with a paragraph devoted to "the Standley collection of ivories and curios," more than one thousand pieces valued at $10,000.[53] For several years the purchase appeared to be a reality, although Standley seems to have had grander ideas about it than did the association. A Curiosity Shop catalog published in 1910 boasted "My Private Collection, 2253 Specimens of Alaska Curios, displayed at the Alaska-Yukon-Pacific Exposition . . . was sold entire to Seattle Museum of Arts and Sciences." The 1915 catalog reported the ivory collection to be at the Washington State Art Museum, Fifth Avenue and Seneca Street, and the 1916 catalog placed it in the Washington State Art Gallery and Free Museum, on Fifth Avenue.[54]

The association had been plagued with problems. Member communities complained about not getting the traveling exhibitions that had been promised, and voters defeated a September 1911 bond issue to fund purchase of a museum site after it was determined that association assets were largely imaginary. Less than 20 percent of the Tozier bill had been paid, and it is unlikely that Standley's bill had been either.[55] An investigation of association records commissioned by the Chamber of Commerce in June 1913 recommended its amalgamation with the rival Seattle Fine Arts Society. After several years of reluctance, the two groups merged in February 1917 and the Washington State Art Association was no more. The Seattle Fine Arts Society sponsored exhibitions in private homes on Capitol Hill into the early 1930s, when its president, Dr. Richard E. Fuller, and his mother together offered to fund a permanent Seattle Art Museum in Volunteer Park.

Like other interested people in the city, Standley kept abreast of the Washington Art Association's problems. As it became clearer and clearer that the group's financial problems precluded its paying for the collections it had bought and that it would be absorbed into the Seattle Fine Arts Society, which had its own agenda, Standley began looking for another buyer. He may have dawdled; his son-in-law Jules Charbneau was the curator of the association's art gallery, and Standley wanted the group and its museum to succeed. There may have been legalities to consider. It was wartime and there were few potential buyers anyway. Fortunately, one very "ambitious private collector" finally did come forth, in August 1916, just before the association's absorption. George G. Heye, preparing to open a Museum of the American Indian in New York, purchased Standley's Arctic collection.[56]

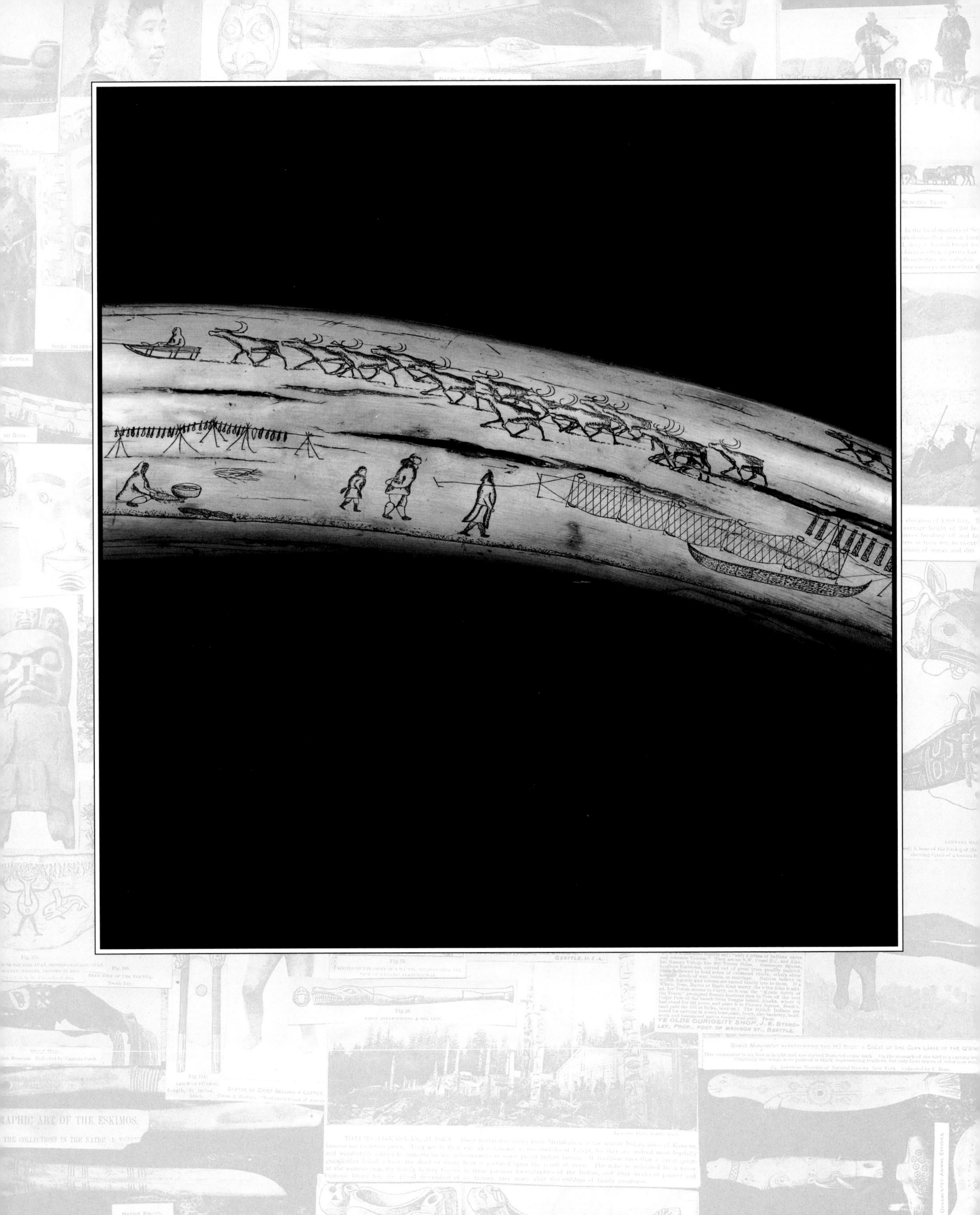

CHAPTER FOUR

"Just What a First Class Museum Should Have": Museum Collecting

In reference to the Curio Arctic Specimens that We sent to you, for Mr. Currelly's inspection . . . I hope he will find nearly all of those Specimens are just what a first Class Museum should have. As the old folks die off in the North, we find that the rising generation are not makeing articles for daily use as did their Parents. They are fast disappearing.
—Standley to C. T. Currelly, March 31, 1930

THE "AMBITIOUS PRIVATE COLLECTOR" THAT JOSEPH E. STANDLEY WAS SEARCHING for appeared in the form of George Gustav Heye of New York. In August 1916 Heye purchased a good portion of Standley's Alaska-Yukon-Pacific Exposition display for $5,000. It was a very important purchase for the shop, constituting almost one-quarter of its annual sales and a major financial boost.[1] Over the following year, as was his approach for all acquisitions, Heye personally cataloged more than twelve hundred objects from Ye Olde Curiosity Shop into the collection of his Museum of the American Indian.

George G. Heye and the Museum of the American Indian

Heye (fig. 4.1) was trained as an electrical engineer but discovered his real life passion on his first job in 1897, when he was sent to Kingman, Arizona, to superintend the construction of a railroad track with the help of Navajo laborers. He later wrote of this experience: "I spent more time collecting Navajo costume pieces and trinkets than I did superintending roadbeds. . . . And then the collecting bug bit me and I was lost."[2] Heye returned to New York with a number of Navajo pieces and began reading about Indians and searching for Indian objects wherever he could find them.

Buying first from Indian owners, Heye quickly graduated to purchasing collections assembled by others. By 1904 his home could no longer hold them all and he began to rent storage space; by 1908 he referred to his amassed collections as "The Heye Museum." Over the next decade storage became an even greater problem, and Heye loaned enough material to fill two exhibit halls to the museum at the University of Pennsylvania (later the University

4.1. Only a few photographs are available of George G. Heye during his Pacific Northwest collecting trips. Here Heye, displaying a carved bowl, stands with Mrs. R. C. Draney and E. S. Robinson, who balances a Nuxalk carved eagle that Heye purchased in British Columbia. Photograph courtesy National Museum of the American Indian, N36887, T. P. O. Menzies, photographer.

Museum) in Philadelphia. In May 1916 Heye established the Museum of the American Indian Heye Foundation, and in June ground was broken for a proper museum building, at Broadway at 155th Street in Manhattan. His "dream museum" was about to become a reality, and he continued to collect for it voraciously. The Heye Foundation board shared and supported Heye's vision, both philosophically and financially, by funding acquisitions and increasingly ambitious anthropological work. Well before Heye's purchase from Standley, he had begun sponsoring excavations in North and South America, hiring some of the most prominent anthropologists of the day to collect in the field for him. In 1919 he established the journal *Indian Notes and Monographs* to publish the results of the foundation's work.

> Many Museums and Universities and the Smithsonian Institution are among our Customers. We have the finest assortment on the coast.
>
> —Ye Olde Curiosity Shop brochure, 1907
>
> In Private Collections and in many Museums in this and Foreign Countries may be seen Curios and Relics secured from this shop.
>
> —Ye Olde Curiosity Shop Catalog C, 1916

Heye purchased Standley's collection in summer 1916, even before the new museum's cornerstone had been placed. Exactly how he came to know of Ye Olde Curiosity Shop is unclear—perhaps from museum trustees, anthropologists, fellow collectors, and friends who had made trips to the Northwest during and after the AYPE. An independently wealthy man and an avid traveler, Heye might have seen the collection himself, but he is not recorded in Standley's Guest Book until the 1920s. Surely he would have been mentioned had he identified himself in the shop. It is quite likely that it was Lieutenant George T. Emmons who at some point recommended Standley's collection to Heye. Emmons had arranged purchase of Northwest Coast material for Heye since the first years of the twentieth century, and he knew Standley and his Arctic collection.

For Heye the decision to buy the collection was probably an easy one. G. B. Gordon at the University of Pennsylvania had collected Yup'ik objects for Heye on his 1907 trip to the Kuskokwim River in southwestern Alaska, but artifacts were more difficult to acquire from the Arctic than from less remote regions, and here was a large, ready-made assemblage from North Alaska.[3] The Standley collection did not date quite as early as the Smithsonian Institution's substantial Bering Sea Eskimo collection, assembled by E. W. Nelson between 1877 and 1881, or as that acquired by John Murdock at Point Barrow (Alaska's most northerly point) between 1881 and 1883, but it came quite close. The material had been gathered mostly in the late 1890s but much of it dated earlier. Although it had not been collected scientifically, nor did it have the documentation of the Nelson, Murdock, and Gordon collections, the objects had been acquired in Alaska and Siberia directly from the Natives themselves. Overall, the material had more documentation than would many of the objects Heye would buy, and the price was excellent. Standley sold the collection to Heye for half of what he had asked from the Washington State Arts Association in 1910.

Most of the more than twelve hundred pieces that Heye acquired from Standley during summer 1916 are pictured in official AYPE photographs (see figs. 3.3a, b). Ivory and bone tools, 136 arrow points from the Columbia River, engraved ivory tusks (fig. 4.2), and small ivory human and animal figures from the Arctic (fig. 4.3) dominate. Some wooden and bone tools are clearly old,

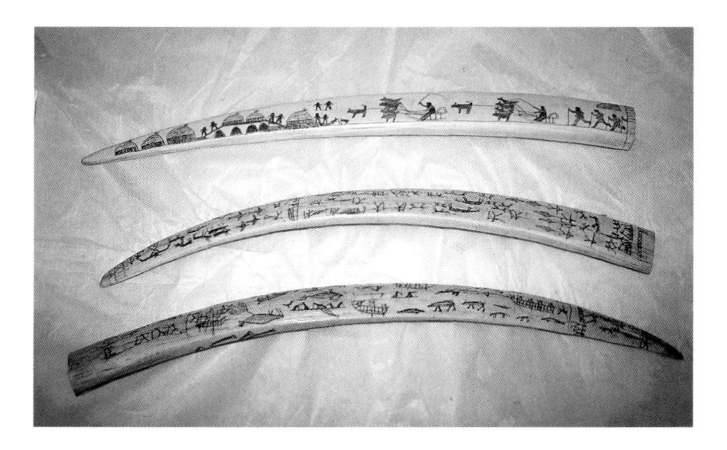

4.2. Engraved walrus tusks, late nineteenth century. Tusks engraved with detailed images of Eskimo life were popular souvenirs in Alaska and in shops that sold Alaskan arts. The lower tusks picture hunting activities engraved in the stylized manner typical of earlier drill bows. The Siberian-style dwellings on the upper, more realistically engraved tusk suggest a Siberian origin. Ivory and graphite. National Museum of the American Indian, J. E. Standley Collection, upper 5/5595, middle 5/4335, lower 5/4331. Photograph by the author.

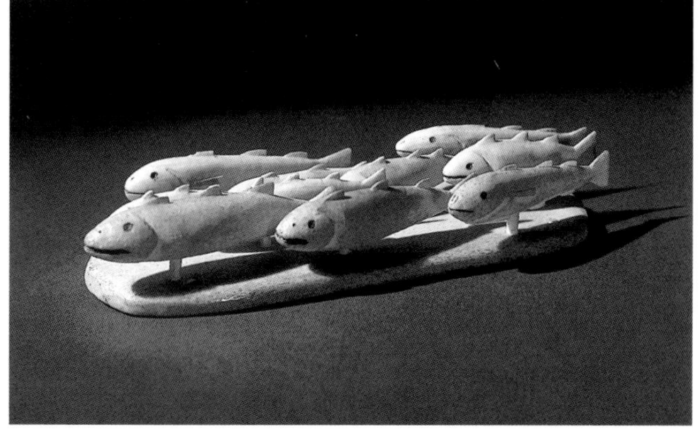

4.3. School of fish, ca. 1900, with each fish individually pegged to the base. This is an unusual subject for Eskimo carvers, who generally preferred seals, walruses, polar bears, and sea birds. Ivory, 7 in. long. J. E. Standley Collection, 5/4325. Photograph courtesy National Museum of the American Indian.

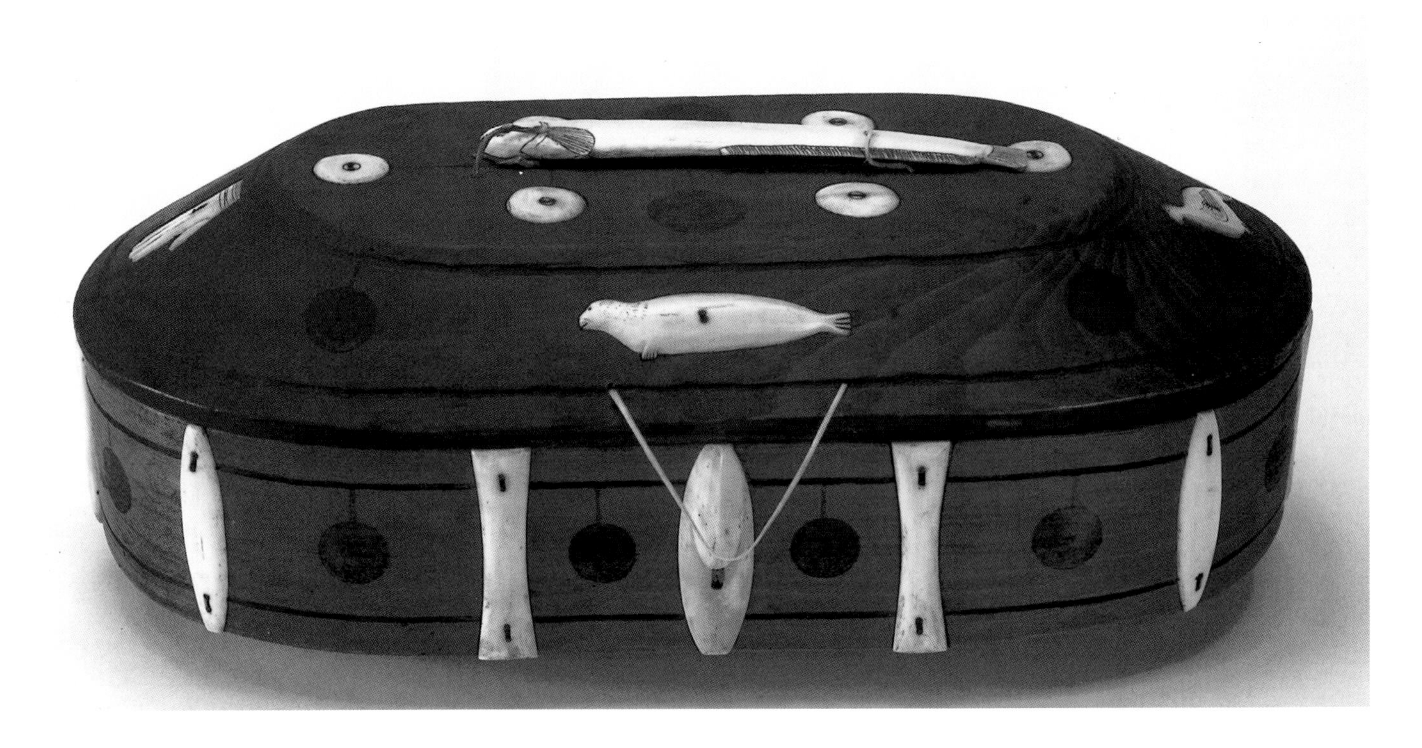

4.4. Wooden toolbox, ca. 1900. Although Standley described this as a "large old and extra fine tool chest," it does not show wear and was likely made near the turn of the century. Men stored their harpoon points and other implements in such wooden boxes. The ivory inlays picture a ptarmigan, seal, adze, and human hand; the handle is a fish, perhaps an Arctic char. Wood, ivory, baleen, 13¼ in. × 7 in. × 5¾ in. J. E. Standley Collection, 5/3747. Photograph courtesy National Museum of the American Indian.

while others, such as several kashim models, snuff boxes, hide balls, and Eskimo bentwood boxes, were seemingly made for the curio trade (fig. 4.4). Images of forty-five of the ivory carvings and engraved tusks have been published in James G. E. Smith's catalog *Arctic Art: Eskimo Ivory* (1980). Official AYPE photographs show that Standley's cases also included a little Northwest Coast material, some of which went to Heye's museum.

When cataloging the collection, Heye worked from the numbered typescript that Standley had put together enthusiastically describing the objects. Standley knew what Heye and other collectors admired and were looking for and thus emphasized quality, age, authenticity, and rarity. Some entries are brief and straightforward—"#560. A pair of very old tom cod hooks"—but most include descriptors like "very ancient," "fine ancient," "rare old," "perfect rare," "unique," "very grand," and so on. Longer explanations include information from the object's collector or Standley's speculative hyperbole. For instance, to Standley the tiny figures in the models of kashims (men's houses) represent medicine men driving out evil spirits.[4] About 5 percent of the objects on the typescript are marked "NC" ("not cataloged—commercial pieces"). These are primarily natural history specimens (whale and walrus teeth, mineral samples, walrus tusks, etc.) and carved ivory pieces made in Alaska at the turn of the century for the curio trade—an "ax," a cribbage board (fig. 4.5), "billicans," and several engraved knives and "hammers" (probably gavels, a popular curio). Despite Standley's earlier boasts that his collection contained no commercial pieces, he had included a number of them in the shipment.

The typescript also includes several bone or tooth ivory pieces described as having Northwest Coast carvings on them. Although marked "NC," these are surely the several small ivory tusks and teeth with shallowly carved totem-pole-like figures, still in the Heye collection (see fig. 3.3a, lower shelf, left). Ivory was rarely used on the Northwest Coast except by shamans carving amulets. These crude pole carvings may have been the work of Eskimo carvers exploring the idea of making a totem pole, or early experiments by Japanese carvers who were just beginning to make ivory totem pole souvenirs. Most of the Standley collection falls into two categories: objects of daily use (implements for hunting, net-making, fire-starting, and such); and ivory items, carved or etched, it appears, for sale. Most daily-use objects were what trader C. T. Pedersen called "old implements," items well worn before they left the North.

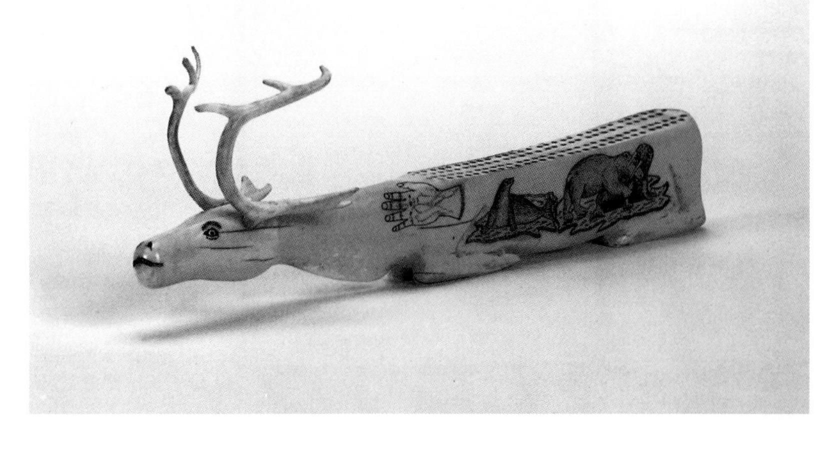

4.5. Engraved ivory cribbage board in the shape of a caribou, 1890s. Cribbage boards were a popular curio made and sold around Nome during the Nome gold rush. The realistic figures of animals, a trophy head, and a hand here were copied from published illustrations, in what has been called the "western pictorial style," introduced by carver Happy Jack. Ivory and graphite, 11½ in. long. Photograph courtesy National Museum of the American Indian, J. E. Standley Collection, 5/3749.

Locations are not common on the typescript Standley supplied, but museum records assign much of his collection to Point Barrow. Heye liked to have locations attached to items and may have added this information himself. There is sufficient significant variety in the many small ivory carvings to suggest that some came from elsewhere, a number from Siberia. Siberian Yup'iks came to Nome in the summers to trade ivory and other items, especially after the influx of population associated with the Nome gold rush, and some of the traders from whom Standley acquired material traded in Siberia. Most of the figural carvings are small; some are quite tiny. Carvers seem to have used whatever ivory was available, often cutting into the textured dentine center of the tusk rather than avoiding it, as would later become a common practice. Some figures are quite detailed, others bold and simple, and the variety in comparison to later ivory carving is striking. A number of ivories in the Heye collection point to a single carver who preferred forceful blunt-nosed forms of animals and men, often involved together in such activities as shooting a bear, dragging a seal, riding reindeer, and running sled dogs (fig. 2.4). Other carvers preferred detailed miniatures emphasizing rhythmic repetitions—of fish traveling in a school (see fig. 4.3), crew members in an umiak, or pairs of wrestlers positioned along the length of a tusk. Some tusk slices, cut through in intricate patterns of alternated whale tails, seem to be hunting tallies, and there are several carvings of rows of schematic animal or human heads emerging from flat bases, the latter said to be carvings of graveyards. The engraved tusks in the collection (fig. 4.2), pipes, and cribbage boards encompass the three engraving styles—old, modified, and western pictorial—described by anthropologist Dorothy Jean Ray as previous to the 1920s.[5]

After the initial purchase, Standley's connection with Heye continued. In November 1916 the shop sent seventy Eskimo and Northwest Coast pieces on approval and Heye purchased half of them.[6] Standley also occasionally donated objects to Heye's museum, which were acknowledged with other gifts in its journal *Indian Notes*.[7] The Curiosity Shop's Guest Book documents a number of Heye's visits to the shop on West Coast trips in the 1920s and 1930s. When in Seattle in September 1922, he purchased twenty-seven items, about one-third of them non-Indian—a cuckoo clock, a sundial, and a set of dressed fleas. On the same trip Heye expressed interest in a large carving of two squat three-foot-tall figures, one smiling and one frowning, supporting a six-foot-tall double-headed serpent.[8] It was the work of Makah carver Young Doctor, of Neah Bay; Standley called it "The Totemic Groupe from Door of Old Totem House." He had had it for at least a decade and agreed to let it go only if Heye would have a copy of it made for the shop.

Young Doctor was an established Makah carver by the time Ye Olde Curiosity Shop began to display his work (fig. 4.6). Born in 1851, the son of Old Doctor and crippled at an early age by an accident, Young Doctor grew up to become a quiet, conservative, and respected carver, singer, and healer who was involved with ceremonial duties. He often lent his house as a potlatch house. In the 1920s anthropologist Frances Densmore recorded some of the songs that Young Doctor had received through dreams. Young Doctor devoted much of his time to carving and to running a small store, and for a while a museum, in his house. He made ceremonial gear for local families on commission and carved for sale, sometimes duplicating traditional items for tourists. He was well-known for his human figures, large model fishing canoes, and head masks.

As arranged, Ye Olde Curiosity Shop shipped Young Doctor's serpent sculpture to New York (fig. 4.7). A replica was made and sent back to the shop, where it was displayed for more than sixty years. It is visible on an upper shelf in several interior photographs (see fig. 2.1, upper shelf, in between the clam shells). In 1990 this carving was purchased by a Seattle gallery that interested a buyer in purchasing and donating the sculpture to the Makah Museum in Neah Bay, Young Doctor's home. By the time it reached Neah Bay, its early history had been lost. Although there is no record, the copy is so typical of Young Doctor's work as to suggest that the artist himself was commissioned

4.6. Makah carver, Young Doctor, photographed at Neah Bay sometime between 1896 and 1903. A respected singer and healer, Young Doctor was well known for his figural carvings and canoe models of various sizes. Here he also displays a two-headed serpent made of canvas and wood. When used ceremonially, the serpent was held up by two men while eight women danced with paddles behind it. Samuel G. Morse Collection, #196, Washington State Historical Society.

4.7. In 1922 Heye purchased from Ye Olde Curiosity Shop a carving by Young Doctor that Standley called "Totemic Groupe from Door of Old Totem House," on the understanding that a replica would be made for the shop. This replica stood on an upper back shelf at the shop until the early 1990s, when it was purchased and returned to Neah Bay. Photo courtesy Makah Cultural and Research Center.

to make it. It seems less likely that in the 1920s a New York carver would have had the sensibilities to capture the artist's style so explicitly.[9] Other figures carved by Young Doctor appear in interior photographs of the shop (see fig. 2.1), and in the shop auction catalogs (1976, 1977, 1980), misidentified there as "Haidah" or Tlingit.

> They were very pleased when he [George Heye] came out because . . . they knew he would be buying a lot of items, you know. During the Depression it was a struggle, and they had all these beautiful things and nobody had any money to buy them except a few of these wealthy people who came out from the East.
>
> —Joe James

On returning home from Seattle in fall 1922, Heye sent Standley an invitation to the November 15 opening of his new museum at Audubon Terrace. World War I had slowed the museum's progress, and it was only now opening officially. Heye's collecting and sponsored anthropological work expanded until the deaths in 1928 of two of his major financial supporters, James B. Ford and Harmon Hendricks, which constricted his purchasing capability. Heye adapted by firing most of the museum staff and cutting the research and publication programs. The stock market crash and Great Depression also took a toll, but by the mid-1930s financial constraints had lessened and Heye began collecting again.

For some years Heye made an annual marathon trip to the West with a driver and a new limousine. He drove a good deal of the way himself, and very fast it is said, stopping at Indian reservations to buy whatever was available, and querying morticians in small towns about recent or imminent deaths of those with Indian collections. He visited Seattle and Ye Olde Curiosity Shop several times during the 1930s. Joe James, Standley's grandson, remembers Heye arriving at the shop in his limousine. He sometimes stayed at Standley's West Seattle home, Totem Place, where he and the Standley family would sit around the stove and exchange stories. Occasionally, he still bought from Standley, who was very proud of his friendship and quoted Heye's comment in the Guest Book and in several catalogs: "Ye Olde Curiosity Shop in Seattle is the only Curiosity Shop today in the U.S." James also recalls a particularly memorable day in the mid-1930s when a box arrived from Heye with something he was sure the shop would be interested in—a group of shrunken heads from Ecuador.

Other Museums and the Shop

After Heye purchased much of Standley's collection shown at the AYPE, other institutions followed suit; some museums bought directly from Ye Olde Curiosity Shop, and others were given single objects or collections that had been purchased there. The Royal Ontario Museum and the Newark Museum, for example, acquired substantial Arctic and Northwest Coast holdings directly from the shop. Smaller collections came to the Portland Art Museum, the Burke Memorial Washington State Museum in Seattle, and the Horniman Museum outside of London. The Smithsonian, the American Museum of Natural History, the Stockholm Museum, the British Museum, and others acquired individual pieces.[10]

Museum personnel from around the world sometimes encountered each other in the shop. In the mid-1940s Russell James, Standley's son-in-law, recalled with sadness the easy relationships of the pre–World War II years: "I've seen representatives from a British and a French and a German museum chatting happily right where I'm standing. Standing by this same whale jawbone and this same early American cherrywood cradle. These men spoke perfect English. They exchanged jokes and laughed heartily and understood each other thoroly [*sic*]. Always there was an easy friendly feeling. Then came the First World War and it's not been the same since. Not even before the Second World War. I wonder if the world can get back to honest, workaday, friendly associations."[11]

In addition to those objects documented in museum records, doubtless there are hundreds of other items that moved through Standley's shop and have made their way into museums without any record of that connection, pieces that were purchased from the shop then slowly lost their personal histories as they were enjoyed or put aside, exchanged at garage sales and flea markets, passed on in families, and eventually donated to museums. Such items may be identifiable now only if there is a Ye Olde Curiosity Shop tag or a price written in code on the object. The shop's letter-code system was used to write prices directly on objects, especially wooden ones, or on attached labels or tags. Only the staff could tell an object's price, which could be adjusted at any time without the customer being aware. The system involved aligning the numbers 1 through 0 (rather than 10) with the letters JOSTANDLEY. Thus, S.YY meant $3.00, OA.YY meant $25.00, and so forth. Standley sometimes used the letter code in his Guest Book to note the amount that a customer had spent.

For a man so interested in faraway places, Standley traveled little and rarely visited museums elsewhere. He appears to have visited the M. H. deYoung Museum in San Francisco's Golden Gate Park in the late 1920s and must have seen Heye's museum in 1930s, when he called on Heye in New York while on a trip to the East Coast. But such trips were rare. Standley knew that some of the items he had belonged in museums, however; accordingly, he routinely gave a 35 percent museum discount. Experience bore him out when museum personnel made purchases while in the shop and ordered from shop catalogs. Standley's connection with a museum was usually first made when someone associated with it visited the shop. Later on he might notify the staff that he had something rare and important that he felt sure they would be interested in if they could just see it. Occasionally he also shipped unsolicited objects on approval or sent small gifts to museums. That museums purchased from his shop was a point of pride, confirmation, and personal pleasure for Standley. He advertised these connections for decades, and jotted down remembrances of the visits of museum personnel in his guest book and on scraps of paper. These connections were in his mind in the late 1920s when he updated his address file of sources and suppliers into a small brown book he labeled "Address of Where to Buy" and he devoted the first page to a "List of Museums That Bought from Us."[12]

It is very likely that many more objects in museums were acquired from curio shops than has been recognized. Although a curio shop might not be credited publicly as a source, at the turn of the century such a shop often served a museum's needs well. This was true especially if the museum were seeking material from the indigenous people of the Northwest Coast and Alaska but could not sponsor a field collecting expedition itself. Historian Douglas Cole has demonstrated the critical role that curio shops in Alaska, Seattle, Vancouver, and Victoria performed as middlemen in the scramble by major North American museums for Northwest Coast artifacts.[13] Ye Olde Curiosity Shop was a player in this scramble, but a minor one, because it never had a great deal of Northwest Coast material that was old or had been used ceremonially. Because of the shop's location, however, and because of the connections it established early on, it was a dependable source for old, authentic objects from the Arctic.

The intention of a museum—its purpose and mission—informs its collection policy and influences the way it collects. A public commitment to education and preservation, coupled with a degree of concern with entertainment, blend with forces of personal vision, ego, and civic pride. Often one of these factors stands out among the others. This was the case with the museums that purchased Native American artifacts from Ye Olde Curiosity Shop. Those who knew George G. Heye, who established his large private Museum of the American Indian, were aware that ego was a primary factor in his collecting activities. For C. T. Currelly, the archaeologically trained founder of the Royal Ontario Museum, civic pride in a modern museum with world-class collections was a driving concern. John Cotton Dana, the librarian-founder of the Newark Museum, believed that education of the city's schoolchildren and service to its immigrant and primarily working-class population should be his museum's purpose. Education was also the major concern of Axel Rasmussen, whose collection went to Oregon's Portland Art Museum, and to the directors and curators of Seattle's Burke Memorial Washington State Museum.

Charles Trick Currelly and the Royal Ontario Museum

C. T. Currelly of Toronto (fig. 4.8), the force behind the founding of the Royal Ontario Museum, was a more worldly and sophisticated collector than was Heye. After a short-lived missionary career in Canada, Currelly studied in

London, where he became interested in antiquities and for several years devoted himself to archaeological work in Egypt, with Sir Edmund Petrie and the Egypt Exploration Fund, and in Palestine.[14] Artifacts discovered during the Fund's excavations went to its subscribers, both individuals and museums. On his trips home Currelly curried Toronto patrons and convinced some to pledge funds so he might build important collections to form a major museum in Toronto for the teaching of science. During his time in Egypt, the Near East, London, and Europe, he also established lifelong connections with scholars, dealers, and collectors who would assist him in his passion. Over the decades, with an eye for a bargain, Currelly sought to find quality examples of the particular ranges and types of items he believed should be in the museum. While visiting Seattle in 1912, he found that even Ye Olde Curiosity Shop could help in these endeavors.

4.8. During the early years of the Royal Ontario Museum, its creator and director, C. T. Currelly, found that Ye Olde Curiosity Shop provided a convenient way to acquire some of the types of Northwest Coast objects he felt his museum should have. He also purchased several large arctic pieces from the shop. Photograph courtesy Suzanne Currelly Hamilton.

In 1903, Currelly first "brought home" to Toronto's Victoria College ancient artifacts from Egypt and the Holy Land. Within little more than ten years he had formed sufficiently large collections to fill an entire museum. When Toronto's Royal Ontario Museum opened on March 19, 1914, the collections were larger than those of any American museum at its opening.[15] The modern building, contemporary exhibition techniques used, and broad and extensive collections garnered wide admiration. The ROM, as the new museum affectionately came to be called, was a magnificent accomplishment that satisfied both the personal ambitions of its founder and the competitive ones of his country.

Currelly's interests were broad and eclectic. Boyhood experience observing the manufacture and craftsmanship of objects in the tiny Ontario town in which he had grown up had led him to a philosophical commitment to the object as the most trustworthy source of information. Later, William H. Holmes of the Smithsonian Institution counseled Currelly that his duty was to science. Collections of objects were essential for long range scientific inquiry, because researchers could go back to them again and again as new kinds of questions became interesting.[16] Currelly envisioned a museum where one could learn by comparing and analyzing comprehensive collections that would show something of the greatness of the various peoples represented. Typical of the time and true to his archaeological training, he sought collections to allow the museum "to follow the full evolutionary pattern in the development of the crafts . . . from the countries where we could obtain the material."[17]

Although his personal interests were strongest in the Near East and later the Far East, Currelly recognized from the beginning that it was important for the ROM to include collections from North America's indigenous peoples.

No doubt this was in part due to his brief early experience in the mission service of the Methodist Church. His second mission assignment had taken him to live among the Bungee (Salteaux) Indians and the Metis (Indian-European mixed bloods) in the Duck Mountains near Lake Winnipegosis in western Manitoba. There he came to appreciate their arts and even insisted on learning how to roll sinew, handle moosehide, and make mitts and moccasins, although these tasks were considered women's work.

When the Royal Ontario Museum of Archaeology (one of five museums that made up the original institution) first opened to the public in 1914, there were two ethnographic galleries, one dedicated to African, Oceanic, and Inuit material, and a second illustrating "the life of the American Indian" in paintings by Paul Kane and Edmund Morris.[18] There were also displays of North American Indian objects, some of which had come from Ye Olde Curiosity Shop. Currelly encountered the shop in late winter 1912, while on a western lecture and collecting tour that took him to the U.S. Southwest then up the coast to arrive finally in Victoria, British Columbia.[19] The Seattle connection he made at this time became a valuable and long-standing one, extending over twenty-four years and entailing considerable correspondence.[20] Several transactions with the shop are also mentioned in Currelly's 1956 autobiography, *I Brought the Ages Home.* Although he never cites Standley or Ye Olde Curiosity Shop by name in the book, at several points he discusses objects acquired there. One of the first was a carved stone figure (fig. 4.9). He wrote: "Just before I left Seattle I had bought a fine piece of stone carving for a small sum—I think in fact the freight to Toronto cost more than the carving itself—and it is the only piece of Totemic art in stone that I have seen. Two sailors had landed from a little ship and found it lying some distance in the woods."[21] The stone carving was included in the shop's first shipment to the museum. It was unusual in that it was not of argillite, the black slate-like stone from which Haida carvers had created thousands of model totem poles and other objects.

The correspondence from this first transaction between the ROM and Ye Olde Curiosity Shop follows a pattern that was maintained throughout their lengthy relationship.[22] The shop would notify the museum that a shipment of artifacts had been sent on approval—in this case in 1912, a 400-pound group of items that included the "large dark stone carved totem" that Standley recalled Currelly showing interest in while in Seattle, and other artifacts he had chosen per Currelly's instructions. A list of individual pieces briefly described each item and gave its price; the sum total was adjusted to reflect the 35 percent bulk discount that the shop accorded to museums.[23] Standley's accompanying letter pledged authenticity and age; his later letters would also emphasize quality and rarity: "Curios shipped today under instructions of your

Mr. Currelly. I have very carefully selected Genuine Indian Relics of interest . . . out of my own Collection that was exhibited at the A.Y.P. Exposition here in 1909 in U. S. Government Bldg. of Alaska. I guarantee the articles of real Indian and Eskimo make and old time at that."[24]

When the shop received an initial payment in early July 1912, Standley acknowledged it immediately: "Hope that you will find lots in the goods I sent for approval that will appeal to you because the good old stuff is getting very hard to get hold of. The Arctic boats returning to Seattle did not bring any curios at all."[25] In late September, Currelly sent the remaining payment. After more curios were shipped in early February 1913, there was another delay. Finally, in mid-May, Standley wrote again: "What has become of the 3 cases curios shipped last Feb. 4th. I hope they have not gotten lost or wrecked. I took considerable care to select a choice lot of Relics and trust that you will find much of interest to your museum."[26]

4.9. Stone totem pole. One of the earliest purchases that Currelly made from Ye Olde Curiosity Shop was an unusual model totem pole carved out of dark stone. It pictures two major Haida crests, a raven and a bear, and is probably Haida, but the pole is unusual in that the stone is not argillite. During the nineteenth century, Haida artists carved thousands of small argillite totem poles, figures, containers, and ship-style and Haida-style pipes as market art. Stone, 26 3/8 in. tall. Royal Ontario Museum, HN194. Photograph courtesy Royal Ontario Museum, Department of Ethnology Archives.

The pattern and wording of the correspondence around this first acquisition in 1912 tells a good deal about both Currelly's and Standley's ways; it also reveals much about the times. Standley was eager and efficient in responding to Currelly's interest in his artifacts, assuring him that they were sufficiently rare and valuable to be worthy of a museum's collection. He was patient with the museum's ever more tardy payments, diplomatic but sometimes urgent in his reminders. For his part Currelly had grabbed an opportunity and agreed to a purchase, although he may not have had the needed funds in hand. Over the years it was common for him to first make commitments, then approach donors begging the needed funding. Here, even before his museum opened, Currelly had apparently overextended himself financially.

Standley's comment about the lack of old material speaks to the times as well. Whaler-traders, revenue cutter personnel, and others had carried artifacts from Alaska to Seattle and San Francisco for decades. By 1908 shore whaling had almost decimated what was left of the bowhead, both the whale oil and whalebone (baleen) markets had nearly collapsed in favor of alternatives, and the Arctic whale fishery had nearly come to an end. Whaling captains had been gradually increasing trading as an adjunct occupation for decades, and by the early twentieth century most of the few captains who still made annual trips to the Arctic had given up whaling entirely in favor of trading. The San Francisco-based Pacific Steam Whaling Company sent only three ships North in 1909, primarily for trading. After that until the end of World War I only one or two large ships and a few small schooners went North each year, to supply coastal communities and to trade.[27] Standley's statement about no Arctic boats with curios was not hyperbole. In contrast to a decade earlier, in 1912 there were few boats returning from the Arctic. The time when "piles of Eskimo Relics" came out of the Arctic annually was past.

After the large purchases of 1912–13, there were few shipments of artifacts sent on approval to the ROM from Ye Olde Curiosity Shop. Most later purchases were of single objects, made after Standley notified Currelly of something he hoped would interest him. Over the next twenty years the Royal Ontario Museum made several important purchases from the shop in this way. During World War I both the Curiosity Shop and the museum were strained for funds. In 1917 Standley contacted the ROM about a standing offer that Currelly had left during his visit in 1912 "to purchase a Tusk of a Mammoth . . . at $400 and if I ever concluded to sell for that price he would be glad to get it" (fig. 4.10).[28] Standley had refused the offer at the time—"I did not need money then"—but now proposed to accept it for "this remarkable specimen" that he described in detail:

> It is the only Ivory Tusk of the Mammoth that ever Came out of Alaska with the Scenes of arctic life engraved all over it done true to nature by the Eskimo. The tusk is Natural Color, from Age, being about 30,000 years since the Prehistoric Elephants Called Mammoths lived in Alaska. This Tusk was dug out of the frozen Gravel by Miners in the Eskimo Village of *Unalakleet* near Nome Alaska in 1898—Then it was taken to Nome Alaska in 1899 and Happy Jack The Eskimo carver spent the long Winter Cutting a history of the Every day life of his home. First he put the Eskimo Village his home furnished by the U. S. Government. Then he put The Woods, with Animal Traps fixed by bending Young Trees and baiting, a large Omiak.[29]

The letter continued with a list of the vignettes pictured. In Standley's supplier book "Where to Buy," under "Relics Eskimo" he noted "Tom Powers, Unalakleet Alaska. That etched tusk came from there," implying that Powers was the miner who had found the tusk and perhaps commissioned a carver to engrave it.

Although Standley attributed the engraving on the tusk to Happy Jack, the Eskimo artist from Nome famous for his representational engraving on ivory, it was more likely the work of Joe Kakarook, who lived near Unalakleet.

Eskimo art scholar Dorothy Jean Ray has pointed out that the style, although more naturalistic than that of many Nome area carvers at the time, is far less so than the work of Happy Jack, and that it emphasizes village scenes, which Happy Jack rarely engraved. Although she suggests that Standley probably provided the attribution "knowing that Happy Jack was the most famous of all carvers," it is equally probable that the attribution came from Powers, who was no doubt also aware of Happy Jack's reputation.[30]

Once the ROM expressed an interest in the tusk, Standley appealed to Currelly's spirit of competition and love for a bargain with an offer of exclusivity: "I am going to hold off offering that carved mammoth tusk to any one else until you have had a chance to interest some Friend of the Museum. These are strenious Times but it is always in such cases that Bargains are obtainable to the best advantage."[31] Currelly asked for the tusk on approval, to allow "bringing it before the gentleman who suggested that he would probably put up the money for it," and offered to pay freight both ways if it had to be returned. This letter probably crossed in the mail with one from Standley indicating that he would send it directly by pre-paid express, because "on account of the war all freights are delayed except for the government," and possibly with another letter sent two days later in which he sweetened the deal with a bargain: "To make a quick turn I will stand all costs of Delivery except duty and for the Museum exhibit there should be free entry." He also mentioned that he could now offer rare shaped arrow points of flint and ivory from the Banks Land Blond Eskimo.

When payment for the tusk had not arrived almost a month later, Standley diplomatically advised that he had received the customs declaration and hoped there would not be a tie up. After yet another month he wrote that his Wells Fargo Tracer has reported "finding the tusk in Toronto." Currelly was

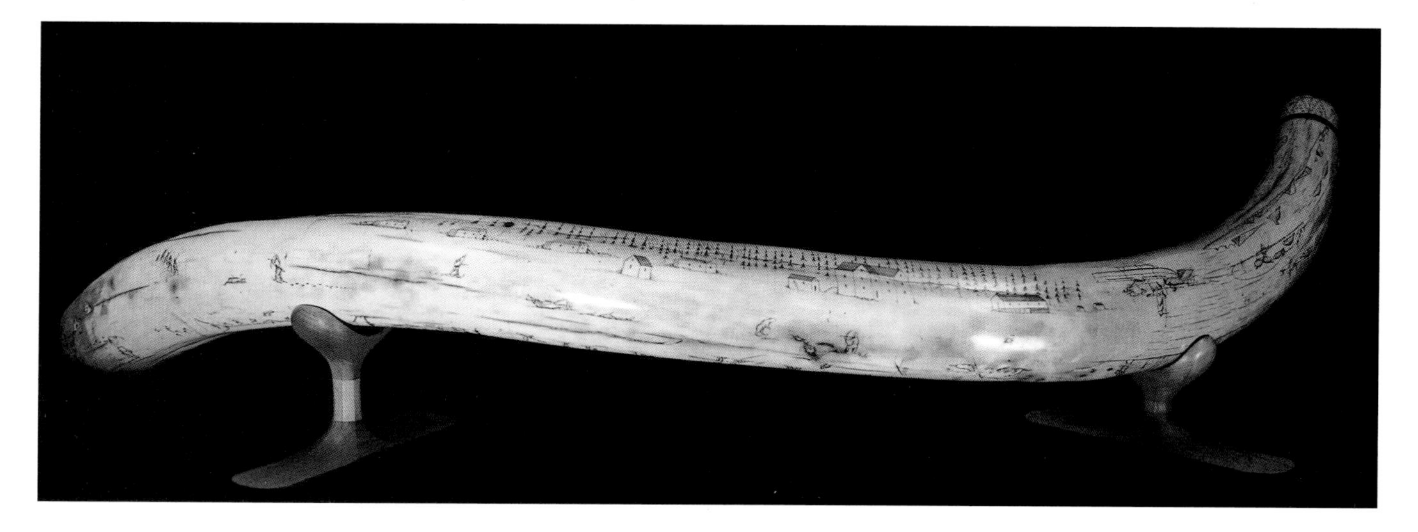

4.10. Engraved mammoth tusk. Standley's letter of June 2, 1917, to the Royal Ontario Museum described this rarity: "The Tusk is natural rich brown aged color in perfect Condition. Measures 79½ inches in length, 15½ in circumference large end and 13 in circumference smallest end. Pictures are all over the tusk representing fishing, Hunting, trapping herding Lassoeng. Games & the daily life among Reindeer, Seals, Walrus, Whales game Bird life, Sledges & etc even the Eskimo Village of unaklet [Unalakleet] near Nome, Alaska." Royal Ontario Museum, 917.11. Photograph courtesy Royal Ontario Museum, Department of Ethnology Archives.

well-known for tardy payments and accruing enormous debt on behalf of the museum. His eye for a bargain and desire to purchase all he believed the museum should have often collided with a meager acquisition budget, and convincing patrons took time. At one point Currelly was in such arrears for museum purchases that the trustees forbade the Bank of England to extend him any more credit. After finally receiving a check for the tusk in late October, Standley sent a thank-you note. It was wise to be gracious. He also included a postcard picturing himself with a polar bear rug and assorted other items (see fig. 2.8) and a list of prices for each. Tough times required aggressive salesmanship, even with straggling payment of bills.

More than a decade passed before the ROM again purchased from Ye Olde Curiosity Shop. After Captain Alfred H. Anderson, one of the last of the Arctic whalers, left articles in the shop on consignment, Standley renewed the contact with Currelly in October 1928. He had just received a stove—"a wonderful Prehistoric relic that was discovered on Victoria Land in the Arctic, perfect carved of solid stone, black with age"—and an accompanying rectangular "kettle" (fig. 4.11).[32] Both objects, acquired when Anderson's vessel had wintered over in the ice at Coronation Gulf, were "wonderful specimens for a museum." On the back of Standley's note to the museum he included drawings of the two pieces, a *Seattle Times* newspaper clipping announcing that they "probably will go to a museum in New York after being exhibited in Seattle" at Ye Olde Curiosity Shop, and a reminder of Currelly's earlier bargain from the shop, the ivory tusk that "is worth double what you paid."[33]

After Currelly requested the price, Standley assured him of his special commitment to him: "I have made you the 1st one to receive a Photograph." Aware that Currelly relished besting the competition, Standley also included a list of the largest such stoves in the major American museums. Standley had written to several institutions, and their replies proved his stove to be a full eleven and a half inches longer than the next largest one, in the American Museum of Natural History.[34] He would ship both the stove and the kettle for $600. Currelly deferred, however, perhaps because he had already acquired sizable Arctic collections that included similar pieces from Vilhjálmur Stefánsson and Robert Flaherty. "Much as we would like to have your Eskimo stone stove and cooking pot, there is only the question of unusual size to account for its value." Two weeks later, having "heard from the old whaler who has cut down the price," Standley offered the lot for $385 cash with the whaler paying the shipping. Currelly leapt at the opportunity.

As the correspondence over the stone lamp provides a glimpse of how both Ye Olde Curiosity Shop and the Royal Ontario Museum operated, it also contains elements that validated Standley's view of himself as a legitimate

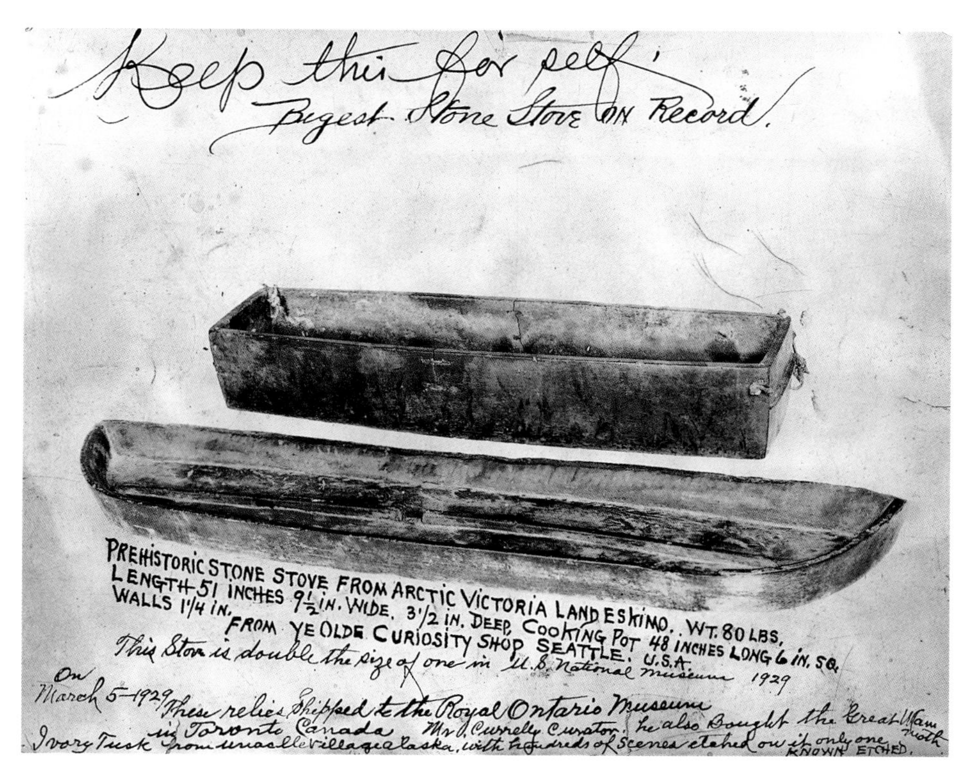

PREHISTORIC STONE STOVE FROM ARCTIC VICTORIA LAND ESKIMO. WT. 80 LBS,
LENGTH 51 INCHES 9½ IN. WIDE. 3½ IN. DEEP, COOKING POT 48 INCHES LONG 6 IN. SQ.
WALLS 1¼ IN.
FROM YE OLDE CURIOSITY SHOP SEATTLE. U.S.A.
This Stove is double the size of one in U.S. National museum 1929
On March 5-1929 These relics Shipped to the Royal Ontario Museum
in Toronto Canada Mr. Currelly Curator.

4.11. Not his usual procedure, Standley had a commercial photograph made of the stone stove and kettle that Captain Albert Anderson left with him on consignment. It may have been a factor in convincing the Royal Ontario Museum to purchase the two items. The writing on the photograph is in Standley's hand. Pierson Photo Co. Commercial Photographers, Seattle, 1928.

museum supplier. Curators at the major natural history museums took his queries for information seriously enough to answer them and showed interest in his wares, thus to his mind they were in competition for them. A letter Standley sent to Currelly after his purchase of the stone relics reported that the Smithsonian was interested in the stove but had no funds at the moment: "Its really laughable for Uncle Sam to be so hard up. I guess its to much Red Tape to go thru so I told them so." A post card sent the same day begged, "Please don't let Mr. Geo Heye of American Museum N.Y. know what you Paid for the Stone Relics, he is a good customer of mine etc—your bargain is easily Worth a Thousand Dollars." The rejoinder was not just flattery. By 1929, Heye had been in the shop several times on collecting trips to the West Coast. He did not buy a lot, but Standley considered him a friend, entertained him at the Standley home, and surely did not wish to offend him.[35]

After Currelly's requests for "stone tools with the wooden handles, from either the West Coast Indians or the Eskimos," Standley sent a list of twenty-one "Alaska Eskimo curios."[36] His understanding of Arctic geography was vague, however, for all were from Coronation Gulf in the Canadian Northwest Territories. Several items were shipped on approval four days later, about the same time that the stove and kettle arrived in Toronto. An echo of earlier times followed when a post card asked that payment be hastened: "I've got to meet important obligations. Now is my Dull Business time of the year." A response assured that the bill was going through channels "to get as rapid payment as possible." It also asked for good Eskimo material "as old whalers must have brought down things which they would still have in their homes" and reiterated the request for tools with handles. The card about Heye had caught Currelly's attention too, for he concluded, "So please make us your special friends by sending us all of the really fine things of mounted stone you can get hold of."[37]

Encouraged by the speedy transactions, Standley sent a two-page letter emphasizing the rarity and antiquity of his items: old muk muk bowls, an ancient bow of musk ox horn, a perfect pointed tusk of the narwhal (now extinct on the Pacific Coast), a rope of braided sinew "used in Primitive times for whales . . . before the white man was on the coast," and "rare old ivory tools." An afterthought, written on the back of the letter, mentioned arrow points from the Columbia and Snake Rivers, "the finest and rarest in the world . . . from [sketch] this size used in water beach ceremonies up to 12 inches . . . of obsidian, jasper, flint, chalcedony, etc."[38]

Mail moved quickly and six days later Currelly expressed interest in a range of items, including "your very choicest arrowheads from the Columbia River. . . . We have a pretty good lot already and should not like any more except remarkably choice ones." The shop responded with an enthusiastic list of relics valued at $1,067.45 to be sent from Seattle. Although Standley had assured Currelly that he was sending "the cream of my stock," there were many duplicates of material the museum already had. Currelly and T. C. McIlwraith, who was now in charge of the anthropological collections, chose a portion coming to less than a third of the total asking price. This included a jade axe (with hopes that Standley would lower its price—he did), some Eskimo implements, and twelve Columbia River arrow points.[39]

In his autobiography Currelly rarely talked of purchases that came from Ye Olde Curiosity Shop, but because of an earlier experience these arrow points caught his fancy and provided an anecdote. As in the case of the stone totem earlier discussed, the shop was not mentioned by name. Instead, the acquisition became a little drama, helped along by a bit of exaggeration. While in England, Currelly had seen some fine Columbia River points in the collection of Dr. Allen Sturge: "For some reasons these arrow points, which were the most beautiful I had ever seen, very small and probably used for birds, had nearly hypnotized me, so that I used to wake up at night wondering if I had left any stone unturned that might bring a few of them to the museum, as they were in such striking contrast to our coarse Ontario points that are largely made of chert. One day I received a letter from a man offering me a collection that he made many years before along the Columbia River. He had found this collection in an old trunk, together with the price that they cost him at the time."[40] That the ROM owns no Columbia River points except those received from Standley suggests that Currelly was indulging in a bit of posturing in his initial correspondence with the shop, so that he would be sent Standley's choicest examples.[41]

Correspondence continued for several years, but there were fewer and fewer items that Standley had to interest the museum. In January 1930 he offered a skin kayak, which was declined; in February he received permission to send a "very nice collection of small Eskimo curios," which he later described as "just what a first class museum should have." Although several of these objects were not Eskimo, the museum purchased most of them—all but the most expensive items. Because of Currelly's travels, the choice of what to purchase was not made until June, and a check was not forthcoming until October, after Standley's plea: "I have so many obligations coming due 1st of the month that I am asking all my debtors to help me out—surely will appreciate it." The museum was also having cash flow problems.[42]

In March 1931 Standley sent to the museum "a wonderful lot of fine old Eskimo curios," fifty items totaling $719.85. Currelly was abroad at the time, but three months later he and McIlwraith decided to return most of the shipment, noting that "many of the hafted tools appear to have been rehafted by Eskimo in relatively recent times." It was not uncommon for Natives to repair old tools for their own use as well as to make them complete before selling them. Tools were for using and should work, was the sentiment, but museums saw this differently. An obviously new repair disturbed both an object's antiquity and the accompanying, if unspoken, idea of Native life as an essentialist construct, timeless and unchanging. Although the final sale netted Standley only $50, he again offered to send "some exceptionally fine old genuine curios."[43]

Several years elapsed before the next correspondence. In July 1935 Standley wrote: "When I get something very unusual from the Arctic Eskimo I think of you," and he offered "the biggest finest made Dog Sled that has ever come out [of Alaska]," with the runners "cut from a whales jaw bone all in one piece 1/2 inch thick, 3 inches wide and 12 feet long." He would sell it for $75 and, referring to the University of Washington, lamented that "our museum wants it here but have no funds." Currelly requested a photograph: "We are still anxious to add to our collections, although the depression has hit us as it has everyone else." Edwin Ewing handled the correspondence in Standley's shop, and he sent the sledge and a small group of other items, mostly ivories, on approval in early January. McIlwraith's reply was diplomatic: the ROM would keep only seven of the pieces, including the sled. A letter from elsewhere in the museum was blunter: "As five of the twelve pieces of the shipment were misrepresented

In our Eskimo and Indian curio stock are many rare curios and prehistoric relics, among which there are no duplicates and are not listed in this catalog. Also articles of rare interest, collected from all parts of the globe. Private collectors and museums supplied. All orders and correspondence will receive our prompt attention, with care and determination to give satisfaction. We warrant every article to be as represented.

—Ye Olde Curiosity Shop Catalog G, early 1930s

to us, we are returning them. One is an old tool to which a handle has been added later, thus spoiling its archaeological value; other pieces are not really old."[44] The shop requested more invoice forms from the museum, but there is no record of further purchases. In 1936 the twenty-four-year relationship between Ye Olde Curiosity Shop and the Royal Ontario Museum ended. It was the longest connection sustained between the shop and any museum. Currelly died in 1957.

John Cotton Dana and the Newark Museum

In 1904 the Free Public Library in Newark, New Jersey, found room among its books to display minerals and other scientific materials belonging to a local collector. By 1909 the area devoted to the display had expanded and collections of objects had become such an important part of the library that a Newark Museum Association was incorporated to manage them. At its head was John Cotton Dana, the library's innovative and crusading director, who believed that the museum's primary purpose should be to educate the public (fig. 4.12). He wrote that "no more useless a public institution, useless relative to its cost, was ever devised than that popular ideal, the classical building of a museum of art, filled with rare and costly objects." Instead, a museum should be "everyday useful, helpful, instructive, entertaining." As an "institute of visual instruction," a museum housed in a library actually provided the optimum learning environment because both objects and the books explaining them were at hand. Dana believed that a museum should even lend out its collections.[45]

Dana's populist ideas about a museum's function, based in his library background, were not entirely new to museums, but his tenacious application of those ideas and ideals were well ahead of their time. He believed that individuals and groups should be able to borrow from a museum whenever it was clear that the objects would be of more service to the community than when "resting relatively unseen and unused, in the museum's headquarters." To this end he established the "lending department" in 1914, and the Newark Museum Association began building both permanent and lending collections. Ye Olde Curiosity Shop would help in these endeavors. Also in 1914 the museum initiated a northern component in its permanent collection with the purchase of thirty-five Northwest Coast, Eskimo, and Subarctic Athapaskan objects from Ye Olde Curiosity Shop. In later years the museum would purchase from the shop for the lending department as well.[46]

At the time that Dana was developing his museum philosophy in New

Jersey, Standley, on the opposite coast, was developing a merchandising procedure that he would use until his death. Over a period of nearly forty years Ye Olde Curiosity Shop would produce at least fourteen catalogs—some modest brochures of several-pages, others over forty pages long—and send them "presented with our compliments" to such potential buyers as museums.[47] Several of the earliest catalogs included a section titled "1001 Curious Things," a numbered list of single and limited-stock items encompassing an amazing array of merchandise for the reader to peruse with intent or abandon. Each time a new catalog came out the list was changed, eliminating what had been purchased since the last catalog and adding new items.

4.12. John Cotton Dana, May 1926. The scientific collections displayed in the Free Public Library in Newark, New Jersey, expanded to become the Newark Museum, with librarian Dana as its first director. Dana's museum philosophy emphasized education, and the list of "1001 Curious Things" in Ye Olde Curiosity Shop catalogs provided a convenient way to acquire Alaskan material for both the museum's permanent and its lending collections. Portrait by Koenig Photographers. Photograph courtesy Newark Museum.

Dana had been in Seattle twice, coming and going from an American Library Association tour to Alaska in 1905, and although his name does not appear in Standley's Guest Book, he surely became acquainted with the shop at that time, for he appears to have been sent one of its first catalogs.[48] Although there are no records to clarify whether the museum used the shop's "1001 Curious Things" list in its first purchase in 1914, it is almost certain that it did, from Catalog A. In 1919, when the Newark Museum Association requested several items on approval, it definitely ordered by number from the list in "Catalog and Price List of 1001 Curious Things from Ye Olde Curiosity Shop" (hereafter called Catalog C). The catalog appears to have come out in late 1916 after George Heye's August purchase of Standley's AYPE display, which the catalog mentions. After the items ordered were received (along with a few others Standley hoped would be of interest), eleven objects were chosen for the museum's lending department, mostly dolls and miniatures useful in teaching.[49]

The shop's lists of "1001 Curious Things" intersperse in no discernible order ethnological objects, Native North American and otherwise, with natural history specimens, crafts, manufactures, and oddities from around the world. Two of the items that the Newark Museum purchased in 1919—"#546. Fire kindler, Wood, Rawhide String with Ivory Handles, Primitive and Rare, from Point Barrow Alaska" and "#560. A Skin Kayak (Canoe, 1 hole), Alaska, Native, Miniature" (for $3.50 and $4 respectively)—are listed among Oriental cloisonné teapots, old Civil War powder horns, and a "Perfect Petrified Fish." Two additional museum purchases from the shop in 1921 were the last on record. With the latter, Standley enclosed his own Seattle Booster card on which he wrote that the Chamber of Commerce, Merchants Exchange, and

Marine Board had merged and a big new chamber building was in the offing. His enthusiasm for his city extended to educating those on the East Coast about it.

Despite a seven-year relationship with the shop, the Newark Museum is not included in the list of museums at the front of Standley's supplier book "Where to Buy." A lack of personal connection may explain this, for all of the correspondence with the museum was between Standley and the Newark Museum Association; none was with Dana himself, although Dana undoubtedly was involved in the choice of items to purchase. The museums Standley remembered and listed in his book were those he associated with a particular individual.

Copyrighted

PRICE LIST

OF

1001 CURIOUS THINGS

Ye Olde Curiosity Shop

SEATTLE, U. S. A.

The Pioneer in Seattle Curio Business

The Most Unique Shop in the World
Located on the Colman Dock

Delivery of Goods guaranteed by insured Parcel-Post. If remittance accompanies order, send Bank Draft, Express Order or Postal Money Order.

WRITE PLAIN DIRECTIONS

Order by numbers also number of the plates

Address

Ye Olde Curiosity Shop

SEATTLE, U. S. A.

J. E. STANDLEY, Prop. EDW. V. STANDLEY, Mgr.

4.13. Cover, Catalog B, 1915: "Copyrighted Price List of 1001 Curious Things Ye Olde Curiosity Shop, Seattle, U.S.A." 10½ in. × 4½ in. The "1001 Curious Things" list is in many parts identical to that in the 1914 Catalog A, from which Currelly purchased for the Newark Museum's Lending Department.

Dana's choices from Ye Olde Curiosity Shop were for the most part technological and utilitarian—everyday tools and utensils, clothing, and handwork like baskets and bags (figs. 4.14, 14.15a, b). Some of the objects showed clear evidence of use, others were new, perhaps even made quickly for sale. His choices were similar to those of other museums installing ethnological exhibits at the time; they reflected the emphasis of the evolutionary-based scientific model on basic tools and manufactures as best demonstrating a culture's way of life and level of development. Display of modern technologies was also prominent in the museum, for Dana felt it was important to educate the people of Newark about their own industries. Whether by design or not, the museum visitor was allowed a comparison of "primitive" and advanced technologies, similar to what had been posed at world's fairs for some decades, a comparison that demonstrated a one-way trajectory in humankind's cultural-evolutionary development.

As his involvement in museum administration and planning increased, Dana developed a philosophy and plan for what he called the "New Museum." The theory held that in such a museum an object's value was based in its direct applicability to education rather than its rarity or cost: "Much of what the old type of Museum . . . would consider quite useless and even unworthy of acquisition, has an admirable utility in the vast field that opens to the Museum of the new type. . . . In addition to being authentic, these objects must have the advantage of being useful, low in cost, easily transported, and not easily damaged by use."[50] Ye Olde Curiosity Shop filled this mandate nicely, especially for the Newark Museum's lending collections. There was little economically priced Northwest Coast material available on the East Coast, and even fewer items from the Arctic. Although Dana appreciated field collecting, he was a pragmatist and felt that objects sent out to schools

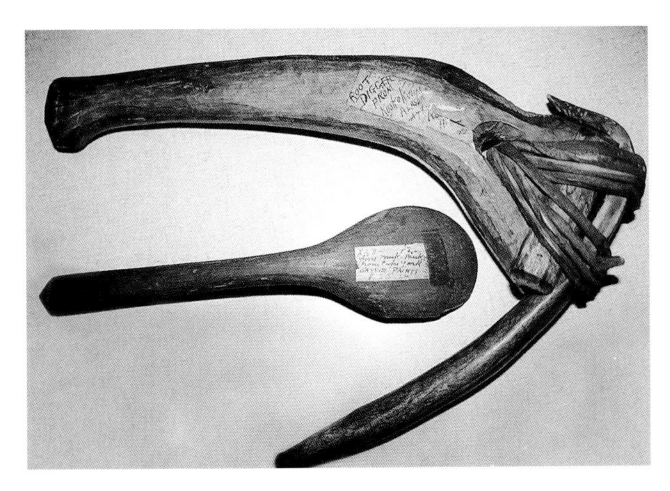

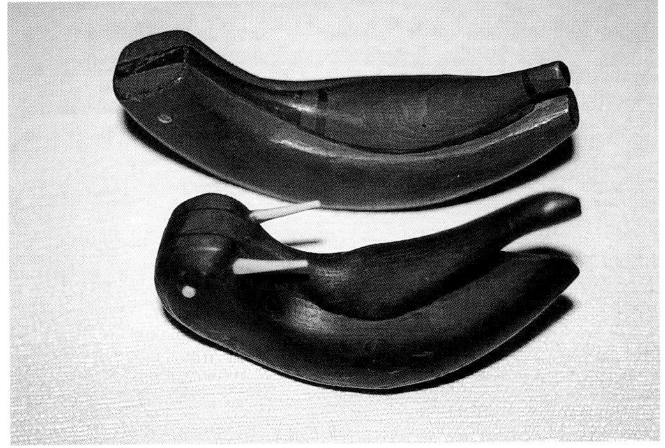

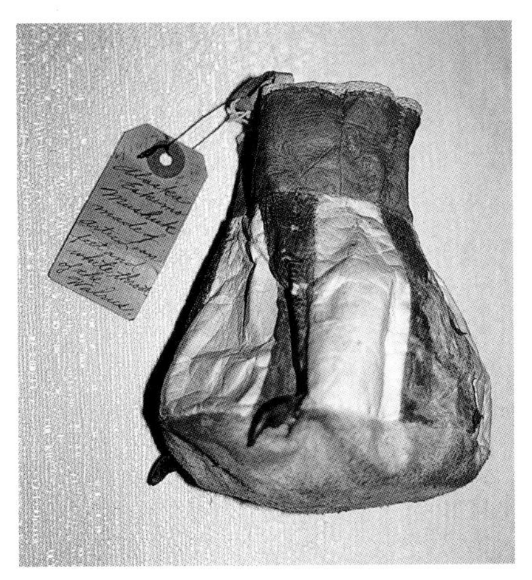

to be handled could not be too expensive. If they were, replicas could sometimes serve the purpose just as well. Since the Curiosity Shop offered a broad, eclectic, and economical assortment of authentic Northwest Coast and Eskimo material, Dana did not even have to compromise. Ordering ethnographic material by mail from the shop made perfect sense, and Standley's lists of "1001 Curious Things" provided an efficient way to find what was needed at affordable prices.[51] With such a source, Newark's own "New Museum" could become a reality.[52]

Axel Rasmussen's Collection at the Portland Art Museum

Although entries in Standley's guest book include the names of a number of private collectors, few of them are easy to trace. An exception is Axel Rasmussen, a Presbyterian minister turned educator, who collected Northwest Coast and Alaska Eskimo material from the late 1920s to the mid-1940s. Although he was in a position to purchase Northwest Coast material from its Native owners, Rasmussen also turned to Ye Olde Curiosity Shop and other curio dealers in Seattle for some Northwest Coast and Arctic items. After several years of pastorate and another several years teaching school in his native Indiana, Rasmussen moved to Alaska in 1926 to become the superintendent of public schools in Wrangell. In 1937 he settled in Skagway, where he lived until his death in early 1945. A longtime friend in Skagway remembered Rasmussen as a quiet, rather lonely man, absorbed in the church, education, and a desire to gather and save the art of the Alaska Indians.[53]

4.14. Old tools and implements were useful in the Newark Museum's collections to illustrate the objects that other cultures used in their lives. In the shop's early years Standley often pasted a label or wrote directly on utilitarian objects. The "AYY" penciled on the Kuskokwim root digger indicated its $5.00 price, using the shop's letter code. The "fine muk-muk [food] spoon" from Cape York was priced at twenty-five cents. *Muk-muk* is an abbreviated form of the Chinook jargon term *muck-a-muk,* meaning "food" or "to eat." Newark Museum: root digger, 21.2039; spoon, 21.2041. Photograph by the author.

4.15 a. Small and elegant animal-shaped boxes that Alaska Inupiat men carved to hold snuff inspired simpler versions to sell to visitors. Here, simplified walrus are surmounted by seal-shaped lids that open by tilting upward. Newark Museum. Front, 21.2040, Cook's Inlet; rear, 14.240, Kuskokwim River. Photograph by the author.

4.15 b. Loon foot bag. The bag is identified on the back of the Ye Olde Curiosity Shop card as: "Alaska Eskimo Mushuk made of Arctic loon feet and white throat of the walrus." Newark Museum, 21.160. Photograph by the author.

Rasmussen began to collect seriously in Wrangell, where he eventually bought Chief Shakes's House on nearby Shakes Island and for a while operated it as a museum, displaying the Native artifacts he had acquired. When he moved to Skagway, he took his collection with him, installed it in his home and opened it to the public as a museum. Rasmussen also collected paintings of Indians and took scores of slides. After his death in 1945 his artifact collection was purchased by the Portland Art Museum, which later published a catalog of the large Northwest Coast portion.[54] Although Rasmussen acquired much of his Northwest Coast material from Indians he knew well in the two communities in which he lived, he also bought from such traders as Walter Waters of Wrangell, such collectors as George T. Emmons, and curio shops in Alaska and Seattle. In Seattle his major source for Northwest Coast material was the Hudson Bay Fur Company, but he also purchased from Ye Olde Curiosity Shop a fine old Salish mat creaser (fig. 4.16), and a Haida mask, a raven rattle, and three horn spoons, all made for sale. Not until Rasmussen's third buying visit to the shop, on August 12, 1932, did Standley write about him in his Guest Book.

Rasmussen's Arctic collection is little known. Purchased primarily during his three visits to Ye Olde Curiosity Shop in the early 1930s, it includes more than seventy ivory objects. A few are small carvings of animals and humans, typical turn-of-the-century tourist work, but most are Thule-period flat-bottomed, bird-shaped gaming pieces and tools, especially bear-headed

4.16. Mat creaser, western Washington, probably Makah, nineteenth century. When making cattail mats, wooden creasers with a V-shaped groove along the bottom were pressed over the needle and cord moving through the leaves to minimize splitting. Photograph courtesy Portland Art Museum, Axel Rasmussen Collection, 48.3.221.

toggles and parts of sewing kits.[55] As with his Northwest Coast collections, Rasmussen's Eskimo purchases reflect his commitment to saving objects related to past customs and sharing them with others for educational purposes. By the early 1930s, the Curiosity Shop's stock of older ivory tools and carvings was well depleted, so he no doubt had to search carefully. That Rasmussen could still find seventy worthy ivory pieces conveys what large quantities the shop had once been able to offer.

The Smithsonian Institution and the American Museum of Natural History

Standley admired scientists and was eager to have ties with the country's major natural history museums. Records at the Smithsonian Museum of Natural History and the American Museum of Natural History document his inquiries and attempts to interest the museum's curators to collect from his shop. Standley's notes indicate that he also corresponded with the Field Museum of Natural History, but there are no verifying museum records.[56] He was well acquainted with reports from the Smithsonian's Bureau of American Ethnology as the authoritative sources on Indians and Eskimos. He used photographs from several of these reports in the photomontage displayed outside his Madison Street shop location and inside at later locations.

It was logical, therefore, to go to the authority when he had questions. On several occasions (always accompanied by one or more cards advertising his shop and Seattle), Standley contacted the Smithsonian, requesting information about types of objects in his own collection or offering items for sale (fig. 4.17). He had just settled into his second location on Colman Dock when in March 1917 he wrote to the Smithsonian (sending four different cards boosting Seattle). He asked for "the length of the largest jaw bones you have of a whale," no doubt in hopes of establishing a record with a set he had acquired to arch in front of the new shop.[57] At twenty and a half feet long, the Smithsonian's jawbones (of the sulpherbottom whale) were longer than those that Standley had photographed in front of his first Colman Dock shop just before the AYPE (see fig. 1.12), and just slightly shorter than his new twenty-one-foot-long jaws. The shop could therefore advertise them as the longest on record! A later request for the length of the Smithsonian's largest Eskimo stone stove (lamp) helped Standley to sell his even larger stove to the Royal Ontario Museum. No doubt there were other requests as well. One inquiry asking the length of the museum's largest flint spear is documented only in a brief article Standley wrote for the *Pacific Sportsman.*[58]

Over the years Standley held many special items or collections on consignment, and he approached museums on behalf of their owners. This was

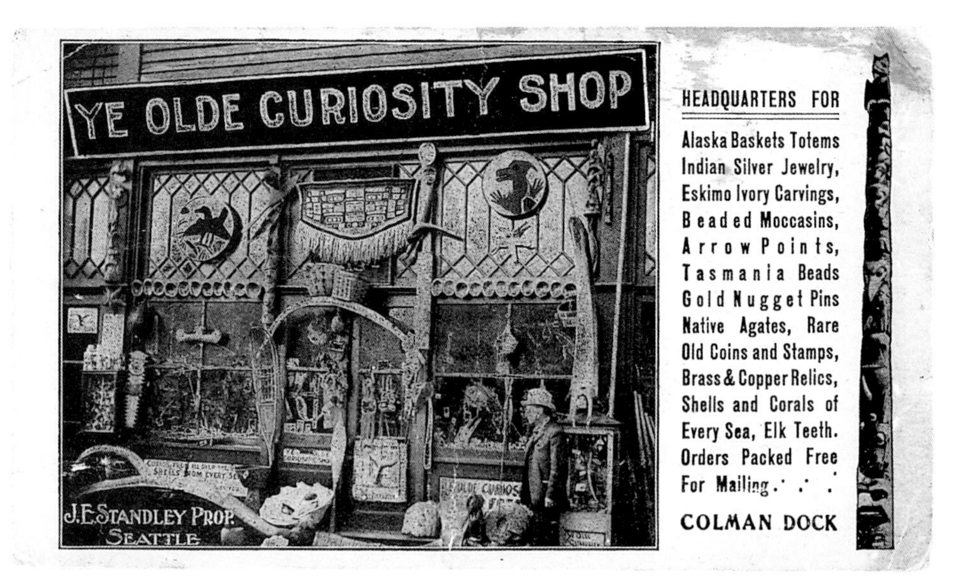

4.17. The shop usually enclosed postcards and booster cards in its correspondence with museums. This card was sent to the Smithsonian Institution in 1908.

almost exclusively the case with the Smithsonian, to whom he offered both ethnological and natural history specimens. In 1903, for example, he contacted the museum about two black clay pots brought out from the Kuskokwim River by L. L. Bales, but the museum already owned a nice collection of the type. In 1904 he offered to arrange for a Smithsonian purchase of the skeleton of the largest shark ever captured in the Seattle Harbor, a female pregnant with seventeen young sharks, and to send on approval the preserved body of a rare two-and-half-inch-long fish with "the appearance of a Bird with Beak & Wings" that had been caught two hundred feet under Puget Sound. The museum declined both, but identified the fish as the "curious Rhampocottus."

In 1913 Standley again approached the Smithsonian, this time with a photograph of two pots carved of steatite (soapstone), "not the production of the American Indian but of a race that lived long before them," which he held on consignment from an owner in Oregon. Museum personnel asked to be informed of the price if the location and conditions of discovery were known. Standley referred them to the owner and included his letters (now lost), which explained both concerns. The reply was brief: the Smithsonian was not prepared to devote $1,000 to such a purchase. The museum also declined Standley's offer the following year to sell Puget Sound rock oyster shells. Ten years later, in 1923, Standley again wrote the museum, offering to sell several Alaskan Eskimo masks. He also sent on approval a "parka and apron of a Banks land Maiden, brought out of the Arctic in 1920" by Joseph Bernard, a maritime trader with an interest in curios. The National Museum already had enough of the items offered and returned to Standley those sent but suggested that local collector Victor J. Evans might be interested.

Smithsonian records indicate that in the bequest of collector Victor J. Evans's estate in 1931, the museum received several other pieces that had been acquired at Ye Olde Curiosity Shop. Standley had recorded Evans's name under "Museums Who Bought from Us" in his address book "Where to Buy." Evans had purchased from a wide range of sources, including shops of various kinds, and most of his enormous collection came to the National Museum with little or no documentation. It is likely that in this collection and others in the Smithsonian, there are even more unidentified items that had been acquired in Standley's shop.

Although the Smithsonian's correspondence with Standley fills a file, and despite his including the Smithsonian on his "List of Museums that Bought from Us," the museum has no record of purchasing from him. It did a lot of "dealing" with shops like his, mostly in the form of exchanges, but rarely purchased from them.[59] However, the museum did accept gifts, including several from Standley. Among the papers Standley marked for safe keeping was a certificate from the Smithsonian, gratefully acknowledging a gift listed in its 1908 *Report of the National Museum* as an "unmounted photograph of native Hawaiian runners or message carriers." It was not so unusual that Standley should have donated something he thought might be of interest to his country's national museum. Other gifts listed on the same page in the 1908 Annual Report include a cicada, a tapeworm, a mountain beaver skull, and a Philippine raincoat contributed by individuals in New York, Oregon, Kansas, and Washington, D.C., respectively.

In 1920 the museum again accepted a gift from Standley, a "freak growth of the tooth of an arctic walrus, 4½ inches longer than natural and has forced its way through a mass of skull bones," sent from Seattle for "the museum's medical department." There is no record of a response to the photo postcard sent in 1934 of two of his shop's most astounding and popular curiosities, the skull of a "New Guinea cannibal girl" and a shrunken head "claimed to be the smallest in the U.S.," but the postcard was placed in the museum's correspondence files. The final transaction between the Smithsonian and Ye Olde Curiosity Shop also concerned a gift. In 1938 eighty-four-year-old Standley asked Smithsonian-associated anthropologist Aleš Hrdlička to take an Alaskan Eskimo feather cape back with him to Washington. The museum's thank-you acknowledgment noted that three species of ducks were represented in its colorful design.

Standley's requests for information and his gifts sent to the Smithsonian Institution reflect the pride and sense of personal connection that many Americans still feel for their national museum. One might never be so fortunate as to visit there but could harbor a sense of personal ownership nevertheless.

To the average citizen, the Smithsonian was a major repository of the nation's knowledge, a place to which anyone could write for answers to questions relating to anything in the institution's broad purview. As the country's national museum surely it was interested in receiving unusual and important objects discovered by the citizenry. The care the staff took in keeping records and responding to the requests of Standley and others helps explain the nation's affection for this museum that treated the concerns and contributions of all with respect and courtesy. Standley obviously felt the same personal ownership that thousands of others did.[60] Although it was limited, the correspondence between Standley and the American Museum of Natural History clearly demonstrates this same respect accorded to his and hundreds of other inquiries from average citizens.

Standley made contact with the Smithsonian in 1904, just four years after his shop opened, but transactions with the American Museum of Natural History in New York are not recorded until late 1928, when he was surveying to determine the size of the largest Arctic Eskimo stone stove. At this time Standley also offered to sell the museum a collection of "rarest old carved tools & implements from the Kaiser Augusta River in New Guinea," which included a skull of a maiden with "the natural features made on the skull of a plastic native art . . . reproducing her life like appearance."[61] Like the shrunken head that accompanied this skull in the photograph sent earlier to the Smithsonian, to Standley it was a fascinating and amazing artifact created in part by human ingenuity; it did not offend sensibilities in the way it would today. Anthropologist Clark Wissler's brief reply to Standley provided the stove's length and declined the New Guinea material.

Standley and Northwest Coast collector George T. Emmons had maintained a friendly connection for more than twenty years when in fall 1931, while reading a book about petroglyphs that had once belonged to Emmons, Standley thought of him. He mailed to Emmons for the American Museum of Natural History "a bunch of sketches that were taken near the Dalles on the Columbia River by a friend of mine named A. G. Colley, in 1926. I have no use for them but I thought you, or some [of] your government friends might be interested in these Prehistoric Rocks. Mr. Colley is a wandering curio hunter [who] makes a living out of natural curiosities . . . an old acquaintance of mine." It was not unusual for local amateur naturalists like Colley to bring collections into Standley's shop when they wished to dispose of them.

Emmons turned the Colley drawings over to N. C. Nelson, curator of prehistoric archaeology at the American Museum, who accepted them "for reference and comparative studies" and suggested that some of the petroglyphs were not very old. Standley thanked him right away and wondered "why some of your museum force never drop in to my shop. There are numerous very rare small relics that appeal to other museums" that "generally find some interesting thing, even if only to look at." In an immediate reply, Nelson explained that the museum had collected a lot in the Northwest from the 1870s through the 1890s and that it now needed materials from other locales. However, he promised to drop in when he would be in Seattle for the Pan-Pacific Congress in 1933. Standley promptly mailed Nelson a small gift, a "dried fish from Japan," speculating that some day American fisheries might be selling fish powder "as a handy wholesome food product." Perhaps the curator felt it best to quell the correspondence before it got out of hand, because a secretary sent thanks on Nelson's behalf.[62]

Museums in Washington State and Abroad

Museums were new to Seattle during the early years of Ye Olde Curiosity Shop, but Standley sought to encourage their growth and to be associated with those few that existed. For a short while he called his shop a "free museum," a title that turn-of-the-century curio dealers sometimes used to draw people in with the promise of displays of special importance. In 1904 he loaned out his collection of ivories to the Alaska Club's informal museum, and after exhibiting it at the AYPE in 1909, Standley sold the collection to the Seattle-based Washington State Art Association for its planned museum. When that enterprise failed because of the association's lack of funds, much of the collection was sold to Heye's Museum of the American Indian in New York.

Twenty years later, after a Seattle museum had become a reality, in the form of the Seattle Art Museum, and on Standley's eighty-second birthday, Standley announced that he would present the museum with "an old and valuable sword made of steel and inlaid with gold of the Ming dynasty, together with a rare Chinese war bow and arrow made of bone."[63]

Although the private Washington State Museum of Arts and Sciences proposed for Seattle after the AYPE never came about, a state-sponsored Washington State Museum had been established in 1899, and Standley was involved with it until his death.[64] Ye Olde Curiosity Shop and the Washington State Museum (renamed in 1964 the Burke Memorial Washington State Museum and again in 1999 the Burke Museum of Natural History and Culture) expanded simultaneously and with similar emphases.

The Washington State Museum began as a grassroots effort. Although the Territorial University did not employ anyone with advanced scientific training to teach science until the end of the nineteenth century, there was interest in the field among several young men who began in 1880 to meet weekly at the home of university founder, Arthur Denny. Calling themselves the Young

Naturalists Society (YNS), they prepared and delivered reports, sponsored essay competitions, gathered natural history collections, and learned how to prepare museum specimens. By 1882 the club had twenty-seven enthusiastic members. Under the influence of the eminent, self-trained naturalist Orson B. Johnson, newly arrived to teach at the university, the YNS began to build a library, sponsor lectures and classes, and increase its collection of specimens, with an eye toward establishing a public natural history museum. In 1886 the group constructed its own building, with exhibition space, on land leased on the university's original campus in downtown Seattle. The Hall of the Young Naturalists served a teaching function, became a popular local attraction, and was visited by naturalists from around the country. Through the YNS the Puget Sound region became known as a rich place for collecting, and the Smithsonian, the American Museum of Natural History, and other institutions exchanged specimens with the society. By the 1890s the group had clearly left its amateur status behind.

After the university decided in 1895 to move from downtown to its current location on Lake Washington, the YNS collections being used by university faculty were moved to the new site and installed in relevant departments and in the Administration Building (now called Denny Hall). In 1899, the year that Standley first arrived in Seattle, the legislature had designated the university collections to be the Washington State Museum, the state's official scientific and historic museum. In 1904 the YNS disbanded and moved the remainder of its collections to the new museum, housed since 1902 primarily in Science Hall (now Parrington Hall).

For many years the Washington State Museum was the only public museum in Seattle. During the first decade of the twentieth century the museum's operation fell to several professors, especially to Edmond Meany of the history department. Standley got to know Meany, who was put in charge of the ethnological collections. Meany sometimes sent visitors to the shop, and Standley often contacted him with questions, even after the museum had an official director. Much of their communication occurred verbally, so the correspondence record is limited. In 1909, Standley expected Meany to know what had happened to the whale bones he had given the university, and in 1937 to identify a canon he had acquired.[65]

An August 6, 1905, article in the *Seattle Post-Intelligencer* also brought Meany and Standley together. The headline trumpeted: "Precious Historical Indian Relics Neglected in Seattle. State Makes No Provision for Preservation of Its Valuable Collection at the University." The impetus for the article may have been a tired Meany, who felt that the university's neglect of its ethnological collections had to be put before the public, or it could easily have been

Standley, who was well accustomed to contacting the newspapers about worthy stories. The article noted that Meany had given his own time and resources to finding relics in the state, often purchasing them with his own money and donating them, and he then had to find time to take care of the objects as well. A photograph of a cluttered university museum room stacked with piles of papers, books, and artifacts was captioned: "Indian Relics Stored at the University. Rare Garments and Cloth Curios Are Said by Private Collectors to Be Suffering from the Ravages of Moths." The disorder at the university was accentuated by including contrasting photos of neatly arranged local private collections: the wigwam and Indian baskets of Mrs. Thomas Burke at Illahee, the collections of Mrs. Samuel Rosenberg and J. B. Krautz, and the "Indian corner" of J. E. Standley (fig. 4.18). A second headline suggested that "Washington Should Follow Colorado's example and Establish Indian Museum." Several years later this occurred.

One of the reasons for holding the AYPE on the University of Washington's new Lake Washington campus was to provide buildings that would become a part of the university. After the exposition closed, the state museum's collections were moved from the Administration Building and installed in the fair's California and Forestry Buildings, then several years later consolidated in the latter. The Forestry Building was an impressive Greek-inspired structure, a temple to the Northwest logging industry with 126 columns constructed from giant Douglas fir trees. Bark beetles, moisture damage, and dry rot plagued it, however, so it was not a good home for a museum. In 1923, before the state legislature considered the problem, the *Seattle Post-Intelligencer* asked Standley's opinion. He deemed the building a firetrap and urged a museum on the model of the Golden Gate Park Museum in San Francisco.[66] The Forestry Building museum site was closed, and four years later its contents were installed in a more suitable place, the AYPE's Washington State Building, recently vacated by the library.

In addition to expanding its natural history collections, the Washington State Museum had by now established a place in the emerging study of ethnology. It was one of many museums that benefited from the collections accrued officially for a world's fair. The museum had received important Northwest Coast material at the close of both the Chicago World Columbian Exposition in 1893 and Portland's Lewis and Clark Exposition in 1905. With the purchase in 1912 of most of George T. Emmon's Northwest Coast collection shown at the AYPE, the museum now housed a major Northwest Coast collection. After anthropologist Erna Gunther took the helm in late 1929, ethnology would become the museum's main emphasis for the next three decades. Standley felt an affinity with the Washington State Museum. Both the Curiosity Shop and

Prof. Meany, University of Washington, Dear Sir:

The Mammoth Pair of Jaw bones of a Whale, The 2 great Vertabra, the 6 Largest Ribs and whales Shoulder blade that were exhibited at the Eskimo Village during the Fair are still there. Captain Baber suggests that they would form an interesting attraction if the Jaw bones were placed upright and Wired to a tree somewhere upon the University grounds with the other bones surrounding. If desired I will be glad to loan them to the University. Mr. Baber will deliver them free of expense to any place you suggest. The 2 Jaws are the Largest on record of a Sulphor Bottom whale being 19 feet six inches in length weighing half a ton each.

Hoping to hear favorably,
I remain Respectfully J. E. Standley,
Colman Dock.

—Letter, October 22, 1909

the museum collected ethnographic relics and natural history specimens, and he thought of his shop as a kind of museum. How the museum's scientists perceived Standley and his knowledge is not recorded, but they were well aware that amid his shop's clutter lay significant Indian and Eskimo artifacts.

In the early twentieth century, curio shops that handled ethnographic material were integral to the museum community in the way that galleries and art dealers would become in later years. Although they might vary in their depth of knowledge about the cultural meaning and use of objects they carried, curio dealers knew their objects' market value and had the connections to help in acquiring special items. Standley was no doubt one of the "Seattle dealers in Indian relics" to whom the university had turned in 1908 when it sought to establish the value of an important Columbia River collection made by Dr. Stewart of Goldendale, Washington, in order to lobby the state legislature for a special purchase appropriation.[67] Museum staff referred interested parties to Standley's and other local shops and sometimes assisted in connecting a potential buyer with a shop that had a special collection.[68]

There is evidence of only one object that the Washington State Museum actually purchased from Ye Olde Curiosity Shop, a Nuu-chah-nulth bark beater of whalebone; however, the museum accepted almost all of the loans and gifts that Standley proffered. The most imposing one was the group of whale bones that he had lent Captain A. M. Baber for use at the AYPE's Eskimo Village in 1909, then loaned to the university when the exposition closed. The loan was expedient in that it solved Standley's problem of where to put the bones, but Standley also saw them as serving an educational purpose. He and Baber suggested that they be displayed outside on the university grounds.[69] In September 1916 Standley officially contributed the shoulder blade, vertebrae, and ribs to the university, but at the same time he took back the jawbones. It seems odd, because he was facing a move to an interim shop in just five months and would have no space for them. His West Seattle home, Totem Place, had become a bit of a tourist attraction, however, and he must have taken them there, where over a number of years he displayed several different sets of whale jawbones on the parking strip.

As already mentioned, Standley sometimes sent unsolicited gifts and

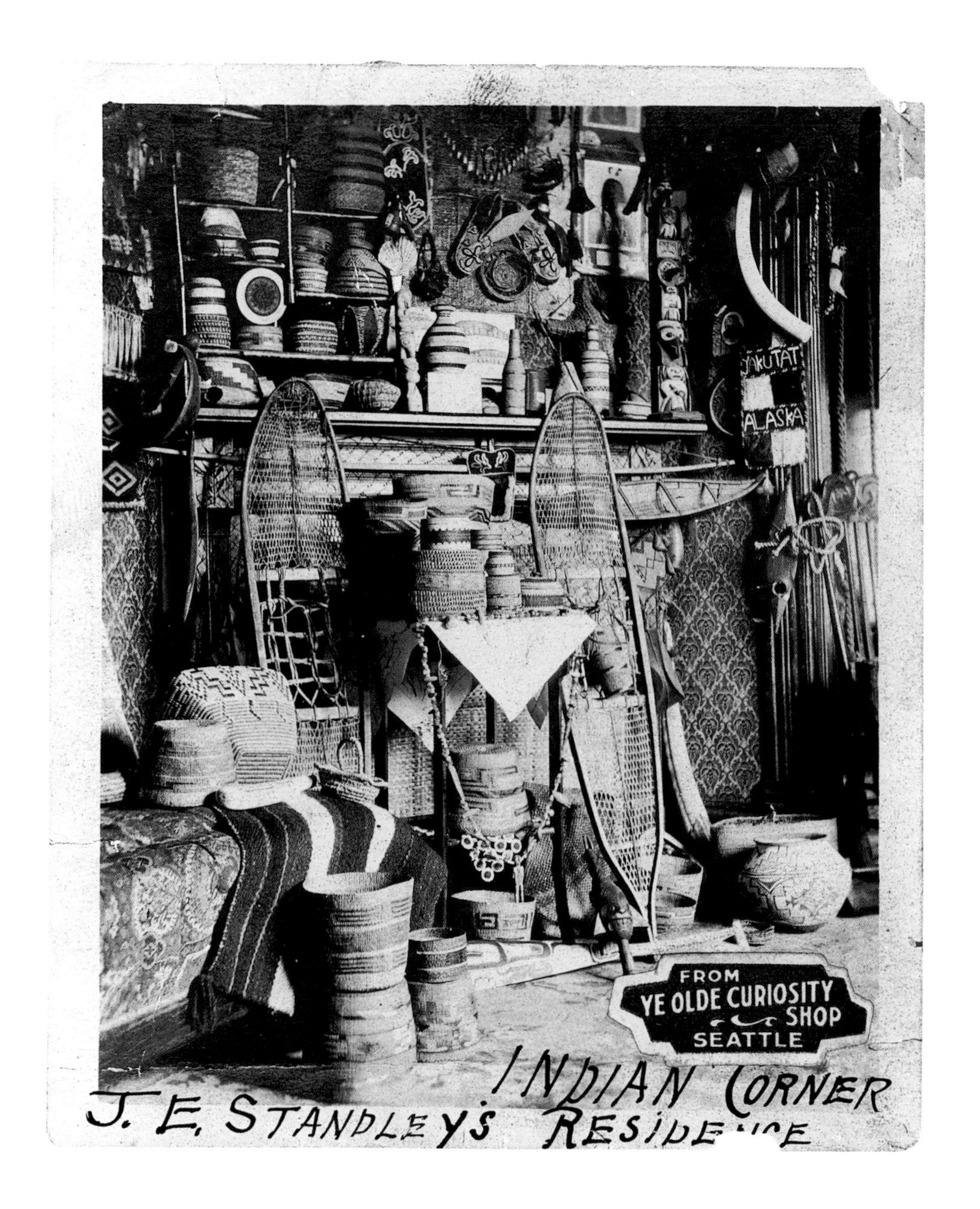

4.18. A 1905 article in the *Seattle Post-Intelligencer* decried the neglected state of Indian relics belonging to the University of Washington. Photographs of well-cared-for collections included this one of an Indian corner that Standley had arranged in his home.

even advice to museums, and the Washington State Museum was no exception. The "wonderful collection of nuts from all over the World" that he offered the museum in June 1919 was declined. In a 1929 letter he advised: "There are Collections of rare articles and Relics in Seattle that you can have if you make a public call for same. Look at the hundreds of Donor's names on Collections in Golden Gate Park Museum."[70] The fate of this advice—that the museum solicit public donations—goes unrecorded. Later in the year Standley simply notified the museum that "a Show Case containing a rare large Cluster of Coral, from the South Seas had been delivered to our State Museum as a Gift from myself." His only request was that an inscribed copper or brass plate acknowledging the shop be screwed to the case. He had a particular standard in mind, so in a follow-up letter he was more specific, asking that "labeling be for permancy and Legibility, and not like the faded, grimy labels upon the specimens exhibited in the Seattle Chamber of Commerce." He also identified the corals as having been brought from the Australian Coral Reefs about 1899 by a schooner captain and suggested helpfully that "corals are fuly described in the Encyclopedia."[71]

For some years the Puget Sound Academy of Science, made up of a group of University of Washington professors, was associated with the Washington State Museum. Its office was at the state museum but its Marine Museum, supported by the academy rather than the university, was located on the full-rigged ship, *St. Paul.* The local Foss Companies, operators of tugboats and scows, had purchased the picturesque old ship in 1930 to save it from being dismantled and presented it to the Puget Sound Academy.[72] Standley was an enthusiastic booster of the new museum. He asked the newspaper to write about it and to solicit donations, and he made some himself.[73] It was F. W. Schmoe, the academy's director, who acknowledged Standley's gift in 1935 of "one case of shells, ivory, etc" and a "display case containing corals, sponges, etc.," which Standley delivered to the *St. Paul* and the state museum, respectively. Schmoe picked up another box from the shop himself, and promised the donations would be on display.[74] The academy's collections were eventually consolidated with those of the Washington State Museum. Most of these donations are still in the museum's natural history collections, along with other gifts from the shop, which include Standley's whale bones, the bones of a prehistoric horse, and some willie willie beans, the toxic red Circassian seeds of the sandalwood tree that for a while were made into tourist necklaces.

Standley also made a few small ethnological gifts to the Washington State Museum, although what motivated these remains a mystery. Museum records document that in 1916 he donated a piece of "Indian bread," a long-keeping Coast Salish foodstuff made of pounded-together kelp, sea weed, berries, fish eggs, and clam juice—"keeps for all time"—and a Makah feather skirt, "said to have been made by old Squaw Yokum in 1879 out of Eagle feathers and Swan down." The skirt's identification, no doubt provided by Standley, is typical of information associated with Makah items in the shop at the time. It probably refers to Rosa Yokum, a Makah basket maker with whom Standley dealt, along with her brother, carver Louis Yokum. The museum also owns several items purchased from the shop and later donated, as well as the four totem poles that Standley had acquired for the Becks to display in their private Ravenna Park during the AYPE.

What is known of the Curiosity Shop's association with other museums in Washington State is uneven. The Department of Anthropology at Washington State University owns two wooden model totem poles that came from the shop. Maryhill Museum, housed in the French chateau built by the eccentric businessman Sam Hill overlooking the Columbia River near Goldendale, documents a set of walrus ivory chess pieces that definitely can be traced to Ye Olde Curiosity Shop. However, baskets and other items in the collections may have come from Standley, since Hill often purchased from Seattle shops. In 1928 the Washington State Historical Society in Tacoma acknowledged a gift from the shop of one of Standley's favorite token contributions, another specimen of "Indian Bread," and a sample of "Madame Pelee's Hair."[75] The latter was a natural curiosity of the sort that fascinated Standley. When Mount Pelée (on the island of Martinique, Lesser Antilles, West Indies) erupted in 1902, some of the highly viscous lava solidified into needle-like strands that came to be referred to as volcanic hair. There are no doubt hundreds of curios purchased at the Ye Olde Curiosity Shop that have made their way without documentation into private collections and museums in North America.[76]

European museums also house items from the Curiosity Shop. The Horniman Museum in Forrest Hill outside London (referred to by Standley as the Hadden Hall Museum) acquired the greatest number of Eskimo and Northwest Coast articles from the shop, through the purchases of Alfred Cort Haddon (see figs. 1.1, 1.3). The British Museum received material from the shop through the estate of Sir Henry Wellcome.[77] Wellcome is best remembered for his large collection of medical artifacts, well-known during his lifetime because they were on display, but the medical museum was actually only a part of a grand plan Wellcome had to create a museum to illustrate human thought from all of the world, over all of history. To this end, he acquired thousands of artifacts, often using agents and at auctions. Wellcome rarely hired specialists to assist him and did not like to pay high prices, so his collections varied considerably in quality and authenticity. After his death in 1936 the enormous collections of his Wellcome Medical Museum were dispersed to other museums in Britain and the Commonwealth. Two Northwest rattles purchased at Ye Olde Curiosity Shop that passed to the British Museum in the Wellcome dispersals are tourist pieces. The museum also owns fossil ivory and what a staff member describes as "marginal Northwest Coast carvings."[78] The National Museum of Stockholm, Sweden, bought mastodon tusks from the shop.

The End of Museum Collecting from the Shop

In his 1907 brochure Standley advertised that museums were his customers. In the catalogs that followed in 1910 and 1915, he noted that he supplied museums and universities and gave a discount. The 1916 and circa 1920 catalogs boasted "In Private Collections and in many Museums in this and Foreign Countries may be seen Curios and Relics secured from this shop." After 1920 the connection with museums is referenced only in the statement "Private collections and museums supplied," which appears in all of the catalogs from 1916 through 1940. Standley always hoped for museum patronage, but through the 1920s and later it was rare. The Great Depression was a factor in this decline, but a changing emphasis in collecting was equally important.[79] At the turn of the century many museums, seeking to illustrate cultural evolution, had been intent on salvaging the last of what was considered to be the vanishing Indian and Eskimo, and filling in any perceived gaps in their ethnographic inventories of Native material culture. The Curiosity Shop's old tools and implements from the Arctic had been of particular interest at that time because Arctic material was not easy to acquire. Ordering from the shop's catalogs was far cheaper than mounting an expedition or even supporting a collector in the field, especially in the Arctic. Then, however, devastation wrought by World War I shook faith in the cultural evolutionary model that had motivated turn-of-the century collecting. After the war anthropologists turned away from material culture to concern themselves with social aspects of culture.

Ironically, although the carved ivory items and totem poles that became more prominent in Ye Olde Curiosity Shop's stock as older material diminished reflected the cultural change within social systems that anthropologists were now interested in, the same scholars and museums had little interest in such Native arts made recently for sale and rejected them for their perceived cultural impurity. Such art was produced for external consumption rather than internal use and was usually stylistically hybrid, incorporating materials, designs, forms, and functions that had been borrowed. In general, the more of these categories borrowed, the stronger the rejection by academicians. The recently carved or engraved walrus tusks from Alaska remained of interest to museums because they were made of an exotic material and pictured activities clearly culturally different. They appeared to relate to the older engraved bow drills with schematic pictographic engraving and to carved ivory implements whose form and function were also culturally different, and *might* be old. But when an engraved or carved tusk was also drilled to function as a cribbage board, its introduced function was obvious. Cribbage boards had been rejected as inauthentic by both shop owners like Standley and museum collectors like Heye, who shared the same concept of authenticity.

The sorts of quickly produced model totem poles most available at Ye Olde Curiosity Shop were even more soundly dismissed. (Even today many museums are slow to collect or even accept into their collections examples of what has become the ultimate cliché of Indian tourist art.) Large or small, model poles did not follow the classic styles of the old Tlingit and Haida poles collected by major museums and known to others primarily through photographs. Most of the shop's totem poles appeared crude by comparison and their brightly painted surfaces were offensive to prevailing understanding of Northwest Coast style. Only recently have tourist totem poles begun to be examined as products of complex transcultural negotiations involving economics, evolving identities, and intertribal connections. Although rejected by museums that were knowledgeable about nineteenth-century Northwest Coast art, such poles had great appeal to individuals who wanted colorful symbols of the mysterious for their estates or to install in public attractions. B. J. Palmer's Little Bit O' Heaven and Robert L. Ripley's Believe it or Not!® museums were among them.

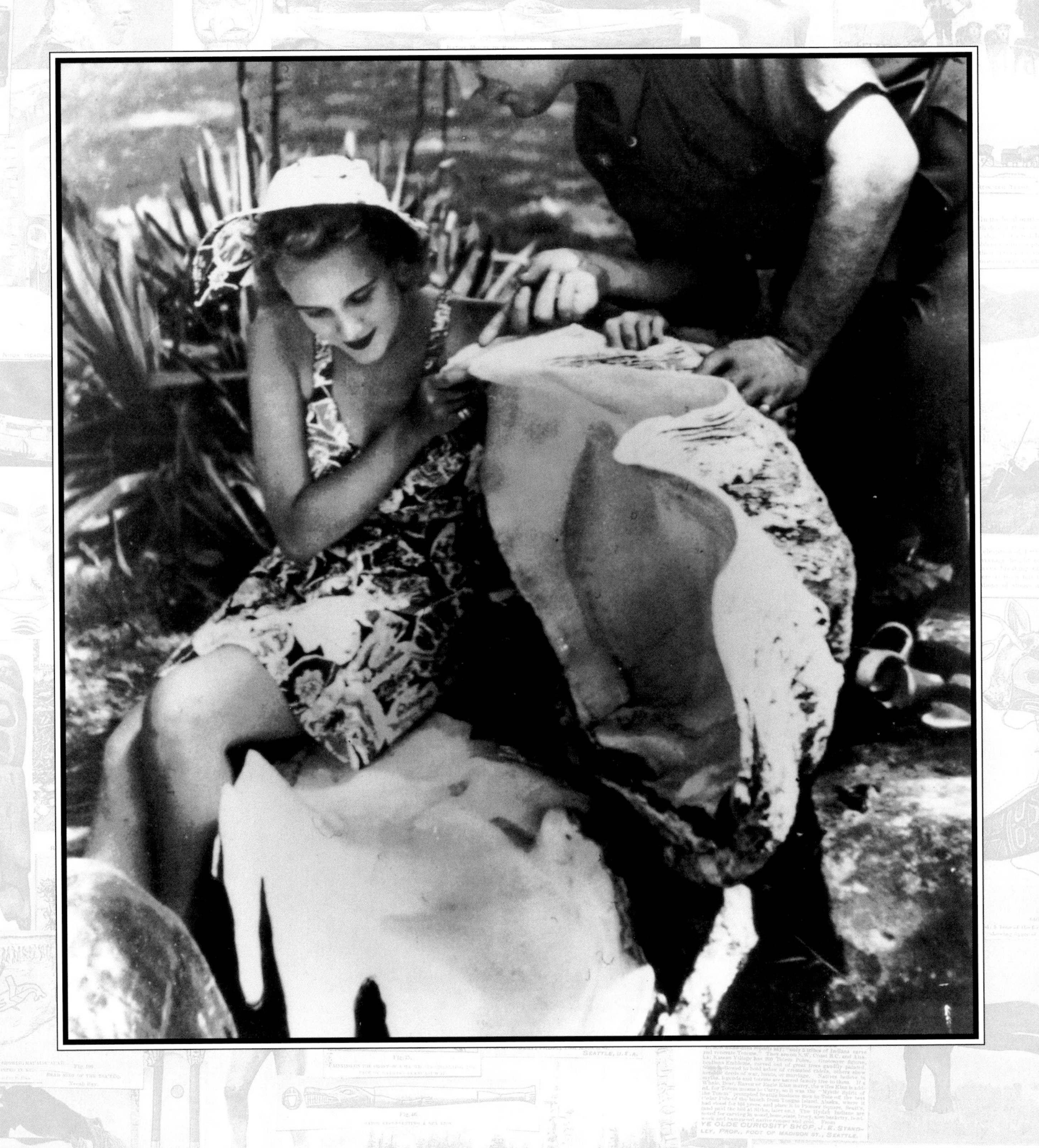

CHAPTER FIVE

Uncommon Treasures for Attractions and Amusements

Ye Olde Curiosity Shop, on Colman Dock.
Everything from a flea uniform to a whale jawbone.
—shop listing in *Seattle and the Pacific Northwest,* (1909)

SOME PEOPLE WHO PURCHASED FROM YE OLDE CURIOSITY SHOP WERE PRIMARILY interested in exotic collections that would entertain and inspire fascination, amazement, and awe. One such customer was Bartlett Joshua Palmer (always called B. J.), who installed purchases from Standley's shop in a fantasy garden of grottoes, shrines, and sculptures that he opened to the public at the Palmer Chiropractic College in Davenport, Iowa. Another client was Robert L. Ripley, who entertained friends and visitors in his Manhattan apartment and upstate New York mansion with a plethora of the unusual, some of which came from Standley's shop. Father Paul M. Dobberstein came to the shop for materials for his largest grotto in the world. Ye Olde Curiosity Shop engaged exotic fascinations because there was always the possibility of discovering yet another uncommon treasure.

B. J. Palmer and "A Little Bit O' Heaven"

Perhaps the most entertaining person of all who collected at the shop was a man who loomed large in Standley's mind and in stories remembered by the Standley family. B. J. Palmer (fig. 5.1), the flamboyant developer of chiropractic healing, was a prominent public personality in the 1920s and 1930s, as he traveled the country giving impassioned motivational lectures about aspects of chiropractic and such topics as self-awareness and selling oneself. Chiropractic was a new and contested field at this time, and he also offered frequent and fervent depositions in support of its practitioners who had been accused of, some jailed, for quackery.

Palmer visited Ye Olde Curiosity Shop several times from 1924 into the early 1930s. Clearly he made a strong impression on Standley because his name appears more times in

B. J. Palmer came into the shop said that's my Totem Pole, a 12 foot fine old Alaska Indian carved. The Chiropractic Club here (all former students of the Doc) told him look over Seattle & the one he wanted they would Buy it—and not introducing himself it was a queer introduction. He once later came in and looked at my 10 shelves full of seashell and said I want 2 or 3 times more than all the shells I see here. This was for his Conservatory 80 × 40 feet for Grottos waterfalls & curbs. 1st trip to Europe he told me if his wife would stand for it he would buy my nice ivory snuff bottle, Obscene carving ancient one. She balked but 2 years later he said she will stand for anything after our Tour of Asia. He gave me his book that he published took his own pictures. He Bot spears, harpoons, Chinese Beheading swords and lots of trim for his big fireplace on [indecipherable].

—Standley, Guest Book, p. 1

Standley's jottings than that of any other individual. Near the end of his life, Standley wrote down his cumulative memories of this man he called "a wonderful collector" in the Guest Book.[1] In many ways "B. J." and "Papa Joe," as the two men came to be known, were soulmates under the skin. Both were showmen, self-made entrepreneurs for whom their work was an obsession, strong personalities with loyal fans and disdainful detractors. And, most important, both relished the unusual, the exotic, the bizarre. For seeking to understand the connection between the two, it is helpful that Palmer left extensive papers. In addition to the Palmer Chiropractic College's administrative, financial, and academic records, he retained multiple copies of every draft of his numerous articles, speeches, and depositions, every letter he received, every check, receipt, trip ticket, scrap of paper on which he wrote, and thousands of newspaper clippings. In the early 1980s, when college officials decided to install an elevator in the unused three-story elevator shaft that had been constructed in 1924 in the clinic building, they faced more than one thousand file boxes stacked inside.[2] It is because of Palmer's "vault" and chronological filing system, the sorting of which will occupy archivists and scholars for decades, that information on his links with Ye Olde Curiosity Shop was retrievable.

Palmer was a larger-than-life individual who raised both passions and hackles across North America for decades. His father, D. D. (Daniel David) Palmer, was a magnetic healer who in 1895 discovered the healing benefits achieved by adjusting the vertebrae of the spine to relieve pressure on pinched nerves. In 1897 D. D. Palmer opened what became the Palmer School of Chiropractic in Davenport, Iowa. After graduating from the school in 1902, his son B. J. gradually assumed its reins and those of the fledgling profession. A stormy career followed as the younger Palmer expanded the college and fought impassioned battles to promote, develop, and legitimize chiropractic through decades of attacks. On behalf of embattled practitioners, he traveled extensively to speak at local chiropractic, business, and service organizations across the country. Two extended trips, one to Asia in 1921–22 and another around the world in 1924–25, relieved the pressures Palmer and his family were under from swirling controversies and allowed him to indulge what he considered a major stress reliever, his hobby of collecting.[3] When he encountered

Ye Olde Curiosity shop in winter 1924 while on a lecture tour through the Pacific Northwest, he, his wife Mabel, and their son David had already been to Asia, where collecting had become Palmer's passion. During the foreign trips of the early 1920s, Palmer freighted back to Davenport what he described as a three-ton bronze Wishing Buddha, which he installed in a specially built shrine in the school's courtyard; several Chinese fou dogs; four carved "idols" from the Igorotte of the Philippines; and numerous other figures related to the Oriental religions he liked to study. He displayed these objects in various ways inside and outside college buildings and referred to them as his "museum."[4] Exhibits varied over the years. At one point the museum displayed the Barnum and Bailey Two Hemispheres Band Wagon, and at another time, the family's pet Saint Bernard, Big Ben. Notified during the trip around the world that Big Ben had died, Palmer telegraphed instructions that Julius Warmbath, Teddy Roosevelt's taxidermist, should stuff the dog so the family could pay its last respects after returning. Big Ben reposed next to the piano for some time thereafter, sometimes startling visitors. In association with his profession, Palmer's museum also boasted the largest collection of spinal columns in the world.

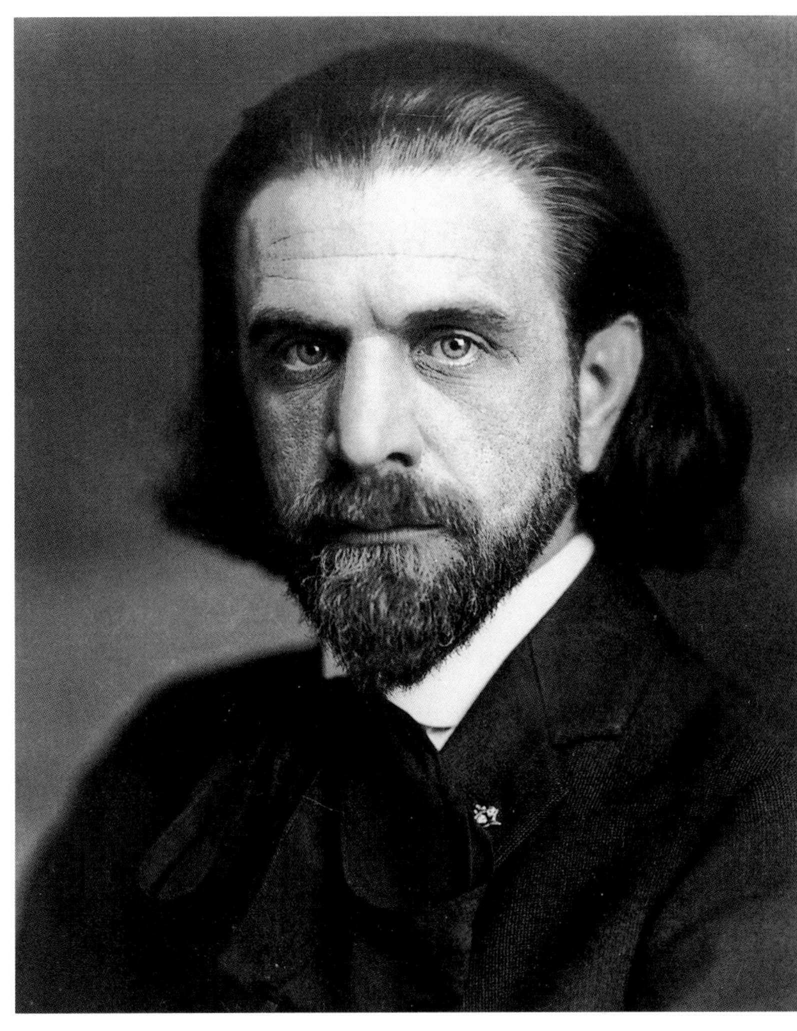

5.1. B. J. Palmer, the intense and charismatic developer of chiropractic healing, made an indelible impression on all he encountered, including J. E. Standley when he visited Ye Olde Curiosity Shop. Photograph courtesy Archives, Palmer College of Chiropractic, Davenport, Iowa.

One can imagine stay-at-home Standley relishing the flamboyant doctor's exciting narrations about being on the scene during fighting in Shanghai, a typhoon on the Yellow River, and uprisings in Palestine. Standley may have listened eagerly to descriptions of Palmer's ongoing project, "A Little Bit O' Heaven," and his adventures collecting the treasures displayed there. During one visit to the Curiosity Shop, Palmer gave Standley a copy of his book *'Round the World with B. J.* (1926), in which he detailed the pleasure and necessity of haggling when collecting. Palmer reported with gusto how he had acquired the largest Buddha that had ever left Japan, the finest Japanese cloisonné vases available, the rarest solid silver bell from China, and a chess set that had actually belonged to Russian czar Nicholas.[5] Because Standley also reveled in owning the largest, the rarest, the most unusual, he was an appreciative audience.

After the 1924–25 round-the-world trip, Palmer appears to have made far fewer extravagant purchases. When his son David returned in 1929 from studying business at the University of Pennsylvania to find the chiropractic college nearly bankrupt, he helped it struggle through the Depression with an assortment of ventures. There was revenue from Palmer's Radio Station WOC, which he had started in August 1920 (and where the young Ronald Reagan was an announcer). Over the years further income came from a variety of enterprises operated on the school's grounds—at various times a window-washing firm, a roller-skating rink, a speakeasy called "The Barn," and the Coconut Grove Root Beer Hut and drive-in theater. The most successful venture was Palmer's A Little Bit O' Heaven.

Soon after completing the West Seattle home, which he named Totem Place, in 1907, Standley had built a fountain and lined the walkways in the yard with seashells, so Palmer's descriptions of a similar project surely interested him. In 1920, while recovering from a nervous breakdown, Palmer and the Palmer College yardman began what eventually became a forty-by-eighty-three-foot-long, forty-foot-high greenhouse fantasy of grottoes and shell-lined paths. The attraction opened to the public on July 1, 1924, and was named, so legend says, by a woman so overcome by its beauty that she fell to her knees, exclaiming, "This is a little bit o' heaven!" The structure grew over a number of years, becoming more and more elaborate, eventually to wrap around two sides of the Palmer Mansion. A sea turtle and alligators swam in the ponds along the driveway. Cast-metal deer, an ox, and other creatures grazed casually on the lawn or stood among boulders hauled into the courtyard that separated the mansion from the school's classroom buildings. Visitors first strolled through the gardens and the courtyard, marveling at an enormous Buddha enshrined in its special grotto and at the dancing Philippine idols and four totem poles overseeing the courtyard (fig. 5.2). They then entered a special door into a narrow channel encrusted with tiles, pebbles, bits of crockery, small mirrors, and other objects embedded in concrete. After pausing at the Chapelle Petite, billed as the world's smallest chapel, spectators emerged into a brilliant glass-enclosed tropical fancy of pebble and shell grottoes, equatorial foliage, ponds, and a forty-foot waterfall (fig. 5.3). Objets d'art posed playfully among lush palms and flowering plants. There were South American macaws and exotic goldfish.

After taking it all in, perhaps from one of the carefully sited benches, the visitor might return to the courtyard and pause to have an ice cream or a root

beer before purchasing postcards or novelty mementos from a kiosk glittering with embedded tiles, bits of glass, and shells. Most of the souvenirs sold came from the Midwest or South—cedar ash trays, salt and peppers shakers, and such—but there were small totem mementos as well.[6] From the late 1930s into the early 1950s, Herman Krupp's Alaska Fur Company and its successor, Oceanic Trading in Seattle, supplied A Little Bit O' Heaven with the same types of totem novelties that it wholesaled to Ye Olde Curiosity Shop. Totem mustard spoons, pickle forks, letter openers, bookmarks, bridge pencils, and pen holders carved of bone were the mainstays, along with thunderbird charms on cards and a few six- to twelve-inch model totem poles of wood. Clearly there was sufficient interest in the totem poles in the courtyard to warrant carrying a variety of totem souvenirs.

As had Standley's shop in Seattle, Palmer's A Little Bit O' Heaven quickly became a tourist draw in Davenport, touted as "a famous spot in our city which you want to see while here."[7] During its first twenty-five years the attraction entertained more than one and a half million visitors.[8] Clearly it helped to support the struggling college, but its maintenance was taxing. Among other

5.2. Totem poles from Ye Olde Curiosity Shop were placed in the Wishing Buddha courtyard of Palmer's A Little Bit O' Heaven. The third pole from the left, with the crescent at the bottom, was a gift to Palmer from his former students practicing in Seattle. Photograph courtesy Archives, Palmer College of Chiropractic, Davenport, Iowa.

5.3. Palmer and his long-enduring wife, Mabel, sit in the glass-enclosed tropical gardens of A Little Bit O' Heaven. Palmer and his yardman incorporated shells from Ye Olde Curiosity Shop when building the attraction's grottoes, waterfalls, and ponds. Photograph courtesy Archives, Palmer College of Chiropractic, Davenport, Iowa.

difficulties, the alligators had to suffer the frigid Iowa winters in the basement of the family home, while the teenaged David suffered the despised responsibility for their care. Cleaning up after the creatures was particularly disgusting, and it was a great relief when his mother insisted that the alligators had to go after the odors emanating upstairs became unbearable. Refused by the Davenport Park Board, approximately a hundred alligators, large and small, were eventually freighted "express collect" to the Lincoln Park Zoo in Chicago.[9]

Palmer acquired material from Ye Olde Curiosity Shop in person, during periodic visits to Seattle, rather than by using Standley's "1001 Curious Things" order list. He was there in late winter 1924 on a Pacific Coast lecture tour, again in summer 1930 when leading a WOC Radio-sponsored tour to Alaska, in fall 1932, and likely for shorter periods as well.[10] His name does not appear after 1932 in Standley's Guest Book (which stops in 1940). Despite Standley's notes, it is not entirely clear what all of the items were that Palmer acquired from the shop, but one definitely was a large totem pole, presented while Palmer was lecturing in Seattle in late winter 1924. His hosts, local graduates of the Palmer College, showed him the city's best-known sights, among them Ye Olde Curiosity Shop, where Palmer decided that he wanted a totem pole. Standley wrote in his notes, "The Chiropractic Club here (all former students of the Doc) told him look over Seattle & the one he wanted they would Buy it." According to Palmer's account, it was during a gala country club dinner, before the dancing, that the state and local chiropractic associations "presented us with a genuine old Totem pole from Alaska the history of which is worth reading . . . [and] tonight they presented us with a small miniature as symbolic of the large one."[11] Directly a large pole was on its way East.

The Palmers brought back from Seattle a folding color postcard of the Seattle Totem Pole, the Tlingit pole that had been removed from Tongass Village in Alaska and installed in Pioneer Square (see fig. 1.4) in 1899. They also brought copies of Standley's information card "History of the Totem Pole," which identified the figures on the pole. Of the four large totem poles still at the Palmer College (see fig. 5.2), the one based most closely on the Seattle Totem Pole is most likely the gift pole, the emblem of the esteem in which Palmer's former students held him.[12] The model pole in the college collection that has a Curiosity Shop tag is surely the miniature one that Palmer mentioned, for its three figures are also based on the original Seattle Totem Pole. The three other large poles in the Palmer collection (now badly damaged) were not made by the same carver as the gift pole, but they appear to have come from Ye Olde Curiosity Shop.[13] Thousands of shells were incorporated in the construction of Palmer's A Little Bit O' Heaven. When he wrote Standley a check for $82.50 on July 8, 1930, it may have been for the two giant clamshells that still sit in the college garden and smaller shells chosen from the ten shelves of seashells in which Palmer had expressed interest.

In addition to his collections of objects associated with non-Western religions, Palmer was fascinated with what he termed *blades,* and he amassed more than a thousand fighting and ceremonial knives of all types—mostly Oriental swords, borongs, and krises. Weapons were never a prominent part of Standley's stock, but he considered them intriguing enough that when some became available from the Philippine exhibit after the Alaska-Yukon-Pacific Exposition closed, Standley acquired bolos, borongs, krises, daggers, and other exotic weapons. The bolo, a single-edged slashing dagger, and the broad-bladed borong of the Moros were Philippine weapons. The kris, with its double-edged wave-shaped blade, was used in both Malaysia and India. He included these items in his "1001 Curious Things" lists in the earlier shop catalogs. In a newspaper announcement after the Palmer family's Seattle visit in February 1924, Standley reported that the doctor had bought "spears, swords, shields, beheading knives, head baskets, masks, etc."

5.4. Stone maul purchased by Palmer for his "phallic museum." Photograph courtesy Palmer College of Chiropractic, Davenport, Iowa.

Palmer also kept what he called a Phallic Museum, a display cabinet "not open to the public" because of "the inability of the occidental mind to understand and appreciate the oriental mind without condemning it."[14] This is where he would have kept the "nice ivory snuff bottle, Obscene carving, ancient one" that Standley mentioned in the Guest Book. This note seems to actually reference different objects. Two small ivory and wood snuff bottles in the Palmer collection, which might be perceived as phallic, may have come from the shop.[15] The Curiosity Shop tag on a prehistoric Northwest Coast stone carving clearly referencing a phallus definitely indicates the shop as its origin (fig. 5.4). The carving, about eight inches tall and shaped out of a hard stone by percussion is actually a multifunctional tool called a hand maul. The broad, flat bottom was used for pounding, and the narrower end could function as a pestle. Palmer's maul is similar to a number of other prehistoric ones from the Columbia and Fraser Rivers in the Pacific Northwest. Such items were of special interest to certain buyers and the shop had some in stock for many years, usually acquiring them from people who found them and brought them in. There was the titillation of perceived obscenity, and Standley, Palmer, and many others at the time imagined such mauls to represent mysterious primitive beliefs and rituals. So focused on possible exotic uses as to eschew a practical one, Standley called them phallic stones and believed that women rubbed them against themselves to induce fertility.[16]

Although Standley wrote that Palmer had bought masks from him, none exist today in the Palmer collection. Considering Palmer's interest in world religions, about which he often wrote and spoke, it is curious that he collected so little American Indian material related to Indian spirituality.[17] Perhaps he did not consider it quite exotic enough; his interest was in Oriental religions. Palmer spoke of his displays as a museum, but other than his profession-associated collections of bones and chiropractic equipment and his "blades," his collections were neither focused nor systematic. Collecting was a hobby that traveling allowed him to indulge, and in times of stress it served a psychological need. Palmer wrote in *The Bigness of the Fellow Within* (1949): "Hobbies are escape valves, where busy men with crowded hours can blow off excess steam. Hobbies are things men do when they relax, crawl in a hole somewhere and 'forget it.'"[18] The book lists and describes twenty-two of his most important collecting conquests. It was not merely the act of collecting but also the statement that Palmer's choice of objects made about him that helped relieve the ongoing pressures from attacks on all that he believed in and believed himself to be. The exotic collections he shared with the public enhanced his image as a daring, worldly, and knowledgeable man, as well as an eccentric. On a much smaller scale, his treasures in A Little Bit O' Heaven played the same self-validating role that C. T. Currelly's conquests had when they were installed in the Royal Ontario Museum. Although in his autobiography Currelly did not credit his connections with curio shops, preferring to report instead his interchanges with well-known dealers in London and the Orient, Palmer did, unabashedly so, in his *'Round the World with B. J.*[19] Tourist and curio shops in the Orient and on the West Coast were important sources for Palmer's collection.

Robert L. Ripley and "Believe It or Not!"®

There are only two men for whom Standley would close Ye Olde Curiosity Shop to the public during regular business hours, or open it after hours: George G. Heye, founder of the Museum of the American Indian, Heye Foundation in New York, and Robert L. Ripley, the creator of the "Ripley's Believe It or Not!"® cartoon, which was carried daily in hundreds of newspapers across the world. One can imagine that Ripley and Standley got on famously, what with their mutual fascination with freakish facts and people who had accomplished amazing feats. Not only was Ripley an international celebrity and a man who shared Standley's passion for the odd and the amazing, but even during the Depression he had substantial money to spend.

December 11, 1936:

His visit was before Christmas. 1st in morning and at 11 pm to 1:30 pm. Mr. Robert Ripley, Taylor's Lane, Mamaroneck NY, his island, his home on it and his lake, his museum. Ripley said its the greatest shop he ever got into.

—Standley, Guest Book, p. 102, next to a signature reading, "Ripley—Believe It or Not"

Born Leroy Ripley in 1893 in Santa Rosa, California, he had grown up as a shy boy most interested in sports and drawing.[20] He worked as a sports cartoonist on several newspapers before joining the *New York Globe*, where other reporters convinced him to change his name to Robert. On a day in December 1918, when he was at a loss for a cartoon idea, Ripley gathered together several sports oddities and drew them up, labeling the strip "Champs and Chumps." The editor changed the title to "Believe It or Not!"® and Ripley's future was launched. The Ripley cartoon branched into other subjects, became a daily, then was syndicated and eventually translated into seventeen foreign languages. At one point a staff of sixty assisted Ripley with research for his cartoons. Financed after 1929 by newspaper magnate William Randolph Hearst, Ripley traveled the world collecting hard-to-believe things and lived well as a flamboyant playboy in a large Manhattan apartment, a thirty-four-room upstate New York island estate in the Long Island Sound, and a home in West Palm Beach, Florida. In addition to drawing cartoons, he became a sought-after lecturer, made movie shorts, and had his own radio show.

Therefore, it was an important occasion when Ripley came to Ye Olde Curiosity Shop, as he did more than once, in winter 1936–37 while he was giving stage appearances in the Pacific Northwest and Alaska and buying Indian art.[21] On an exciting day in December 1936, when Standley opened the shop for Ripley after a show, he proceeded to spend $1,000, an unprecedented amount during the Depression. He bought the shop's tallest totem pole, its "Potlatch Man," and other items, including a giant "man-eating" clamshell from the Equator Islands. All of the items went to Mamaroneck, his upstate New York mansion. The pole and Potlatch Man were installed as outdoor sculpture and the giant clamshell became a birdbath. Ripley was always looking for material for his daily cartoon, and while in Seattle he took a photograph of the shop's aberrant three-tusk walrus head, from which to sketch. The cartoon (fig. 5.5), which featured the tusk and identified its source, gave Ye Olde Curiosity Shop important national publicity.[22] The thirty-seven-foot totem pole that Ripley purchased had stood outside Ye Olde Curiosity Shop for more than a decade. It was the work of Sam Williams, a Nuu-chah-nulth carver from Vancouver Island who lived in Seattle, and had been made in the 1920s (fig. 5.6). For years Williams was one of the mainstay carvers of big poles for the shop, and he and his work were among Standley's favorites. With another rebuilding scheduled for Colman Dock and the shop facing a move to a smaller interim location in just a few weeks, selling the pole and

5.5. Robert L. Ripley cartoon, published in syndicated newspapers, January 10, 1937. "Ripley's Believe it or Not!" cartoons typically combined a random assortment of odd facts. Cartoon courtesy Ripley Entertainment, Inc., Orlando, Florida.

other large items would solve awkward storage problems.[23]

The ten-foot Potlatch Man had also been carved by Sam Williams. Ripley exhibited it at the 1939 New York World's Fair (fig. 5.7).[24] The explanation in Ripley's guidebook combined information from Williams as lensed through Standley's imagination.[25] The identification of the twins on the knees, the Thunderbird, the Eagles on the arms, and the Killer Whales under the feet came from Williams. The "Haidah Shaman" identification and other meanings appear to have been Standley's contribution. Williams's Potlatch Man was actually an unusually elaborate and brightly painted version of a Nuu-chah-nulth welcome figure, a very tall male figure that Nuu-chah-nulth and Kwakwaka'wakw chiefs sometimes erected on the beach in front of their houses to welcome potlatch guests. At Ye Olde Curiosity Shop, the Potlatch Man had stood along the street in front of the shop to draw in and welcome visitors. In the late 1950s Williams recorded for the figure a welcome speech of the sort that would be given at a potlatch:

> [On the north side, the welcome side:] My friends, I welcome you into my humble home, I will give you what I can to make you happy. I wish nothing in return, because someday your grandchildren will give me good time. I promise there will be no war between your tribe and my tribe. If any tribe wars on your tribe, I shall be there to help you. Ask me nothing because all is given what I shall give. Go forth and have a good time. That is all.
> [On the south side:] Eating frog because he defies any ever to come forth and fight him. And there will be nobody coming to him unless it's some other big chief bringing daughter to marry off to him.[26]

After this first Potlatch Man left the shop, Sam carved at least two other versions, one of which still remains at the shop.

The giant "man-eating" clamshells (fig 5.8), some of which Ripley purchased during this 1936 visit, had also engaged Palmer. Standley typically

5.6. This thirty-seven-foot pole carved in the late 1920s by Vancouver Island Nuu-chah-nulth carver Sam Williams was photographed outside Ye Olde Curiosity Shop before its sale to Ripley.

5.7. Ripley and friends with Sam Williams's Potlatch Man at Ripley's New York estate, Mamaroneck. Photograph courtesy Ripley Entertainment, Inc., Orlando, Florida.

set out giant clamshells for official shop photographs and sold a postcard of his grandchildren sitting in them as infants. He bragged that not only were these shells astounding in size, but they could actually eat a man! The story stretched the truth a bit, but it was based in fact. In at least one case a man diving for the world's largest pearls (found in these shells) caught his arm when the shell closed and drowned. Ripley's shell weighed two hundred pounds and was more than three feet long at its greatest length and a foot thick at its hinges. It would have been an appropriate subject for a "Believe It or Not!"® cartoon. A few of the many other items that Ripley purchased from Standley over the years appear in Ripley photographs—a narwhal tusk and a large mask are displayed in interior photographs of the 1916–37 shop location. Some of the smaller totem poles, especially those used to frame Ripley's doghouse, may also have come from the shop.

After Ripley's death in 1949 his estate and much of his collection were auctioned. Ripley Entertainment, Inc., was established in 1951 to continue the cartoon; to merchandise Ripley books, films, and later videos; and to open Ripley Believe It or Not!® museums. The first museum, in Saint Augustine, Florida, was followed by others in Niagara Falls, San Francisco, Ocean City, Maryland, and other tourist locations.[27] The museums continued a tradition begun by Ripley himself in the 1930s, when he mounted temporary "Odditoriums" at world expositions. The labels in Ripley displays and those from Standley's days in Ye Olde Curiosity Shop have much in common in their emphasis and their explanations of the art and culture of indigenous people around the world. Both men blurred the past with the present, used the ethnographic present (speaking of the past as if it were the present), and focused on the strange and odd, but they also withheld value judgment.

There is another link between Ripley and Ye Olde Curiosity Shop. In 1904 Standley's youngest daughter, Caroline, married twenty-one-year-old Jules Charbneau.[28] Charbneau, who worked for a while in Standley's shop, shared his father-in-law's fascination with the minuscule; he had bought his first miniature as a teen in 1900 at the Paris Exposition. Charbneau later turned to selling life insurance, and for a while was curator of the gallery run by the Washington State Art Association in Seattle. He and his family moved to San Francisco in 1937, where he lived until his death. His wife and one daughter, Isabella, shared his passion for miniatures, and both joined him in collecting, showing, and lecturing about their collection around the world for decades.

By the 1960s the Charbneau collection numbered some thirty thousand objects. The dressed fleas, Siwash bread, tiny cast-metal totem poles, and grains of rice and human hair with writing on them were duplicated in displays at Ye Olde Curiosity Shop and had been obtained from, or in conjunction with, the shop.[29] Ripley displayed some of Charbneau's miniatures in his "Odditorium" at Chicago's Century of Progress fair in 1933 and San Francisco's Golden Gate Exposition in 1939. After her father's death, Isabella Standley Charbneau Warren and her husband Clair continued to show parts of the collection until they sold it in 1969. Ripley Enterprises was among the buyers.[30]

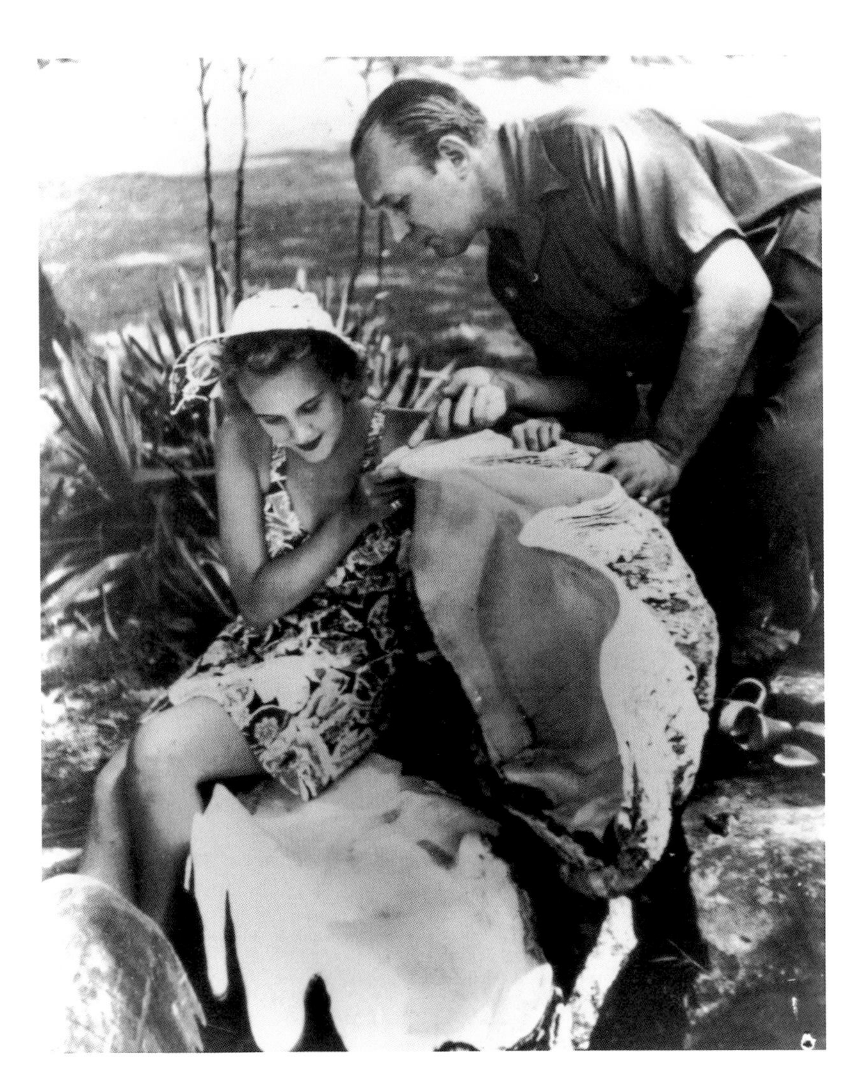

5.8. Ripley and visitor, ca. 1940, admiring the giant clamshell installed at his estate. "Man-eating" clamshells were popular for birdbaths and garden decor. Photograph courtesy Ripley Entertainment, Inc., Orlando, Florida.

Home Decor and Sacred Grottoes

Just as Palmer and Ripley purchased mostly totem poles and shells, especially giant clamshells, so did less well-known buyers with a range of modest or expansive reasons for collecting. Totem poles displayed in the front yard or on the grounds of a mansion made a statement about the owner's worldliness, eccentricity, even daring. The shells of giant "man-eating" clams safely domesticated as birdbaths or garden planters raised exclamations of amazement at their size. Small sea shells referenced nature and took on various kinds of symbolism when cemented into shrines and grottoes. All such objects were guaranteed conversation starters.

Standley's Guest Book records the names of sixteen buyers of large totem poles, the sort used for exterior display, and several dozen buyers of small model poles (fig. 5.9). There were scores more no doubt. In 1913 the comedian Wright Lorimer chose a twelve-foot pole for his Thousand Island summer home. Several years later the Simon J. Gray family, on their way from Dawson City, in the Yukon Territory with a husky dog, bought several big totems with which to decorate their home in Alameda, California. In 1926 a fifteen-foot pole was purchased for Jenner's Zoological Amusement Park in Loup City, Nebraska, and in 1929 author Zane Grey purchased a pole of the same size for his home on Catalina Island. In 1931 two huge poles went to J. Mile Barbour, maker of linen thread, for his estate in Ulster, Ireland.[31]

When large quantities of shells were purchased from Ye Olde Curiosity Shop, they were often combined with stones in the construction of grottoes

5.9. A totem pole sentinel on the lawn of an estate stimulated conversation. These, carved by Sam Williams, who lived in Seattle much of his life, were photographed along with Standley in 1933 on their way to a Virginia estate. Webster & Stevens photograph.

and shrines, especially after concrete was reintroduced into the building arts late in the nineteenth century and its possibilities captured the fancy of many. Usually very personal projects of imagination, devotion, and sometimes compulsion, outdoor grottoes were particularly popular in the United States during the early twentieth century with Catholic German immigrants who settled in the Midwest. Shells from scores of wharfside shops along the world's coasts made their way into these private creations, great and small. The largest of all, to become the largest man-made grotto in the world, was constructed by a Catholic priest who traveled great distances to gather his materials. In 1927 Standley noted in his Guest Book that Father Paul M. Dobberstein had been in the shop and "bought barrells of Sea shells to build great grottos at West Bend, Iowa, Wonder of the World." He also pasted in a postcard photograph of the priest (fig. 5.10).[32]

In 1912, Dobberstein had begun to create a place on the flat Iowa landscape to inspire meditation, a place that would use "silent stone made eloquent" to tell the story of man's fall and redemption. Over a period of more than forty years he and an assistant built the Grotto of the Redemption, creating large forms from concrete in which they arranged local flat field stones, augmenting them with other precious and semiprecious stones, petrified wood from Arizona, stalagmites from New Mexico, Venetian glass, and thousands of shells. They eventually created nine separate grottoes, each devoted to an event relating to the life of Jesus. Most of these are elaborate architectural constructions with inspirational statuary (fig. 5.11).

When Standley discovered Dobberstein's interest in grottoes and semiprecious stones, he took the priest home for dinner and to show him his own creations at Totem Place. Standley had done the same with Palmer, whose concrete-based grottoes in A Little Bit O' Heaven in Davenport, Iowa, had probably been inspired by Dobberstein's grotto just across the state to the west. Furthermore, it may well have been Palmer, who, after seeing Standley's agate fireplace and shell garden structures in 1924, told Dobberstein about Ye Olde Curiosity Shop as a source. The shells the priest acquired in Seattle in 1927 are believed to have been used in the grottoes of the Stations of the Cross and the Sermon on the Mount in Dobberstein's enormous Grotto of the Redemption.

5.10. Father Paul Dobberstein worked for decades creating the Grotto of the Redemption in West Bend, Iowa. Standley pasted into his Guest Book the postcard that Dobberstein sent him after he visited the shop. Photograph courtesy Grotto of the Redemption, West Bend, Iowa.

Special Kinds of Collectors

Standley, Palmer, and Ripley had a lot in common. Each became interested in the unusual at an early age. Each was a creative, intelligent individual whose life situation limited his schooling. Had they been raised in more affluent circumstances and encouraged to higher scientific education, their interests in the unusual in nature and their fascination with people and culture might have led to careers in biology or to the exciting new field of anthropology. Instead, each man began working at an early age and found a way, through entrepreneurial ambition, to exercise and share his passion through popular culture. Although Standley had followed his father in becoming a grocer, he also nourished and shared his boyhood habit of collecting natural and cultural curiosities by collecting and displaying them in his Denver store before he decided to devote his livelihood to such items in Seattle. Palmer's father's interests as a magnetic healer led his son to explore alternative modes of healing and non-Christian spiritual systems and the objects associated with them. Ripley dropped out of school to help support the family after his father died and never finished high school, but he parlayed his drawing skills and interest in oddities into his daily "Believe It or Not!"® cartoon, for years the most popular reader-interest feature in newspapers.

The limited scientific education, and perhaps the natural inclination

5.11. Entrance, Stations of the Cross, Grotto of the Redemption, West Bend, Iowa. Dobberstein integrated shells from Ye Olde Curiosity Shop and other stores into his enormous concrete and stone grotto dedicated to the life of Jesus. Photograph courtesy Grotto of the Redemption, West Bend, Iowa.

of the three, meant that their interests remained at the popular culture level. Standley acquired a few scientific books and talked occasionally with such anthropologists as Aleš Hrdlička and George T. Emmons and with scientists at the University of Washington, but he depended for explanations of things primarily on the stories his visitors told him, on the family encyclopedia, and on newspaper articles. Ripley's cartoon, printed daily in the *Seattle Post-Intelligencer,* was one of Standley's sources. The snippets of information that Standley attached to individual objects displayed in his shop evolved into stories about their meaning that ranged from true or partly true to the fantastic. He purposefully invented some information, like his explanation of the "Puget Sound mermaid" that hung from the shop's ceiling, but he also believed much of the information he provided. Ripley's interests were broad ranging and, as a "disseminator of the incredible truth," with the help of a large staff he sought to be sure that the claims in his cartoons were legitimate. In at least one case—that of Sam Williams's Potlatch Man—he succumbed to fantastic explanation when he trusted the information that Standley had provided rather than searching for what would have been harder-to-access information.

In a world where natural history and art museums were increasingly defined by a mainstream academic paradigm, Standley's Ye Olde Curiosity

Shop, Palmer's A Little Bit O' Heaven, and Ripley's "Odditoriums"—all called museums by their creators—harkened back to the first museum in the United States. Opened by Charles Wilson Peale in Baltimore, Maryland, in 1814, this museum was a place that focused on education and entertainment simultaneously, combining important scientific collections with constructions of human artifice such as "Fiji Mermaids." Standley, Palmer, and Ripley would have agreed with Peale that a museum should be a "rational amusement."

CHAPTER SIX

Curiosities and Charisma: Exotica and Daddy Standley

Curiosity is one of the permanent and certain
characteristics of a vigorous mind.
—Samuel Johnson

YE OLDE CURIOSITY SHOP WAS THE PLACE IN SEATTLE WHERE THE VIGOROUS MIND could always be exercised amid a comprehensive collection of the minuscule, the gigantic, the enigmatic, the forbidden. The shop's generous assortment (and sheer quantity) of natural and artificial curiosities meant that even frequent visitors could always enter, not knowing quite what they might find but sure that there would be something to amaze, delight, or shock (fig. 6.1). Nationally syndicated journalist Ernie Pyle commented on the shop: "Best of all you can browse around for hours as if you were in an old book store. It's more edifying than a museum, more fun than a roller coaster."[1] The shop presented an endlessly interesting world as "artificial curiosities" joined with "natural curiosities" to awe and engage the visitor. Objects of Native American culture, the primary subject of this book, were a main attraction, but there were certain other articles that drew customers in and in many people's minds formed an essential part of the shop's identity, as they continue to do today. Repeatedly, the first question from those familiar with the shop who have heard about this book has been, "Do they still have the shrunken heads?" They do.

"Natural curiosities" were defined in the days of the *Wunderkammer,* or cabinet of curiosities, as those elements of the natural world that invited study and enlightenment. They have always been an important part of the Curiosity Shop's stock—shark eggs, a narwhal tusk, a whole bear's foot, "man-eating" clamshells, a glass sponge from Pitcairn Island (labeled "the rarest animal known"), and dozens of other oddities. Some of these objects could even be purchased. Over time, the most popular natural wonders for sale in the shop have been the "living" ones—sea horses advertised as swimming vertically with their rear dorsal fins whirling like propellers

> $10,000 expended in travel will not afford you the opportunity of observing a similar variety of articles which may be seen within an hour's time at this famous shop
>
> —Ye Olde Curiosity Shop brochure, mid-1920s

and Mexican jumping beans. "Artificial curiosities," objects of wonder made by human artifice, have been even more important to the shop's identity over the years. The minuscule were the sorts of attractions one might find on a circus or world's fair midway, and the gigantic were primarily the remnants of whales like those in natural history museums. However, most of the thousands of unusual things that the shop contained were the amazing flotsam of human culture. Part of their appeal was the imagination that one could bring to a discovery: a pastoral fancy replete with camel bells from Palestine; a pensive reverie before Sylvester, a prospector mummified in the torrid Arizona sun; a darker vision while fingering a Chinese beheading sword or staring into the eyes of a shrunken head.

Miniatures and Mermaids, Mummies, Shrunken Heads, and Armadillo Baskets

The Curiosity Shop fed a voyeuristic curiosity that allowed visitors to search out the unusual, the impossible, the shocking. Even ordinary objects seemed uncommon in the shop's jumble of the disparate. An object might be something unfamiliar but admirable (an Aleut basket with more than one hundred stitches per inch), or unexpected and startling (a sewing box made from an armadillo shell). It might represent the seemingly impossible. Could the entire Lord's Prayer really fit on the head of a pin? Could the mermaid truly be real? Perhaps the object strayed from the norm (a deformed pig in a jar) or supposed the mysterious (a grimacing mask, a medicine man's rattle). Or it might be something shocking or forbidden like stone hammers in the shape of phalluses, human mummies, and shrunken human heads.

Some objects were made of unusual materials using uncommon techniques, showed unexpected fineness of craftsmanship, or featured abstracted designs that were not easily understood. Some originated in unfamiliar cultures and places, or were said to have unusual, even bizarre uses, supposed or real. Whatever they discovered there, viewers were allowed to wonder, speculate, and argue what they saw at Ye Olde Curiosity Shop against what they knew or expected or thought. As in Charles Wilson Peale's museum a century earlier—the first in the United States—the visitor in Standley's shop was pressed to reexamine the reality of his perceptions and of the world. Unlike the visitor to Peale's museum, however, the spectator in the Curiosity Shop could purchase a memento, a connection to the experience.

> The Lord's Prayer on the Head of a Pin. We had a thousand of them. Believe it or not, we sold them for 25 cents a piece, and then one day the die got broken and that was the end of it.
>
> —Joe James, 1995

Miniatures engage a sense of wonder, inquiry, and admiration—at their seeming impossibility, the patience and discipline they evidence, and the delicate tools and skills necessary to create them.[2] Ye Olde Curiosity Shop's most popular miniatures (some of which are still in the shop today) have been those with minuscule writing that is visible only through magnification. Over decades a largely churchgoing public was fascinated to see the Lord's Prayer engraved on the head of a pin or on a grain of rice. The "Original Lord's Prayer Pin," attributed to an A. Schiller, was exhibited at the Chicago Columbian Exposition in 1893. A few other makers followed. According to Standley, the Curiosity Shop sold nearly all the Lord's Prayer pins made by a Godfrey Lundberg over a period of eighteen years.[3] The shop's example of the Lord's Prayer engraved on a grain of rice was surely the work of the man called Homma who demonstrated engraving on rice at the Ripley's Believe It or Not!® exhibit at the Chicago Century of Progress Exposition in 1933. The example of Robert Ripley's name written on a gray human hair by E. L. Blystone is still in the shop. Shop visitors were also fascinated by minuscule carvings: seven Chinese gods of good fortune sculpted inside a nut the size of an acorn, thirty-six elephants small enough to fit into a hollow bean, and what were billed as the smallest carvings in the world—four grains of rice with husks on which were carved the Virgin Mary with the infant Jesus, Christ upon the cross, Confucius, and Buddha.[4] There were also seashells the size of rice, the "Widow's mite," and the famous fleas in dresses (fig. 6.2).

6.1. J. E. Standley sometimes wrote identifications directly on photographs such as this one taken in front of his first Colman Dock shop ca. 1904 by photographers Webster & Stevens.

Even more tantalizing than the Curiosity Shop's miniatures, however, have been the unthinkable and the shocking—a mermaid, mummies, and a group of shrunken heads. Early in the twentieth century the shop acquired (and still owns today) a mermaid, which has for years hung from the ceiling (fig. 6.3).[5] In his 1910 catalog Standley advertised mermaids or "Dugong" from

FLEAS IN DRESSES
PHOTOGRAPHED
By THE TIMES MICROSCOPIC
LENS
Oct. 1919
FROM
YE OLDE
CURIOSITY
SHOP
SEATTLE

6.2. Ye Olde Curiosity Shop's set of dressed fleas from Mexico joined the Lord's Prayer on the head of a pin and other minuscule curiosities to amaze visitors for almost a century.

twelve to thirty inches long, for $2 to $5. In 1923 a local paper published a tale about the shop's "dugong," or "Mare puella geodukus Puget Soundiensis," that would have been suitable as an April Fool's Day feature. According to Standley, a fisherman on Hood Canal had caught her in his net, killed her, then stuffed her and brought her to Ye Olde Curiosity Shop. The article concluded: "People believe it is a fish story until they examine it. Then they will think so."[6] Dugongs are actual herbivorous marine mammals with flipperlike forelimbs and a deeply notched tail fin that live in tropical coastal waters. Because of certain characteristics (their cry, perhaps?), stories arose about their luring ancient mariners. The dugong in Ye Olde Curiosity Shop, today referred to as "the Thing" by the shop's staff, is actually one of at least four (and likely more) "mermaids" or "mermen" constructed by an Asian taxidermist by sewing monkey torsos to fish bodies. Similar creations hung for years in a curio shop in Banff, Alberta, at the Cliff House in San Francisco, and in one of Ripley's Believe It or Not!® museums.

Had he been alive, Standley would surely have approved of the Curiosity Shop's acquisition of several mummies. In the late 1940s the shop purchased its first mummy, a small female whom the staff named "Gloria." Shop history relates that the mummy had been found in an Arizona cave about 1900, was between five hundred and a thousand years old, and had been displayed for a while at the Smithsonian then stowed in a Seattle closet until her owner, a "female explorer," offered her to the shop.[7] The second mummy, named "Sylvester," became the shop's most popular attraction after it was acquired in 1955 (fig. 6.4). Cowpokes are said to have found Sylvester, who had been a prospector, in 1895 in the desert near Gila Bend, in southwestern Arizona. The "drying and chemical action of the desert" had preserved him so well that the bullet

MISS ELSIE MARCUNE is shown chumming with a stuffed Puget Sound mermaid or "dugong," the property of J. E. Standley, proprietor of Ye Olde Curiosity Shoppe here. People believe it is a fish story until they examine it. Then they will think so.

hole from which he probably died was still visible. Sylvester stood propped up in a secondhand store in Yuma, Arizona, for a while, was exhibited in Texas as a carnival attraction, then was displayed at the Alaska-Yukon-Pacific Exposition in 1909 and San Francisco's Panama-Pacific Exposition in 1915. The mummy then changed hands several times before being offered for sale to the shop. Occasionally shop visitors insist on a different history. One, in 1998, claimed that Soapy Smith, the legendary Skagway, Alaska, bunco artist, had the mummy fabricated and sold him in Seattle on his way to the Klondike gold rush.[8] In the late 1960s Sylvester gained a companion when the shop acquired another standing mummy, "Sylvia." Somewhere along the way a desiccated dog found during the excavation for a dance hall in Everett, Washington, joined the pair and was christened "Petrifido."

Certainly not the most endearing objects, but by far the most widely known, in Ye Olde Curiosity Shop's collection are its shrunken heads. In the mid-1930s George G. Heye decided to sell some of the shrunken heads that

6.3. A picture of a pretty girl and a monster, and a story about Ye Olde Curiosity Shop's Puget Sound mermaid or "dugong," could always liven up a slow news day. The article accompanying this August 24, 1923, photograph in the *Seattle Post-Intelligencer* recounted bizarre tales about the physical characteristics of the creatures and Indian chiefs offering their daughters in marriage in exchange for a mermaid.

6.4. "Sylvester the Mummy," said to be a prospector who had died of natural causes in the shifting sands of Arizona, became an object of public fascination as soon as he was installed in Ye Olde Curiosity Shop in the mid-1950s.

he had in his Museum of the American Indian, Heye Foundation, and he thought Standley would be interested. The two men had become staunch friends and this was a way to help him acquire an especially astounding curiosity. Standley's grandson Joe James, then a youngster, happened to be in the shop on the exciting day when Heye's shrunken head collection arrived. James's father and uncle anguished over the purchase—"it was right there in the Depression and they didn't have much money you know, but they wanted 'em"—and they finally decided to buy several shrunken heads, including a female one that included a torso.[9] The head of the latter broke off in the shipping and Ed Standley, James's uncle, repaired it. Several other shrunken heads passed through the Curiosity Shop before it became illegal to sell them in the United States, but the shop never sold any of the original ones from Heye. As happened with the mummies, the smallest head was given a name, "Jo Jo," much as if it were a pet, distancing it from its grisly origins (fig. 6.5).[10]

European and American fascination with shrunken heads began in the mid-nineteenth century. A practice of the Shuar and Achuar Indians of the Ecuadorian lowlands (two of four tribes known as the Jivaro Indians), it riveted the imagination and generated a scientific and pseudo-scientific literature.[11] An authentic shrunken head, a *tsantsa,* was most often made from the head of a seized male enemy of another tribe, shrunk to capture his avenging soul and prevent him from seeking revenge for his death. The tsantsa was used in a ceremony that sent the soul away to its own neighborhood. The head might then be kept as a trophy of valor and to provide strength and prosperity, and perhaps later be sold for export.

Counterfeit tsantsas were made as early as the 1870s in Columbia, Ecuador, and Panama by non–Shuar and Achuar people, but their production increased when a market developed for them abroad and they could be exchanged for guns. To create them makers used bodies from morgues, monkey heads, sloth heads, and even goatskin. Counterfeit heads lack certain traits that are characteristic of real ones.[12] It has been estimated that about 80 percent of the tsantsas in private and museum hands are fraudulent. The shrunken female head and torso and some of the shrunken heads that Heye sold to Ye Olde Curiosity Shop appear to be counterfeit. It is generally agreed that an authentic tsantsa is seldom female and that it never includes a torso or full body, although some full shrunken bodies were made by the Jivaro about 1890 as demonstrations. In the United States there was a strong market for shrunken heads in the 1930s, and many natural history and private museums acquired them until importing them was made illegal in the 1940s. In 1999 the National Museum of the American Indian, Smithsonian Institution (formerly George Heye's Museum of the America Indian, Heye Foundation) repatriated the

Collection of shrunken human heads
from upper Amazon, and "Gloria" the
mummy. Seen at Ye Olde Curiosity
Shop, Colman Dock, Seattle, Wash.
Ellis
9070

6.5. Directly after he received the shipment of shrunken heads from George G. Heye, Standley had them photographed for this and other black and white postcards. He was not aware that several of the heads, including the shrunken torso, were among the hundreds of counterfeit *tsantsas* made expressly for sale to eager collectors. In their array of disparate items, Ye Olde Curiosity Shop's display cases echoed eighteenth-century "cabinets of curiosities." Gloria the Mummy, an ornamented skull from New Guinea, and the shrunken heads were grouped with Aleut baskets, ivory carvings, and a large ship model of ivory.

authentic shrunken heads in Heye's collection to Ecuador.[13] Ye Olde Curiosity Shop's collection of shrunken heads has elicited enough visitor interest over the years to inspire a gag "shrunken head kit"; although offensive to many today, this was not always the case. A box with a small knife, a mysterious powder, and a needle and thread, the kit came with instructions that suggested: "For further information or for especially large (swelled) or dense heads contact Contracted Heads, Inc., Upper Amazon. . . . Remember our Motto: 'Don't lose your head . . . shrink it!'"

Another unusual curiosity in Seattle and elsewhere, especially during the 1920s, was a sewing basket made from the armorlike shell of the Mexican armadillo, a variety of anteater common in south Texas and Mexico (fig. 6.6). Standley kept addresses for six suppliers of armadillo shell baskets, all in Texas, and wrote in his "Address of Friends" in 1928 (page J): "Johns, Boerne, Tex. he has best armos of all."[14] The baskets can be seen on display in several interior photos of Ye Olde Curiosity Shop. Armadillo shell supplier Charles Apelt of Comfort, Texas, advertised that it was he to whom "the possibility of converting it into baskets of original design suggested itself" (fig. 6.7). The armadillo shell was turned on its back and the tail bent and attached at the neck end to form a handle. The baskets, then about eleven to fifteen inches long, were

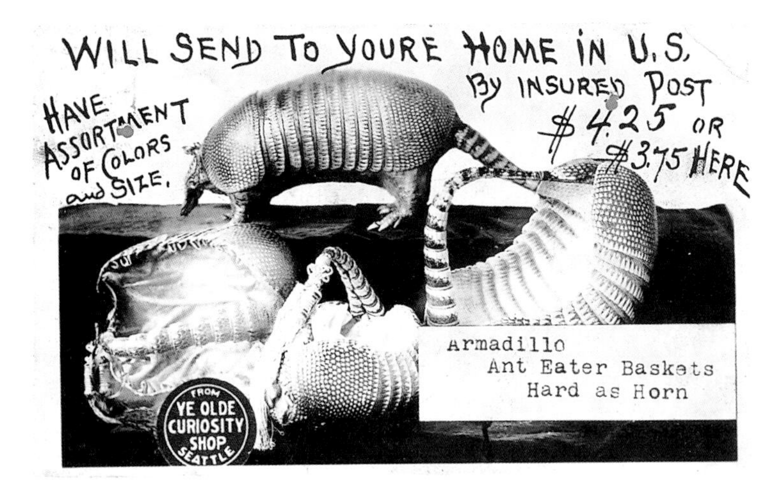

THE WORLDS ONLY ARMADILLO FARM
Scene on the Drying Ground, showing about 500 Armadillo Shells. (See Other Side.)

6.6. Ye Olde Curiosity Shop advertised its armadillo shell sewing baskets using this black and white postcard on which prices were written directly. After the shells arrived from Texas, turning them into fabric-lined baskets was an intergenerational Standley family enterprise.

6.7. Color postcard, Apelt Armadillo Farm, Comfort, Texas. Charles Apelt claimed to have invented the armadillo shell sewing basket, a curiosity that was popular across the United States during the 1920s and 1930s.

lined with satin. Apelt and other suppliers wholesaled both lined and unlined baskets. The Curiosity Shop chose to buy the unlined ones and finish them in the shop (see fig. 2.1, right side). All of Standley's family was involved at one time or another in the operation of the shop, and one of Joe James's first jobs there was to come in after school and drill holes in the shells, about a quarter-inch from the rim and one inch apart. He hated it because the odor was similar to that of burning hair. Edward Standley's wife, Edna, would then line the shells with brightly colored satin by running a cord in and out through the holes to hold the fabric to the shell.

"Daddy Standley" and Seattle

Standley was an outgoing and gregarious man, enthusiastically intrigued by everything and everyone. He loved to show people around the shop, telling the stories behind his curios, explaining how he got them and how they worked. He would sometimes become so excited about an object that he would then refuse to sell it. Curio dealers from across the country visited the shop when they came to Seattle, some of them after having read an article in *Hobbies* magazine, written by publisher O. C. Lightner. Lightner believed that Standley's shop was an exhilarating model for what a curio store could be.[15] For such a store to be successful, money had to be invested in real curios, but what really attracted the public was the "bally," or ballyhoo—"the noise out in front." Ye Olde Curiosity Shop's "bally" was visual—the record-sized whalebones and mammoth tusks, a ten-foot rattlesnake skin, and other smaller items that its proprietor attached to the front each morning, as well as the unusual curiosities displayed in the windows to attract attention. Said Standley of these wondrous objects: "It's my advertising." None of it was for sale.

Within a few years of its opening in 1904 on Colman Dock, Ye Olde Curiosity Shop was heralded by the local business community as "the attraction of the waterfront" (fig. 6.8). Its reputation grew steadily. A 1933 article in the *Seattle Star* named it number one in a list of "The Seven Wonders of Seattle," followed by the harbor, the Ballard Locks, the Boeing airplane

factory, the Seattle Art Museum, the public market, and the University District's Edmond Meany hotel.[16] A *Seattle Times* reporter described the shop as a "'must see' item on every tripper's list, as much a part of the flavor and character of Seattle as the hills, lakes, ocean-going commerce and distant view of majestic Mount Rainier."[17] Standley, the jovial proprietor, was ever there, "puttering among the endless and amazing things he had gathered . . . greeting thousands of visitors with a smile and a card listing the wondrous curiosities of his shop."[18] If nothing else, a visit to the shop was bound to amuse. A local writer, drawn to the devotion this "untiring host" put into his work, observed: "One is made welcome by the joyful interest he seems to feel as he ushers you about showing you curios. He beams genially as does the amused onlooker while displaying his dressed-up flea for the millionth time. One may leave Ye Olde Curiosity Shop empty handed, but never empty headed or hearted."[19]

6.8. Shop interior, ca. 1923. Standing at attention for this formal portrait after the shop had moved one door south in 1923 are son-in-law Ed Ewing, Standley, and his son Ed. The Navajo rugs, placed on the floor only for photographs, were available for sale. At the lower left corner of the Indian basket display case stands a brass shell casing on which a sailor from the U.S.S. *Pennsylvania* had pounded out a totem pole in repoussé.

"The Old Curiosity Shop"
That whale's old jawbone marks the spot
Where you will find me, like as not;
When covering the waterfront
I can't resist its blandishment.
For near that bony sentry stands
The gateway to the Wonder Lands.
No flying carpet has the power
To speed so far in one short hour
As I am carried by the spell
Of what these relics have to tell.
And as I zoom from place to place
A kind old man with smiling face
Will spin a yarn that fits each piece—
Egyptian, Mayan, Siamese—
And every land I would explore.
The yarns that he has told before
A thousand times, but even so,
So quaintly that you'd never know.
And so content is he in telling
He seems to have no thought of selling.

—Sprague O. Smith, n.d.

The Curiosity Shop became a place that children begged to visit, where they could explore on their own and discover, be shocked, titillated, and thrust into gales of laughter in the course of but a few minutes. The small old man in the skull cap might give them a shell or a bead or another tiny memento. Standley loved children, but his gifts were also astute investments in the shop's future. He believed that these presents and the shop where they had been received would remain in their memory, and the child, grown to adulthood, might become a regular customer. Shop visitors today occasionally approach Standley's great-grandson Andy James, who now manages the shop, with a tiny treasure and recall, "Your grandfather gave me this when I was a child." Although an entertainment, even an irritation to some, Standley was clearly well liked. He traveled little; people came instead to him, and after their visits he corresponded avidly. At Christmastime Standley sent holly all over the world. He was generous with friends and acquaintances, and in turn those who shared or were amused by his fascinations sent things to him. One gift was a mounted duck-billed platypus—"the strangest freak in nature"—which arrived from a sailor on the U.S.S. *Pennsylvania.*

In its early years Ye Olde Curiosity Shop acted as an unofficial waterfront post office, where letters arrived from all over the world for sailors and adventurers, to be held until they docked.[20] The shop's fans were legion and it continually received mail, especially in the early 1940s, when thousands of sailors came through Seattle. It might be hard to remember the shop's exact address, but identifying characteristics easily stuck in the mind and the postal service was up to the task. Letters addressed as variously as Colman Dock Est. 1899, Thousand and One Store, Whalebone Curio Shop, Shop of 1001 Curios, Mr. Colman Duck, and Alaska Eskimo fur doll, Ye Olde Curiosity Shop made their way to Standley's shop. Seattleites came to think of Ye Olde Curiosity Shop as an icon in their city. Whenever a guest visited, a trip to the shop was an essential part of the hosting. Visitors told others of it, and locals returned again and again. In the late 1930s city police said that the question most asked of them by tourists was how to get to the shop.[21] A few fans wrote ditties of genuine affection (if questionable literary merit) to Standley and his shop. Like the Seattle Totem Pole, Ye Olde Curiosity Shop became a visual symbol around which private and public emotion centered, a construct that would for decades resonate within the community.

> A bouquet to: Joseph E. ("Daddy") Standley, because through the maintenance of his "Ye Olde Curiosity Shoppe" over a period of years he has helped to make Seattle famous the world over.
>
> —"Flowers for the Living," *Seattle Star,* November 21, 1929

A Singular Chamber of Commerce

Standley was a passionate advocate of Seattle from almost the moment he arrived. His collections and the city were his two favorite topics. He extolled Seattle's virtues in booster cards that he gave out, in his advertising, and in his catalogs. He believed that a businessman should be committed to the city in which he did business. Standley had produced and distributed booster cards in Denver also, but his love for Seattle was clearly genuine and never faltered. He went to some trouble to obtain a copy of the comments that Theodore Roosevelt had made in a 1903 address about Seattle's natural advantages and potential greatness, and saved this and other clippings with statistics about the city so he could quote from them at length. He wrote letters to the editor of various city papers with suggestions about how to develop the city's beauty and uniqueness, to encourage more visitors and entice them to settle on the West Coast.[22] He held that Midwestern farmers should be interested in this region, "where there are never any crop failures" and in Seattle, the "1st city in the world to run street cars with electric."[23] Standley believed passionately in the local litany of optimism and progress that boasted: "Chief among Seattle's assets is the historic *Seattle Spirit,* which knows no obstacle it cannot overcome."[24]

Files at the Royal Ontario Museum, the Smithsonian, and other museums with which Standley corresponded, include cards advertising the city and the shop that he typically enclosed in his communications. Over the years he printed and distributed thousands of booster cards, ranging from two by four inches to standard postcard size. On them Seattle became variously "The Gateway of Alaska and Orient," "The New York of the Pacific," or "Seattle, the Queen City of Puget Sound." Standley's earliest cards were clearly modeled on the "Sights around Denver" cards he had distributed while running a grocery there, although the cards about Seattle, a less established city, listed slightly fewer attractions. Several lines at the bottom of each card directed the reader to Ye Olde Curiosity Shop. One 1904 card titled "Washington, the Evergreen State" pictured Standley's new Colman Dock shop on one side and listed tourist attractions on the other.[25]

There were also information cards describing the shop and its contents. Although the general card—"You are invited to visit Ye Olde Curiosity Shop"—was altered several times to update it as shop merchandise changed, cards on

And young Teddy Roosevelt, when he returned from Alaska, stood right here and picked out Alaskan curios.

—"Standley Adds Milestone at Old Curiosity Shop," *Seattle Times,* February 24, 1931

specific subjects changed little over the years. Such information cards covered topics about which tourists wondered and provided information on types of frequently purchased objects. The cards titled "History of Chief Seattle and Princess Angeline, Seattle" and "Story of the Indian Carved Totem Pole in Seattle" dealt with local history. Cards such as "Wonderful Baskets Made by Indians," "Alaska Indian Totem Poles," and "Wonders of Nature—Corals" dealt with shop stock. The information provided was cursory, usually a general sentence or two about the topic followed by a list of shop merchandise.

Standley preferred to stay in the shop, and to the best of his family's knowledge he never joined civic or fraternal organizations other than the Chamber of Commerce. He modeled civic duty by ardently supporting the chamber, weighing in regularly in the newspapers with his opinions and ideas about encouraging tourism, and by helping local causes financially or by loaning objects. Of course, all of this served to keep Ye Olde Curiosity Shop in the news and the public mind as well. Standley lamented civic apathy and spoke out about it.[26] As a public service he encouraged friendly journalists to write about and publicize such local attractions as George Jaeger's frozen fish museum at the Port of Seattle's cold storage plant and the Puget Sound Academy of Sciences Marine Museum located on the ship *St. Paul.*[27] Standley made the city of Seattle a present in 1939, the totem pole that came to be called the West Seattle Pole. His major gift to the city, however, was his shop's far-flung reputation as a tourist attraction worth coming to Seattle to see.

Local businesses, organizations, theater companies, and convention organizers sometimes turned to the Curiosity Shop when they needed Indian items.[28] When the New Washington Hotel opened in 1908, its striking faience fireplace was framed by totem poles that had been replicated from two in the shop. Planners for the 1909 Alaska-Yukon-Pacific Exposition and the 1911 Seattle Potlatch Carnival used Standley's copy of Franz Boas's 1897 study of the Kwakiutl Indians for ideas.[29] The President Theater used the shop's Eskimo chair in 1928, and the Federation of Women's Clubs borrowed a teepee, "a proper cedar head band, a real duck rattle and a necklace of teeth" for the Medicine Man when it presented the play "Blue Wing" at the Moore Theater.[30] When Miss Agnes Spotted Feather made a war bonnet for Washington state Governor Roland Hartley in 1931 while sitting in a window of the Frederick & Nelson Department Store, curios from the shop provided ambiance.[31] The props that Standley loaned out were not all of Indian origin, however. The shop's large, blue semiporcelain Fou dog, its small ivory replica

Chiccalina the famous Italien "Tenor" had dinner with us at Totem Place with Harry Green & Wife, Orpheum Cir. Chic Bot Lantern for his song in Prison scene, he offered to sing his whole opera for my ivory polar bear & walrus.

—Standley, Guest Book, p. 58, ca. 1920

of the revenue cutter *Bear,* and other special objects graced commercial and industrial exhibits.[32] The shop has continued Standley's tradition of loaning things.

Over the years the shop has also loaned both its objects and its site for movies and television. In 1923 Kiser Studios of Portland, Oregon, used canoes and other "relics" for the film *Rock Where the Winds Whisper,* "illustrating an old Indian myth."[33] Standley and the shop were featured in the Paramount Pictures series "Unusual Occupations" in the late 1930s, and when television's Faye Emerson Show featured Seattle in the mid-1950s Emerson chose as backdrops the Boeing Company, Mount Rainier, and Ye Olde Curiosity Shop. Joe James's office doubled as the center of drug operations in the film *Scorchie,* with Connie Stevens, shot in the mid-1960s.

Famous Visitors

Standley was fascinated by celebrities and particularly admired those with special skills or accomplishments. Like other visitors to Seattle, many of them did not want to miss the shop either. Standley made celebrities especially welcome and invited some to his home, Totem Place, for dinner. Some signed the Guest Book, but more often Standley wrote about their visits, sometimes gluing in photographs clipped from the newspaper. Officers from the revenue cutter *Perry* thrilled him with the story of their discovery of an island created by a volcano (fig. 6.9). Presidents also visited—Warren G. Harding and earlier, Teddy Roosevelt and his son Teddy—as did the political cartoonist Clifford Berryman, creator of the "Teddy Bear." There were opera stars, dancers, and entertainers performing in local theaters, especially the venue run by Standley's friend Alex Pantages. Actor Charlie Chaplin came in to the shop, as did actresses Jean Harlow, Leslie Carter, and Ruth Clifford, with her dwarf squirrel monkey. The Snake Dancer at the Pantages found something essential when she "bot [a] wooden flexible snake."

The pianist Ignace Jan Paderewski visited the shop, as did Buster Brown and his dog Tige. Radio artists Dobbsie "the Greatest radio announcer" and Little Mickey, James A. Bailey of Barnum & Bailey, and the boxer Jack Dempsey are all recorded in Standley's Guest Book. The Countess Vanderbilt bought pearl beads for her friends, and Louis Tiffany, "the old jewelry gent," purchased Alaska curios, idols, and a mammoth tusk. The dancer Ruth St. Denis and banjoist Eddie Peabody both bought small totem poles to take to friends. Even the near-great were worth recording—a Mr. Pinkham, a relative of Lydia Pinkham, Mark Twain's daughter, and Thomas Edison's son, Charles. George

Perry Island, Bogosloff Group, Rose in Behring Sea,
Spring of 1906. This Island is of Volcanic Eruption.
about 5 years later this Island
disappeared in to the sea
The officers on the U.S. Revenue
Cutter Perry
discovered
it

6.9. A color postcard sold in the shop pictured officers of the U.S. revenue cutter *Perry* and the island named after them after they watched its creation from an undersea volcanic eruption.

Sutton, the armless billiard champion, particularly amazed and thrilled Standley, who wrote about him several times. In 1908 he invited him home for dinner. Afterward, at a friend's home, Sutton "gave us a display of all his fancy and trick shots with Billiards. Think of it he has no arms only stubs. He could jump a Ball off the table to floor and then another jumped off to hit [the] one on floor."[34]

Another memorable visitor was Queen Marie of Rumania, whose trip to parts of the United States and Canada in fall 1926 created a stir across the continent.[35] It was advertised as a goodwill tour that would educate the queen about the United States firsthand. She would also dedicate a museum built by Sam Hill at Maryhill, Washington. Newspapers suspected other motives for the trip, ranging from finding a husband for her daughter, Ileana, to selling Hollywood on movie scenarios she had written, to influencing a positive settlement of Rumania's World War I debts. Of the three, only the latter was accomplished. Traveling with the queen were her son and daughter, her friend Loie Fuller, the well-known American dancer, and personal attendants. The Baltimore & Ohio Railroad sponsored a special train and other railways assisted the entourage throughout the tour.

A successful, eccentric businessman, Sam Hill, had fallen in love with the Columbia River gorge while involved in the construction of a rail line from Spokane to Portland. In 1914 he began to build a French-style chateau for entertaining, situating it high on the plateau overlooking the river. Hill named the building Maryhill, after his daughter. After World War I interrupted construction, Hill decided to turn the building into a museum instead, and hearing that Queen Marie wanted to visit America, he invited her to come as his guest and dedicate the museum. Such impulsive actions inspired the popular expression, "What in the Sam Hill?" Queen Marie arrived in the United States in mid-October 1926. Traveling aboard "the Special Train conveying Her Majesty the Queen of Roumania," she spent a few hours on November 3 dedicating the museum, then continued on to the coast.

While in Seattle Queen Marie visited its most famous curio shop, where she sat in the Chinese chair. There was criticism of her trip, not only by the press but by political, labor, and ethnic groups as well. Conflicts within her entourage also made the news. Was it her reputation—there had been a most embarrassing row over who would introduce her in Portland—or Standley's experience when she and her daughter Ileana visited, which caused him to write in his Guest Book: "Queen Marie of Romania and Elena. Joy, scraps, snubs, disappoints. Peace & rows. Sam Hill with her. I sent her a Totem Pole, got letter." Whether there were two gifts or a lapse in memory is unclear, for a note in Standley's hand on the thank you from the queen's secretary says "a fine native-basket."[36] Years later, in February 1931, just after Hill had died, Standley relished an irony: "I'll always remember how Mr. Hill, the railroad magnate, brought a friend of his down here who wanted to see the most outstanding 'art' gallery in Seattle."

Standley's Guest Book also offers an overview of tourist and harbor activity during these years that brought excitement and business to the shop. He noted Elks, Kiwanis, Rotary, Shriners, and other fraternal organization conventions that brought in thousands of customers. During a Knights Templars convention in July 1925, for example, as many as three thousand people came through the shop on several nights. He also recorded the names of large ships that brought an influx of sailors, especially in wartime and during the annual Fleet Week in late summer. Most were American battleships, but over the years there were also British dreadnoughts, German gun boats, and Japanese ships.

Totem Place

By 1906 Ye Olde Curiosity Shop was doing well enough that Standley could join other successful businessmen in moving his family from a downtown apartment into a home on the outskirts of the small city. He chose a lot in West Seattle, just across Elliott Bay from the shop, and built a craftsman home, where he lived until his death in 1940. Always the regional booster, Standley later attributed his health and longevity to his "grandest view in the world"—that of Puget Sound, the Olympics, the city lights, and the stars. "It's like a tonic, and anyone with a love of the beautiful and nature at her very

Totem Place is . . . one of the most unusual private residences in the city.

—*Philatelic West,* 1919

best in their hearts, should certainly live to be a hundred on Puget Sound."[37] The home was conveniently located near the end of the streetcar line, which allowed Standley and his family to trolley down to the ferry dock at the base of the hill and ferry over to the shop.[38]

Standley's home became his pride and joy, and he kept it in shape with the motto "paint or prune." Like his shop and his earlier Denver home, it reflected "his passion for the earth's amazing flotsam" and his enthusiasm for sharing it.[39] In Denver he had built a mound of shells, petrified wood, and cactus in the side yard where passersby could study it and had incorporated his name into the front fence using small limbs and roots. Some of his Denver treasures came with him to Seattle and were used again in his new home. Over time Standley planted monkey puzzle trees and created a sunken garden with mounds of shells and stones neatly embedded in cement, installed totem poles, and christened the residence "Totem Place" (fig. 6.10). There came to be shell-lined walkways and birdbaths made of giant clamshells, armadillo shells and whale vertebrae used as flower baskets, a Chinese Mandarin sundial, and a pair of whale jawbones laid along the parking strip to form the shape of a canoe. On the grounds Standley built a log cabin playhouse and an authentic Japanese teahouse of bamboo for his daughter Ruby, which he furnished with Oriental curios. His grandchildren, Joe and Emabelle James, and their cousins found it a wonderful house in which to grow up, with totem poles to hide behind, whalebones to play among, and enough unusual things to fire any child's imagination. For several years Totem Place won a contest sponsored by the city's public schools for the "best home play yard" in Seattle.[40]

For some years, on entering the gateway, visitors stepped over a two-foot-square swastika made of blue and white tiles embedded in cement. Standley had placed it there as an Indian good luck symbol but became worried in the late 1930s that someone would think him a Nazi sympathizer and covered it over with concrete. The Standley residence was best known for what one journalist called its "mementos of 'lost races'"—its totem poles (fig. 6.11). The number of poles varied over the years; in 1925 there were nine, and at one point later as many as thirteen. Although the poles were said to be from Alaska, or carved by Bella Bella Indians, those shown in the pictures of Totem Place were, for the most part, the work of the Nuu-chah-nulth carvers who lived in the Seattle area. There are several individual carving styles represented, but with the exception of some Williams family members, the carvers remains anonymous.

After the 1906 move to the new house, with its expanded room there was not just an Indian corner (see fig. 4.18); rather, there were curios everywhere. Carved chairs of black Chinese teak joined a group of sword canes, a case displaying his wife Isabelle's collection of more than 250 miniature pitchers and another of shells from around the world. There was a glass case of carved ivory, an Igorrote war shield, and a cannonball fired from the U.S. warship *Decatur* in 1856 when it sailed into Elliott Bay to assist in the Indian War. Standley's special pride was the ornate fireplace that he had made himself by inlaying semiprecious stones in cement (fig. 6.12). Polished Brazilian agates including a rare tiger-eye from the Johannesburg mines dominated, but there were also topaz and amethyst crystals. The house contained so many uncommon things that some suggested that if the shop ever burned, it could be reopened the next day with the curios that Standley kept at the family home.

6.10. In his later years Standley liked to putter in his garden, sit outside his West Seattle home, and talk with visitors who arrived on tour buses. He installed totem poles against the house and in the side yard and christened the home "Totem Place."

6.11. At times there were as many as thirteen totem poles installed among the monkey puzzle trees, shell constructions, and shrubs in the side yard at Totem Place.

Newspaper articles talked about the Standley home and its totem poles, the shop sold postcards of the house and its embellishments, and Totem Place became a sometime stop on tour bus routes. Standley loved to work in the garden or to sit on the porch in his elk horn chair and walk out to talk with visitors. As one interviewer put it, he had a "penchant for retailing . . . the odd tales that are woven around the things . . . the peculiar manners in which they fell into his hands."[41] If visitors had the time, he might invite them inside. His daughter Ruby James never knew who was coming for dinner, as Standley was also prone to inviting important customers to his home on the spur of the moment, especially those who shared his special passion for agates, shell-and-cement structures, or other curiosities that he could show there.

When Ruby married Russell James, they moved into Totem Place. After Standley's wife, Isabelle, died in 1920, the Jameses stayed on to keep house for him and to raise their own family. After Standley's death in 1940, Totem Place was sold. The agates were taken out of the crumbling fireplace and reused in the home to which the James family moved. Eventually the one totem pole left at the house as a marker disappeared, the side yard land was sold, and a three-story home was built there. The house passed through several hands until it

6.12. Standley liked to show off the agate fireplace he had constructed in the living room at Totem Place. The editor of *Hobbies* magazine was so impressed that he featured it on the cover of the February–March 1919 issue, flanked by photographs of Haida and Tsimshian totem poles.

was purchased in the 1990s by a family that has restored many of its original interior and exterior features.[42] Totem Place lost its unique identity when all but one of the totem poles in the side yard were put back into Ye Olde Curiosity Shop's stock after Standley's death. But the shop's identity, bound to the totem pole from almost its beginning, remained. Its founder, Standley, had been a major player in establishing the totem pole as a symbol for Seattle and the Pacific Northwest.

CHAPTER SEVEN

Totem Poles, Ye Olde Curiosity Shop, and Seattle

Indian totem poles carved by natives of
Alaska and British Columbia. Descriptive
cards explaining the Indian mythological
geneology [*sic*] of a fast disappearing race.
—Ye Olde Curiosity Shop Catalog C, 1916

IN FALL 1899, JUST ABOUT THE TIME THAT J. E. STANDLEY AND HIS FAMILY MOVED to the Northwest, Seattle installed a large Alaskan totem pole in its downtown. It was the city's first large public sculpture. Although there was controversy over the pole, especially because it had been simply cut down and hauled away from a Tlingit Indian village in Southeast Alaska, in the public mind it quickly became known as the Seattle Totem Pole, a symbol for the city. The pole, which pictured a combination of animals rendered in forms unlike any with which Standley was familiar, captured his fancy, and he believed it would intrigue others as well. Most curio and gift shops in Seattle would come to carry miniature totem poles, many of them loose copies of the Seattle Totem Pole, and some would offer a few large poles, but Ye Olde Curiosity Shop's emphasis on tall totem poles would set it apart.[1] Over the next few decades, totem poles would become a mainstay of both the shop's image and its stock.

Only the earliest shop photograph, taken in 1901 at the Madison Street location, when it was called The Curio (see fig. 1.6), shows no totem poles (although pictures of Kwakiutl houseposts appear in the framed photomontage hung outside the shop). By the second photograph, however, taken a year or so later at the same location (fig. 1.8), Standley displayed two small totem poles at the left edge of the window. An eleven-foot pole appears in the 1908–09 Asahel Curtis photograph of the Wrst shop on Colman Dock (fig. 1.12), and there are large poles in all exterior shop photographs thereafter. The Curiosity Shop would maintain the greatest stock of large poles in town. During the 1930s it stored them at the rear of the shop, and after the 1937 move, along the entrance and exit ramps to the ferry. A photograph of the shop's interior from about 1912 (fig. 2.1) demonstrates that by this time miniature totem poles had become an important part of the shop's regular stock.

The Seattle Totem Pole: City Symbol and Public Art

In 1899 when a group of prominent Seattle businessmen on excursion to Southeast Alaska came to the village of Tongass and found it seemingly deserted, they chose one of the most elaborate totem poles in sight, chopped it down with an ax, and hauled it home. There they presented the pole to the Chamber of Commerce. News articles from the late 1930s, when a crisis had arisen over what to do with the then decaying pole, detail much of its history and disclose that Seattleites harbored mixed understanding and feelings about the pole even after its several decades in the city. The Tongass Raven pole had been erected by the Kyinanuk (Kininnook) family of the Raven lineage as a memorial to an ancestor, Chief of All Women, who had drowned in the Nass River. As was traditional, the pole had been raised in conjunction with a memorial potlatch, an occasion when family members and visitors of both lineages came together to honor the deceased and to validate the transfer of inherited privileges. As was also tradition, the pole had then been left to slowly weather and eventually return to the earth.[2]

The carving on the Tongass Raven Pole referenced three myth-time stories of the Kyinanuk family. On top, Raven the trickster holds the crescent moon in his beak, referring to his gift of light to humankind. Below him, the woman who married a frog perches atop her frog husband and holds their frog child. Below is Mink, often Raven's helper; then comes Raven standing atop a whale (blackfish) holding a seal in its mouth. Greedy Raven had consumed much of a whale, refusing to share the bounty with others nearby. Raven's grandfather, from whom Raven stole the light, stands at the base of the pole. These Raven stories reflected the Kyinanuk family's Raven moiety; the frog and whale stories were clan stories.[3]

The Tongass Raven pole was erected in Seattle on October 18, 1899, in a small triangular park created at First Avenue and Yesler Street in what would become known as Pioneer Square (see fig. 1.4, fig. 7.1). For Seattleites and visitors it was now known as the Seattle Totem Pole. Over the years the pole gradually suffered changes: some were cosmetic while others altered the pole's original meaning. For example, before the pole's installation, the lower figure's down-curved beak, which had been broken in transit, was replaced with a short blunt one. The original black, red, and blue-green painting, following the principles of classic Tlingit style, was altered by painting and repainting in various colors, in the city's attempt to keep the pole bright. Eventually putty was dabbed into holes that had been caused by dry rot, and guy wires were added to provide support.

The transformations in the meaning of the pole were more profound. In Tongass the pole had reminded village members daily of the ancestor whom it memorialized, of the power and prestige of the family who had raised it, and of that family's inherited and owned stories about myth-time ancestors whose activities were cited on the pole. In Seattle, however, few people held any knowledge about these meanings. The *Seattle Post-Intelligencer* described the pole as "emphatically unique, barbaric, bizarre . . . each fantastical figure facing resolutely up First Ave." In a sort of salvage paradigm, Will H. Thompson, who had been part of the excursion to Alaska when the pole was taken, defended the "acquisition," insisting that in Seattle "the totem will voice the native's deeds with surer speech than if lying prone on moss and fern on the shore of Tongass Island."[4]

7.1. "Unveiling the Seattle Totem." The totem pole taken from the Tlingit village of Tongass by local businessmen on a cruise was dedicated in downtown Seattle on October 18, 1899. It quickly became known as the Seattle Totem Pole. Photograph courtesy Museum of History and Industry, Seattle.

Misinformation about the pole's meaning was commonplace, and Standley was in part responsible. In 1910 he copyrighted and published on five-by-twelve-inch cardstock a "History of the Indian Carved Totem Pole."[5] The text came in part from Standley's friend L. L. Bales and his article "Totem Poles," published in 1908 in *Outdoor Life*.[6] Bales's explanation of the pole, probably composed as he observed and interpreted it at Standley's request, combined fantasy with misinformation. According to Bales (and Standley's information card), Raven held not the crescent moon but a herring, and the woman who married a frog was interpreted to be a medicine man, distinguished as such because he held his clan totem, the frog, upside down and by its hind legs. Mink was misidentified as Annihoots the brown bear, and Raven atop the whale was thought to be an eagle rampant.

Bales correctly identified the blackfish (orca) as a variety of the whale family, but he did not know that the small face just forward of the fin was a personification of the whale's blow hole. Instead, he took it to be a human, a signal that the pole's owner had slaves. Bales misidentified Grandfather Raven as an eagle rampant and, in an extraordinary leap of imagination, he explained the formline ovoids on its wings as halved eggs signifying embryonic life. Although Bales had lived in Sitka, Alaska, and had previously written about totem poles, his knowledge was obviously limited. He did not recognize even the widely known legend of Raven giving the light to humankind and was unfamiliar with the northern Northwest Coast formline system that was typically used on flat areas such as wings.

Despite these errors in interpretation, Bales's explanation was perpetuated for many years. Although university history professor Edmond Meany had acquired a true account of the pole's stories in September 1904 from Tlingit David E. Kininnook of Ketchikan—and published it in the *Seattle Post-Intelligencer*—these facts had been forgotten.[7] The fledgling University of Washington did not yet have an anthropologist, and Meany fielded any questions about Native culture. Information about such arcane subjects as totem poles was almost nonexistent in 1910 when Standley first published his Totem History card. As is often the case in such a vacuum, the one who publishes first becomes the expert, and to Standley and no doubt countless others, Bales's article had in effect credentialed him as a knowledgeable source. Also, with Standley's combination of visibility and certainty, the information he offered had come to be generally trusted.[8] Not until after the Seattle Totem Pole burned in late October 1938 and the *Seattle Post-Intelligencer* again published Bales and Standley's Totem History would university anthropologist Viola Garfield set the record straight with her 1940 publication, *The Seattle Totem Pole.*[9]

In October 1938, after forty years of slow deterioration and during a period when Seattle was experiencing a rash of petty arsons, "firebugs" stuffed papers into a dry-rot hole at the base of the Seattle Totem Pole and lit them.[10] Over the next several months, articles and letters to the editor in local newspapers followed, debating the meaning and symbolic value of the damaged pole and how (or even whether) it should be replaced. The debate can be traced through the *Post-Intelligencer.*[11] There were reservations and explanations about how the pole had been originally acquired. One woman, who had been on the excursion boat in 1899, reported that Fort Tongass had not been abandoned as was originally claimed. Rather, the local men were merely away fishing, and those on board had treated taking the pole "as a sort of Halloween prank." The ship's captain, R. D. McGillivray, told reporters that after he chopped the pole down and cut it in two, he tied the parts together, straddled them, and paddled them out to the ship.[12]

Another reader, whose grandfather had been among those who took the pole, captured conflicting perspectives in a story based on what she had been told as a child. In the story a hired hand tells the children about "that great big totem pole that the brave men stole from the Injuns!" Their father returns and insists that the men were not thieves because they had paid for the pole; after "some lawyer got wind of the matter and talked it up to the Indians," each man involved paid out several hundred dollars.[13] What from a century's distance represents at best ignorance and blatant insensitivity—at worst an inexcusable theft—was thought of little other than as a prank, even after Tongass people complained to Alaska Governor John G. Brady and a payment was eventually negotiated. Several years before this renewed discussion in 1938, a *National Geographic* illustration had already subtly altered history when it described the pole as "purchased from the Indians, who carved it and gave it its original coat of paint."[14]

As the city pondered what to do about the damaged pole, the public discussion was not about whether Seattle was an inappropriate context for a totem pole, but about whether a totem pole was an appropriate emblem for the city. Captain A. J. Goddard of the Alaska-Yukon Pioneers proposed instead a thirty-five-foot bronze statue of an Alaskan prospector to be faced looking north.[15] Some were fond of the pole and begged for its repair; still others saw its being made of wood as the problem, and there were several suggestions to cast the pole in concrete.[16] True to form, Standley's idea was the most ambitious of all. The city could create a unique world attraction by casting electric light poles in the shape of Alaskan Indian totem poles of three or four different designs and placing them on concrete balustrades at the foot of each street entering Alaskan Way.[17]

Dozens of citizens watched in April 1939 as the Seattle Totem Pole was taken down and transported to the Seattle City Light building. Short on funds, the city asked for bids to repair the pole, then after some weeks of consideration, decided on replication instead. The park board hoped that someone would donate a red cedar log, sturdier than the hemlock from which the original had been carved.[18] New differences then arose as local carvers, both Indian and white, vied for the job. The Indian communities of Neah Bay and Queets submitted bids, as did Swinomish carvers from La Conner, who were invited to Seattle for discussion.[19] Belle Simpson, who ran the Nugget Shop in Juneau, Alaska, offered a genuine pole for $3,000, and Ye Olde Curiosity Shop submitted a bid much the same.[20]

An arrangement was eventually made with two Puget Sound Suquamish Indians to do the carving in Woodland Park, where visitors might watch; funding would come from the WPA, the federal government's Works Progress Administration. A news columnist interviewed the two carvers and wrote a sympathetic but not so thinly veiled caution. Although neither had ever carved a totem pole, the men were not apprehensive about the job because they could take measurements from the original pole. The carvers said that "it would help vastly . . . if [they] could only know what they were supposed to be carving on the Seattle pole," but the old totem was related to the tribal history of distant Alaska Indians rather than their own. Within days University of Washington anthropologist Viola Garfield intervened, pointing out to the park board that totem carving was never a Native art among Puget Sound tribes, and declaring that "it would be no more paradoxical for a white man to carve the new totem than for a couple of Suquamish Indians to do it." An advisory committee was appointed.[21]

During the fall a new and far more satisfactory arrangement fell into place. The Tongass Raven Pole would be shipped to Alaska, to Saxman on the Tongass National Forest near Ketchikan, where a U.S. Forest Service–sponsored Civil Conservation Corps workshop was restoring old poles. It would be duplicated and the original returned to those from whom it had been taken years ago. Washington state Senator Warren G. Magnuson would ask the U.S. Congress to pass a special bill permitting the Forest Service to furnish the pole free to Seattle; the Alaska Steamship Company would transport both the old and the new pole free of charge.[22]

In January 1940 the old pole was shipped north to Saxman, where it was replicated by Tlingit head carver Charles Brown, assisted by his father William H. Brown, who did the adze work, and several helpers.[23] The downturned beak and colors of the original pole were restored, and the new painting was slightly elaborated. On April 17, 1940, the new Seattle Totem Pole arrived on the S.S. *Tanana* and was stored while the title was transferred and officials argued over two proposed locations. The original site, now called Pioneer Place, was ultimately chosen, and the pole was raised, facing north, like its predecessor. After a day's delay because of rain, the new Seattle Totem Pole was dedicated on July 27 as a part of the annual Seattle Potlatch festivities.[24]

The Seattle Totem Pole is one of the earliest examples of public art on the West Coast, the first in Seattle. A century later, installing a large public sculpture in the city would involve layers of bureaucracy. Private and public debate about needs, meetings to establish guidelines, and a search for funding would be followed by artist competitions, engineering reports, and finally discussion about the success of the art project itself after installation. In 1899, however, local government officials made the public sculpture decision on the spot when they saw a totem pole they considered abandoned. They simply acquired it, assuming that any details could be worked out. There were no debates, designs, engineering reports. It was not until forty years later, when the pole needed replacing, that extended public discussion took place; even then it was primarily informal, through the newspapers. By the time the Seattle Totem Pole was set afire in 1938, it had become a public symbol, a facilitator of civic consciousness, meaningful enough to local citizens to be worthy of debate.

Public art often draws directly on local historical memories and traditions. There were other images unique to young Seattle, a city that had quickly grown from its ambitious pioneer roots. Some suggested the image of a logger or a goldminer, although the latter would also have been considered an appropriated symbol, alluding to Seattle's proprietary attitude toward Alaska. It was not the past, however, that Seattle was intent on celebrating; rather, city boosters looked to an expansive vision of Seattle's future. When rebuilding the downtown, which had been destroyed by the great fire of 1889, city fathers had chosen to emulate such eastern cities as Chicago and Pittsburgh by constructing substantial stone buildings in Romanesque Revival style. Placing public sculptures in city parks and squares was also a well-established tradition in the East, and in 1899 serendipity had made a truly unique sculpture, the Tongass Totem Pole, "available" to Seattle.

Despite the public's general ignorance of the pole's real meaning and use, by the 1930s the sculpture had come to meet what has been called "the challenge of public art." It had become a visual symbol around which private and public emotion centered, an image that resonated within the community and would continue to do so.[25] Throughout the debate over the Seattle Totem Pole there were catchy headlines in Seattle newspapers, such as "Totem Pole Hollow! It's Only a Shell of Its Former Self," "Totem's Waistline Dimensions Reduced by One Foot," and "Totem Will Be According to Indian Hoyle." The ongoing discussion ignited new interest both in totem poles and in their use as public sculpture. Standley's 1938 letter to the editor suggesting that multiple totem poles be cast in concrete to mark the streets entering Alaskan Way may have inspired a group of four identical cast concrete poles mounted in 1940 at either end of the Capital Boulevard Bridge at what was once the entrance to Olympia.[26]

Just as Seattle had appropriated the Seattle Totem Pole as its first public sculpture, Standley and others immediately appropriated it for use in association with their businesses.[27] The pole was featured in city booster and tourist literature from almost the day it was erected. A loose sketch of it appeared on the cover of each Official Daily Program of the AYPE in 1909. The first known catalog put out by the Ye Olde Curiosity Shop, about 1910, offered the Seattle Totem Pole in cast antimony, on the handle of souvenir spoons, and burned into natural wood plaques.[28] Standley used the pole on his letterhead and in advertising (see fig. 7.2) and published his "fully copyrighted" explanation of it titled Totem History. Vague on the history and distribution of totem poles, Standley believed them to be an emblem of the entire Northwest, to be "one of our big bets" in tourism. He encouraged local carvers to replicate the Seattle Totem Pole, especially in miniature, and offered wooden models of it and other

7.2. Like some other businesses, Ye Olde Curiosity Shop used a drawing of the Seattle Totem Pole on its letterhead and in advertising. This pamphlet from the mid-1920s was printed in red and black on a yellow background.

poles in sizes ranging from four to forty-eight inches in all of the shop's catalogs. Standley's letterhead image, based on a drawing of the pole, retained a relatively close likeness, but the locally carved miniature poles quickly became simplifications.

Explanations of Totem Poles

Shops that sold totem poles were expected to provide explanations and be able to answer questions about them. Like the Alaska Steamship Company and others who took visitors to see poles in situ, curio shops developed brochures and descriptive cards about them. There was little published material available to writers of such tourist literature, and they often combined bits of information from various sources, including each other's brochures. The clippings and pamphlets saved in the records of Ye Olde Curiosity Shop provide only a sampling of information that was popularly disseminated on totem poles during Standley's lifetime, but they include some of the most common misinterpretations. Standley did not have much formal schooling, but his attitudes and confusion about Native cultures cannot be blamed on limited education alone. The misinformation that he and his information cards and catalogs perpetuated for decades echoed the era's widely held assumptions and beliefs (fig. 7.3).

Most explanations in advertising brochures and published articles focused on the concept of totemism, the meaning and use of totem poles, and the identification of the figures on them. Ignorance and preconceptions influenced both by the Christian faith of many of the writers and Darwinian concepts informed value judgments and clouded attempts at explanation. The stylized animal creatures appeared strange to many and aroused Christian anxieties about demons, evil, witchcraft, and the worship of idols. From a Darwinian perspective the poles represented the less developed thinking and artistic skills of primitive man as compared with those of civilized man. If Darwin was correct—that humans had in fact evolved from animals—then the totemism that totem poles represented bore this out.[29] Although the long discussions in such works as Bales's "Totem Poles" (1908) and Reverend J. P. D. Llwyd's *The Message of an Indian Relic* (1909) reflect these ideas more fully, the same are also implicit concerns in the short explanations that Standley and other businesses put out in their advertising.[30]

Standley first distributed his card called "History of Totem Poles" at the AYPE to advertise the Ravenna Park "Totem Village" and his "Free Priced

Booklet '1001 Curious Things.'" The card explained: "Totemism embraces forms of Deity, Demon, Myths, Charms, Evil Spirits, Legend and Witchcraft. These Totemic symbols are regarded with superstitious, almost sacred, reverence." Figures on the poles were called "grotesque": "Many are gaudily painted, elaborately carved, tracing the geneology [*sic*] of a once semi-savage, barbarous people." In a silly play on words Standley referenced the Seattle Totem Pole: "Tote means to carry, so the mystic spirits prompted Seattleites to tote off the best 60-foot cedar Totem Pole in the bunch from Tongass Island, Alaska, 1897, where it had stood for 110 years and place it in Pioneer Square, settling the bill later." Over time, as Standley learned more—perhaps under the influence of friends like George T. Emmons—he tempered his language a bit in the information card, replacing the terms "Deity, Demon" with "forms of Geneaology [*sic*]" and dropping the mention of "toting" the totem. He also eliminated "gaudily painted" and "grotesque."[31] Although the term *grotesque* (derived from the word *grotto*) had once been neutral (meaning fanciful, bizarre, something markedly departing from the natural), it was becoming more and more pejorative.[32]

Standley's early information cards, as did information from other shops, explained the genealogical relationship with animals referenced in totemism as the transmigration of human intelligence to animals.[33] Totemism was a difficult concept for people who experienced animals primarily as domesticated and considered humans superior. But Northwest Coast Indian traditions referenced a time when ancestors depended on hunting to survive, when hunters knew animals intimately and respected their special and enviable sensory and physical skills like flying or surviving underwater. Standley's explanation of transmigration was thus backward. In Northwest Coast stories about the encounters between their ancestors and animals in myth-time, it was the animals who gave their knowledge and power to humans so that *they* might survive. By virtue of this ancestral relationship, some animals and other beings came to be regarded as totems—emblems of kin groups—and were represented on totem poles. Totemism is the belief in that affiliation.

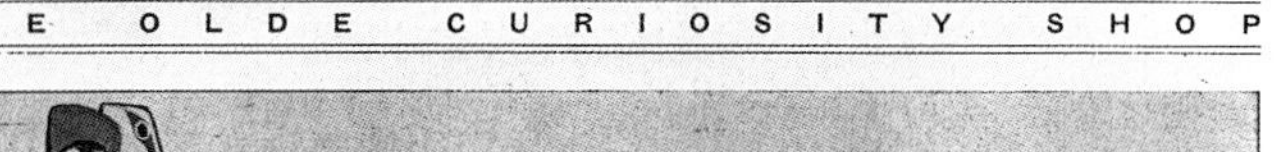

INDIAN TOTEM POLES ***carved by the Natives of Alaska and British Columbia***

Totemism embraces forms of genealogy, myths, evil spirits, legends and witchcraft. Totemic symbols are regarded with superstitious, almost sacred reverence, but not idoltary. Family Clan Totem is transmitted by inheritance. In marriage the wife's Totem is added, be it whale, bear, frog, fish, raven, eagle or wolf; some times two Clans are joined together, such as half bear and half whale, signifying his ancestors belonged to the bear and whale Clan. We have a great many Totem Poles in miniature, from 4 to 20 inches high.

64—Sitka Totem 12-in. 2.25; 16-in. 3.00; 19-in. 4.50
65—Kassan Totem 10-in. 1.50; 12-in 2.25
66—Facsimile of 60-ft. Totem in Pioneer Square, Seattle, with complete history and meaning of figures....8-in. 1.10; 11-in. 1.50
67—Yakatat Totem ....5-in. .45; 6-in. .65; 8-in. 1.00
68—Toyet Totem ....4½-in. .30; 6-in. .65
69—Alert Totem ....4½-in. .30; 6-in. .65; 8-in. 1.00; 10-in. 1.50; 12-in. 2.25
70—Stickine Totem 8-in. 1.10; 10-in. 1.50
71—Haines Totem 10-in. 1.75; 12-in. 2.25; 14-in. 2.50

We have larger sizes from 3 to 10 feet high, at $5.00 to $10.00 per foot, according to the width and carving. 10 to 20 feet high at $7.00 to $15.00 per foot, according to the width and carving.

Write for Information

All Prices include prepaid delivery charges.

PAGE ONE

7.3. Ye Olde Curiosity Shop began carrying wooden model totem poles based primarily on well-known Alaskan poles as soon as Standley could arrange for some. This photograph, last used in the 1939 Fortieth Anniversary Catalog (Catalog I), appeared in brochures and catalogs beginning in the early 1920s.

Some writers interpreted totem poles in terms of Euro-American institutions—as "family registers," "emblems of brotherhoods, clans and families," "for the most part a history of the families owning them."[34] One writer explained, "Instead of being preserved in a written or printed form as civilized people do, [the crest] was recorded by a series of carvings or paintings."[35] Seattle's Hudson Bay Fur Company and Walter Water's Bear Totem Store in Wrangell, Alaska, erroneously suggested that clan symbols related to hunting: "The clan of the mighty bear hunter were therefore known as bears, of a whale hunter as whales, etc."[36] In actuality, Native explanations of totems, the kin group emblems also called crests, is that they were acquired through myth-time encounters of ancestors with supernatural creatures who gave them special powers, or by purchase with an ancestor's life.[37]

The figures on totem poles were often wildly misinterpreted. Many believed that the poles actually told stories (rather than simply referenced them), and they were thus frustrated by their inability to find out about the specifics of the creatures and tales. A recurring complaint was that it was difficult to acquire true knowledge about poles. Writer Lloyd W. MacDowell explained: "The legends which the totem poles illustrate are the nursery tales and traditions of a primitive people. . . . Due to reticence and deliberate misconception on the part of the Indians themselves many weird and untrue stories have been circulated about the Alaska totems."[38] He made the point that the older Natives were reluctant to talk with white people, and the younger ones said they knew nothing about these ways (which was often true because by the 1890s when MacDowell was writing, Northwest Coast tribal cultures had suffered severe disruption and many young people had been sent away to boarding schools and knew little of their Native traditions). Explanations had not been written down because the tribes had no written languages. In such encounters, the Euro-American belief in the democratization of knowledge—that all have a right to know—collided with a cultural system in which oral tradition rather than written language carried history and culture, a system in which knowledge was owned. Because knowledge held power, it must be protected and shared only with a receiver who was experienced and wise enough to respect that knowledge and use it with care. It is doubtful that many readers thought deeply about the confused explanations of totem poles offered in what they read, and more likely that readers invested their own interpretations.

The Rookwood Pottery Totem Poles and the New Washington Hotel

On October 21, 1908, the *Seattle Daily Times* reported that earlier that day patrons had rushed the doors of the elegant New Washington Hotel even before its official noon opening, vying to be the first to buy a cigar or curio or to eat in the largest and most elaborately decorated dining room in the Northwest.[39] In addition to picturing the hotel's front desk and marble staircase, the article showed the Lounging Room and its focal point—an elaborate fireplace with flanking totem poles and a tile mural of Mount Rainier, made by the famous Rookwood Pottery (fig. 7.4). As both the totem pole and Mount Rainier had come to represent Seattle and the Pacific Northwest in civic consciousness, what better way to create a regional ambiance in the new hotel than to combine the two symbols.

7.4. Totem Fire Place, New Washington Hotel, Seattle, 1908. The photographer did not distinguish between the two Washington Hotels when he labeled the photograph. Standley was also incorrect when he wrote on the back many years later: "They were made of pottery in New Jersey about 1910. I loaned my 2 big totem poles for the Hotel to copy these 2 totem poles." The faience mantle, totem poles, and tile mural above and to the sides were made in 1907 or 1908 by Rookwood Pottery of Cincinnati, Ohio.

Standley wrote on the back of his photograph of the new hotel's fireplace that the totem poles were based on ones loaned by Ye Olde Curiosity Shop. Although this is unconfirmed, it is easy to imagine that Standley himself could have enthusiastically suggested the Mount Rainier–totem pole tableau, offering his poles to be copied. Could the New Washington Hotel's architects have concurred, having heard of the elaborate tile work that Cincinnati's Rookwood Pottery had recently created for fashionable hotels, banks, and railway stations in the East? Perhaps they had seen its prizewinning architectural faience (an opaque glazed earthenware) exhibit at the 1904 St. Louis Exposition, or its new 1907 catalog of architectural embellishments. An installation by Rookwood could place Seattle's new hotel in league with those of cities it hoped to emulate.

Rookwood Pottery had built an international reputation for art pottery in the years since Maria Nichols founded it in 1880, a time when china painting was a popular and acceptable occupation for women. The company had grown steadily, experimenting with special vase forms and glazes, and had won top prizes at expositions in Buffalo, Chicago, Paris, St. Louis, and Turin. It would again, in 1909, at the AYPE in Seattle. The Rookwood architectural department, which worked directly with architects to produce interior and exterior embellishments of faience, expanded in 1901. Hotels, businesses, theaters, and a host of public and private buildings across the country ordered mantel facings, large tile murals, and even entire rooms. Rookwood fabricated fountains for department stores, designed garden installations, and produced moldings and decorative panels for twenty-three New York subway stations. The years 1907–13 were the most successful for the architectural department, but it was never as profitable as hoped. The hand-tailored design and double-fired process were intensive and expensive.[40] No wonder that the order from Seattle's New Washington Hotel for an elaborate faience fireplace—fourteen and a half feet by twelve and a half feet, of special design and framed in totem poles—was noted in Rookwood records with care. Its $1,250 price was significant.[41]

After consultation with a client, a Rookwood artist made watercolor sketches of all of the project details. For murals the sketches were then photographically enlarged to actual size to serve as full-scale blueprints. The Mount Rainier mural at the New Washington Hotel would have been created in this way. How the design of the totem poles was handled is not recorded. Although Standley could have shipped the poles so drawings or castings could be made, it appears that he sent photographs. The pole at the left of the Rookwood fireplace is a version of the local landmark, the Seattle Totem Pole, and that at the right represents the Chief Shakes Pole at Wrangell, Alaska. Both were among Standley's favorites and, along with the Alert Bay Pole, were the most often replicated throughout Ye Olde Curiosity Shop's history. The Rookwood poles appear to have been based specifically on two model poles that are pictured in the shop's 1915 Catalog B (fig. 7.5) as well as two subsequent ones and an undated postcard that the shop sold for years.[42] In the postcard both poles are visible in the upper left-hand corner, the Shakes-type pole on the left with the Seattle-type pole to its right. Misinterpretations of details suggest that the pottery studio was working from both the Catalog B photograph and the postcard. The poles in the photographs and the faience poles share the same figures in the same form, with some license taken in how the figures are combined.[43] What happened to the Rookwood mantle and mural is not known. In 1964 the New Washington Hotel was purchased by the Catholic Archdiocese of Seattle and remodeled into the Josephinum, a residence for senior citizens.[44]

Other Totem Poles for Seattle

The totem poles that Standley acquired for William W. Beck for Ravenna Park during the AYPE were the first group of poles erected in Seattle and among the first large poles Standley commissioned (figs. 3.9–3.11). After the originals were deposited in the Washington State Museum in 1913, they were rarely displayed; however, at least two poles very similar to these were carved locally and installed on either side of Standley's new shop when it reopened in January 1917 after the rebuilding of Colman Dock (see fig. 1.14).

7.5. The Rookwood faience totem poles appear to have been replicated using photographs, including this one that advertised model poles about 1915, in Catalog B. The Rookwood Architectural Department worked from poles two and seven, versions of the Seattle Totem Pole and the Chief Shakes Pole.

On July 21, 1939, a news article announced that not one but two totem poles had been given to the city.[45] The Daughters of the American Revolution had donated a pole that would be dedicated in Woodland Park the following week. The other, a gift from Standley, would soon be set up in Belvedere Park, on Admiral Way in West Seattle. The Woodland Park pole was the work of Snohomish Chief William Shelton, whose last pole, a much taller one, was given to the state the following year, to be erected on the state capitol grounds in Olympia.[46] Both Shelton poles were rendered in a style that Salish carvers developed after WPA programs in the 1930s provided funds for several Washington state tribes to carve poles. Totem poles were not part of native Salish culture, and Shelton and other carvers turned to the sculptural tradition associated with the interior "story poles" of their traditional shed-roof houses. On these posts individual figures relating to family and personal guardian power stories of the maker were carved in relief against a flat background. Because of their distinct differences in form from Northern and Central Coast totem poles, Salish poles like Shelton's have sometimes been erroneously confused with totem poles carved expressly for the tourist trade. These twentieth-century Salish totem poles erected outside relate, however, to closely held family and individual knowledge and are an expansion of deeply held spiritual traditions.

The totem pole (fig. 7.6) presented to the city by Standley was to be installed at Grand View Point in West Seattle near his home. The information that Standley provided reporters about what came to be called the West Seattle Pole contained more fiction than truth. A short newspaper article announcing the gift alleged that it had been "carved by the Bella Bella Indians of Vancouver Island" in 1901 and perpetuated L. L. Bales's explanation of the ovoid as an egg cut in half symbolizing embryonic life."[47] The pole was actually the work of Sam Williams, a Nuu-chah-nulth carver from Vancouver Island, who supplied poles to Ye Olde Curiosity Shop for more than half a century. It had been made in the early 1930s and stored with other poles along one of the ferry automobile ramps that bracketed the shop. Throughout the twentieth century, four generations of the Williams family carved for the shop.

During the earliest years of his shop Standley began to associate the name Bella Bella with Nuu-chah-nulth carvers from Vancouver Island. Tribal misidentification of Northwest Coast Indians and objects was common at the time in both the United States and Canada, but Haida was the more typical

What a View

Star Oct 12 1939

Here is Naomi Stone, 4219 W. Atlantic street, examining the totem pole which Daddy Standley erected in West Seattle, overlooking Elliott Bay.

View From New Totem Pole Draws Praise

While the rest of the city argued whether totem poles are beautiful or ugly—an attraction or a menace—Daddy Standley has put up a real totem pole in West Seattle.

"The people from the east come to Seattle expecting to see totem poles," Daddy Standley, who has the Ye Olde Curiosity Shop, declared. "The doggone fools who want to put up statues that the tourists can see in every other city in the country, just don't seem to be able to understand that Seattle is in the northwest and that totem poles are one of our big bets."

The pole which Daddy Standley erected at the head of Admiral way, which is one of the finest view spots in West Seattle to see the city, was carved by the Bella Bella Indians 40 years ago.

"I picked that spot because 30 years ago when Frank G. Carpenter of the New York Herald was here, he declared that the view from this point was not excelled by any city he saw during his whole world tour," Daddy Standley declared.

75 Per Cent of U. W. Students Self-Supporting

A good 75 per cent of the 10,500 students now attending the University of Washington contribute to their own expenses by working part time or by piling up enough ready cash during the summer to pay for part of their schooling themselves.

Figures released today by Norman Hillis, head of the University employment service, showed that 2500 of the students are entirely self-supporting.

Most of those employed are working as houseboys, dishwashers or waiting table, or do all sorts of odd jobs. However, they are filling all sorts of positions from steeplejack to mortician, Hillis said.

7.6. With discussion hot in local newspapers over whether the totem pole should be an emblem for Seattle, Standley weighed in in the affirmative by donating to the city what came to be called the West Seattle Pole. Although newspapers identified it as old and Bella Bella, the pole was actually made in the 1930s by Nuu-chah-nulth carver Sam Williams.

misattribution. Exactly who the Bella Bella of British Columbia were was confusing and remains so today. Early observers applied the name Bella Bella to the principal Heiltsuk Reserve allotted in 1882; to the speakers of the northern Wakashan language, Heiltsuk, who later moved to Campbell Island on the central west coast of British Columbia beginning about 1933; and to two communities, Bella Bella and New Bella Bella.[48] The name Bella Bella has no relation to Vancouver Island or the Nuu-chah-nulth, however. How Standley came to use the term as he did is not clear. A carver may have identified himself as Bella Bella. Bella Bella was one of the villages where excursion steamers sometimes called, and Standley would have heard or read about it. Perhaps he decided that because it had pleasant connotations and was easy to pronounce, he would identify Williams and other Nuu-chah-nulth carvers as Bella Bella.[49]

The West Seattle totem pole suffered the ravages of weather that other poles in the city did. When Parks Department employees repainted it in 1955, the *Seattle Times* provided the pole with a new history: it was "believed to have been carved by the Haida Indian Tribe of the Queen Charlotte Islands."[50] Despite the misidentification, unlike articles written in 1939 when the pole was originally donated, this article reflected an increased understanding of what totem poles were actually about, a trend that continued through the century. Repainting the West Seattle Pole did not preserve it from rot, however, and in 1965 it was taken down for replication. As had been the case with the Seattle Totem Pole, there were those who believed that they could make the copy, although they had not carved totem poles before. The Parks Department accepted the volunteer services of two Boeing engineers with wood-carving experience and provided them a log. The new pole was dedicated in August 1966, with speeches by park board officials and the introduction of the new Miss West Seattle and her court. Curiously, the old pole was now reported to have been carved by the Bella Bella of the Queen Charlotte Islands.[51] The plaque on the original pole, which cited Standley as the donor, was replaced with one acknowledging only the Parks Department.

The appropriation was now complete. The original West Seattle Pole, made for sale by an Indian carver with little tribal tradition of totem poles, was already distanced from what totem poles are really about. The copy was simply another piece of publicly owned sculpture, in a totem pole form now associated in the public mind with Seattle, and an emblem of the largesse of local government. Like the Seattle Totem Pole, the West Seattle Pole became a popular image on postcards, usually colored in bright yellow, green, and orange-red.

Early Suppliers: Nuu-chah-nulth Carvers and Commercial Souvenir Suppliers

Ye Olde Curiosity Shop never carried a great many totem poles from the northern Northwest Coast. The supplier books from the 1920s record only two sources for northern poles: Thomas Deasy, the Indian agent at Massett for "black jadeite totem poles," and "Capt. Edenshaw, Old Massett, B.C. he is a big man among the natives."[52] Standley was surely referring to the famous Haida artist Charles Edenshaw, although he confused him with his relative James Edenso (Edenshaw), who was called Captain.[53] About 1820, Haida men began carving argillite pipes to sell to visitors, and throughout the century they added other forms, including model totem poles. Charles Edenshaw was the best known of the Haida carvers who carved model poles in both wood and argillite, the black slatelike stone that was available only in the Queen Charlotte Islands. He made carvings for general sale and groups of model totem poles and house fronts that were commissioned by museums to replicate masterpieces in Native villages now abandoned.

Standley could easily have purchased Tlingit wooden model poles from John Feusi or Walter Waters, both of whom were shop dealers in Alaska who supplied him with other Tlingit articles. What he needed most, however, was to assure himself a large, affordable, and dependable enough supply of wooden model poles to be able to advertise them in the catalogs he began putting out about 1910 (see figs. 7.3, 7.5). For these he came to rely on carvers living locally. He also turned to Japan for inexpensive totem pole souvenirs carved in ivory and bone. One of the local men on whom Ye Olde Curiosity Shop came to depend was Nuu-chah-nulth carver Sam Williams, probably the man pictured sitting with his carving tools in the later photograph of the Madison Street shop (see fig. 1.8). Williams was born about 1880 and raised at Nitinat, a tiny community near Cowichan Lake on Vancouver Island.[54] Little is know about his early years. Although he had a traditional upbringing in a family with traditional artistic lines, Williams probably had limited if any training as a carver. Around the turn of the century he moved to Seattle and settled on the Duwamish River flats between Seattle and West Seattle in what Standley called the Indian Village. About 1901 Standley arranged for him to carve for the shop.

The Nuu-chah-nulth on Vancouver Island and the Makah in Washington were related and had freely moved back and forth across the Strait of Juan de Fuca for centuries, so they were allowed to travel between the United States and Canada without documents or customs restrictions during the early years

7.7. Standley wrote "Our old Tillicum Sam" on the back of this photograph taken of Sam Williams outside Ye Olde Curiosity Shop in March 1933. "Tillicum" meant "very good friend" in the Chinook trade jargon that Standley and others with Alaska ties still used during the first decades of the twentieth century. Neither pole in the photograph was carved by Williams.

of the twentieth century. They usually rode second class on the lower deck of the Canadian Pacific ferries. Multiple factors encouraged Nuu-chah-nulths to come to Washington, and a number of families lived semipermanently in the Puget Sound region. The Canadian policy of removing Indian children to boarding schools caused a number of families to move across the Strait during the early twentieth century. Some Indians felt that they were treated better in Seattle than in Vancouver or Victoria. There were economic reasons as well for relocating. Washington offered seasonal work in the strawberry and hop fields, and in Seattle's flourishing tourist trade, they were paid more for their carvings.

In 1904, Franz Boas's Kwakiutl-speaking assistant George Hunt verified an economic difference. While collecting Indian artifacts for the American Museum of Natural History, he wrote Boas about the high prices that the Nootka of Friendly Cove were asking: "I never see any Body like these People for asking so a High Price for there things as this People, for they say that they can go to seatle and tacoma and get High Price for What Ever they Bring there." For those who chose to live in Seattle, there was a steady market for all they could carve. Again, historian Douglas Cole's observation that Natives entered and exploited the art and artifact market themselves, and welcomed the opportunity, comes to mind.[55]

Williams was accommodating and popular with Standley and other curio proprietors such as "Mack" McKillop and Herman Krupp, for whom he also carved. Standley felt proprietary, however, and using the Chinook jargon term for "very good friend," he wrote "Our old Tillicum Sam" on the back of a photograph he had taken of Williams outside the shop in March 1933 (fig. 7.7). He encouraged Williams to carve exclusively for the shop and sometimes undermined his competitors. Carmen McKillop recalls that Williams would begin a pole for her husband, who ran Mack's Totem Shop, and Standley or Krupp would come along and buy it before Mack could pick it up.

Although he made miniature totem poles, Williams preferred to carve large ones. Several poles that Joe James identifies as Sam Williams's work appear in shop photographs; some still belong to the shop. The earliest poles attributed to Williams are two tall ones, probably dating from the 1920s. One stood at Standley's West Seattle home, Totem Place. The other stood outside the second Colman Dock shop (see fig 5.8) and was purchased by the cartoon-

ist and adventurer Robert L. Ripley in 1936. Both poles exhibit characteristics that would become typical of Williams's style. Across the Northwest Coast, the height and width of totem poles has been influenced by the size of the trees available. Sam's poles varied, from the tall narrow ones of the 1920s, to shorter ones of "monumental" girth in the 1930s, to short narrower ones later. The sizes of his poles were determined by the size of the logs he could salvage after they broke free from logging booms and washed onto the tide flats near his home (fig. 7.8).

Several of Williams's poles from the 1930s are among groups photographed in 1938 leaning against the back of the Curiosity Shop (fig. 7.9). They are distinctive and unlike classic poles from any Northwest Coast tribe. He appears to have developed his own style after coming to Seattle, influenced especially by the Kwakiutl carving style and by the interior and exterior poles carved about 1877 at Friendly Cove for the Nuu-chah-nulth Captain Jack, a chief of the Mowachat.[56] Williams would have been familiar with the poles, located north of where he grew up. Figures on many of Williams's poles share the very narrow foreheads; thick, curved, blunt-ended brows; eyes with flat round pupils and open, defined eyelid lines; and wide chinless mouths with a single row of large separated teeth characteristic of the Captain Jack poles.

7.8. Sam Williams carved his poles near his home on the Duwamish Flats. Like several of Williams's children, his youngest son, Ray (pictured here), became a carver and produced hundreds of model poles for Standley's and other shops in Seattle. Photograph, 1930s, courtesy of Carmen McKillop.

7.9. The largest totem poles were stored in back or alongside the shop. Of these, photographed in 1938, the pole on the right exhibits characteristics typical of Sam Williams's poles from the 1930s: large flared teeth, blunt noses with large cut-in nostrils, bulging eye orbs with large pupils, and a particular asymmetrical split-U form. The second and third poles from the left are also thought to be his work.

There are also idiosyncrasies on several early Williams poles, including an inexplicably tall triangular nose on some creatures, stretching from above the mouth to the top of the ears (see fig. 7.8, third pole from the left).

Williams developed a distinctive mouth form. The lips, drawn back along the sides of the pole, are formed by cutting in sharply to create a ribbon around an almost rectangular open mouth. Large white rectangular teeth with rounded corners flare out distinctly. On the broader poles he carved in the 1930s, the lips are cut in less deeply and the lower lip forms the chin, rounded at the bottom. Humanlike noses are shaped like an upside-down T and flattened, or more often, a triangle cut with large flaring nostrils. The eyes are more dominant than earlier, with large bulging pupils encircled in white; individual facial components are bolder, adapting to the girth of the poles, and the carving is less exact. On his poles from the 1940s the carving is flatter, more cursory, and shallower than earlier.

Williams's son, Wilson, who may have worked with his father in the 1920s on the tall poles made for Standley, went on to carve both large and small poles and a range of other forms. Wilson Williams developed a related but more fluid style than his father's, with greater detail and a more refined handling of features.[57] He referenced Nuu-chah-nulth activities and stories in his work more often than did his father. Whales, whaling canoes, a dragon with scales, a thunderbird, and head-dressed dancers appear on some of his large poles, on a set of panels carved for the front of Mack's Totem House, and on canoe benches, carved settees, and chests sold at Ye Olde Curiosity Shop and elsewhere (figs. 7.10, 7.11).

With no strong Nuu-chah-nulth tradition of totem poles for the tribe's carvers to reference, Williams and other Nuu-chah-nulth carvers working in Seattle developed their own styles. Trained neither in a traditional apprenticeship system nor in carving for traditional use, they were free to experiment and they did, at the same time maintaining a boldness that was typically Nuu-chah-nulth. Because they were producing primarily for dealers, Williams and his son were influenced by their various suggestions. Nuu-chah-nulth art leaned toward bold forms and bright reds, blues, and later yellows and greens. These characteristics also appealed to Standley, and he encouraged the Williamses to carve deeply and paint the poles with bright colors in weather-hearty enamels. Williams's wife, Nellie, who carved four- and six-inch poles herself, painted most of her husband's poles.

Like the Ravenna Park poles, the Williams poles and thousands of others carved to sell in the Curiosity Shop and other shops in Seattle, British Columbia, and Alaska, are transcultural arts. They developed expressly through an interaction between a producer from one culture and a consumer from another,

7.10. The Williams family also carved for Mack's Totem Curio Shop. Wilson Williams, one of Sam Williams's older sons, carved the central Three Brothers Pole and the panels above the windows. The panel below the left-hand window was carved by Sam Williams, and that below the right-hand window was the work of "Mack" McKillop himself. Photograph, ca. 1940, courtesy of Carmen McKillop.

7.11. Wilson Williams included several of the important Nuu-chah-nulth figures that he carved on the panels for Mack's Totem Shop on this chest, photographed at Ye Olde Curiosity Shop in the late 1930s. On the lid the Thunderbird holds a whale and a sea serpent in his talons. On the front two sea serpents flank a central totem pole.

and represent a group of pragmatic accommodations on the part of the carver, the merchant middleman, and the buyer. These poles are also transtribal; they share characteristics of form and style of several Northwest Coast tribes. Standley needed totem poles to sell, and it was important that they be Indian-made. The Nuu-chah-nulth makers in Seattle needed income, and carving was a skill they knew or were willing to learn and apply to the making of poles. In the process they created a new identity for themselves as totem pole carvers. Most buyers looking for a small memento or a large eye-catching statement for their yards had not seen totem poles, but they held expectations based in the descriptions and explanations of poles in newspapers, travel information, and business advertising such as Standley's. A brightly colored totem pole with frontal stacked animals, especially those like birds, bears, beavers, or wolves that could be easily identified, filled their expectations. A large pole might be too unwieldy and expensive, but there were miniature poles to fit into even the smallest suitcase and budget.

In its 1915 catalog the Curiosity Shop offered wooden poles beginning at fifty cents. The large Chief Shakes Pole copied by Rookwood Pottery was the most expensive at $7.00. The 1916 catalog offered "Hidah" poles in "Black Jade" (argillite) at $1.50 per inch, and "exact reproductions of the Famous Seattle Totem" starting at thirteen inches for $1.50 to four feet for $7.50. Other totems were priced about the same if finely carved, and slightly less if not. By the mid-1920s Standley had few argillite poles to offer, and priced the wooden ones only slightly higher than a decade earlier. Prices held relatively steady throughout the 1930s, dropping slightly by 1940.

The miniature poles pictured in Ye Olde Curiosity Shop photographs and catalogs were the work of a number of different carvers (figs. 7.9, 7.12). Carvers did not sign their poles in Standley's time, but there are definitely identifiable styles that future art historical analysis may isolate. Individuals usually preferred to carve a given pole—the Alert Bay Pole or the Chief Shakes Pole, for instance—and would bring in several dozen almost identical ones at a time. A thunderbird with outstretched wings above a grizzly bear signified an Alert Bay pole. To be "a Chief Shakes," a pole must include a few figures from the original pole—usually the lower "Atlas" figure, encircled

7.12. The legend on this color postcard, still sold in Ye Olde Curiosity Shop in the 1990s, identifies the miniature totem poles as: (1) Alert Bay, (2) Bear Totem, (3) Chief Kyan, (4) Chief Shakes, (5) Seattle Pioneer Square Totem, (6) Raven Flood, and (7) Alert Bay.

raven's head, box, and upper raven with a conical hat. Few visitors would ever see the real Chief Shakes Pole, located in Wrangell, so they were unlikely to feel cheated if a miniature by that name was missing a few figures. Miniatures of the Seattle Totem Pole typically included at least schematic reference to all of the figures of the original pole. The buyer in the shop could see the actual pole nearby and notice if a creature were missing, so its proximity was a factor. Local carvers were also familiar with the pole and could consult it directly rather than having to work from a photograph. Each carver interpreted the figures of a given pole a little differently, varying the proportions of certain features and details.

7.13. In August 1939, a few days after an article announcing that a white man might carve the replacement for the Seattle Totem Pole, the *Seattle Post-Intelligencer* interviewed Haida Chief White Bird (Raymond L. Ready) about his dismay at many of the model poles being sold in Seattle. In the accompanying photograph, Ready contemplated a model of the Chief Shakes Pole in Ye Olde Curiosity Shop. *Seattle Post-Intelligencer* files, 23833, Museum of History and Industry, Seattle.

Most of Williams's children and many of his grandchildren and great-grandchildren have carved for Ye Olde Curiosity Shop. During the seventy-plus years of Joe James's memory, the Williams family has provided more than half of the shop's poles. Ray Williams, Sam Williams's youngest son, liked to carve miniatures of the Seattle Totem Pole and the Alert Bay Pole with many small cuts; his children's work is similar. Other pole carvers who have worked for the shop include Jimmie Johns, Simon Charlie, and Katie Archer. In the 1950s another woman carver specialized in tiny poles, two to two and half inches tall, and brought them in several hundred at a time. Popular as banquet favors, they sold for twenty-five cents each.

Some shops in Seattle sold wooden totem poles that were made in Japan. During the ongoing discussion in the late 1930s about replacing the Seattle Totem Pole, Raymond L. Ready, called Chief White Bird (fig. 7.13), contacted a newspaper to talk about the inauthenticity of Japanese-made model totems that were "peddled to tourists." He decried the rearrangement of characters to fit mass-production methods so that "these totems simply don't tell any story whatever. An Indian would go crazy trying to figure them out." He was also saddened "that there had been such demand for small totems that Alaska Indians who should know better and who should have more respect for their tradition are manufacturing poles out of their imagination, then inventing stories to explain them."[58] Ready may also have been thinking of the poles made by local Nuu-chah-nulth carvers, or by others like Chief White Eagle from the Southwest, who carved both kachina dolls and totem poles for the shop. Through

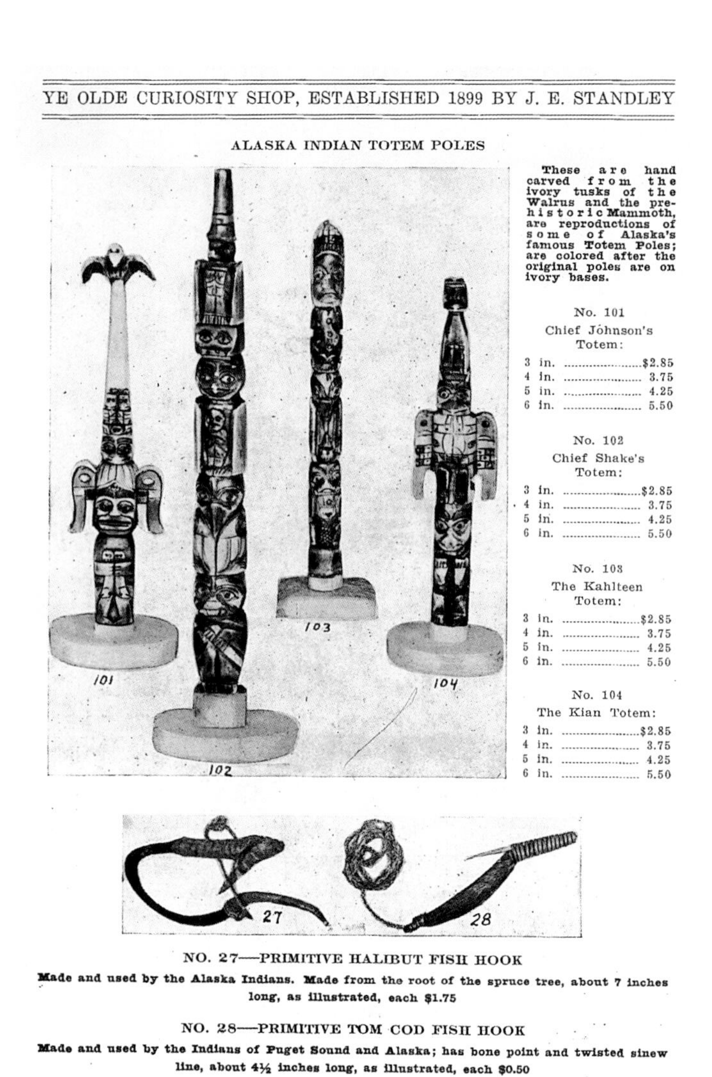

YE OLDE CURIOSITY SHOP, ESTABLISHED 1899 BY J. E. STANDLEY

ALASKA INDIAN TOTEM POLES

These are hand carved from the ivory tusks of the Walrus and the prehistoric Mammoth, are reproductions of some of Alaska's famous Totem Poles; are colored after the original poles are on ivory bases.

No. 101
Chief Johnson's Totem:

3 in.	$2.85
4 in.	3.75
5 in.	4.25
6 in.	5.50

No. 102
Chief Shake's Totem:

3 in.	$2.85
4 in.	3.75
5 in.	4.25
6 in.	5.50

No. 103
The Kahlteen Totem:

3 in.	$2.85
4 in.	3.75
5 in.	4.25
6 in.	5.50

No. 104
The Kian Totem:

3 in.	$2.85
4 in.	3.75
5 in.	4.25
6 in.	5.50

NO. 27—PRIMITIVE HALIBUT FISH HOOK

Made and used by the Alaska Indians. Made from the root of the spruce tree, about 7 inches long, as illustrated, each $1.75

NO. 28—PRIMITIVE TOM COD FISH HOOK

Made and used by the Indians of Puget Sound and Alaska; has bone point and twisted sinew line, about 4½ inches long, as illustrated, each $0.50

16 WE PAY ALL DELIVERY AND INSURANCE CHARGES

7.14. In Ye Olde Curiosity Shop Catalogs E through G, Standley advertised "Alaska Indian Totem Poles" on stands and similar but smaller "Totem Pole Pendants," both carved of ivory. The title was accurate, for the poles copied were all Alaskan, but it did not reveal that the carvings had been made in Japan and imported by Takenoya Brothers of Tokyo, a longtime supplier to the shop. Catalog F, p.16.

Standley's lifetime the shop purchased model poles and other wood carvings from unnamed Alaskan and Canadian carvers who were in town briefly, just as it bought ivory from visiting Yup'ik and Inupiat carvers. A sign-off book begun in the 1940s records carvers and the work they brought in. Some, like Tlingit artist Abner Johnson, sold to the shop over decades; others, non-Native carver Duane Pasco among them, sold pieces to the shop when they were just getting started.[59]

The catalogs that Ye Olde Curiosity Shop distributed over at least thirty years of Standley's life display some of the commercially produced totem pole souvenirs the shop offered. Because of its connections with local carvers, the shop could acquire all the wooden poles it needed rather easily, but it also stocked ivory and bone totem pole souvenirs that had been produced in Japan, as did several other Seattle shops. In the early 1920s Standley wrote to the Tokyo Chamber of Commerce asking for the name of a potential supplier for ivory carving.[60] He was put in touch with Takenoya Brothers, a business established in 1898 by Daisaburo Takenoya. Standley provided photographs of the same totem poles that the shop had carried for at least a decade, cast in silver by the local Joseph Mayer company. By the mid-1920s, Takenoya was sending two-inch-tall ivory totem pole pendants, hand carved and colored, and three- to five-inch versions of some of the same poles carved from walrus and mammoths tusks and mounted on bases (fig. 7.14).[61] They were pictured in shop catalogs during the 1920s and 1930s. In Catalog G from the early 1930s, the poles mounted on bases were also offered at about one-quarter the price in "carved whale ivory, a fine grade bone," actually cow bone (fig. 7.15). Takenoya also supplied a "whale ivory" cigarette holder with a crudely scratched in and colored totem pole.

The Curiosity Shop purchased from Takenoya Brothers until the bombing of Pearl Harbor and later after the company resumed exporting in the late 1940s. Takenoya's early records were lost in the bombing in 1945.[62] The sole postwar catalog from Ye Olde Curiosity Shop pictures an assortment of Takenoya's crudely painted post–World War II totem pole pins, bookmarks, and

paper knives of "boneware or 'whale ivory.'" The pendants and mounted poles that the shop bought from Takenoya were not as refined and detailed as some that had come from Japan. A number of imported ivory poles were the work of Japanese artists who produced *netsuke,* the tiny intricately carved toggles used to fasten a purse or other items to the kimono sash. The shop carried netsuke for years, as well as ivory totem poles. Joe James believes that in Seattle wholesaler Herman Krupp handled the most finely detailed ivory totem poles from Japan (fig. 7.16).[63] Although his supplier is not recorded, Krupp also imported and wholesaled Japanese totem pole souvenirs made from bone. B. J. Palmer, of the Palmer Chiropractic College in Davenport, Iowa, was one of Krupp's customers (see chap. 5). Before and after World War II, Palmer ordered thousands of totem pole mustard spoons, bridge pencils, letter openers, and other souvenirs made of bone, to sell at the gift kiosk that was a part of his showplace A Little Bit O' Heaven. Although miniature totem poles of bone or ivory displaced the reality of the totem pole even further than did the tiny

7.15. This six-inch-tall "whale ivory" totem pole purchased at Ye Olde Curiosity Shop in 1941 for $1.50 was actually carved from fine-grained cow bone and imported by Takenoya Brothers. Bone totem poles like this that the company supplied before World War II were detailed more skillfully than those sent after the war. Private collection.

7.16. Japanese *netsuke* carvers also produced miniature ivory totem poles for export. Although this pole replicates the Chief Shakes Pole, the facial expressions and detailing betray its Japanese origin. Walrus ivory, 6 in. tall. James Collection.

wooden model poles that the shop sold, they were quite satisfactory as souvenirs. Many pictured a symbol that had become associated with Seattle and represented a memento of having visited the city and its famous shop.

The second Curiosity Shop catalog, Catalog B from 1915, pictures among other jewelry three tiny "totem pole brooches of silver" and very narrow silver bracelets with heads identified as Alaskan birds or animals at one end. All items are said to be Indian-made. The next catalogs, from 1916 and about 1920 (Catalogs C and D), include the same photographs, plus another showing an assortment of sterling silver "Alaska Indian totem pole pins." A third photograph in Catalog D introduces both a bracelet and two rings stamped with totem pole designs. The totem pole pins, bracelets, and rings can all be traced to Mayer & Bros. Company in Seattle.

In the late 1890s German immigrant Joseph Mayer went to the Klondike and founded jewelry companies in Skagway and Dawson. He moved to Seattle by the first years of the twentieth century and established a metal stamping company called Jos. Mayer & Bros. in the Colman Annex Building. It specialized particularly in stamped souvenir spoons, medals, and jewelry for fraternal orders, but the company also created lines of gold nugget jewelry. For a while the largest jewelry manufacturing operation west of the Mississippi, the company survived the Depression, but financial problems caused Mayer to take his life in 1942. Now called Northern Stamping Company, it was purchased by E. J. Towle, who ran it until 1987, when it became Metal Arts Group. The business was located in the building on Dexter and Harrison that Meyer had moved to in 1932, until 1999, when it was sold to a Portland company. Until that time it owned more than fourteen thousand of the original hand-carved Mayer Bros. stamping dies, including those for the items that appear in the Curiosity Shop catalogs.[64] Mayer Bros. souvenir spoons celebrating the dog musher, the prospector, Chief Seattle, Princess Angeline, the Seattle Totem Pole, and the city of Seattle became staples in Alaskan and Seattle gift and curio shops. Mayer Bros. also operated a concession at the AYPE. Ye Olde Curiosity Shop carried Mayer Bros. spoons in its catalogs for decades, beginning in 1915.

7.17. For nearly twenty years Ye Olde Curiosity Shop catalogs (Catalogs D–G) advertised this assortment of silver "Alaska Indian Totem Pole Pins" cast by Joseph Mayer & Bros. of Seattle (later Northern Stamping Company). Some of the original dies were dated 1909, indicating that some of the poles were first made for sale at the Alaska-Yukon-Pacific Exposition. Only four poles are represented (E50, Yaadaas crest pole; E53, Kian pole; E56, Kahlteen pole; E60, One-Legged Fisherman pole). E50 and E56 were cast together, base to base, then bent into bracelets or cut into segments to create pins. Catalog F (late 1920s), p. 37.

The catalog photograph titled "Alaska Indian Totem Pole Pins" shows nineteen pins (fig. 7.17). Pictured full size, they range from slightly more than three-quarters of an inch tall to just shy of three inches. Only four poles are actually represented—a Yaadaas crest corner pole from the Haida village of Old Kasaan, Tlingit Chief Kahl-teen's pole at Wrangell, Tlingit Chief Kian's (Kyan) pole at Ketchikan, and the upper half of the One-Legged Fisherman Pole, which Tlingit Chief Shakes erected in the graveyard at Wrangell in honor of his uncle, Kauk-ish, who died in 1897. All were available in photographs

ALASKA INDIAN TOTEM POLE PINS

Order by Numbers. All are Guaranteed Sterling Silver

History of the Indian Totem Pole Free with Each Pin

Actual Size Shown

	Each
E-50—Brooch	$1.00
E-51—Brooch	.75
E-52—Brooch	.75
E-53—Brooch	.75
E-54—Brooch	.50
E-55—Brooch	.75
E-56—Brooch	1.00
E-57—Scarf Pin or Tie Clasp	.40
E-58—Scarf Pin or Tie Clasp	.40

	Each
E-59—Brooch, Scarf Pin or Tie Clasp	$0.50
E-60—Brooch only	.50
E-61—Brooch, Scarf Pin or Tie Clasp	.50
E-62—Brooch, Scarf Pin or Tie Clasp	.40
E-63—Scarf Pin or Tie Clasp	.40
E-64—Brooch, Scarf Pin or Tie Clasp	.40
E-65—Scarf Pin or Tie Clasp	.40
E-66—Scarf Pin or Tie Clasp	.40
E-67—Brooch, Scarf Pin or Tie Clasp	.40
E-68—Brooch, Scarf Pin or Tie Clasp	.40

taken by Juneau photographers Winter & Pond and others in the 1890s and marketed widely through magazines and other publications.[65] The shorter pins are actually segments of three of the complete poles; only the One-Legged Fisherman Pole is not segmented. (The Kahlteen and Kian poles are also among the Japanese carved ones that Standley offered in ivory.)

The tiniest cast totem pole figures also lent themselves to attachment. Bracelets in Curiosity Shop catalogs from the 1920s were bent from cast totem poles or include stampings of the One-Legged Fisherman Pole or the upper section of the Kian Pole, attached amid stamped Southwestern motifs. Rings were also made in the same way. Joe James remembers Standley's son Edward soldering the tiny silver poles onto silver bands, then making them into bracelets and rings. It is unclear whether the Southwestern-style bracelets and rings pictured in the shop catalogs were made in the shop or received from elsewhere and Edward Standley then added totem poles to some. The catalog description of this "Indian Design Silver Jewelry" does not claim that it was Indian-made, but could easily have been misconstrued to mean that, as the statements alone are themselves true, but in their juxtaposition give a false impression (fig. 7.18).

PLATE Y

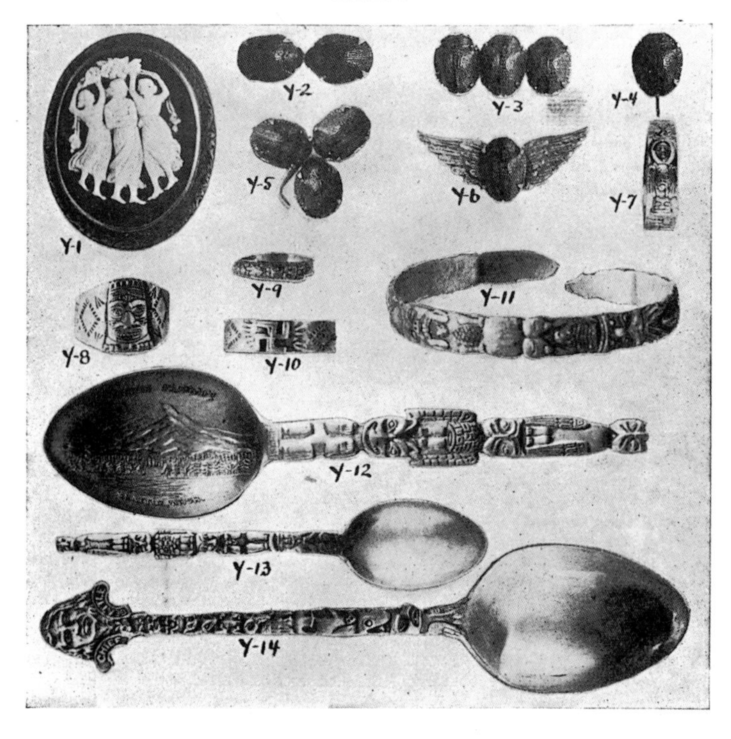

Illustrations Exact Size

Y-1	RARE CAMEO BROOCH, "THREE GRACES." We have these in several sizes, in the Dark Brown, Brown and White shell, and also in the Agate shell, unmounted and mounted. Write for prices.	
Y-2	Genuine Brazilian Beetles, mounted in Sterling Silver Brooch	.75
Y-3	Genuine Brazilian Beetles, mounted in Sterling Silver Brooch	1.25
Y-4	Genuine Brazilian Beetles, mounted in Sterling Silver Scarf Pin or Brooch	.50
Y-5	Genuine Brazilian Beetles, mounted in Sterling Silver Brooch	1.25
Y-6	Genuine Brazilian Beetles, mounted in Sterling Silver Brooch	1.50
Y-7	Silver Ring made by Alaska Indian, Totem Pole Design	1.25
Y-8	Silver Ring made by Alaska Indian, Potlatch Bug	1.75
Y-9	Silver Ring made by Alaska Indian, Totem Pole design	.75
Y-10	Silver Ring made by Alaska Indian, Swastika Cross	1.25
Y-11	Silver Bracelet, Totem Pole Design	2.25
Y-12	Silver Spoon, Totem Pole Handle, heavy	2.60
Y-13	Silver Spoon, Totem Pole Handle	1.00
Y-14	Silver Spoon, Totem Pole Handle	2.25

46

7.18. Catalog D, ca. 1920, p. 46, includes a number of Mayer Bros. castings. Bracelet Y-11 was formed from poles E50 and E56, cast base to base then bent to fit the wrist. Tiny silver totem poles first sold as brooches in Catalog B (1915) are here soldered onto rings Y-7 and Y-9. The Chief Seattle spoon with the Seattle Totem Pole handle (Y-14) and Kian totem pole souvenir spoons (Y-12, Y-13) also appeared in Catalog B (1915).

Influence on Expectations of Totem Poles

Totem poles played a major role in Ye Olde Curiosity Shop's image from almost its beginning. Along with the misinformation about their meaning and use, the totem poles in the shop reinforced certain visual expectations as well. Standley believed that large, brightly painted poles placed outside his business would catch visitors' eyes and lure them inside, where they would find that the substantial stock of economically priced miniature poles in a range of sizes placed owning such a pole within everyone's reach. The bright primary colors and bold forms that Standley liked were also a part of Nuu-chah-nulth and neighboring Kwakwa̱ka̱'wakw visual traditions, and both traditions came to dominate the transtribal styles that Sam Williams and other Nuu-chah-nulth carvers developed while working for Standley and others in Seattle. Their poles, in turn, influenced the consumer's expectations.

In the years after Standley's death in 1940, Curiosity Shop personnel continued to influence carvers with suggestions and through their decisions about what to buy. Like Standley, Joe James has encouraged deep carving and sharply defined features. In the 1950s he showed carvers a Japanese-made pole that included a bird with a long beak created by cutting wood out from behind. Ray Williams then others began creating similar beaks on some of their poles and calling them "Mosquito Poles." They delivered the poles unpainted to the shop, where staff then stained them brown or black and buffed them to a light sheen.

There is a certain circularity between a symbol and commodification. The commodification of an image helps to distill it into a symbol, and being a symbol encourages its commodification. The Seattle Totem Pole erected in Pioneer Square in 1899 blurred the boundary between Alaska and Seattle, merging the two regions and subsuming the idea of the totem pole within a broad definition of the Pacific Northwest. The many replicas of the Seattle Totem Pole and others poles sold at Standley's and other Seattle shops have perpetuated this connection for a century, as did the catalogs that Ye Olde Curiosity Shop distributed during the last three decades of Standley's life.

"1001 Curious Things": Merchandizing Native American Goods

This catalog is presented with our compliments. The perusal of it will afford you information concerning the wonders of Alaska and the Great Northwest.
—Ye Old Curiosity Shop, Catalogs C (1916) and D (ca. 1920)

CURIO CATALOGS ARE EPHEMERA THAT WERE ISSUED, PERUSED, USED, AND DIScarded. For this reason early ones are rare, and today's collectors search hard for them. It is unusual to have as many brochures and catalogs from one source as exist from Ye Olde Curiosity Shop (figs. 4.13, 8.1, 8.2, 8.3, 8.4). Like other curio catalogs offering Native American material during the early decades of the twentieth century, they astound with their low prices in comparison to today and sometimes startle late twentieth-century sensibilities with their rhetoric. They include such items as Tlingit baskets and Navajo textiles, which have come to be considered fine art, and other objects that have been deemed tourist or souvenir art. The catalogs include both Indian- and Eskimo-made items and commercially produced replications sometimes sold with the implication that they were Native-made.

Ye Olde Curiosity Shop began distributing catalogs advertising its natural and human-made curiosities by at least 1910 and continued through 1940. Brochures were produced in 1907 and 1923, and a final catalog was put out in the 1950s. It is unclear how many catalogs there were altogether, but the numbers on several of them in conjunction with all the others that have been found suggest that about fourteen catalogs were issued before J. E. Standley's death in 1940.[1] The 1923 brochure was put out to alert readers of a change of address when the shop moved one door south. The 1939 and 1940 catalogs are very similar, except in the 1940 one the "Navajo Lucky Swastika" ring, carried for decades, has been eliminated. An ancient cosmic or religious symbol, the swastika was believed to be a Navajo good luck symbol. A left-facing version is basic to certain Navajo dry paintings. The swastika on the ring faced to the right, as did the Nazi swastika, and it was essential to remove the ring and reissue the catalog. None

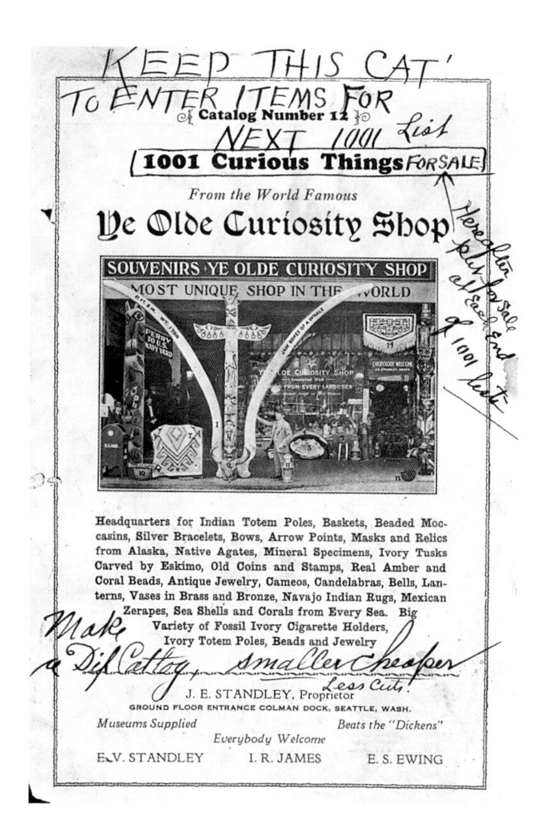

8.1. Cover, Catalog G, early 1930s. Several Ye Olde Curiosity Shop catalogs include Standley's notes in planning the next catalog. The instructions for changes noted on this cover do not appear on any known catalogs; rather, they suggest that another catalog from the 1930s has yet to be discovered. For the catalog Standley has enhanced a photograph of the 1923–37 shop by pasting on cutouts of totem poles and other merchandise.

8.2. Cover, Catalog E, mid-1920s. Catalogs E and F (late 1920s) feature covers of a heavy paper (gray for E and red for F), embossed to suggest leather. The three-masted bark is suggestive of a pirate ship, emphasizing the global reach of the treasures one might find within the catalog.

but the 1939 anniversary catalog includes a date, although the catalog numbers printed on three have been helpful in sequencing. The two brochures and the nine catalogs currently known to have been produced through 1940 have been ordered and dated through cross-referencing photographs and text with each other and with other shop records. Through the catalogs and brochures one can trace the Curiosity Shop merchandise and merchandising over the first four decades of the twentieth century—from the exciting, expansive time of the Alaska-Yukon-Pacific Exposition (AYPE), through World War I, the Great Depression, and the buildup to World War II.

"1001 Curious Things" and Display Pages in the Catalogs

A folded four-page brochure on which Standley wrote "1907" predates the known catalogs and is the earliest shop advertising found to date that includes prices (see p. 5). Two-thirds of its text is devoted to natural curiosities, coins, stamps, postcards, and shells, and the remainder to "Relics and Curiosities from the Primitive Races, who are fast disappearing from Bering Sea, Alaska, Puget Sound." Merchandise is listed in paragraphs, some of which include prices.

The brochure served to entice a potential buyer but would have been difficult to purchase from, so Standley decided to organize his offerings into a list from which one could order by number. Good fortune and hard work

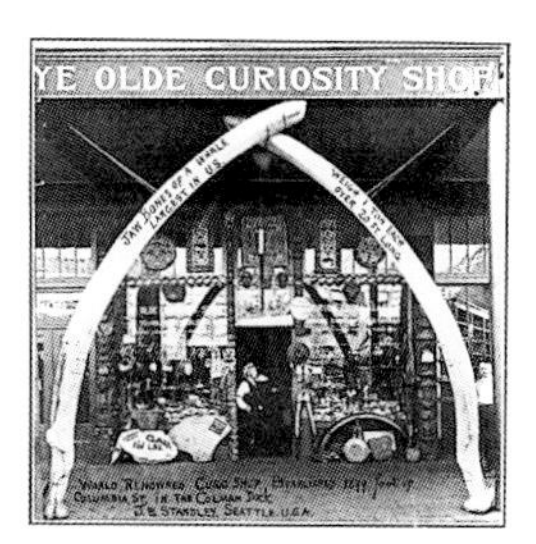

PIONEER CURIO SHOP
of Seattle
Established 1899

Built upon Piling near the Ships and Steamers that ply to all parts of the Globe. This Shop is a famous one for visitors, who are always welcome.

In Private Collections and in many Museums in this and Foreign Countries may be seen Curios and Relics secured from this Shop.

In trading with the Indians and Eskimos there accumulates a lot of curios not listed, or never are duplicated.

It is a veritable free museum and most unique of its kind in existence.

SNAPSHOT OF PART OF SHELVING, SHOWING HUNDREDS OF INDIAN BASKETS AND NO TWO ALIKE

CATALOG AND PRICE LIST
OF
1001 CURIOUS THINGS

FROM

Ye Olde Curiosity Shop
ESTABLISHED 1899
THE MOST UNIQUE SHOP IN THE WORLD
LOCATED ON THE COLMAN DOCK
SEATTLE, WASH.

8.3. Cover, Catalog D, ca. 1920. The front cover is identical to that of the previous Catalog C, except for a narrow black border on the earlier one. Both include "1001 Curious Things" lists.

SEATTLE *the playground of the West*

The Gateway to Alaska and the Orient . . . the playground of the West. Her beautiful harbors of fresh and salt water are unsurpassed anywhere in the world, either for depth or extent. 40 Steamship lines ply from Seattle to all parts of the globe. Surrounded by fertile valleys, wooded hills and snow-capped mountain ranges and paved highways which lead to all the scenic grandeurs of the great Northwest, Seattle offers the utmost in healthful recreation and material resources. The tourist may take launch, steamer and yachting trips: go camping, fishing, hunting, dig clams, gather flowers, berries, nuts and ferns the year 'round.

Make Seattle the first stop on your Western trip

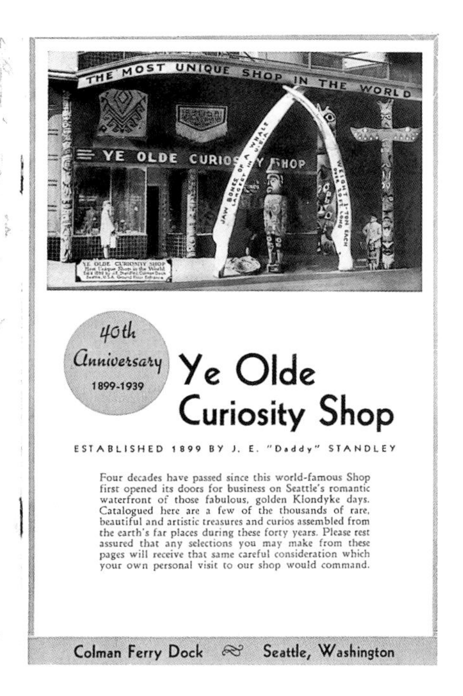

40th Anniversary 1899-1939

Ye Olde Curiosity Shop

ESTABLISHED 1899 BY J. E. "Daddy" STANDLEY

Four decades have passed since this world-famous Shop first opened its doors for business on Seattle's romantic waterfront of those fabulous, golden Klondyke days. Catalogued here are a few of the thousands of rare, beautiful and artistic treasures and curios assembled from the earth's far places during these forty years. Please rest assured that any selections you may make from these pages will receive that same careful consideration which your own personal visit to our shop would command.

Colman Ferry Dock ~ Seattle, Washington

8.4. Cover, Catalog H (1939). The photograph for the cover of the shop's Fortieth Anniversary Catalog was also a photomontage with added cutouts. The shop shown opened in June 1937.

had allowed him to acquire a tremendously diverse quantity of unusual items during his first years in business, but communicating what the shop offered presented a challenge. In the popular story "1001 Arabian Nights" the bride Scheherazade beguiled her king each evening with a tale, thus saving her life. Perhaps Standley's brief descriptions of "1001 Curious Things," diverse and amazing curiosities from around the globe, would enchant the reader into placing an order. There was intense curiosity at the time about natural and man-made wonders and the "1001 list" engaged clients who simply liked to browse. It worked especially well for those looking for specific types of objects, as was Newark Museum director John Cotton Dana. In 1919 Dana put together an order from the list in Catalog C and had probably ordered earlier from Catalog A.

Standley included a "1001 Curious Things" list in six of the seven catalogs published between 1910–13 and the early 1930s. During that time only Catalog E was without one. The twenty-six pages of the earliest catalog (Catalog A) were devoted entirely to a "1001 list," along with a few interspersed pictures and light text on the front and back covers. Standley must have decided that pictures of merchandise and prices would be helpful, for in Catalog B, also twenty-six pages long, he fit the list into slightly more than eleven pages by setting it in smaller, closer type and devoted the remaining pages to photographs of groups of related objects and their prices. Subsequent catalogs with "1001 lists" (Catalogs C, D, F, and G) followed this format. Catalog E may have been an experiment to see how orders fared without the list. A list returned in the next two catalogs before it was retired altogether.

The earliest "1001 lists" include the greatest variety of Native American merchandise, much of it acquired during the shop's earliest years when large quantities of material were coming out of Alaska. Standley's purchases at the close of the 1909 AYPE of Philippine objects and other items that were sold rather than returned to their countries of origin had also expanded his inventory's variety. In later catalogs items in the numbered lists became increasingly redundant and non-Indian objects were emphasized in the catalog section. The six "1001 Curious Things" lists are similar. Each includes many entries from the previous list but new items appear, to replace those sold or no longer available. The list in Catalog B (1915) is typical. Despite the stress on Native American items in the text on the front and back covers, only 18 percent of the list is devoted to such. The bulk of the list embraces an array of minerals, shells, sea creatures, and natural oddities from around the world: teeth, tusks, and bones from Alaskan animals; Oriental weapons and novelties; coins and jewelry from other countries; and souvenirs from the AYPE and the Seattle Potlatch Carnival.[2]

The descriptions of Indian and Eskimo objects in the "1001 lists" contain a good deal of fact, some half-information, and occasional myth. Adjectives emphasize rarity and age. There are dozens of one-of-a-kind objects, especially from Alaska: an "Eskimo's Ivory Needle Case with Ivory Needle," a "Rare Old Indian Halibut Fish Hook, Curious," an "Old Time Indian Dress, made of

Beaten Cedar Bark," a "Pipe from Siberia, Carved Figures on Ivory Tusk." Some listings are for categories: Indian masks, argillite totem poles from the Queen Charlotte Islands, beaded seal skin wall pockets, and model canoes and umiaks. The "Muk-Muks, Indian spoons of mountain sheep horn" and some of the "cedar bark hats" were likely wholesaled from Alaska, along with baskets, moccasins, and a few dolls. "Zuni rain gods," small seated human figures made primarily at Tesuque but also at other pueblos in New Mexico, surely came from J. S. Candelario of Santa Fe, one of Standley's recorded suppliers, who shipped thousands of the figures to curio dealers from 1905 through the 1930s. The "Pottery bowls from the Aztec Indians and cliff dwellers" probably did as well.[3] The "Small Square Tiles from Cliff Dwellers' Ruins" were likely tiles made as curio items on the Hopi mesas and acquired through a wholesaler, along with the "Moki Indian Basket Plaques." Appealing to the needs of schools and universities, as well to as private collectors using baskets and other Indian items in home decor, the lists also offer prepared assemblages: "A Collection of Ethnological Curios from Alaska," "Museum Collections for Universities," "Interesting Collections, Indian Curios for Den," and for postcard aficionados, "postals" (postcard sets) of Puget Sound scenes, Alaska, American Indians, and Indian and Eskimo Chiefs.[4]

The later "1001 lists" (in Catalogs F and G, from the late 1920s to early 1930s) offer fewer Native American items and less variety in merchandise in general. It is common for the same object to be listed more than once, in different sizes or with slightly different descriptors. Commercial manufactures dominate the Indian and Eskimo offerings. By the time the list was dropped from the catalogs in the late 1930s, museums had almost ceased to be customers. During the Depression fewer individuals had the luxury to purchase the unnecessary, sight unseen, simply because it sounded intriguing. Also, direct experience and increased media coverage of events surrounding America's emergence as a colonial and military power during the Spanish American War and World War I had forged a more sophisticated awareness of "the unfamiliar" and of unknown peoples. As the century unfolded, Standley's stock of unique items from Alaska had slowly diminished at the same time that Americans' knowledge of the world had steadily expanded. Now, far less seemed exotic.

Although Standley made the shop's catalogs available (exactly how they were distributed is not clear), he experimented only briefly with selling wholesale, probably because he did not want or need to. His grandson Joe James has characterized Standley as a curio lover first, an entertainer second, and a businessman third. Enjoying his curios was important to him, and there was sufficient traffic through the shop once it relocated to Colman Dock to keep it financially sound and in some periods quite successful.

Ivory Relics from the Eskimo of Alaska, carvers of ivory teeth of Polar bear, Walrus and Baluga (white whale), reproducing in miniature animals and birds, used as wampum (money). Also ivory knives, spear-heads, labrets . . . gavels, pipes, skin scrapers, watch chains, sacred charms . . . ; walrus ivory tusks 10 to 30 inches, many have arctic scenes, also a cribbage board and pegs. . . . Be a collector. The Fad Pays.

—Ye Olde Curiosity Shop information card, "Ivory Relics"

Native American material comprised about a third of each Curiosity Shop catalog. The remainder was various, changing a bit with each catalog. Jewelry, clocks, and desk and dressing table accessories made variously of agate, abalone, or mother of pearl were important in the conventional catalog sections during the 1910s and 1920s, as were shells of specific collectible types, brass candelabras from Russia, and armadillo shell sewing baskets. The late 1920s brought gold nugget jewelry, brass from India and China, Japanese carvings and jewelry of elephant ivory, and Chinese cloisonné.[5]

The nine catalogs range in length from sixteen to forty-eight black and white pages. Seven catalogs have covers of the same paper stock as the catalog itself, and two of heavier stock. The continuities of merchandise, photographs, and prices in the catalogs and brochures suggest that should interim catalogs come to light, they will not dramatically alter the picture that emerges from those now available. The catalogs trace the changes in merchandise and prices throughout the first four decades of the twentieth century. These in turn reflect influencing factors: the availability of items, trends in taste, and price fluctuations based in the economic realities of the time.

Ivory and Bone Work and the Commercial Production of Souvenirs

Within a few months of his arrival in Seattle in fall 1899, Standley had made contact with men working in the Arctic. He quickly introduced both raw and worked ivory from Alaska into both his private collection and his shop's stock. Some of the ivory relics in his personal collection were old tools or parts of tools. There were also scores of ivory carvings similar to those collected in the 1870s and 1880s by ethnographic collectors John Murdock and Edward William Nelson, as well as somewhat different carved figures and engraved tusks, pipes, and cribbage boards that were being produced for sale in Alaska at the turn of the century. The Curiosity Shop's "Ivory Relics" information card randomly associated both the old and the new, the traditional and the made-for-sale. In the shop's early years Standley kept the ivory collection apart from the regular merchandise. He displayed it first at the Arctic Club, then at the AYPE, and later in the Seattle gallery run by the Washington State Art Association. After George G. Heye's purchase of the collection in 1916. Standley kept some that remained in a small private collection at home; the rest went into shop stock and was referenced in entries in his "1001 lists."

Although Standley's earliest made-for-sale ivories shown at the Arctic Club and the AYPE had been made by Eskimo carvers from Alaska and Siberia, ivories of more uncertain origin soon joined them in the shop's stock. His 1907 brochure advertised, "We have hundreds of old Ivory articles used in fishing, hunting, games, dances of the Eskimo," but also "Wampum [identified in the 1915 catalog as Little Carved Animals], Beads, Lucky Emblems, Tools, Ivory Jewelry," whose origins are more difficult to identify. Some of the latter items could have been made in Alaska by Eskimo artisans, by Eskimos or others working in commercial operations in Seattle, or even in the Curiosity Shop itself by Standley's son Edward.

The offerings in the shop catalogs chart the changing availability and market for ivories associated with the Eskimo. In Standley's "1001 Curious Things" list in Catalog A (1910–13), published after the close of the AYPE, his collection was so large that he simply grouped the items together as "Ivory Carved Relics, from Arctic Eskimos Hundreds, No Duplicates." In Catalog B (1915) he introduced the first photograph of a group of ivories, then used an even larger one showing more examples in Catalog C (1916) (fig. 8.5). Most of the items in the earlier photograph, and many in the 1916 one, parallel those that had been made and sold by Eskimo carvers in Nome, Alaska, since the turn of the century—a pipe with carved animals, a cribbage board, a letter opener, a gavel, a cigar holder, a billiken, napkin rings, etched tusks, and freestanding animal figures.[6] The desire for ivory souvenirs among the thousands who went to Nome for the gold rush precipitated a fluorescence of ivory carving by both local Inupiat and those from King and St. Lawrence Islands, who brought their winter's output to Nome each summer. Siberian carvers also came to Nome in the summers to trade. Although Standley's supplier books list no Nome sources for ivory, some may have come via Charles T. Wernecke's Nome fur supplier, during the years he ran a small fur business in the rear of Ye Olde Curiosity Shop. Standley's friend and supplier L. L. Bales traveled between Seattle and

BEAUTIFUL ARTICLES, HAND CARVED BY THE ALASKA ESKIMO OUT OF IVORY TUSKS OF THE WALRUS.

Plate No. 9

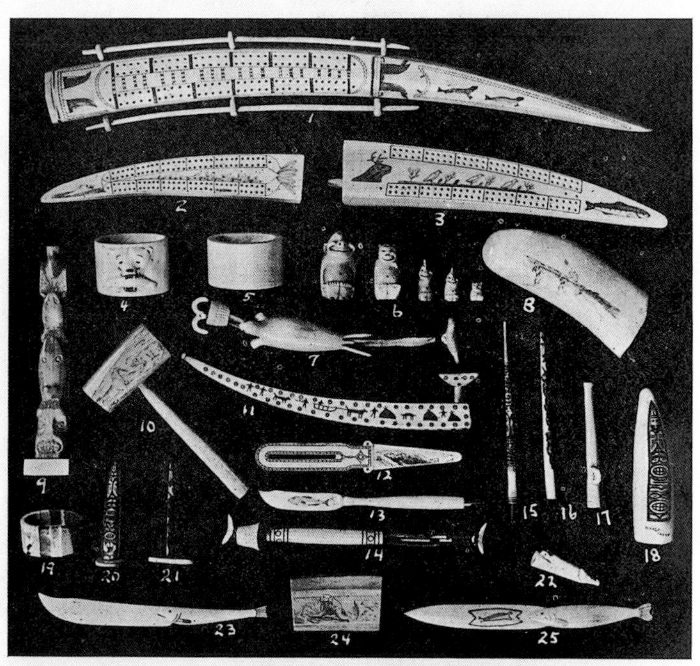

Nos. 1, 2 and 3 Ivory Cribbage Boards, Hand Carved by the Eskimo, from the Tusks of the Walrus.

The prices of these vary, according to the size of the tusk and quality of the carving. Approximate sizes, as follows:

9 inches long	$3.00 to $4.50	13 inches long	$6.50 to $ 8.00
10 inches long	3.50 to 5.50	14 inches long	7.50 to 9.00
11 inches long	4.00 to 6.50	15 inches long	8.50 to 10.00
12 inches long	5.00 to 8.50	17 inches long	9.00 to 12.00

A Set of 4 Ivory Pegs with Each Board.

We also have large ones up to 30 inches long, at prices up to $50.00 each.

Nos. 4 and 5 Napkin Rings carved from Ivory Walrus Tusk by the Eskimo.

No. 4 shows one of the finer carved Napkin Rings, some carved with a Seal, Walrus, and Polar Bear. Price as to carving, each .... $3.50 to $5.00

No. 5 shows one plain, as to size .... $1.00 to $2.50

Also have these etched with native or animal scenes. Price according to size and etching .... $1.50 to $3.50

No. 6. The Lucky Billican carved from Ivory. Eskimo work.

½ inch high at	$0.50	1½ inch high at	$1.75
¾ inch high at	.75	2 inch high at	3.00
1 inch high at	1.00	3 inch high at	4.00

Nos. 7 and 14. An Eskimo Woman's Needle Case and Thimble. These rare curios are all carved from Ivory. The case has a piece of Raw Hide run through it in which they stick their Ivory needles, and thus keep them from breaking. These come in dierent designs to represent dierent animals such as Seals, Foxes, Walrus and Polar Bear. Prices according to carving from .... $3.00 to $7.50

Also have some in plain holder with little figures pictured on like No. 14 at $1.50 to $3.

21

8.5. This photograph in Catalog C pictures an assortment of ivory cribbage boards, billikens, napkin rings, paper knives, and such that were common in curio shops in Nome after the gold rush brought an influx of people to the region. The totem pole pen, cigarette, and cigar holders (nos. 15–17) probably came from Japan. The price list continued on the following page. Catalog C (1916), p. 21.

YE OLDE CURIOSITY SHOP, ESTABLISHED 1899 BY J. E. STANDLEY

IVORY CIGARETTE HOLDERS

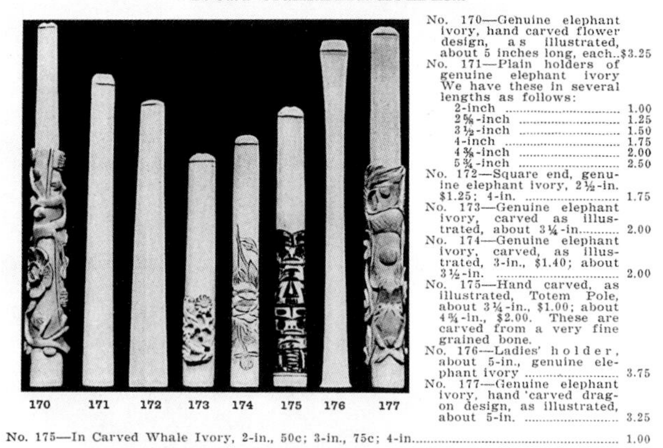

No. 170—Genuine elephant ivory, hand carved flower design, as illustrated, about 5 inches long, each..$3.25
No. 171—Plain holders of genuine elephant ivory We have these in several lengths as follows:
2-inch 1.00
2⅝-inch 1.25
3½-inch 1.50
4-inch 1.75
4⅜-inch 2.00
5¾-inch 2.50
No. 172—Square end, genuine elephant ivory, 2½-in. $1.25; 4-in. 1.75
No. 173—Genuine elephant ivory, carved as illustrated, about 3¼-in.......... 2.00
No. 174—Genuine elephant ivory, carved, as illustrated, 3-in., $1.40; about 3½-in. 2.00
No. 175—Hand carved, as illustrated, Totem Pole, about 3¼-in., $1.00; about 4¾-in., $2.00. These are carved from a very fine grained bone.
No. 176—Ladies' holder, about 5-in., genuine elephant ivory 3.75
No. 177—Genuine elephant ivory, hand carved dragon design, as illustrated, about 5-in. 3.25

No. 175—In Carved Whale Ivory, 2-in., 50c; 3-in., 75c; 4-in.......... 1.00

ALASKA ESKIMO CARVINGS

The Eskimos are noted for their carved ivory cribbage boards, paper knives, gavels, pen holders and other useful articles. Carved out of ivory tusk of Arctic Walrus.

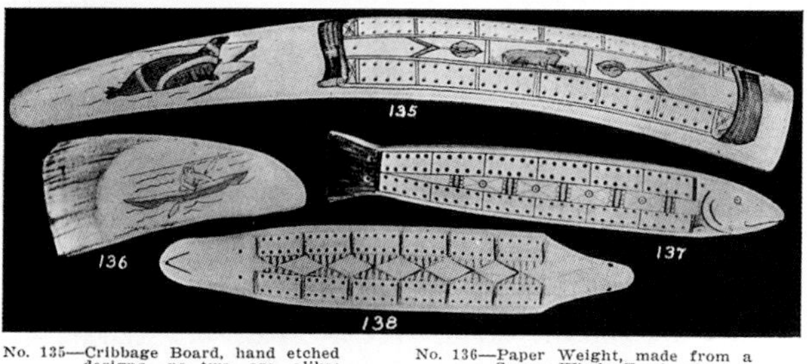

No. 135—Cribbage Board, hand etched designs, no two are alike; about 14 inches long..........$10.00
No. 137—Cribbage Board similar to illustration, about 8 inches long 5.25
No. 138—Cribbage Board, similar to illustration, about 8½ inches long 5.50

No. 136—Paper Weight, made from a Sperm Whale Tooth, about 4 inches long, with various etched designs, each.......... 2.75

We also have other Cribbage Boards in Stock from 7 to 30 inches in length, at prices from $4.00 to $35.00 each.

We Carry Large Stock of Ivory Gavels—Write for Prices.

22 WE PAY ALL DELIVERY AND INSURANCE CHARGES

8.6. Walrus ivory cribbage boards such as these carried by the shop for some years were made by Inupiat and Yup'ik carvers living in Alaska or visiting Seattle, but the cigarette holders of elephant ivory, including one featuring a crudely carved and colored totem pole, were imported from Japan. Catalog G (early 1930s), p. 22.

the Seward Peninsula rather regularly, and the trader C. T. Pedersen brought out worked ivory he traded for in villages along Alaska's coast.[7]

By the time of the second catalog, the billiken—the chubby, pointy-headed, seated figure introduced in 1909 at the AYPE as a good luck souvenir—had become one of the best-known ivory souvenirs of all time. After the fair, at the suggestion of a Nome shopkeeper, well-known Eskimo artist Happy Jack carved the first billiken in ivory. Already familiar to the public from the exposition, the ivory billiken quickly became associated with Alaska. Over the next decades Eskimo carvers and non-Native manufacturing companies in Seattle and Japan would produce thousands of ivory billikens for the souvenir trade, as figurines, letter openers, salt and pepper shakers, jewelry, and more. A variety of billiken forms, such as billikens in action and billiken families, appeared, and mythologies developed about the figure's origin and meaning. Female figures were sometimes called "millikens." In many shops the billiken's AYPE role as a source of good fortune was perpetuated, and it was sold with instructions to rub its belly or tickle its toes to bring luck.[8] For decades the shop displayed little trays of billikens, and they sold well.

The photographs of ivory in the 1915 and 1916 catalogs (Catalogs B and C, as well as the "Supplement Price List" to Catalog C) also picture ivory "totem pole pen holders" and totem pole designs carved into sperm whale teeth and baby walrus tusks. Several of the latter were displayed in Standley's AYPE cases and later purchased by Heye (see figs. 3.3a, b). These items may have been experiments by Eskimo carvers, but subtle style similarities with later ivory totem pole souvenirs made in Japan suggest that they could possibly have come from Japan. If so, they date the beginnings of Japanese-carved ivory totem poles even earlier than suspected. The photograph of ivories used in Catalog C (1916) also appears in Catalog D (ca. 1920).With the exception of cribbage boards, prices have risen in Catalog D, for both old items like needle cases and newer ones like souvenir paper knives and billikens. In Catalogs E and F (from the mid-1920s to early 1930s) cribbage boards (with prices still steady), gavels, pen holders, and letter openers "carved by Eskimos" are still present, pictured in small photographs, and the space given to the ivory totem poles from Japan discussed in chapter 7 has increased.

Catalogs E and F also introduce a new group of ivory carvings, with Standley's statement: "Very true to nature are the miniature bears, dogs, foxes, walrus, seal and other animals hand carved from the ivory tusks of the walrus; teeth of the Sperm whale and tusk of pre-historic mammoths." Made in Japan, these items are not identified as Alaskan or Eskimo, although a casual reader might have assumed that being of ivory, they were. The more observant may have thought it strange to find a camel and a buffalo among the Arctic animals and, if familiar with Eskimo ivory carving (which was unlikely), would have noticed a degree of detail uncharacteristic of Eskimo carving.

Both a reasonable price and the need for a dependable supply were factors in Standley's turning to Japanese wholesalers. To offer items in the catalog, other than singly in the "1001 lists," he needed to be reasonably sure he could keep such objects in stock and doing so had become more and more difficult. As old Eskimo material from Alaska diminished, and carving from Alaska became harder to depend on and more expensive for the customer, Japanese and other commercially made ivory souvenir items became increasingly integral to catalog offerings. The small Catalog G from the early 1930s offers in ivory only the Eskimo cribbage boards, the Japanese totem poles listed in the two previous catalogs, and a crude totem pole cigarette holder (see fig. 8.6). The ivory in Catalog H (1939) is limited to unworked pieces and a few ivory animals pictured together (fig. 8.7). Some are Alaskan but most are Japanese; grouping the carvings as such has diluted the importance of distinguishing between them. No ivory is mentioned in the small Catalog I (1940) except a few examples in a partial "1001 list."

In addition to ivory animals and billikens, Eskimo carvers made ivory beads and an assortment of usable items

8.7. The shop purchased ivory animals from Yup'iks and Inupiats visiting or living in Seattle but assured a dependable supply by importing also from Japan. The Japanese-carved ones like these in Catalog H (1939, p. 12) were often made of elephant rather than walrus ivory and lacked the Eskimo carver's stylizations based in deep understanding of the habits and gesture of Arctic animals. They were instead stiffer and emphasized precise surface details and a highly polished surface. The dolls pictured on p. 13 include several Eskimo ones that could have been made in Alaska, a commercial doll called Siwash, and a kachina doll probably carved by Chief White Eagle, who also made miniature totem poles for the shop while he lived in Seattle.

Y E O L D E C U R I O S I T Y S H O P

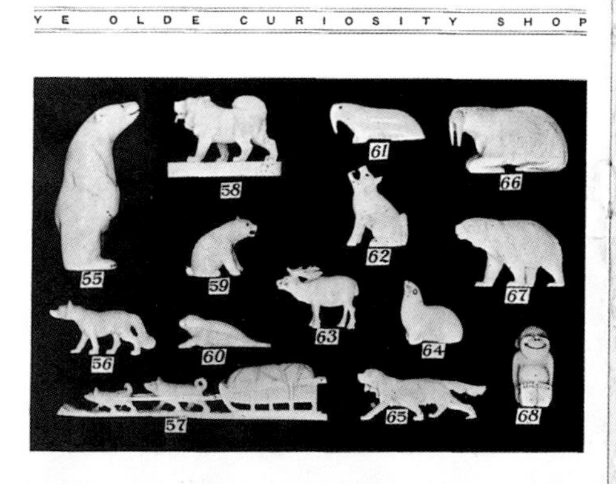

BEAUTIFUL IVORY CARVINGS

55-I—Alaska Ivory Bear, 3½ inches high 7.00
56-I—Ivory Foxes .... from 1.50
57-I—Alaska Ivory Dog Teams, from 1.00 each up to 35.00
58-I—Ivory Dog, 2 inches long 3.50
59-I—Alaska Ivory Bears, 2 inches 2.50
60-I and 64-I—Ivory Seals, 1½ inch 1.00, 1¾ inch 1.50
61-I—Ivory Walrus, 1½ inch 1.00, 1¾ inch 1.50
62-I—Ivory Dog, 1 inch 1.00, 1½ inch 1.50
63-I—Ivory Deer and Moose .... each 4.00
65-I—Whale Ivory Dog, 2½ inches long 1.35
66-I—Ivory Walrus, 2½ inches long 5.00
67-I—Ivory Bear, 2½ inches long 4.25
68-I—Ivory Billikens .... 1.00 up

Approval Shipments Sent to Responsible Customers

Except where noted, all prices include prepaid delivery charges

PAGE TWELVE

COLMAN FERRY DOCK - - SEATTLE, WASHINGTON, U. S. A.

DOLLS FROM THE FAR WEST AND NORTHLANDS

36-D and 40-D—Russian Dolls, 3" high, Native Costume .... each .35
37-D—Kachinas Dolls, made by Hopi Indian Priests of carved wood and highly colored—
2½" high .... .50
3½" high .... .75
5" high 1.00
38-D—Eskimo Doll, 11" high 2.00
39-D—West Coast Siwash Character Doll, 6½" high .... .75
39-DD—Same as above, 10¾" high, Chief, Squaw or Papoose 1.65
Write for Larger Sizes
41-D—Alaska Eskimo Doll with Carved Wooden Face 2.50
42-D—Alaska Eskimo Doll, Native Constume, 6" high .85, 8" high 1.00
42-DD—Same as above with Carved Wooden Face 1.50
44-D—Rare Eskimo carved Ivory Ikon Doll, 1½" to 4", 2.00, 3.00, 5.00 and 7.50
45-D—Doll made of Sea Shells, 8" high 1.00

Except where noted, all prices include prepaid delivery charges

PAGE THIRTEEN

such as napkin rings, paper knives, and gavels with etched Eskimo scenes. Because these items were easy to replicate, commercial operations in Seattle began producing them too. Curio and gift shops were interested in a dependable, economical souvenir supply, and these objects became more and more commercially important during the 1930s and 1940s. The "1001 Curious Things" list in Standley's Catalog G from the early 1930s demonstrates how only subtle wording distinguished between Eskimo-made and commercial ivory work. It offered "Ivory Net Sinkers used by the Eskimos," "Eskimo Footballs," and "Napkin rings . . . Eskimo make" but also "Whale teeth polished, have Eskimo scenes etched on," "Eskimo dog team . . . hand carved from a walrus tusk," and "Pickle fork with hand carved Totem Pole."

Curio shops often created jewelry from walrus tusks and teeth themselves. Standley's son Ed preferred making ivory jewelry in the back room to selling. So did Albert (Mack) McKillop who opened Mack's Totem Shop in the 1930s. During the first half of the century walrus teeth were readily available from Alaskan suppliers, and Standley's shop bought thousands of them by the pound. They were often wholesaled already tumbled and sanded, and the shop gave them a fine polish on a buffing wheel and sometimes stained them green, brown, or black. They were then drilled to be used on key chains, as pendants and earrings, or connected together at the top and bottom with elastic cord to become bracelets. The shop also purchased quantities of walrus tusks that Ed cut crosswise into thin slices to show the granular center. He then stained them with a spirit-based wood stain that brought out color, and drilled them, also for use on key chains and bracelets or as pendants.

The jewelry made from walrus ivory was described in a general way in the catalogs but not pictured. During the 1910s and 1920s, however, the imitation elk teeth that Ed created were pictured. The mid-1920s catalog (Catalog E) described them as "Reconstructed Elk Teeth," available singly and in matched pairs, and noted: "We are the originators of the Elk Teeth made from the teeth of Arctic Walrus. These teeth have a natural eye like the real Elk Teeth and can hardly be told from the genuine." Curiously, in the 1916 catalog (Catalog C) they were titled "Hello Bill—Elks' Teeth," perhaps in reference to Buffalo Bill Cody. There was obviously sufficient market for elk teeth to warrant replicating them, and the Hudson Bay Fur Company and others also sold them. In about 1916 Standley noted in his guest book, "Old Indian bot 200 elk una [ulna] teeth to sew on Buckskin jacket shirt and sell the tourists at 50c a pick off the shirt."

Although Ed did not engrave "Eskimo" images on the ivory objects he made, nor label them Eskimo-made, consumers could have assumed they were because they were made of Alaskan ivory. Other commercially made ivory and bone work the shop carried may have been even more confusing, because it emulated work produced by Eskimo carvers in Alaska and often incorporated "Eskimo" motifs. During Standley's lifetime, Herman Krupp's Alaska Fur Company, later called Oceanic Trading, was the shop's most important local supplier of commercially worked ivory. The Alaska Fur Company, a wholesale rather than retail firm, was both a fur and curio provider. It was first listed in the *Seattle City Directory* in 1917, but items in Standley's 1916 catalog suggest that it may have operated earlier. Krupp developed several lines of merchandise. Jewelry made from "Alaska black diamond" (black hematite) or from jade was the most prominent, but he also wholesaled etched ivory items. Although businesses in Seattle bought from him, shops in Alaska were his most important customers. Krupp also purchased miniature wooden totem poles directly from the same carvers who supplied them to Standley's and other local shops then wholesaled them to Alaska. Krupp's line of etched ivory, "signed" *Nuguruk,* included jewelry (bracelets, pendants, and earrings), and such household items as cake breakers, pie servers, knife sets, and paper knives.

Eskimo carvers were hired in some smaller commercial ivory operations in Seattle—especially Leonard F. Porter, Inc., and the James L. Houston Manufacturing Company—and an Eskimo employee may have originated the initial Nuguruk designs, but the unsigned and slickly etched pieces themselves were made mechanically by longtime Krupp employee Karl Lemke. Houston's company, although known especially for its gold nugget jewelry, also produced ivory knife sets and curios signed Weyahok, the Inupiaq name of the young Point Hope artist Howard Weyahok Rock. When Rock needed work while studying art in Seattle, the Houston Company employed him for several years to apply color by hand to Eskimo-subject designs that had been etched mechanically onto ivory. They were then signed "Weyahok" (fig. 8.8). As walrus ivory became less available, many objects were made of elephant ivory. For a time Rock also produced small oil paintings of Alaskan scenes for Krupp's company, signing them "Kunuk." He later returned to Alaska, where he became an important Native leader and newspaper editor in Nome.[9]

Ye Olde Curiosity Shop continued to buy from Krupp after he sold his Alaska Fur Company name and

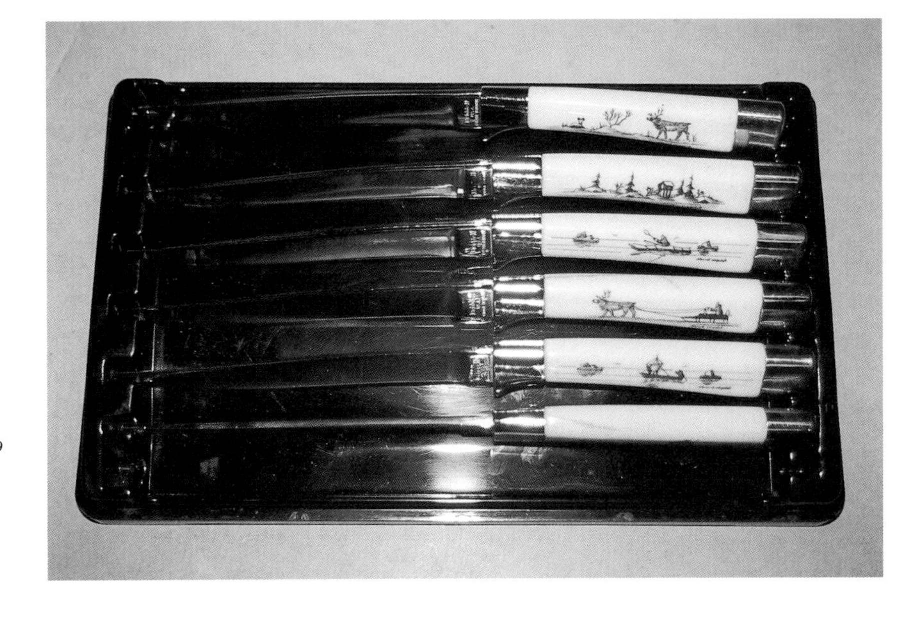

8.8. Commercial operations such as Herman Krupp's Alaska Fur Company (later the Oceanic Trading Company), Leonard F. Porter, Inc., and the James L. Houston Manufacturing Company made carving and steak knife sets, paper knives, and other items engraved with Eskimo-type images and signed them with Eskimo-sounding names like Nunuk and Nuguruk. Howard Weyahok Rock, a young Inupiat artist who worked for the Houston Manufacturing Company while in college in Seattle in the 1940s, added finishing color to these steak knives, signed Weyahok. Alaska State Museum, Juneau, TD 98-11-13. Photograph by the author.

Wonderful Indian Baskets

When the cycle is right, the natives gather grasses, roots of spruce trees, and inner bark of cedar trees. They bury, wash, scrape, beat, bleach and dye the strands, with colors obtained from herbs, bones, minerals, then weave most beautiful baskets, mats, hats, bottles, card cases, fans, etc. (from 50 cents to $50 each), using their fingers for needles and teeth for scissors. Superstition bars copying patterns. Designs are from nature.

—Ye Olde Curiosity Shop basket information card included with each basket purchased

took the name Oceanic Trading in 1943, until the company closed in the late 1980s. The shop also bought ivory from the Houston Company. In 1974 the Federal Trade Commission took Oceanic Trading, the Houston Company, and several other manufacturers and wholesalers in Seattle and Portland to court, alleging that they misrepresented their products. The suit was thrown out. Several years earlier a growing concern about fraudulent Alaskan arts and crafts had induced the Alaska Division of Economic Enterprise to develop a "Silver Hand" emblem to be attached to authentic items.[10] As in the Curiosity Shop's early years, the ivory available to buyers was a matter of supply and demand, with supply being the major factor. Collectors and some tourist buyers searched out authentic, Eskimo-made carvings, but most buyers were most interested in a souvenir of their visit.

Baskets from Puget Sound and Alaska

Ye Olde Curiosity Shop has always sold baskets. Standley liked them and enjoyed buying directly from women who brought them into the shop. Puget Sound baskets were readily available when he first arrived in Seattle, and he quickly made connections in Alaska to acquire Tlingit and Aleut ones as well. Photographs of shop interiors and Standley family memories corroborate that in the shop's early years, baskets sold well, but the market later dwindled. Standley kept a copy of George Wharton James's *Indian Basketry* (1903) and distilled from it a mixture of information on materials and techniques that he published on his all-purpose basket information card. The card was more accurate in its list of basket shapes the shop carried than anything else. The descriptions of baskets in his "1001 lists" were not much more specific: "Klickitat Hard Water Tight Baskets, Natural Colors, From Roots $3.50 to 20.00," "Hats Woven on the West Coast out of Cedar Bark $3.00 to 6.00," "Flasks Covered with Grass Weaving by Indians $1.25 to 7.00" (from Catalog A).

The 1907 brochure advertised "Beautiful baskets for the dresser, also for jardinerres . . . 25c to $25.00, occasionally $50.00" and proclaimed with exaggeration "Indian Baskets. There are so many hundreds of patterns of tribes and weavers shown in our stock that it is impossible to catalog them. Some of the old Indian women send us all their output, not many, if it takes 2 months to create a fine woven basket." An interior photograph on the cover of the brochure (see page 5) included the same basket shelves pictured on Standley's basket postcard (see fig. 2.9); the postcard photograph was used in the first four shop catalogs (Catalogs A–D). Although Standley carried some baskets from elsewhere in the Puget Sound region, California, and further afield, Makah and Quileute baskets from the Olympic Peninsula and Tlingit baskets from Alaska dominated.

The Makah and Quileute baskets were rarely utilitarian ones; rather, they were smaller basketry "bowls" and what have come to be called "trinket baskets." Small, round, and lidded, the trinket baskets are constructed with a plaited bottom of flat strips of cedar bark and cylindrical sides of wrapped-twining. The fine strands of an added outer weft of bear or elk grass wrap the warp and inner weft of cedar bark to create a pale, glossy, and finely textured outer surface. Dyed grass is used for contrasting stripes or figures. Although such "trinket boxes" are usually attributed to the Makah, neighboring Quileute women taught by Makah women also made them. Stanley's supplier books list women of both tribes as suppliers.[11] Trinket baskets were also made by Canadian Nuu-chah-nulth women. They are difficult to distinguish in photographs from those of their Makah relatives, although baskets with knobbed lids tend to come from Canada.[12] Because the Nuu-chah-nulth were allowed to move back and forth between Washington and British Columbia with impunity, many of them probably brought baskets to Seattle to sell. Wives of the Nuu-chah-nulth men living on the Duwamish River, who carved thousands of totem poles for Seattle curio shops, surely did as well. A number of Makah-type trinket baskets were purchased in Alaska as Alaskan baskets early in the twentieth century, suggesting that Seattle companies that wholesaled to Alaskan gift shops may have been purchasing them in quantity for that purpose.[13]

Although James G. Swan wrote as early as 1870 that Makah women made "a small basket of bark and grass dyed various colors with realistic and geometric designs," the Makah trinket baskets he collected for the Smithsonian are almost all geometric. Photographs taken about 1900 of the collection of Samuel Morse, a missionary at Neah Bay, show piles of small trinket baskets and bowls with stripes but none with figures.[14] Photographs from the same time of women selling baskets on Seattle's streets also show striped trinket baskets (see page 9). Yet, Ye Olde Curiosity Shop's basket postcard also pictures Makah and Quileute baskets with schematic birds or canoe and whale figures similar to those long woven on ceremonial whaling hats. In a view of the shop's interior from 1912 (see fig. 2.1), almost all of the Makah and Quileute baskets include such figures.

Marketers often influence tourist art, and when recounting early times to a local reporter, Standley took some credit for the innovation: "The baskets in those days were all plain. Tourists wanted something fancy, so I influenced the local Indians to incorporate designs in their work. This custom spread all over the Sound."[15] Certainly, Standley did not invent the idea of using figures on trinket or other baskets made for sale, but it does appear that his encouragement induced such baskets to become more common, certainly in his stock, until they came to be considered typical. In his address and supplier books from the 1920s and his address book "Friends" (dated 1928), Standley recorded some of the basket makers with whom he was dealing. He noted that Mrs. Agnes Ward of Neah Bay made fine oval baskets with gulls, fish, swastikas, and whales that she sold for fifty-five cents, and Rosa Yokum "covers bottles and makes dandy $1.50 baskets with covers on." Florence Greene of Port Angeles, Washington, made pretty baskets at forty, fifty, and seventy-five cents each, while Quileute weaver Mrs. Mary Chips sold her tiny thimble baskets for fifty and sixty cents.[16] Quileute basket maker Ida Penn Taylor of Mora (the mailing address for the La Push community), the daughter of Standley's longtime friend Dan White, was named several times. Her baskets with fish, gulls, canoes, and swastikas were "extra fine" and "very swell." Although Standley listed Washburn's Store in Neah Bay as also selling Makah baskets, he does not appear to have bought there.[17] He did not need a middleman because Olympic Peninsula Natives came into Seattle often enough to deal directly with them.

Because the supplier books do not denote the size of the baskets sold, it is not possible to directly correlate what a maker received for a basket of a particular size with what the store sold it for. The markup for larger ones appears to have been substantial, however. In the early catalogs and within the store itself, Makah-type "trinket baskets" were priced by size, ranging from fifty cents for one about two and a half inches across and two inches deep to $3 for one seven inches across and four and a half inches deep (fig. 8.9). Small but very finely woven examples and tiny "thimble baskets" were higher. Unlidded bowl baskets were less expensive relative to their size than were trinket baskets. Both bowl and trinket baskets were considered attractive souvenirs suitable for display on a dressing table or mantle, or, as was also popular at the time, in a basket, Indian, or curio corner. They sold well during the shop's early years. Although Standley also carried baskets from elsewhere in Washington, his catalogs suggest that the supply was inconsistent. He sometimes bought baskets from Yakama Indians who brought them to the shop, but he recorded no names. His source for Klamath baskets was Orville Elliott, the agent on the Klamath Indian Reservation in Oregon; W. T. Paul & Curios of Portland provided Klickitat ones.

At the time Standley opened his first Seattle shop, Alaskan baskets were coveted tourist mementos and requisite to the complete basket collection. By 1884 the Pacific Steamship Company offered regularly scheduled excursions along Alaska's Inside Passage, taking visitors to Juneau, Killisnoo near Angoon, Sitka, and Wrangell. The 1,650 tourists in that area in 1884 had more than tripled by 1890.[18] The Inside Passage tour offered multiple opportunities to purchase Tlingit baskets and other curios, often directly from the makers. For travelers who could go only so far as Seattle, Tlingit baskets and a few Haida and Aleut ones from Alaska were available at curio and gift stores, including Ye Olde Curiosity Shop.

Standley's basket postcard (see fig. 2.9) pictured about two dozen Tlingit baskets, most of them open topped and slightly flared. Typical of those sold to cruise passengers, these baskets were twined of spruce root and ornamented with two or three geometrically patterned bands of false embroidery using dyed grass and maidenhair fern stem. The patterns on those in the photograph include swastikas, crosses, diamonds, and named patterns such as *wave, tying,* and *tattoo.*[19] To acquire the famous Tlingit baskets, Standley depended on Alaskans who ran curio shops themselves, particularly Walter Waters of Wrangell and John Feusi of Douglas.

In the Aleutian Islands finely woven grass baskets were important long before European contact. By the late 1860s the sale of Aleut grass baskets, particularly those from the island of Attu, were important to the Aleut economy. These flat-bottomed baskets and card and cigar cases, constructed of two pieces that fit together, were considered by many to be the finest basketry in the world. Constructed with two-strand twining, some baskets numbered as many as a hundred stitches per inch, and many incorporated intricate eccentric patterning and colored touches of worsted wool. By the 1890s collectors were willing to pay high prices for the especially delicate work from Attu and Atka. Likely because they were expensive and not easily available, Ye Olde Curiosity shop advertised Aleut baskets in its catalogs for only a short time, and then only card cases (also called cigar cases). These baskets were difficult to obtain as early as 1915, and it is not clear from whom Standley acquired them.

In the mid-1910s Standley's catalogs advertised "wonderful Indian baskets of Washington State and Alaska. Made from grasses, cedar bark, spruce roots, native dyes, many rare designs. Hundreds to select from." A grouping of photoclips of baskets with prices first appeared in Catalog C (1916) and was used throughout the 1920s (Catalogs D–F) with essentially the same descriptions but some changes in prices (see fig. 8.9). Offerings included Makah baskets with and without covers as well as napkin rings and thimble baskets, Skokomish baskets, Attu card cases, and Klamath baskets. There were also

No. 9 Reproduction of Whale Hutners Totem, 19 inches high $3.50
No. 11 Reproduction of Chief Shakes Totem from Wrangle, Alaska, 33 inches high.... $6.50
No. 12 Shows one of the many designs of Totems we have in stock, no two of which are alike. Prices are as follows:

8 to 10 inches high	$0.50	Same size, finer carving	$0.75
11 to 14 inches high	1.00	Same size, finer carving	1.50
15 to 18 inches high	1.75	Same size, finer carving	2.50
19 to 24 inches high	2.50	Same size, finer carving	3.75
25 to 30 inches high	4.50	Same size, finer carving	6.00
30 to 40 inches high	5.50	Same size, finer carving	7.50

We have larger sizes from 4 to 10 feet high, at $2.00 to $4.00 per foot, according to width and carvingg.
10 to 15 feet high, as to carving and width, $2.50 to $5.00 per foot.
For larger sizes, write for prices.
No. 13 Raven and Frog Totem from Kwakiutl Indians, B. C., 15 inches high........ $2.00

WONDERFUL INDIAN BASKETS OF WASHINGTON STATE AND ALASKA, MADE FROM GRASSES, CEDAR BARK, SPRUCE ROOTS, NATIVE DYES, MANY RARE DESIGNS. HUNDREDS TO SELECT FROM.

Plate No. 14

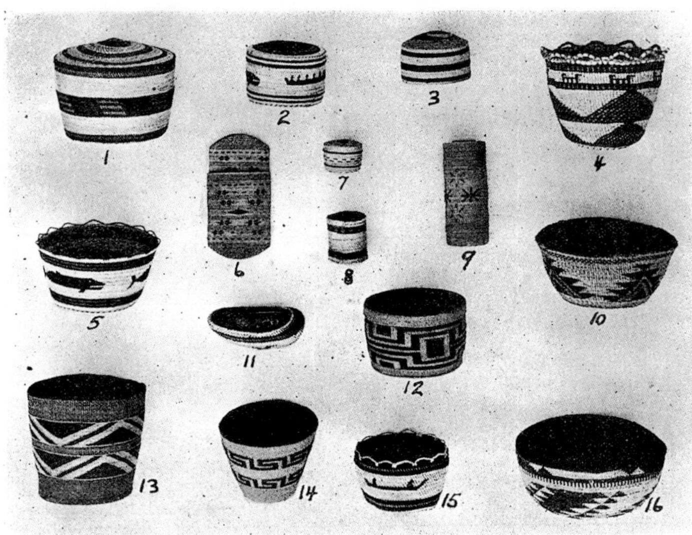

MAKAH BASKETS

Like Nos. 1, 2, 3, 7, with cover.		Like Nos. 5 and 15, without cover	
2½ in. across by 2 in. deep	$0.50	4 in. across by 2½ in. deep	$0.75
3½ in. across by 2½ in. deep	.75	5 in. across by 2½ in. deep	1.00
4½ in. across by 2¾ in. deep	1.00	5¼ in. across by 2¾ in. deep	1.35
5 in. across by 3 in. deep	1.50	5½ in. across by 3 in. deep	1.50
5½ in. across by 3½ in. deep	1.75	6½ in. across by 4½ in. deep	1.75
6 in. across by 3½ in. deep	2.00	8 in. across by 6½ in. deep	2.00
6½ in. across by 4 in. deep	2.50	9 in. across by 7 in. deep	2.50
7 in. across by 4½ in. deep	3.00	10 in. across by 7 in. deep	3.00

No. 4 Napkin Ring made same as Makah Baskets, each 50c
Same as Nos. 1, 2, 3 and 7 only much finer.

Thimble Basket, fine weaving	$1.50
Thimble Basket, extra fine weaving	2.00
Basket about 1¼ in. across by 1¼ in. deep	1.50
Same size, finer weaving	3.00
Basket about 2 in. across by 1¼ in. deep	$2.50 to $3.25
Basket about 2½ in. across by 1¾ in. deep	$5.00 to 7.50
Basket about 3½ in. across by 2½ in. deep	$7.50 to 12.50

27

8.9. This photograph was reused in shop catalogs through the 1920s (Catalogs D–F), although the shop's stock of several types of baskets was declining precipitously. By 1930 only Makah and Tlingit baskets were easily available. The price list and caption continued on the following page, listing baskets from the Skokomish (no. 4), Attu (nos. 6, 9), Klamath (no. 10), "Thlinket" and "Hidah" (no. 12), Taku, "Thlinket," or Yakutat (nos. 13, 14), and Shasta (no. 16). Basket page, Catalog C (1916), p. 27.

"Thlinket" and "Hidah" baskets "with rattle top covers. Prices according to fineness of weave"; Taku, "Thlinket," or Yakutat baskets, "prices according to fineness of weave and design"; and Shasta squaw caps and jar shape, "prices according to weave." Despite their considerable differences, Standley referred to "Thlinket" and "Hidah" baskets as if they were similar. It is unlikely that he ever held many Haida baskets, but a few fine Haida woven hats appear in early photographs.

Shop catalogs after 1916 document an uneven decline in basket making and availability in general. In 1920 (Catalog D) prices for Makah and Klamath baskets were the same or only slightly higher than earlier, but other baskets (especially Tlingit and Haida ones) were more expensive. Skokomish and Attu baskets had become "almost impossible to obtain. Write for List and Prices." Prices during the mid- and late 1920s (Catalogs E and F) were little different, but Klamath baskets now required one to "write for list and prices." Catalog G (ca. 1930) reflects a dramatic decline. In a small corner of a single page a Tlingit and a Makah basket are pictured with instructions to write for information on larger sizes. Interior shop photographs from the 1930s also document the shrinking stock of baskets. Both availability and interest were now too limited to warrant much catalog space. Baskets are not listed at all in subsequent catalogs.

As the basket collecting craze subsided, basket makers suffered from this decline. Stores serving Indian communities, like Washburn's at Neah Bay, accepted baskets in payment for groceries because they were sometimes a family's only livelihood, but they could not sell them (fig. 8.10). Ye Olde Curiosity Shop continued to buy some occasionally too. Standley's grandson Joe James recalls that in the 1940s and early 1950s, the shop still had "a beautiful selection of baskets at fantastic prices," but "you could hardly give them away."[20] The shop also offered corn husk bags from the Plateau for years. Basket makers still occasionally brought in finely woven little baskets that the shop would buy for $20 apiece, but selling one was rare compared with the market for totem poles. The market for baskets did not begin to strengthen again until the 1960s.

> The Top Row is the wonderful Hair Seal Moccasin made by the Alaska Indians; are made of Indian Tanned Skins prettily beaded, and are fur trimmed. Seldom do we get two designs alike. Guaranteed to be Genuine Indian Made.
>
> —Ye Old Curiosity Shop Catalog C, p. 28

Moccasins

Indian moccasins came to be expected in a curio shop, and Ye Olde Curiosity Shop began carrying them shortly after its opening. The 1907 brochure promised moccasins in hair seal, soft and hard tan, varying from seventy-five cents to $5, depending on quality, size, and bead or porcupine quillwork decoration. The 1910–13 catalog (Catalog A) listed cute baby mukluks from Point Barrow and Eskimo walrus and hair-sealskin boots for adults. The 1915 catalog (Catalog B) introduced a photograph of hair-seal moccasins from Alaska Indians (75 cents–$2.25), pictured along with four pairs of commercially made "Pocahontas" ones made of leather. The photograph and text are the same in the next two catalogs (Catalogs C and D) with prices rising slightly about 1920. In the mid-1920s catalog (Catalog E) commercial moccasins with "Indian beaded designs" dominated the display page, but the shop still offered Indian hair-seal moccasins from Alaska and had added a more expensive "Alaska Eskimo moccasin" with soles of ice-tanned seal skin. It also advertised Sioux moccasins with rawhide soles and fully beaded buckskin tops. All three types were carried through the late 1920s and the 1930s but were not necessarily listed in each catalog. Catalogs F and G do not mention commercial moccasins, as do the other catalogs.

Over the years "the wonderful Indian hair-seal moccasins made by the Indians of Alaska" dominated Standley's stock of Native-made moccasins (fig. 8.11). Those that he ordered were a standard Tlingit type, rather quickly constructed with the sole and body made of one piece of seal skin usually turned so that the hair was on the outside, seamed at the heel, and gathered at the toe around a large vamp or instep. The vamp was of wool fabric, typically red but sometimes blue or green, and beaded with eagles or simple flowers. The shop also carried similar moccasins in moosehide. The more shaped Tlingit moccasin with a blunt, T-shaped toe seam and small vamp with open foliate-scroll beading that is

8.10. Indian family, probably Makah, vending baskets in front of the Frederick and Nelson Department Store, 1912. Makah and Quileute women from the Olympic Peninsula brought cash into their families by selling baskets by the thousands on the streets and to shops in Pacific Northwest coastal cities. The wares here include cedar-bark rain hats, bowl baskets, and lidded trinket baskets in a range of sizes. *Seattle Post-Intelligencer* collection, 83.10.PA2.1, Museum of History and Industry, Seattle.

ADDRESS: COLMAN DOCK FRONT, SEATTLE, WASHINGTON

ALASKA INDIAN HAIR SEAL MOCCASINS

No. 650—The wonderful Hair Seal Moccasins, hand made by the Indians of Alaska. These are made from the skin of the Leopard or Hair Seal; soft Indian tanned, trimmed with wool seal and other Alaska furs. The beaded toe piece is of flowers, birds, animals and other Indian designs; seldom do we get two pairs alike:

Men's, sizes 7 to 12, as to quality, pair	$3.00	to	$3.50
Ladies', sizes 3 to 7, as to quality, pair	2.75	to	3.25
Misses', sizes 11 to 2, as to quality, pair	2.50	to	3.00
Children's, sizes 6 to 10, as to quality, pair	$1.75	to	$2.25
Baby's, sizes 1 to 5, as to quality, pair	1.00	to	1.50

No. 648—Alaska Eskimo Moccasins

These Moccasins are made by the Eskimos of Alaska from walrus, seal and reindeer skin. The soles are of ice tanned seal skin, the uppers of seal or reindeer and are lined with reindeer, rabbit or gray squirrel; are sewed with sinew. Ladies' sizes 3 to 6. Per pair, $5.50.
Gents' sizes 7 to 11, as to quality, $5.50 to $6.00 per pair.

THE ARMADILLO BASKET

The Armadillo is a most interesting and curious animal and is found in Western Texas and Old Mexico. It is protected by a shield of armour, which is fashioned into a basket, the tail being bent and attached to the head to form a handle; the shells, which are very durable, vary in length from 11 to 15 inches; are thoroughly cured and finished with a waterproof varnish. Are as hard as bone.

No. 801—Plain Basket $3.25
No. 802—Basket lined with fine quality of silk, in colors of pink, lavender, turquoise blue, dark blue, red, yellow, orange and green, each 4.50

WE PAY ALL DELIVERY AND INSURANCE CHARGES 21

8.11. Ye Olde Curiosity Shop has always offered both Native-made and commercially manufactured moccasins. Beginning very soon after the shop opened and until such moccasins became prohibitively expensive in the 1950s with the advent of the ANAC (Alaska Native Arts and Crafts) association, it sold thousands of hair-seal moccasins made by Tlingit women in Alaska. The "Alaska Eskimo Moccasins" with ice-tanned sealskin soles were especially popular in the 1920s and 1930s. Catalog G (early 1930s), 21.

common in museum collections does not appear in the catalogs, probably because it was more expensive.[21] Beaded moccasins began to be made for sale in earnest in Tlingit communities about 1890, as more and more visitors on steamer cruises through the Inside Passage sought mementos to take home. Tlingit men often went barefoot, using moccasins only when snow shoeing, and women wore them inside the house, but moccasins did not become an important Tlingit manufacture until a tourist market developed. Neighboring Athapaskans to the east and a few Cree bands that had settled in British Columbia, both of whom made beaded moccasins, were influential in the design of Tlingit ones.

While Tlingit women in Sitka, Wrangell, and other southeastern Alaskan communities vended moccasins along with beaded wall pockets, baskets, and silver bracelets on the streets of town and on the wharf when steamers docked, local traders acted as middlemen to fill orders from shops elsewhere, Ye Olde Curiosity Shop among them. Standley bought Tlingit hair-seal moccasins from at least a dozen providers in Southeast Alaska, mostly stores that bought from local sewers and acted as middlemen. His supplier books from the 1920s and 1930s indicate that John Feusi, who ran a general store in Douglas, Alaska, across from Juneau, and Walter Waters of Wrangell were major suppliers, but there were also R. J. Peratrovich of Klawock, Alaska; Peter Kastrometinoff of Sitka; William Gray and his wife, Betty, of Yakutat; and others.[22]

In the mid-1920s the shop began to offer Alaska Eskimo moccasins with "ice tanned seal skin soles," bent up and crimped, then attached to an upper of seal or reindeer skin (see fig. 8.11). This type of stiff sole, similar to rawhide, is normally termed "hard tanned" or "oil tanned" because the dehaired hides are stretched and left outside in the dead of winter to allow the action of wind and dry blowing snow to polish them white, but Standley's term "ice tanned" held more romance. The moccasins were usually fur lined, had a fur cuff, and might be ornamented at the toe with a touch of contrasting fur and/or a simple appliquéd hide or bead motif. The shop bought them directly from both Eskimo women and suppliers living in Alaska and the Puget Sound area.[23]

After the state-sponsored organization Alaska Native Arts and Crafts (ANAC) was established in 1956 to encourage, tag, and market arts made by

Alaska Natives, the Curiosity Shop ordered moccasins through ANAC. From the shop's standpoint, ANAC created a problem. As Joe James explained it, ANAC paid Alaska Natives more for their arts than they had been making, but the Natives were not interested in making a lot of money, so they produced only an amount sufficient to earn enough money to get by. As their return went up, their production went down. The resulting scarcity of items made the price to the shop and subsequently to the consumer rise steadily year after year for both hair-seal items and ivory. Instead of purchasing seven pairs of moccasins for $1 each, the old price, the shop had to pay $7 for one pair and raise the price for consumers. The shop therefore carried fewer and fewer Native-made moccasins. "People just don't want to pay those prices, except collectors."[24] In the 1920s and 1930s the shop also sometimes purchased Athapaskan mooseskin moccasins for $2 a pair through Abe Stein in Fairbanks, Alaska, and Yakima-[Yakama] style miniature moccasins from Susie Joe of Toppenish, Washington, at $1.50 a dozen. Its major commercial moccasin brands were Pocahantos and Minnetonka.

Beadwork and Leatherwork

For over a century Indian beadwork has been standard in curio shops; Ye Olde Curiosity Shop is no exception. The octopus bag and dance shirt in the photograph from about 1901 of the Madison Street shop (see fig. 1.6) show that at the very beginning Standley had acquired a few Tlingit beaded pieces made for dress occasions. In later years he purchased Plateau beaded bags and other articles when Indians from eastern Washington brought them in.

The various shop catalogs support Standley family observations that the shop has always carried a little beadwork, but, like baskets, beadwork has never been the dependable seller that totem poles have. The "1001 Curious Things" lists include not only beaded moccasins but an occasional beaded vest, papoose carrier, or gun case as well as such souvenir items as beaded watch fobs. In the catalogs beadwork appears on both Indian-made and commercially manufactured moccasins and bags. A photograph used in catalogs from 1916 through the late 1920s (Catalogs C–F) pictured beaded leather bags alongside koa seed bags from "Fiji and the Samoa Islands" with a caption reading, "We have also Beaded Bags, Belts and Pow Wow Bags from the Blackfeet and Sioux Indians" (fig. 8.12).[25] Three of the four leather bags shown, each with simple geometric beading and leather fringes to give them an "Indian look," are types produced in Indian arts and crafts enterprises of the period. Catalogs from the mid- and late 1920s (Catalogs E and F) also offered a ladies beaded "tulip bag" made of white kid leather (fig. 8.13). Although Standley did not record where he had acquired such bags, in the 1920s tulip bags were offered by mission-based

YE OLDE CURIOSITY SHOP, ESTABLISHED 1899 BY J. E. STANDLEY

BAGS AND BELTS MADE OF KOA SEEDS
ALSO FANCY BEADED BAGS

These Koa Seed Bags are made by the natives of Fiji and Samoa Islands, from rich brown sea beans, hard as bone. We also have Beaded Bags, Belts and Pow Pow or Tobacco Bags from the Blackfeet and Sioux Indians.

KOA SEED HAND BAGS

I-2	2¾x2¾ in., 34 in. chain	$0.85
I-6	2¾x2¾ in.	.50
I-3	4x4 in.	1.00
I-3-1	4x4 in., 38 in. chain	1.50
I-4	5x5 in.	1.75
I-4-1	5x5 in., 48 in. chain	2.25
I-4-2	6x6 in.	2.25
I-4-3	6x6 in., 48 in. chain	2.75
I-5-1	7x7 in.	3.00
I-5-2	7x7 in., 52 in. chain	3.50
I-0-1	Koa Seed Napkin Ring (Not Illustrated)	.25

LADIES' LEATHER BAGS
Fancy Beaded Designs Exclusive of Fringes

I-7	5¾x3½ in.	$2.25
I-8	8½x5¼ in.	4.00
I-9	9½x7 in.	3.75

I-10 INDIAN MADE BEADED BAGS
These are real creations—beautiful and destinctive.
Sizes from 5x7 in. to 12x15 in. Prices range from $6.00 to $25.00 each

I-1 KOA SEED BELT.......$0.85
(Give Size)

These Hand Bags are made of black Koa seeds and bright red Black Eyed Susan sea beans.

No. 1-1a—3x3-in., no flap......$0.60
No. 1-2a—4x4-in., with flap.. 1.35
No. 1-3a—4½ x 4 ½-in., no flap, ... 1.15
No. 1-4a—6x6-in., with flap.. 2.50
No. 1-5a—6½ x 6 ½-in., with flap 3.00

14 WE PREPAY ALL DELIVERY AND INSURANCE CHARGES

8.12. Most of the Indian-made beaded bags that Standley advertised (1/7–1/9) are types of bags that were produced in mission-based arts and crafts enterprises in the 1920s and 1930s. Photoclip 1/10 is a generic stand-in for a range of other beaded bags purchased from individual makers. Catalog E (mid-1920s), p. 14.

Indian arts and crafts businesses such as the Mohonk Lodge in Clinton, Oklahoma, and the Rocky Boy Mission in Rocky Boy, Montana.[26] Standley's tulip bag and two of the beaded bags in the photograph have the same central "beaded Indian design," linking them to the same supplier.

The shop always had a few beaded Plains or Plateau bags that Standley had purchased from individual makers. They are represented in the photograph by a rectangular beaded handbag with a simple floral motif against a white solidly beaded ground. In the mid-1920s Catalog E also advertised rectangular draw-string bags beaded on chamois skin made by the "Yakima" [Yakama] Indians, priced from $2.25 to $7.50, and Sioux Indian tobacco bags with quill-wrapped lower panels and hide fringes for $15 to $35. According to Joe James, some of the pipe bags came from the Midwest, but most were made locally. Neither the drawstring or pipe bags appear in other catalogs. The Denver wholesale distributor H. H. Tammen Company (Standley's source for decorative clocks, dressing table accessories, and jewelry made from Colorado stones) also provided the shop with many of the leather goods with Indian images. About 1900 the company began to market a range of Indian-related leather goods, among them pennants and pillow tops painted with images of generic Indian princesses and chiefs in Plains headdress, and, for Ye Olde Curiosity Shop, totem poles. Standley included chief pillows in several of his lists and pictured them in catalogs during the 1920s (fig. 8.13.)

Dolls

Indian dolls are another minor, but expected, component of a curio shop's inventory, especially in Indian country. Across the United States those offered have for the most part been the same commercially-produced ones, sometimes augmented with dolls made by local Natives. Dolls were never a prominent part of the Curiosity Shop's stock, but over the years there has been sufficient interest to justify carrying them. The catalogs' "1001 Curious Things" lists included a few Native-made dolls, primarily Eskimo ones, but those shown in the catalog photographs were almost all commercially manufactured. Of the

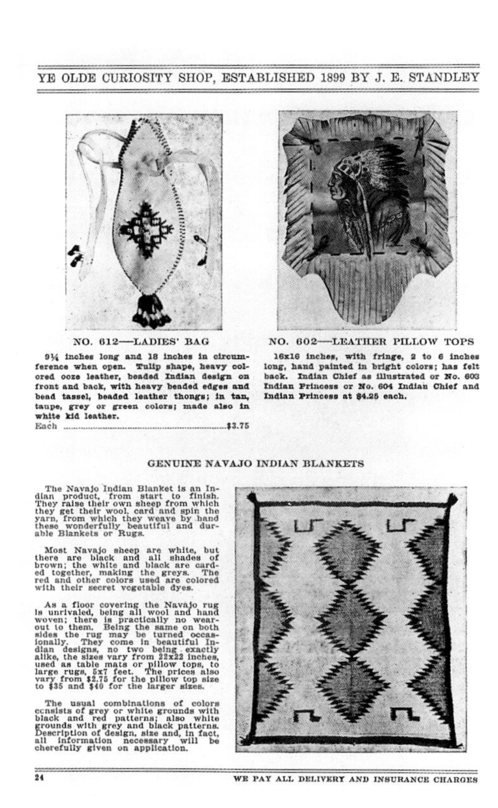

YE OLDE CURIOSITY SHOP, ESTABLISHED 1899 BY J. E. STANDLEY

NO. 612—LADIES' BAG

9¼ inches long and 18 inches in circumference when open. Tulip shape, heavy colored ooze leather, beaded Indian design on front and back, with heavy beaded edges and bead tassel, beaded leather thongs; in tan, taupe, grey or green colors; made also in white kid leather.
Each $3.75

NO. 602—LEATHER PILLOW TOPS

16x16 inches, with fringe, 2 to 6 inches long, hand painted in bright colors; has felt back. Indian Chief as illustrated or No. 603 Indian Princess or No. 604 Indian Chief and Indian Princess at $4.25 each.

GENUINE NAVAJO INDIAN BLANKETS

The Navajo Indian Blanket is an Indian product, from start to finish. They raise their own sheep from which they get their wool, card and spin the yarn, from which they weave by hand these wonderfully beautiful and durable Blankets or Rugs.

Most Navajo sheep are white, but there are black and all shades of brown; the white and black are carded together, making the greys. The red and other colors used are colored with their secret vegetable dyes.

As a floor covering the Navajo rug is unrivaled, being all wool and hand woven; there is practically no wear-out to them. Being the same on both sides the rug may be turned occasionally. They come in beautiful Indian designs, no two being exactly alike, the sizes vary from 22x22 inches, used as table mats or pillow tops, to large rugs, 5x7 feet. The prices also vary from $2.75 for the pillow top size to $35 and $40 for the larger sizes.

The usual combinations of colors consists of grey or white grounds with black and red patterns; also white grounds with grey and black patterns. Description of design, size and, in fact, all information necessary will be cherefully given on application.

24 WE PAY ALL DELIVERY AND INSURANCE CHARGES

ADDRESS: COLMAN DOCK FRONT, SEATTLE, WASHINGTON

SKOOKUM INDIAN DOLLS

The original and greatest Indian Character Doll. Representing the true Indian type; dressed in characteristic Indian headwear, brightly colored blankets and decorated leather moccasins. Solid, indestructable composition faces. Real Indian hair. They stand up.

No. 625—Chippewa Chief, 10¾ inches high, illustrated $1.65
No. 626—Chippewa Squaw with papoose, 10¾ inches high 1.65
No. 627—Navajo Chief, 10¾ inches high 1.65
No. 628—Apache Chief with Indian trappings and fancy blanket, 17 inches high, illus. 3.25
No. [illegible]—Sioux Squaw with papoose, head covering and bead necklace, as illustrated 3.25
No. 630—Sioux War Chief, 21 inches high, with feather war bonnet and fancy blanket, not illustrated 4.50

INDIAN LEATHER DOLLS

Nine inches long, painted leather face and body, with leather fringed trimming

No. 601—Boy, each $0.50
No. 602—Girl, each .... .50

NO. 94—SEA HORSES

One of the strangest animals of the sea is the Sea Horse, known as the Kangaroo of the sea. It has a head like a horse. The male has an abdominal pouch in which he carries the larva and hatches the young. Are rarely over a few inches in length. Male and female about 3 inches long; per pair, 50c.

WE PAY ALL DELIVERY AND INSURANCE CHARGES 17

8.13. The ladies' tulip bag, available from mission-based Indian craft businesses, alluded to "Indianness" yet fit into mainstream fashion. The shop's painted leather pillow tops probably came from H. H. Tammen Company of Denver, although other distributors offered them as well. The information Standley provided about his Genuine Navajo Indian Blankets was based on the text of a catalog put out between 1918 and 1921 by one of the shop's suppliers, Santa Fe trader Julius Gans. Catalog F (late 1920s), p. 24.

8.14. Skookum Dolls were a favorite of curio shops for decades. That they always looked in one direction spawned various authoritative explanations. It was said that those looking right looked to the future, and those rare ones who looked to the left, like the old chief here, looked toward death. Catalog F (late 1920s), p. 17.

six pictured in the first doll photograph (in Catalog D, about 1920), the sole noncommercial doll was actually a narrow five-inch-long sealskin pouch with a tiny rudimentary face peeking from the top. The commercially made dolls included a profile "Cuddle Kid," with two feathers and a tomahawk, and a frontal "Indian doll," wearing chaps; both were soft dolls sewn of hand-colored leather and stuffed. An "Eskimo Doll," which appears to be a fashion doll wearing a white fur coat and a muff, and a blanketed "Little Buck" and a "pappoose" were all hard-body dolls with molded heads. The Little Buck and Pappoose stood in for an assortment of dolls from the same source, "no two alike, each one a little different. Just like real people." In later catalogs from the 1920s (Catalogs E and F) these dolls would be identified as Skookum Indian Character Dolls (fig. 8.14).

The popular Skookum Dolls, first developed in the mid-1910s, sold for decades. Standley ordered them from Denver's H. H. Tammen Company. Mary McAboy of Missoula, Montana, had invented the dolls, patented them in 1914, and established a cottage industry in which women made them in their homes. *Skookum* was both a Chinook jargon word meaning large or strong and a brand of Washington state apples. The original Skookum Dolls were made with apple faces. Those pictured in Standley's catalogs have the molded composition faces that took the place of apple faces beginning in 1920 and the

Skookum Indian Dolls. The original and greatest Indian Character Doll. Representing the true Indian type; dressed in characteristic Indian headwear, brightly colored blankets and decorated leather moccasins. Solid indestructible composition faces. Real Indian hair.

—Ye Olde Curiosity Shop Catalog E, mid-1920s

braided wigs of real hair, horsehair, or mohair, typical of Skookum Dolls of that time. Their armless bodies, tightly wrapped in small cotton blankets from the Beacon Company of New Bedford, Massachusetts, and sometimes wearing beads, were made of straw with attached wooden legs. The suede-covered feet were painted to indicate moccasin decoration. Large display dolls provided by the distributor appear in several interior photographs of Ye Olde Curiosity Shop (see fig. 6.8). Skookum Dolls were produced until 1960 and are now considered collectors items. There were also Skookum Injun coloring books, but it is not known whether Ye Olde Curiosity Shop carried these.[27]

In the early 1930s catalog (Catalog G), dolls were relegated to the "1001" list, but a doll photograph returned in Catalogs H and I (see fig. 8.7).[28] The photograph contained four Eskimo dolls with flat painted faces and rabbit skin "parkas," likely made in Alaska, and a generic female doll wearing a print dress, moccasins, and a bead necklace and headband. Calling it a "West Coast Siwash Character Doll" provided a local connection, perhaps to enhance its salability. By the late 1930s small kachina dolls were common in curio shops in the Southwest. Although the simple kachina doll in Standley's catalog photograph was said to have been "made by Hopi Indian Priests of carved wood and highly colored," few of them were in fact. Chief White Eagle, who carved totem poles for the Curiosity Shop, also made kachina dolls and may have been the source of those advertised in the catalogs. The last catalog the shop put out (Catalog J), in the 1950s, pictured a large assortment of Skookum Dolls.

Northwest Coast Chilkat Blankets and Southwest Textiles

By far the rarest textiles Ye Olde Curiosity Shop ever carried were Chilkat blankets, the elegant finger-woven ceremonial robes with geometricized Northwest Coast crest designs. Standley acquired his first Chilkat blanket in 1900 and draped it across the lap of Indian silversmith Chad George for the second photograph of his Madison Street shop (see fig. 1.6). With the move to Colman Dock in 1904, when Standley had the shop photographed he hung the blanket above the door, obscuring the name of C. T. Wernecke Raw Furs, the business with which he shared the space (see fig. 1.12). Another Chilkat blanket was pictured on the covers of Catalogs C (see fig. 8.1) and D (1916 and early 1920s) to represent those offered for sale inside, for between $150 and $200. In Catalog A (ca. 1910) the price had been $60. In the mid-1920s the Chilkat blanket photograph was moved into the catalog proper (Catalog E) and dropped thereafter. During the late 1910s and early 1920s, Chilkat blankets were sufficiently available that Standley believed he could offer them in his catalogs. How many blankets he actually had at any given time is unclear, likely one or two at most. One of his supplier books, however, indicates that if there was an interested buyer, Standley could turn to basket supplier R. J. Peratovich of Klawock for one. Four different "Chilcats" (Standley used the older spelling) appear in shop and catalog photographs. When Joe James came into shop management in 1946, however, there were none.[29]

> Chilcat Blankets are worn by the chiefs during their ceremonial feasts and Potlatches. The material used is mountain sheep wool, the warp having cedar bark interwoven with the wool; the dyes used are all of native make, and is one of the rarest examples of Indian weaving. The designs are taken from Indian mythology, and show the genealogy of the tribe or family.
>
> —Ye Olde Curiosity Shop Catalog E, mid-1920s

From the beginning, the Curiosity Shop carried a few other types of textiles, and continued to do so over the years, but textiles were only a minor part of the stock. In the first shop photograph Chad George (marked "Indian") is wrapped in a coarse Navajo blanket (see fig. 1.6). A staple in Southwestern curio shops, Navajo rugs were placed on the floor for official shop photographs. For a while in the late 1920s and early 1930s Navajo textiles were offered in shop catalogs (see fig. 8.13).[30] Although there were dozens of Southwestern traders dealing in Navajo weaving, Standley's supplier books list only five, among them the Kirk Brothers of Gallup, New Mexico, and Julius Ganz (Gans) of Santa Fe.[31] Gans put out at least three catalogs between 1918 and 1921, and Standley seems to have had one. As was common at the time when curio dealers put together catalogs, Standley lifted verbatim part of what he published about Navajo rugs from another catalog, a Gans one, and paraphrased the rest.[32]

The Navajo rugs on the floor in shop photographs and pictured in shop catalogs tended toward simple bold motifs and muted, mostly natural colors—black, white, grays, and brown-grays, with a little red—traits especially common from about 1890 to 1920. In contrast, the Genuine Mexican Zerapes (serapes), which Standley imported directly from Mexico and advertised throughout the 1920s and into the 1930s, seemed so bright, at least in the subdued light of the Pacific Northwest, that he hastened to assure customers that they were in fact tasteful. "Characteristic of Mexican taste, the colors are exceedingly bright; however, the combinations are perfectly harmonized and lend a distinctly foreign air not to be encountered in any other form of native weavings." Being lighter in weight than the Indian (Navajo) blankets, larger serapes could serve as portiers (curtainlike hanging), couch covers, and wall blankets. Smaller ones were useful as table scarves and pillow tops.[33] What Standley identified as Chimayo Indian weaving, but was actually Spanish-American weaving from northern New Mexico, appeared in the "1001" list in the late 1920s (Catalog F).[34] For a short while in the mid-1920s (Catalog E)

Indian Design Silver Jewelry. The Haidah Tribes of Southeastern Alaska are the best silversmiths, and from hammered coin silver they make attractive bracelets and finger rings, using the Totem Pole designs. The Navajo Indians of New Mexico use native turquoise to embellish their bracelets and rings. We have hundreds, all different, a few listed here.

—Ye Olde Curiosity Shop Catalog E, mid-1920s

the shop also offered 100 percent wool Pendleton blankets, in four sizes, with fringes or bound in felt.

Silver Jewelry of Indian Design

Over the years Ye Olde Curiosity Shop also carried some individually made Navajo jewelry imported from the Southwest and a few Haida silver bracelets made in Alaska. Although Standley listed only a few sources for Southwestern jewelry in his supplier address books, there were also others, including curio dealers from across the country who were visiting Seattle or in town on buying and selling trips.[35] One such dealer was Allie BraMe of Phoenix, Arizona, the first curator of the Heard Museum. BraMe kept a journal during a trip to the Northwest Coast in summer 1928, during which she and her husband sold curios from the Southwest and purchased Northwest items to add to their stock. On Friday, July 13, she wrote that Max Silver of the Hudson Bay Fur Company came to their hotel room and bought a lot of silver and all the rugs they had brought. Then "Mr. Stanley [*sic*] from Ye Olde Curiosity Shop came and bought silver rings and bracelets. We are going shopping in their shops tomorrow." The visitors spent the next day buying Alaskan curios to sell in Arizona.[36]

Although the Curiosity Shop began advertising Indian silver jewelry in its 1907 brochure, and continued in catalogs throughout Standley's lifetime, jewelry such as the pieces that BraMe sold him is not what was pictured. Although implied (but not directly stated) to be Haida or Navajo, the bracelets and rings in catalog photographs were all, or almost all, commercially stamped ones; some if not all were made in Seattle. Catalog B (1915), the first to include grouped photoclips of merchandise, introduced Southwestern-style silver rings and bracelets stamped with crossed arrows, swastikas, and sunbursts. Some of these items had small turquoise settings. In the 1923 brochure, and catalogs throughout the decade (Catalogs E and F), a new photograph titled "Indian Design Silver Jewelry," pictured twelve bracelets, ten of them stamped with swastikas or other Southwestern designs (fig. 8.15). An 1896 report of the U.S. National Museum that named the swastika as the earliest known symbol had popularized it as an Indian and a good luck symbol.[37] Inexpensive stamped bracelets and rings were made and sold by the thousands in the Southwest at the time, but a close look at Standley's photograph reveals that two of the bracelets feature tiny cast-silver totem poles from the Seattle-based Mayer & Bros. In addition, Ed Standley had soldered them among the stamped motifs and may well have made the bracelets entirely. The last catalogs (Catalogs G

8.15. Although the text here speaks of tribes that make silver jewelry, the title "Indian Design Silver Jewelry" does not state whether what is pictured was actually Indian-made. Much, perhaps even all of the jewelry, was not. Both commercial enterprises and Indian artisans in the Southwest produced thin stamped silver bracelets similar to those here. The Mayer & Bros. totem poles attached to nos. 403 and 405 were added by Standley's son Edward, who may even have made the bracelets himself. Bracelets 410 and 411 are also Mayer & Bros. products. Catalog E (mid-1920s), p. 19. See figs. 7.17 and 7.18.

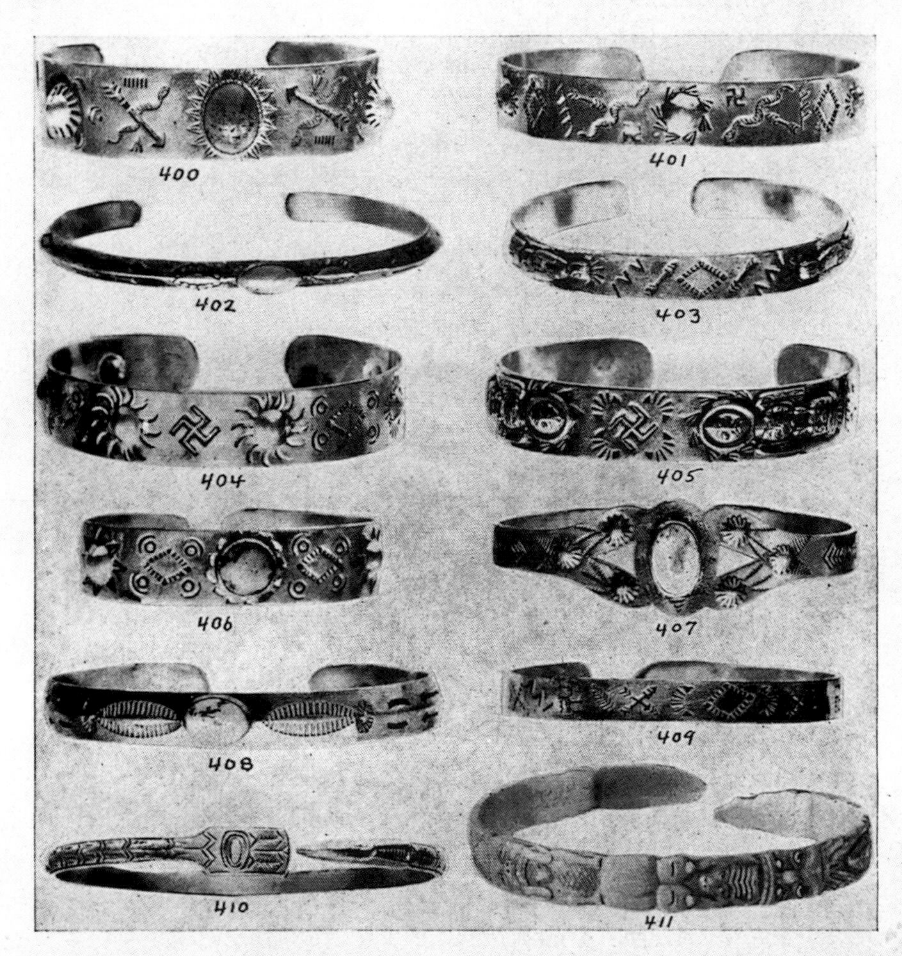

INDIAN DESIGN SILVER JEWELRY

Jewelry from the American Indian. The Haidah Tribes of Southeastern Alaska are the best silversmiths, and from hammered coin silver they make attractive bracelets and finger rings, using the Totem Pole designs. The Navajo Indians of New Mexico use native tourquoise to embellish their bracelets and rings. We have hundreds, all different, a few listed here. The bracelets are adjustable in size and will therefore fit any wrist.

No. 400—Indian design, ladies' size, ⅝-inch wide with turquoise matrix set $4.50

No. 400A—Without turquoise set, three raised designs 2.50

No. 401—Indian design, ladies" size, ⅜-inch wide, has three raised designs 2.00

No. 402—Indian design, ladies' size. Triangular shape, about ¼-wide, with turquoise matrix set 2.35

No. 402A—Without set 1.35

No. 403—Indian design, 5/16-inch wide, with two raised Totem figures, ladies' size 1.75

No. 404—Indian design, ½-inch wide, has five raised designs, ladies' size 2.25

No. 405—Indian design, ⅜-inch wide, with two raised Totem figures 2.50

No. 406—Indian design, ½-inch wide, misses' size, turquoise matrix set, two raised designs.... 3.00

No. 407—Indian design, front is ⅞-inch wide, turquoise matrix set, ladies' size 3.25

No. 408—Indian design, ⅜-inch wide, triangular shape with turquoise matrix set 3.00

No. 408A—Without set 1.85

No. 409—Indian design, ¼-inch wide, misses' size 1.25

No. 410—Indian design, 3/16-inch wide, ladies' size 1.50

No. 411—Stamped Indian Totem Pole Bracelet, ⅜-inch wide 1.50

Red Pipe Stone, Tomahawk Pipe . . . Large Red Pipe Stone, Peace Pipe . . . War Club, Large with Stone Head and Buckskin Covered, Beaded Handle.

—Ye Olde Curiosity Shop Catalog C, 1916

Horsehair, Indian Woven Belts, Hat Bands, Silver Mounted

—Ye Olde Curiosity Shop Catalog A, 1910–13

Dancing Masks, Heidious Carved Wood Faces, Alaska

—Ye Olde Curiosity Shop Catalog A, 1910–13

These queer grotesque faces are carved from wood by the Indians of Washington, British Columbia and Alaska, who use them in their ceremonial dances and Tribal Potlatch Feasts. Usually after the feasts the masks are destroyed.

—Ye Olde Curiosity Shop Catalog E and F, mid-1920s and late 1920s

and I), of 1939 and 1940, picture only the rings of the earlier catalogs, identical except for the removal of the swastika ring from the 1940 catalog.

Other Indian Items

Ye Olde Curiosity Shop catalogs advertised a few other popular Indian items that the shop could acquire from individuals or regional dealers who sold through mail order. At the time those who knew anything at all about Indians were more than likely familiar with Plains Indians. Thousands saw Buffalo Bill Cody's Wild West show during the more than thirty years it toured between 1883 and 1917. In early twentieth-century America the Indian with a feather headdress and tomahawk was still a far more familiar image than the Northwest's regional icon, the totem pole. A shop that offered a range of Indian items needed to carry at least a few Plains objects, and the Curiosity Shop did. Some of these appeared in the "1001 Curious Things" lists and occasionally in catalog illustrations.

Collectors of Plains art and artifacts were primarily men, interested in moccasins, weapons, and pipes. Businesses located on the Plains could supply these items and such regalia as "war shirts" and "war bonnets." Some shops, like Pawnee Bill's Indian Trading Post in Pawnee, Oklahoma, did business through mail order and continue to do so today.[38] For the most part Standley did not cater to the dedicated collector who was concerned with the authentic and the old, but he did advertise a little Plains beadwork, and in one catalog (C) he offered some weapons and peace pipes from Pipestone, Minnesota (fig. 8.16). The latter were inexpensive and satisfied the lower-end customer with a penchant for what in the public mind had become symbols of Plains Indian culture and savagery. Although Standley's written notes suggest that J. H. Austin of Pipestone was the shop's supplier for pipestone carvings, the line drawings used in his catalog are those that appear in a small undated "Indian Curios" catalog put out by James Irving, also of Pipestone.[39] Standley must have cut the drawings from a supplier catalog and reused them, a common practice at the time.

The pipe and pipe-tomahawk in the catalog drawings were cut from red catlinite, a stone named after artist George Catlin who painted and wrote about it after he visited the large quarry, near present-day Pipestone, in 1836. Pipes were rooted in long-established Plains ceremonial traditions, but those

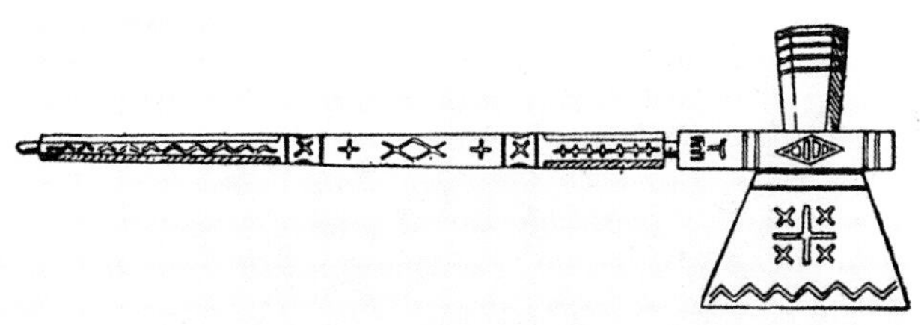

No. A **Red Pipe Stone, Tomahawk Pipe, Wood Stem, about 17 inches long; Price, each $2.40**

No. B **Red Pipe Stone, Tomahawk Pipe, Stone Stem, about 17 inches long; Price, Each. . 3.25**

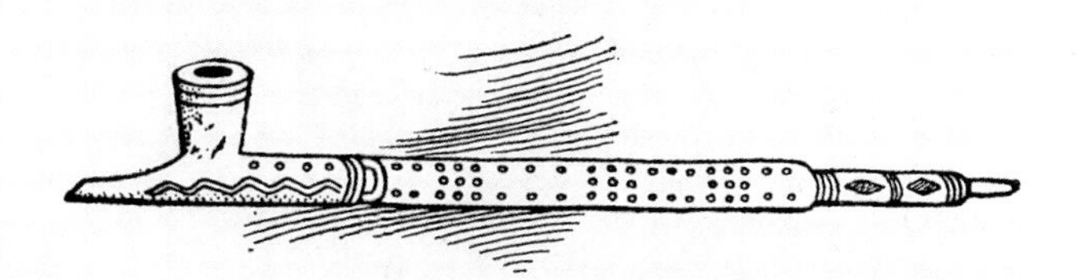

No. C **Red Pipe Stone, Peace Pipe, Wood Stem, about 17 inches long; Price, Each. $2.40**

No. D **Large Red Pipe Stone, Peace Pipe, Wood Stem, about 21 inches long; Price, Each 2.75**

No. E **Large Red Pipe Stone, Peace Pipe, Stone Stem, about 21 inches long; Price, Each 3.75**

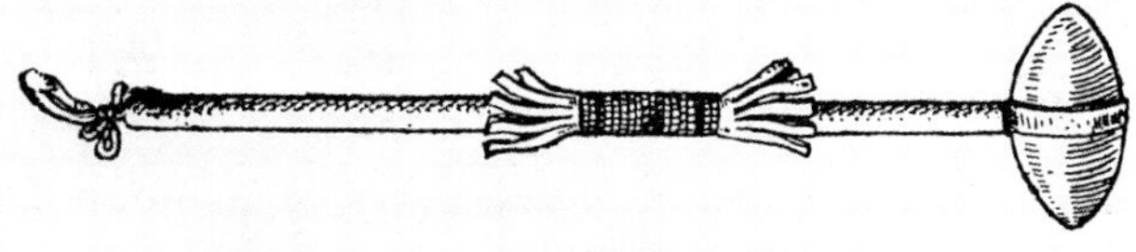

No. F **War Club, Large, with Stone Head and Buckskin Covered, Beaded Handle, Each.$2.50**

8.16. On the one occasion when Standley pictured Plains weapons and pipes in a shop catalog, he used line drawings that appear to have been taken from a small "Indian Curios" catalog put out by James Irving, a curio dealer in Pipestone, Minnesota. The items pictured were made at Pipestone and wholesaled across the country. Catalog C (1916), p. 27.

Standley sold were simple ones, typical of the pipes that non-Indians had begun carving using power machinery by the early 1860s. They became staples in curio shops across the country, along with the pipe-tomahawk and the hide-covered stone warclub.[40]

In addition to pipes, several of the catalogs' "1001" lists include Indian woven belts and hat bands of horsehair. The technique was actually horsehair braiding, a Mexican craft associated with horsegear. It was taken up by cowboys and has been documented among the Pima Indians of Arizona.[41] Standley's sources for horsehair work were state prisons in Deer Lodge, Montana; Florence, Arizona; and Canon City, Colorado.[42] Prison authorities encouraged the craft of horsehair weaving among prison communities because it was time-consuming and did not require sharp tools. The finished products also provided income. No doubt some Indians wove horsehair in prison, but there is no reason to believe that the examples Standley was selling were necessarily made by Indians. Standley also purchased "old horn canes" from the prisons.

The shop also carried masks, although considering Standley's interest in the exotic, it is surprising that he offered so few. A large Nuu-chah-nulth mask (which was purchased by the cartoonist Robert L. Ripley in the 1930s) dominates the upper back shelf in photographs of the 1904–16 store (see fig. 2.1). A few small Yup'ik masks and one of two crudely carved generalized masks pictured in the 1920s catalogs (Catalogs E and F) also appear in interior photographs. An assortment of small crude masks, and a larger carefully carved mask mixing Nuu-chah-nulth and Kwakiutl styles, appear in interior photographs of several stores (figs. 2.1, 6.8, 9.3). The Yup'ik masks came from Alaska, but most of the others were produced nearby, by Nuu-chah-nulth carvers of varying skills.

Ye Olde Curiosity Shop Catalogs

In its 1915 catalog the shop began including photographs of "Indian" and "Eskimo" things, along with other merchandise. Some objects were accompanied with brief descriptions; all included prices. Standley's catalogs bound image and text, hoping to induce the reader to order. The individual photographs had been manipulated to communicate specific messages.[43] The format was a slightly old-fashioned one that was common in curio shop catalogs during the early twentieth century, appropriate because the Indian and Eskimo items were considered to be associated with an eternal past. Most of Standley's catalog photographs were constructed from smaller photos of individual related objects, clipped out and presented in rows against a blank background. Each object confronted the viewer directly and frontally. There were no photographs of Indian or Eskimo makers included and, with the exception of Catalog B, no Pacific or Arctic environments, nothing visual to place the objects in time or space in reference to their makers. In this sense, the items were acultural and ahistorical. After Catalog B contextual photographs referenced only Standley and the shop, picturing Seattle, his collection on display at the AYPE, exterior and interior shop views, and totem poles at the Standley home, Totem Place. The context for the objects advertised in the catalogs thus became the shop. As at world's fairs, the cultures of people foreign and different had been distilled down to objects and presented in organized rows as on a shelf, asking to be safely ordered with the stroke of a pen.

The limited informational text Standley offered in shop catalogs was primarily straightforward—"Totem Poles, Indian Carved from Alaska and British Columbia"—lightly focused with adjectives such as "rare," "old," "fine," even "this is a dandy," and sometimes with misinformation. Tribal distinctions were sometimes given, but the term "Indian" was common. The poles and other objects were ready not only to be appropriated by the prospective buyer, but to be invested with meaning hinged on his or her imagination and the usually limited knowledge most buyers brought to the items. Although the buyer could approach the strange, fierce creatures on a totem pole, the connection he or she captured by owning the pole was with the experience in the shop. The pole was a memento.

Standley's catalogs both enticed and reassured readers as they entered the world of cultures not their own. They urged readers to be inquisitive—"Curiosity is a natural instinct; if developed leads to discovery"—and offered "articles of rare interest, collected from all parts of the globe" to capture potential buyers' attention. Like the shop, the catalogs provided a place of safe encounter. The message was, in part, the message of consumerism—that the acquisition of objects is easy, a fine hobby, a fine investment. But there was more: One could actually own the oldest or the rarest or the finest remaining remnants of vanishing races and feel noble, special, and secure in a sense of sanctioned hegemony.

The shop itself presented art and artifacts in the same push-pull fashion as the catalogs, but with the added excitement of a quest. Sorting through a list of "1001 Curious Things" presented in no particular order was relatively easy and sedate, compared with visually and physically exploring the jumble within the shop itself in hopes of discovering a treasure. The shop's disarray invited one to explore and marvel. Yet the shop was (and still is) reassuring. The disorder was contained within one room and visitors could simply stand outside, studying it through the windows, as early Asahel Curtis and Webster & Stevens photographs document that many did.

Ye Olde Curiosity Shop since 1940

Some people find you [Ye Olde Curiosity Shop] interesting
in a strange sort of way. Others find you strange. But people,
by the droves, come to Seattle's waterfront to find you.
"We never really had anything people have to have,"
muses Joe James. "Guess it goes to show you that curiosity
is innate to us all."

—Robert L. Jamieson Jr., "Curiosities Galore
Keep Luring People to Waterfront Shop," *Seattle
Post-Intelligencer,* October 7, 1999

On June 4, 1937, after six months at the shop's interim site at 814 First avenue during the rebuilding of Colman Dock, Ye Olde Curiosity Shop moved into its fourth waterfront shop, its third on the dock, where it would stay until March 1959. Standley had looked forward to the new store. Earlier in 1937 he had told a reporter: "When the wharf is changed over and Railroad Avenue is finished, I'll be back on the waterfront—going to have a new front on the store—steel and stucco—modernistic. It's going to look pretty nice."[1] The days of displaying a variety of artifacts out front were over, but the new storefront had large pane windows, above a base of smart black tiles, and the name Ye Olde Curiosity Shop shone in neon (fig. 9.1a, b). The dock had taken on a 1930s art deco style, looking to the future—or at least the present, but definitely not back to the past. The interior was less narrow than before, and there were no back windows. A balcony in the rear emphasized the width and a central table made use of the open space, but the displays were installed much the same as always, with small items in showcases and hundreds of objects suspended from the ceiling.

Standley was a sturdy and energetic man who refused to let age slow him down. In 1925 a writer commented, "Although now 72 years old, his business . . . gives him keener enjoyment than when he began as a young man."[2] Through the 1930s it became a tradition that local newspapers would write about Standley each year on his birthday, and each year he emphasized that he was looking forward, not back. In 1935 it was reported that he "celebrated his 81st birthday by showing a farmer friend from Port Orchard Seattle's giddy show places until 2 am" and was found working in his garden by ten the next morning.[3]

9.1 a, b. Ye Olde Curiosity Shop, Colman Dock, 1937–59. In 1937 Standley's shop, like others on the dock, was remodeled in an Art Deco style with signage in blocky neon lettering. The whale bones were not installed until several months after the shop opened.

On July 2, 1937, "Daddy" Standley was hit by a car when crossing Alaskan Way and his leg was broken. New stoplights had been installed but were still set on blinkers. His spirits remained high, however, and he later said, "When you pass eighty it takes more'n a ton of rubber n' steel to put you out of commission permanently." But Standley never quite got over the injury.[4] Because his son-in-law Russell James and his son Ed Standley had taken over the shop's daily operations, Standley divided his time between the shop and his West Seattle home, Totem Place, where he liked to prune his plants and putter about. In November he talked with a reporter in front of his new "modernistic" shop as a rigger arrived to install the whale's jaws to arch over the door: "Now I'm back again and they're back. . . . Eighty four years and good for ten more . . . this is where I belong" (figs. 9.2, 9.3).[5] On his eighty-fourth birthday Standley waited on trade, trimmed shrubbery, and celebrated at a surprise dinner "that my children usually give me."[6] On his eighty-fifth the "grand old man of the waterfront" commemorated the day by "acting in the capacity he loves so well—that of being a one-man-chamber-of-commerce—telling visitors where to go and what to see, singing loud the praises of Puget Sound."[7] On his eighty-sixth he was "still working in the store. Still seeing people. Still going down to a show Saturday nights—alone, too." He handed out booster cards and a fossil ivory tooth to reporters as they left.[8]

9.2. Standley, by the door of his new shop, ca. 1937. The totem pole, by Nuu-chah-nulth carver Wilson Williams, is now at the Makah Cultural and Research Center in Neah Bay.

Nine months later "Daddy" Standley died of pneumonia, on Friday, November 25, 1940. He had gone home from work the previous Monday with a chill. Newspapers wrote of him fondly: how he had helped to preserve the early history of Puget Sound; of his countless friends, large family, and love for his work; how he saw the funny side of everything and would want us to rejoice that he was privileged to live nearly one hundred years. Standley's shop had been a "'must see' item on every tripper's list, as much a part of the flavor and character of Seattle as the hills, lakes, ocean-going commerce and distant view of majestic Mount Rainier."[9] His friend H. E. Jamison, a columnist for the *Seattle Star,* quoted Standley's recipe for longevity: "The fountain of eternal youth is available for everyone—it's simply this—work at a job you like, and live in the Northwest, on salt water if possible."[10]

Continuity and Change after Standley's Death

The late 1930s were challenging for Ye Olde Curiosity Shop. Times were hard financially. Even as a defense boom associated with World War II was building, there were the losses of the Great Depression to overcome and every sale counted. Although foreign travelers and curio collectors dwindled, the thousands of armed forces personnel who traveled in and out of Puget Sound supported a lively business, which kept Russell James and Ed Standley at work until eight or nine on many nights. James had felt it was harder to train someone else than for him and his family to work long hours.

During World War II there were plenty of buyers, but merchandise was difficult to obtain. Travel and import restrictions meant that supply lines across the Pacific for many types of curios that had become shop mainstays were disrupted. As soon as restrictions eased, the shop scrambled to restock. An October 1946 news article announced an eagerly awaited shipment: "Its arteries partially cut by the war, Ye Olde Curiosity Shop will soon unpack its first import from an overseas land in five years." Six hundred ebony elephants one inch to one foot high were on their way from Colombo, Ceylon, on the British steamship *Silver Larch.* By the time imports were again available, postwar prices had increased substantially. While strings of ivory beads from India had been so inexpensive before the war that the shop had sold them for $3.50, exporters now asked much more for them.[11]

Money was tight after the war, and private collectors and their heirs converted old collections into cash by selling them to the shop. Among the collections brought in, it was not unusual to find individual pieces that had earlier been sold by the Curiosity Shop, with stickers attached or the shop's letter code written directly on the items. During this time the shop also sold off valuable older Native American pieces when finances required it, hoping to be able to replace them later. In the 1950s and 1960s businesses gradually began to pull out of the postwar slump. The shop experimented briefly with wholesaling model totem poles and soapstone carvings to small shops on the West Coast and in the Midwest. After a trip to Hawaii in 1955, when Joe James saw that there were few seashells and souvenirs for sale there, the shop wholesaled shells, koa seeds, and black-eyed susan mats and necklaces from the British West Indies to Hawaiian shops, until jet air service opened up more possibilities to retailers there.[12]

For Indian and Indian-type merchandise, the shop depended on already established strategies. It continued to buy model totem poles, wood carvings, and an occasional basket directly from Indian makers, as did other local curio shops and wholesalers, but it also purchased from local commercial suppliers. After 1943 Herman Krupp, operating as Oceanic Trading, supplied the shop with ivory "Nuguruk" items into the late 1980s. Another Seattle wholesaler, Indian Arts and Crafts, had dealt with Standley in the late 1930s, when its founder, Burt Mayers, would visit the shop carrying a cigar box of souvenir samples, not necessarily Indian or Alaska related, and take orders. During the war, when leather was at a premium, Mayers wholesaled a variety of items including canvas moccasins that shop customers swore wore better than leather. In the late 1940s Mayers took in a partner who had Alaskan connections, Walter Lowen, and the business thrived, particularly through wholesaling to shops in Alaska. It handled totem poles bought from local carvers in Seattle, Krupp's line of Nuguruk ivories, and many lower-scale souvenir items. Ye Olde Curiosity Shop came to depend on Indian Arts and Crafts for postcards and inexpensive "Indian-style" souvenir items—dolls, bow and arrow sets, feather headdresses, and pillow tops with Indian designs. In the 1990s Lowen's son took over Indian Arts and Crafts, and in the late 1990s the company was absorbed by Bloom Brothers of Minneapolis.

After Standley's son Edward died on September 2, 1945, his son-in-law, Gordon McGuire, agreed to take care of Edward's interests in the shop. An engineer by training, McGuire never really enjoyed working in the shop, however, and he and his wife sold out to Russell James in 1949. The shop has remained in the James family since that time. After Russell's son Joe James

9.3. Ye Olde Curiosity Shop interior, 1938. The shop has always been a family business. Pictured left to right: Standley's son Edward, Standley, son-in-law Russell James, and daughter Jessie Standley Parker. A Makah mask and the carving by Makah artist Young Doctor of two figures supporting a serpent dominate the center back balcony.

returned from the Navy in 1946, he joined his father in management and eventually became sole proprietor. Russell James died in December 1954.

Colman Dock and the Blackball Ferry Line that operated there were privately owned until the state took over the dock and Blackball's Puget Sound ferry runs in 1948. When a 7.1 earthquake shook the city on April 13, 1949, it was alarming, but the shop suffered little damage other than broken windows; the dock had absorbed most of the shock as it separated then moved back against the sidewalk again and again. Joe James stood inside with two frightened tourists from the Midwest, watching as the ceiling displays suspended on wires rose when the walls bulged, pulling the wires taut, then fell as they relaxed, then rose and fell again. Construction of a double-layered elevated roadway above Alaskan Way began in 1951, disturbing pedestrian traffic along the storefront. At the suggestion of the Port of Seattle, the shop then opened a small store in Fisherman's Terminal at Salmon Bay in July 1952, but this closed in late 1953. When the new Alaskan Way viaduct was completed in 1958, it channeled the through traffic of the main north-south corridor, U.S. Highway 99, and the waterfront returned to its previous quieter, more leisurely pace.

In 1959 a space at the south end of Pier 52's Colman Dock became vacant when Sunde and d'Evers Ship Chandlers moved. Ye Olde Curiosity Shop

9.4. Ye Olde Curiosity Shop, Pier 52, Colman Dock, 1959–63. The new lettering in Old English style on the 1959 shop alluded to the shop's Charles Dickens namesake.

had been located further north on the dock since 1937, but this new site would allow badly needed space, and Joe James decided to relocate the shop. At this time Seattle was deep into planning its second world's fair, the Century 21 Exposition, and in anticipation of the thousands of visitors an expansion seemed to be a wise investment. The shop moved down the dock and opened on March 12, 1959, at 801 Alaskan Way, Pier 52 (fig. 9.4). The new shop's exterior was similar to the previous one, with a black-tiled front, but it was wider, with more large-pane windows. Its sign, now in Old English letters, referenced not modernity but a nostalgic past. James felt that the new shop fitted its nature well. The Century 21 Exposition, which opened in mid-April 1962 and continued into September, brought tripled business during its run.

In the early 1960s talk of rebuilding the ferry terminal again became serious. At the same time developers were making plans to rebuild Pier 51 with an extended tourist complex to include restaurants, an aquarium, and shops. Ye Olde Curiosity Shop would be located at the center of the new project. When the plan fell through, however, James decided to build on Pier 51, but at the street end where the shop would open to the sidewalk. Paul Thiry, the local

architect who had done work for the recent Century 21 Exposition—as well as a friend, customer, and collector of Northwest Coast Indian art—offered to plan the building. Thiry designed a wooden structure loosely patterned on the northern Northwest Coast longhouse (fig. 9.5). Between May and July 1963 the shop moved by buckboard into this new waterfront location and held a grand opening on June 29. Thiry's building won the Downtown New Look Award in 1963 from the Downtown Seattle Association and was featured in several architectural magazines. Although the location was threatened briefly by condemnation in 1979, it would be twenty-five years before the shop would have to move again.

9.5. Ye Olde Curiosity Shop, Pier 51, 601 Alaskan Way, 1963–88, soon after the shop opened in 1963. This shop, modeled on a Northwest Coast longhouse, was designed by Seattle architect Paul Thiry. The totem pole entrance was the work of designer Otis Baxter. The tall segmented poles, made in Tacoma by the Cascade Pole Company, had stood at the south entrance of Seattle's Century 21 World's Fair in 1962.

Two major moves in a six-year period had been arduous and hard on the collection of the older, now quite valuable, artifacts. With each move some suffered breakage and others disappeared as the ceiling display was dismantled and reinstalled; insurance premiums grew higher and higher. It seemed wise to dispose of duplicates and some other pieces in the collection. Nearly two thousand items from the shop, mostly Native American pieces, were sold in three auctions—one held in Cleveland, Ohio, in 1976, and two in Seattle, in 1977 and 1980.[13] It was hard for James when he walked into the first auction and saw so many familiar things slated to leave the family: "It was a traumatic experience and it still bothers me to this day."[14]

In the early 1980s, anticipating that the Washington Department of Transportation might eventually need the property on which the shop stood, James look a lease on space on Pier 55 so the shop would be assured a waterfront location should that happen. In 1985 the family decided to use the lease and open a second store, the Waterfront Landmark. That the shop had often been called "a waterfront landmark" inspired the auxiliary store's name. The new Waterfront Landmark's stock overlapped somewhat with that of Ye Olde Curiosity Shop, and both stores have been run by the James family since that time. In 1988 the state decided it wanted the Pier 51 space where Ye Olde Curiosity Shop stood and purchased the shop's lease. Moving to the Waterfront Landmark's Pier 55 location was a possibility, but an even more appealing option was available: moving to Pier 54, adjacent to the venerable Seattle institution, Ivar's Restaurant, located there since 1938. The current Curiosity Shop opened there in April 1988 (fig. 9.6). The long narrow space was more like earlier shops than the longhouse had been and made it possible to replicate the cases, and wall and ceiling displays of earlier times. In the 1980s the Jameses also opened several other shops for short periods: the Seattle Landmark in the Center House at Seattle Center, 1981–1990; a second Seattle Center store, the Crossroads, 1988; and the Potlatch Gallery on Pier 57, 1988–89.

The Shop at the End of the Century

Ye Olde Curiosity Shop has continued to be cited occasionally in both local and national publications, such as *Holiday* and *National Geographic.*[15] In recent years the shop has been described as "a shop for the curious" and "a store with wacky and bizarre souvenirs."[16] When talk surfaced in 1996 about financial difficulties at the University of Washington, a news columnist recommended tongue-in-cheek that to raise revenue, "the [university's] Burke Museum would be sold to Ye Olde Curiosity Shop."[17] Today for Native American material the shop depends primarily on contemporary Northwest Coast carvings, although a few local and Alaska baskets and ivory carvings occasionally are available as bits of private collections are liquidated. But the "relics" that the shop once heavily dealt in are now rare and expensive, generally in the purview of exclusive galleries and private collectors. A necklace with an old shop tag in Standley's handwriting describing it as an "Alaska Kodiak Bear Claw necklace with the rare old Blue Wampum Beads, $6.50" came up for auction in 1996 in England with a suggested bid of fifteen hundred to twenty-five hundred pounds.[18]

A recent article in the *Seattle Times* listed places for families to see on the Seattle waterfront—a new Maritime Discovery Center, the Seattle Aqua-

9.6. Color postcard of Ye Olde Curiosity Shop at its current location, 1000 Alaskan Way. When the shop moved in 1988 to Pier 54, next to Ivar's Restaurant, the entrance carving from the 1963 shop was maintained, as were the totem poles displayed at earlier shops.

rium and Omnidome, harbor tours, viewpoints, and restaurants.[19] Earlier in the twentieth century, before the advent of museums and the aquarium, in a haphazard but undeniably successful fashion, Ye Olde Curiosity Shop had filled the roles those new attractions do today. In 1999, as the shop celebrated its one-hundredth anniversary, it was still listed widely as a tourist attraction.[20] Today it is one of multiple entertainment possibilities and souvenir shops along Seattle's waterfront, however, and operates in the context of a far more educated, sophisticated, and jaded public. Whereas *National Geographic* magazine was once the major complement to much the shop had to offer, today its public is overwhelmed with media-provided information about the usual, the unusual, the unthinkable. It takes far more to truly amaze. But there is a mystique, something about the personal search, the discovery, and tangibly experiencing the object itself, that a media experience cannot provide. Visitors still rush their friends through cramped aisles to a display case somewhere in the rear of the shop to share a discovery.

For those who vividly remember the excitement of childhood exploration in the shop, "when it was genuinely eccentric and more than a little spooky,"[21] and as adults wish for the old Eskimo tools, argillite model totem poles, and

Tlingit and Makah baskets of Standley's day at affordable prices, the end-of-the-century mix of merchandise disappoints. The shop as it was in its early days would today be an anachronism. But to each new generation of children, despite changes in public sensibilities and taste, the mummy, mermaid, and shrunken heads still bring chills and exclamation, the now shabby dressed fleas continue to amaze, and the Arctic relics and natural history specimens hung from the ceiling still elicit speculation. As in Standley's day, everyone is welcome, and children, as always, free to wander and discover, still rush to their friends in excitement, whispering urgently: "Come see what I found!"

For many visitors the shop still functions as a museum. Alaska Natives visiting Seattle are far less apt to go to the nearby Seattle Art Museum than to Ye Olde Curiosity Shop, to look at its recent Northwest Coast wood carving or old Arctic objects suspended from the ceiling. Although the art museum exhibits extremely important Northwest Coast collections, it displays no Arctic material, is imposing, and charges an entrance fee. In contrast, the Curiosity Shop, as familiar as a general store in the Alaska bush, displays old artifacts from both the Northwest Coast and the Arctic, and is free. As has been the case for a century, everyone feels welcome to wander and reminisce. What cannot be replicated in Ye Olde Curiosity Shop today is the energetic little man in a skull cap and the presence he brought to his beloved shop during the forty-one years he presided. J. E. Standley was a part of the lure and the mystery as he circulated about, enthusing over his collections with visitors, and slipping children a bead or shell, sealing their experience with a tangible memento of the curious and his Curiosity Shop.

Appendix: Ye Olde Curiosity Shop Catalogs and Brochures

Ye Olde Curiosity Shop brochures and catalogs available for examination at the time of research are as follows. Only one item is dated; the others have been sequenced and assigned approximate dates through cross-referencing with each other and with other shop materials and records.

Brochure: "Ye Olde Curiosity Shop," 1907 (titled by sign in shop photograph in circular vignette in center), 8¾ in. × 5¾ in., folded, with paragraphs listing merchandise; black and white cover with central circular photograph of exterior of the first Colman Dock shop flanked by two rectangular interior photographs of same; four pages including cover, unstapled (cover, see p. 5).

Catalog A: "Price List of 1001 Curious Things (Copyright)," ca. 1910–13, 10½ in. × 4½ in.; black and white paper cover with photograph of J. E. Standley and polar bear (see p. 6); thirty-two pages, including the outside and inside of the cover, stapled.

Catalog B: "Copyrighted Price List of 1001 Curious Things Ye Olde Curiosity Shop, Seattle, U.S.A.," 1915, 10½ in. × 4½ in.; black and white cover with photograph of J. E. Standley and polar bear; thirty-two pages, including the outside and inside of the cover, stapled (cover, see fig. 4.13).

Catalog C: "Catalog and Price List of 1001 Curious Things from Ye Olde Curiosity Shop," 1916, 8¾ in. × 5¾ in.; black banded color cover with Chilkat blanket and canoe paddles; thirty-six pages plus the inside and outside cover, stapled. Includes a separate "Supplement Price List to Our Catalog of '1001 Curious Things' from All Parts of the World," 8¾ in. × 5¾ in.; black and white cover with hatched band and photograph of the 1916–23 shop at 811 Railroad Avenue.

Catalog D: "Catalog and Price List of 1001 Curious Things from Ye Olde Curiosity Shop," ca. 1920, 8¾ in. × 5¾ in.; unbanded color cover with Chilkat blanket and canoe paddles; forty-eight pages plus the inside and outside cover, stapled (cover, see fig. 8.3).

Brochure: "From the World Famous Ye Olde Curiosity Shop," 1923, 6 in. × 4¾ in., folded; black and white cover with pasted-up photograph of the exterior of the 1923–37 shop at 809 Railroad Avenue; folded to make eight pages, unstapled.

Catalog E: "It Beats 'The Dickens' Ye Olde Curiosity Shop," mid-1920s, 8¾ in. × 5¾ in.; gray artificial vellum cover with a black and gold drawing of ship; forty-eight pages plus cover, stapled, does not include a "1001 Curious Things List." Separate "Wholesale Price List for Catalog No. 9" (cover, see fig. 8.2).

Catalog F: "It Beats 'The Dickens' Ye Olde Curiosity Shop" (Catalog No. 11), late 1920s, 8¾ in. × 5¾ in.; red artificial vellum cover with a black and gold drawing of ship; forty-eight pages plus cover, stapled, includes a "1001 Curious Things List."

Catalog G: "Catalog No. 12, 1001 Curious Things From the World Famous Ye Olde Curiosity Shop," early 1930s, 8¾ in. × 5¾ in.; black and white cover with pasted-up photograph of exterior of the 1923–37 shop; twenty-four pages plus the inside and outside cover, stapled (cover, see fig. 8.1).

Catalog H: "40th Anniversary 1899–1939, Ye Olde Curiosity Shop," 1939, 8½ in. × 5⅜ in.; black, green, and white cover with pasted-up photograph of 1937–59 shop, sixteen pages plus cover, stapled (cover, see fig. 8.4).

Catalog I: "When in Seattle You Are Invited to Visit the World Famous Ye Olde Curiosity Shop," 1940, 8½ in. × 5½ in.; black and white cover with photograph of interior 1923–37 shop, thirteen pages plus front cover and outside back cover, stapled.

Catalog J: "When in Seattle You Are Invited to Visit the World Famous Ye Olde Curiosity Shop" (Catalog No. 77), early 1950s, 9⅛ in. × 6 in.; green and white cover with a photograph of the interior of the 1937–59 shop with a cigar store Indian; fifty-six pages plus covers, stapled.

NOTES

Prologue

1. Lawrence Weschler, *Mr. Wilson's Cabinet of Wonder* (1995).

2. Many of the shop's records from 1899 through 1940 will be deposited in the Manuscripts, Special Collections, and Archives Division of the University of Washington Libraries by 2005.

3. Richard White, *Remembering Ahanagran: History and Storytelling in a Family's Past* (1998), 4–6.

4. White, *Remembering Ahanagran,* 6.

5. The critical literature relevant to this book is so extensive that I mention here only a few recent works that reference the earlier literature. Many of the essays in Ruth B. Phillips and Christopher B. Steiner, eds., *Unpacking Culture: Art and Commodity in Colonial and Postcolonial Worlds* (1999), address related issues with perceptive insight, as does the book's epilogue by Nelson Graburn, whose pioneering *Ethnic and Tourist Arts: Cultural Expressions from the Fourth World* (1976) essentially initiated serious study of tourist art. Both Phillips, *Trading Identities: The Souvenir in Native North American Art from the Northeast, 1700–1900* (1998), and Marvin Cohodas, *Basket Weavers for the California Curio Trade* (1997), are especially relevant concerning individual and cultural identity and the synthesis of indigenous and introduced influences in arts of transculturation. Susan Stewart probes society's fascination with the miniature and the gigantic in *On Longing: Narratives of the Miniature, the Gigantic, the Souvenir, the Collection* (1984). Beverly Gordon, in "The Souvenir: Messenger of the Extraordinary," *Journal of Popular Culture* 20 (3): 135–47, and *American Indian Art: The Collecting Experience* (1988), studies society's love of souvenirs. On tourist art as a medium of communication, Bennetta Jules-Rosette, in *The Messages of Tourist Art: An African Semiotic System in Comparative Perspective* (1984), builds on Dean MacCannell's discussion of the nature of tourism in *The Tourist: A New Theory of the Leisure Class* (1976). James Clifford's *The Predicament of Culture: Twentieth-Century Ethnography, Literature, and Art* (1988) addresses the fluid nature of the categories art and artifact. Comments in Eric Hobsbawm and Terence Ranger, eds., *The Invention of Tradition* (1983) are relevant to thinking about the creation of new art traditions in Alaska and the Pacific Northwest. Mihalyi Csikszentmihalyi and Eugene Rochberg-Halton, *The Meaning of Things: Domestic Symbols and the Self* (1981); Arjun Appadurai, *The Social Life of Things: Commodities in Cultural Perspective* (1986); Grant McCracken, *Culture and Consumption: New Approaches to the Symbolic Character of Consumer Goods and Activities* (1988); and Simon Bronner, *Consuming Visions: Accumulation and Display of Goods in America, 1880–1920* (1989) probe aspects of consumerism and the meanings of goods to their purchasers.

Chapter One. The Early Years of Ye Olde Curiosity Shop: "It Beats the 'Dickens'"

1. Many visitors signed Ye Olde Curiosity Shop's Guest Book between 1900 and 1940, but throughout the book there are also many instances where Standley himself wrote in notations about certain visitors in blank spots or after erasing earlier penciled signatures.

2. Alfred Cort (A. C.) Haddon's June 30, 1909, lecture took place in the Fine Arts Hall at 4 P.M. (AYPE clipping volume 9-SP, University of Washington Archives and Special Collections). Haddon visited the United States several times during the first decades of the twentieth century, lecturing to raise money to fund his Malaysian expeditions. World fairs provided receptive audiences, and he spoke during at least one other such fair, the 1904 Louisiana Purchase Exposition in St. Louis. Directors of the AYPE viewed it as encompassing the entire Pacific Rim; the subject of Haddon's talk was thus quite topical.

3. Haddon's life and career are detailed in A. Hingston Quiggin, *Haddon, the Head Hunter: A Short Sketch of the Life of A. C. Haddon* (1942). Standley's Guest Book entries and an article, "An Exhibit of Alaskan Curios," in the *Westerner* 11 (1909): 11, document Haddon's visit to Ye Olde Curiosity Shop.

4. Quoted from London County Council, *Guide for the Use of Visitors to the Horniman Museum* (1912), in Douglas Cole, *Captured Heritage: The Scramble for Northwest Coast Artifacts* (1995), 112, 331, footnote 17.

5. The signature E. J. Horniman appears in Standley's Guest Book (p. 17) during summer 1909. Emslie John, the son of Frederick John, a tea merchant who gave his private museum to London in 1901, seems to have accompanied Haddon to Seattle. It was Emslie John who presented to the museum the objects that Haddon had bought at Ye Olde Curiosity Shop.

6. According to Horniman Museum files, billing lists from Standley to the museum include the price paid for each item Haddon purchased: $3.50 for the "fire kindler of Eskimo" (HM 9.792), $3.50 for the "carved wood seal knocker & salmon club" (HM 9.786), and $4 for the "Raven mask" (HM 9.808).

7. A comment in an endnote in Cole's *Captured Heritage* (359, footnote 20) led to reconstructing the history of the Raven mask in the Horniman Museum. Cole reported that art historian Bill Holm had noted that a mask Haddon collected from Standley for the Horniman was based on a line drawing in Franz Boas's *The Social Organization and the Secret Societies of the Kwakiutl Indians* (1897).

8. Haddon actually purchased three masks from Standley in 1909: the replica of the Berlin mask sketched in Boas, *Social Organization and Secret Societies,* fig. 128; a replica of a Kwakiutl Sea Monster mask in the Museum of the Geological Survey, Ottawa, also sketched in the same book, fig. 145; and an old eagle headdress mask from the Nuu-chah-nulth. Standley may have chosen the Berlin copy for his postcard photograph because, of the three masks, it was the more complex, with its projecting beak and feathers.

9. Miscellaneous clippings that Standley kept include an article titled "Rock Carvings on the Ohio River," which describes the petroglyphs at Smith's Ferry, Pennsylvania, and Wellsville, Ohio, the latter just twenty-two miles from Steubenville. "Seattle Thumbnail," *Seattle Magazine,* June 1932; Standley's notes in Guest Book, p. 1.

10. Letter, March 20, 1931, from "Brother Joe Standley" to "My Dear Girls" [Winifred and Lillian Standley, daughters of J. E. Standley's cousin Jake]. My thanks to Standley family relative Eileen Unger for sharing this letter.

11. "Curiosity Shop Keeper 83, but He Has Modern Ideas," *Seattle Daily Times,* February 22, 1937; "Daddy Standley, Venerable Curio Dealer, Dies at 86," *Seattle Daily Times,* October 25, 1940. Most of the newspaper clippings referenced throughout this volume were culled from Standley family scrapbooks; therefore page numbers have not been included.

12. "Making the Rounds, Curios," *Town Crier,* February 21, 1931; "Seattle Man, One of West's Oldest Advertisers, Who Collects Curios," *The Philatelic West* (1919).

13. "Daddy Standley Prunes Shrubbery on His Eighty-Fourth Birthday," *Seattle Star,* February 25, 1928; note in Standley's handwriting on an undated newspaper clipping with a drawing of Denver's Birks Conforth Pioneer Grocer.

14. Standley operated in at least two Denver locations. An undated business card lists his store address as Champa Street and Downing Avenue, while a promotion sticker in the shape of a leaf and dated 1881 cites 434 Larimer Street. The Larimer shop was located under the Alvord Hotel.

15. Business card, "Compliments of J. E. Standley Old Reliable Grocery House, corner Champa Street and Downing Ave. Established 1876"; H. E. Jamison, "Along the Waterfront," *Seattle Star,* February 24, 1936.

16. Guest Book, pp. 5, 61; Standley's notes on a postcard of Buffalo Bill Cody.

17. "Curiosity Shop Keeper 83, But He Has Modern Ideas," *Seattle Daily Times,* February 22, 1937.

18. Standley's note on an unidentified article about a man who collected "roots that look like things"; his notation on the back of a photograph of his Denver house: "Denver residence of J. E. Standley, Cor[ner] 33d and Champa St., 1890." There was evidently another Denver home as well, documented by a photograph of a different house on which is written: "Ruby Standley was born in this house 'the Willow Springs Fruit Farm' just beyond Elitches Gardens, Denver, July 11, 1892." A shakier hand continues: "Home I built in the country 1/2 mile West of Elitches Gardens. Mrs. John Elitch was my wifes Pal. She drove a team of Ostrich. 1892, J E Standley." Here, as in scores of Standley's other late-in-life notations, his memory has hinged on something unusual.

19. For information on early Seattle history, I have relied especially on Roger Sale, *Seattle: Past to Present* (1994); Murray Morgan, *Skid Road: An Informal Portrait of Seattle* (1962); and Paul Dorpat's photographic histories in *Seattle Now and Then,* vols. 1–3 (1984, 1988, 1994).

20. The name Skid Road dates from the 1850s, when pioneer Henry Yesler began logging the hills of Seattle. Logs from his steam-powered saw mill on the hill were skidded down what became known as Skid Road (now Yesler Way) to the wharf and waiting ships that hauled many of them south to be used in building the young city of San Francisco. The term *skid row,* now a universal phrase for an area where derelicts live, derived from the name.

21. When Erastus Brainerd sent copies of an October 4, 1897, special issue of the *Seattle Post-Intelligencer,* "Seattle Opens Gate to the Klondike," to libraries, post offices, mayors, railroads, and such, he created the public perception that Seattle was *the* place in which to outfit and depart from when traveling to Canada's Klondike gold fields. Since the Canadian government required gold seekers to carry a one-year supply of food and other provisions to enter the Yukon, the one hundred thousand who left Seattle purchased their "outfits" there.

22. Guest Book, p. 10, lists steamers. These late-in-life written-in and written-over additions complicate following the chronology of the signatures. Although only a few entries include dates, there are enough to allow most other notations to be dated within a year or two.

23. For discussion of western curio shops, especially those in Santa Fe, New Mexico, see Jonathan Batkin and Patricia Fogelman Lange, "Human Figurines of Cochiti and Tesuque Pueblos, 1870–1920: Inspirations, Markets, and Consumers," in Jonathan Batkin, ed., *Clay People* (1999), 41–63; Batkin, "Some Early Curio Dealers of New Mexico, *American Indian Art Magazine* 23 (3): 68–81; and Batkin, "Tourism Is Overrated: Pueblo Pottery and the Early Curio Trade, 1880–1910," in Ruth B. Phillips and Christopher B. Steiner, eds., *Unpacking Culture: Art and Commodity in Colonial and Postcolonial Worlds* (1999), 282–97.

24. The 1885 eviction of the Chinese from Seattle following the 1882 Restriction Act was slowly forgotten, and Japanese immigrants arrived in the region as well. In the 1892–93 *Polk's Seattle City Directory* there were only two establishments listed as selling Chinese or Japanese merchandise; in 1895–96, eight; and by 1899, fourteen. In each case some were listed under "Curios," but more were found under "Chinese and Japanese Goods." Some establishments came and went, while others, like Mark Ten Suie, remained in business for many years. By 1905 Asian listings had increased to twenty-eight and by 1908 to thirty-six.

25. The Arctic Trading Company (listed at 819–823 First Avenue, Miner W. Bruce, manager) sold arctic curios and furs.

26. City directories give a relatively accurate picture of businesses in operation at a given time, but because of how businesses listed themselves the data given may not be entirely complete. According to listings in the 1901 edition of *Polk's Seattle City Directory,* The Basket Rooms, Henrietta Hamilton, Manager, was located at 614½ Second Avenue. Both Mrs. Marion C. Pearsall, widow of Jacob A. Pearsall, who sold curios at 1014 Second Avenue, and Mrs. Emma M. Rhodes, "curios and Indian baskets" at 309 Columbia Street, operated out of their homes. Some other businesses also dealt a little in Indian curios or carried a few baskets. It was Paul Parker's Northwest Gem & Curio Co. with whom collector-dealer Grace Nicholson corresponded in August 1903 about possibly acquiring some of revenue cutter captain Dorr F. Tozier's excess stock (letter August 9, 1903, to Miss Grace Nicholson from Paul P. Parker, Grace Nicholson papers, box 12, Henry E. Huntington Library, San Marino, California).

27. Beulah Hurst, "Interesting Citizens You Meet in Admiral District," *Admiral District Tribune,* December 23, 1930; H. E. Jamison, "Along the Waterfront," *Seattle Star,* February 14, 1936.

28. Charles Dickens's book *The Old Curiosity Shop* began as a serial in 1840, in a weekly periodical called *Master Humphrey's Clock,* but Dickens soon decided to finish it and publish it as a book instead. Standley may have thought that using "Ye" and "Olde" in his shop's name would add cachet.

29. Inner text of 1907 brochure: "Ye Olde Curiosity Shop, Headquarters for Alaskan's and Globe Trotters on the Water Front, Colman Dock," 1907, p. 5).

30. "Seattle's Interesting and Picturesque Waterfront," *Seattle Post-Intelligencer,* July 16, 1905.

31. Charles T. Wernecke Furs is listed in the 1898 *Polk's Seattle City Directory* at 809 Railroad Avenue on Columbia Dock. In 1903 he moved to Colman Dock, and from 1904 to 1916 shared the same address as Ye Olde Curiosity Shop, 813 Railroad Avenue. Wernecke moved to the Grand Trunk Dock in 1916.

32. The *Historic Colman Dock Exhibit* (1982) brochure outlines the dock's history. See also Paul Dorpat, *Seattle Now and Then,* vol. 2 (1988).

33. Notes and postcards in Standley's Guest Book.

34. Standley wrote about Baber seven times in his guest book. He cherished a letter Baber had written him, saying that "he had been all over the world but [had seen] no shop as interesting as mine." After the AYPE, Baber toured his Eskimo and Igorrote Villages in Europe.

35. Letters, J. E. Standley to Prof. [Edmond] Meany (Burke Museum of Natural History and Culture, Archives 1909–27).

36. "Waterfront Back to Normal, 'Daddy' Standley Is on the Job," *Seattle Times,* November 24, 1937.

37. *Polk's Seattle City Directory,* begun in 1899 and continued to the present, lists both Standley's business and home addresses for most years. Joseph E. Standley appears in it for the first time in 1902, under the heading Curios, at the 82 W. Madison business address. His home is recorded as at 2021 Second until 1905, when the address changed to 2313 Fifth. Standley's new West Seattle home is first listed in 1907, at California and Madrona, West Seattle, and thereafter at 1750 Palm.

38. The Hudson Bay Fur Company listed its Colman Building address, 819 First Avenue, in city directories beginning in 1912 and continuing into the 1930s. Throughout that period it sometimes listed alternative or secondary addresses as well. The February 8, 1931, *Seattle Times* announced the company opening at 1517 Fifth Avenue, but at least one of its undated catalogs lists both this and the First Avenue address. In 1955 it moved to Fifth and Pike. My thanks to the Maxwell Museum at the University of New Mexico for allowing me to work with notes made in 1983 by Bruce Bernstein when interviewing a longtime Hudson Bay Fur Company employee.

39. Mack's Totem Shop was located at 71–75 on the Marion Street Viaduct. According to Joe James, "Daddy" Standley helped Mack McKillop when he was first getting started, by telling him what items sold well and giving him addresses of sources. Over the years animosity developed between the two, however, to the point that McKillop would not tell those who asked where Ye Olde Curiosity Shop was. McKillop's wife, Carmen, remembers that Erna Gunther, the director of the Washington State Museum at the University of Washington between 1929 and 1962,

would send people to McKillop's shop for good service and authentic Indian material. My thanks to Carmen KcKillop, John McKillop, and Mardonna McKillop for information on Mack's Totem Shop and the carvers who worked for it.

40. A number of recent books and articles examine the role that tourism played in the creation of a particular public image of the Southwest's indigenous peoples. Indebted to postmodern theory, these works raise essential questions about how perceptions of cultures and peoples are created out of multiple contexts and forces, among them the interface between the psychological needs and economic aspirations of the creator—in this case white America processing a cultural mandate of manifest destiny. Using, developing, and civilizing what was considered an almost empty landscape populated by primitive people was an important component of this mandate. Among the most accessible of these works are Marta Weigle and Barbara Babcock, *The Great Southwest of the Fred Harvey Company and the Santa Fe Railway* (1996), and Kathleen Howard and Diana Pardue, *Inventing the Southwest: The Fred Harvey Company and Native American Art* (1996). Important articles include Edwin L. Wade, "The Ethnic Art Market in the American Southwest, 1880–1980," in George Stocking Jr., ed., *Objects and Others: Essays on Museums and Material Culture* (1985), 67–91; Curtis Hinsley, "Collecting Cultures and the Cultures of Collecting: The Lure of the American Southwest," *Museum Anthropology* 16 (1):12–20; and M. Riley, "Constituting the Southwest, Contesting the Southwest, Re-Inventing the Southwest," *Journal of the Southwest* 36 (3): 221–41.

41. The Pacific Northwest Collection, Suzzallo Library, University of Washington, houses an assortment of tourist brochures, including all of those cited here. Indian men gaze at Mount Rainier in *Rainier National Park: Summer Fun amid Snow and Flowers* (1920s) and *The Wonder Mountain* (ca. 1910) and travel in canoes in *The Land That Lures* (1911). The wood carrier appears in *Beauties of the State of Washington* (1916), the basket seller in *Snohomish County Washington: The Richest of Puget Sound* (1905). My thanks to Dickson H. Preston, University of Washington graduate student, for research associated with this topic.

42. For discussion of early Alaska tourism, see Frank Norris, "Showing off Alaska: The Northern Tourist Trade, 1878–1941," *Alaska History* 2 (2): 1–17, and *Gawking at the Midnight Sun: The Tourist in Early Alaska* (1985). See also Ted Hinkley, "The Inside Passage: A Popular Gilded Age Tour," *Pacific Northwest Quarterly* 56 (2): 67–74; and Molly Lee, "Tourism and Taste Cultures: Collecting Native Art in Alaska at the Turn of the Twentieth Century," in Ruth B. Phillips and Christopher B. Steiner, eds., *Unpacking Culture: Art and Commodity in Colonial and Postcolonial Worlds* (1999), 267–81, 366, and "Appropriating the Primitive: Turn of the Century Collection and Display of Native Alaskan Art," *Arctic Anthropology* 28 (1): 6–15.

43. See Christopher Steiner on the role of redundancy, repetition, and the familiar in establishing the veracity of information in travel literature ("Authenticity, Repetition, and the Aesthetics of Seriality: The Work of Tourist Art in the Age of Mechanical Reproduction," in Ruth B. Phillips and Christopher B. Steiner, eds., *Unpacking Culture: Art and Commodity in Colonial and Postcolonial Worlds* (1999), 87–103.

Chapter Two. Relics and Handiwork: Early Sources for Native Art and Artifacts

1. Catalog C, 1916; Catalog D, ca. 1920.

2. "Alaska Curios in the Exhibit at the Alaska Club," *Seattle Post-Intelligencer,* September 29, 1907; "An Exhibit of Alaskan Curios," *Westerner* 11 (3): 11.

3. Guest Book, pp. 30, 31.

4. "Demolition of Ye Olde Curiosity Shop Now Complete," *Seattle Post-Intelligencer,* June 11, 1904.

5. L. L. Bales's activities are chronicled especially in Alaskan newspapers. He is listed as Louis L. in Seattle city directories and news articles. Lightner, the name by which Standley called him, was probably his middle name.

6. It has been suggested that L. L. Bales ran a store in Sitka, Alaska, before moving to the Nome area during the gold rush there, but it was instead a T. H. Bale, proprietor of The Ranch Store, General Merchandise *(The Alaskan,* Sitka, September 21, 1895).

7. Bales was well known in Alaska as a dog musher and mail carrier. *The Alaskan* (April 7, 1906) quoted an old friend of his as saying, "You could start this fellow out with a jack-knife and he would go all over Alaska." Bales wrote about a particularly challenging mail run to Nome in 1901 in "A Tale of the Tundra," *Pacific Sportsman* 2 (3):148–49. Bales was commissioned to collect "natural history specimens" for a museum *(Seward Weekly Gateway,* March 17, 1906) and for the 1909 Alaska-Yukon-Pacific Exposition (*The Alaskan,* Sitka, March 10, 1906, 3; April 7, 1906, 2). Two grizzly cubs he lent to the exposition were so neglected that they died soon after their arrival in Seattle, and Bales was awarded a judgment against the exposition *(Seward Weekly Gateway,* May 7, 1910).

8. James Wickersham, *A Bibliography of Alaskan Literature* (1927), 520–22, 694–95, lists some of Bales's articles.

9. Although Standley wrote in the Guest Book, p. 40, that he had purchased the copyright to Bales's article "Illustrated Life among Alaskan Eskimo" from *Outdoor Life and Recreation,* this has not been substantiated.

10. *Polk's Seattle Directory* lists a downtown address for Louis L. or L. L. Bales for the years 1900, 1905, 1907, 1912, and 1913. The 1913 directory entry, "Louis L. (Margaret B.) miner, 2175 Laurel Shade Ave," adds a woman's name, suggesting that the marriage

may have occurred about then. (Seward newspapers reported an earlier marriage that ended in divorce in 1910.) Standley wrote about Mrs. Bales's rare, fine lace trousseau and that Bales's daughter Margaret (Standley's god-daughter) won recognition as a ballet dancer. Both wife and daughter appear to have been named Margaret. When Bales died in December 1929 at Fox Bay, Alaska, better known as Bales's Landing, he had spent more than forty years as an Alaskan resident (obituary, *Fairbanks Daily News Miner,* January 4 , 1930). Margaret B. Bales was listed in the 1930 San Diego city directory as living in that city and running the Alaska Fur and Curio Store. Murdock reported that men at Barrow had been carving ivory and masks for sale since 1881 *(Ethnological Results of the Point Barrow Expedition).*

11. After the whalebone market declined, in 1915, Charlie Brower, the trader at Point Barrow, introduced the craft of making baskets from his overstock of baleen to produce a salable souvenir item. Many of the ivories that George G. Heye purchased from Standley's collection in 1916 were registered into Heye's Museum of the American Indian as from Point Barrow, although the designation often does not appear on the list Standley provided with the pieces. Although there is question as to whether all of the ivories registered as from Point Barrow actually came from there, it appears that Brower was encouraging ivory carving before the baleen enterprise. Murdock (1892) reported that men at Barrow had been carving ivory and masks for sale since 1881.

12. Guest Book, Averill, p. 71; Patterson, p. 85; Anderson, p. 85. Other whalers and traders who signed or are noted in the Guest Book include: "Capt Anson, old Arctic whaler of schooner *Isquaw* [*sic*];" "Capt Carr the Old Eccentric Arctic Navigator;" "Capt Backland, Arctic Navigator wife & son;" "Karl Peterson relics from Coronation Gulf and Victoria Land," and Mr. O. Svenslip, a Norwegian whaler at Akutan island. Svenslip is likely the source for at least one set of whale jaws that Standley acquired. Guest Book, Anson, p. 85; Carr, p. 72; Backland, p. 76; Peterson, p. 85; Svenslip, p. 91.

13. John Bockstoce, *Whales, Ice, and Men: The History of Whaling in the Western Arctic* (1986), 240. Hackman is mentioned in the Guest Book, pp. 10, 84.

14. J. E. Standley, "From the Northland," *Pacific Sportsman* 1, no. 2 (1905): 78–79.

15. In 1900 the shop purchased Siberian curios from the father of Leo Wittenberg, a Siberian trader. Standley also mentions I. N. Grieve of Colima River, Siberia, who worked for the Olaf Swenson Co. as a source, as well as a Russian, Mr. Alexander, who collected in Siberia for the Smithsonian, noting "I Bot his collection icons etc." Guest Book, Wittenberg, p. 95; Grieve, p. 66; Alexander, p. 66.

16. Guest Book, Baber, pp. 13, 15, 20, 59, 81, 83, 84, 96.

17. Guest Book, James, p. 94; Anson, pp. 8, 25. A popular bar joke in Alaska was to convince a newcomer to kiss what looked like a polished tusk of ivory for good luck, then to identify it as an "oosik" (Standley's "kassuke"), the bone of a walrus penis.

18. Among other sources on Roald Amundsen are Roald Amundsen, *My Life as an Explorer* (1927) and Partridge Bellamy, *Amundsen the Splendid Norseman* (1929); sources on Vilhjálmur Stefánsson include William R. Hunt, *Stef: A Biography of Vilhjálmur Stefánsson, Canadian Arctic Explorer* (1986).

19. In addition to the Horlick Malted Milk box incident, Standley confused Amundsen and Stefánsson in other instances. He credited "Capt Louis Lane The Arctic Navigator on the *S.S. Polar Bear"* for "discovering" Amundsen, when it was actually Stefánsson (in 1915 when he was on Banks Island, and newspapers sensationalized Lane's coming on him as a rescue) (Guest Book, p. 52). Later, Standley bought the ship bell off of Lane's ship *Polar Bear* when it wrecked on Pinnacle Rock (Guest Book, p. 24). It was also Stefánsson's rather than Amundsen's men who died on Wrangel Island in 1923, where they had been left to start a colony (Guest Book, p. 52). Ada Blackjack, whom Standley also wrote about, was the only survivor.

20. When recalling information about C. T. Pedersen, Standley confused his initials (C. P., C. S., C. D.) but not his activities (Guest Book, pp. 70, 67, 76).

21. In "My Arctic Adventures," a typescript by C. T. Pedersen (Archives and Manuscripts Department, Library, University of Alaska Anchorage), he cites 1920 as the date of this last killing of a bowhead. Bockstoce, *Whales, Ice, and Men,* cites 1921.

22. Christian T. Pedersen Papers, Northern Whaling & Trading Company Papers (located in the Archives and Manuscripts Division, Library, University of Alaska Anchorage, hereafter called the Pedersen Papers), especially Series 2, *Patterson* Trade Account Books, 1927–29; and Series 3, Account Books of trading posts, 1924–39. The Pedersen Papers also include records associated with Pedersen's involvement in a Canadian trading company and in fur farming in Quebec and the Aleutians.

23. Pedersen's records include invoices to the Seward Drug Co.; Mr. Walter Waters, Wrangell; the Hayes Shop, Juneau; Pruell's Gift Shop, Ketchikan; Arthur Newman, False Pass Alaska; Kirmse's Gift Shop, Skagway; and Mr. Halford Lemke, Seattle. Pedersen Papers, Series 12, Invoices, 1924–32, 1934–37.

24. Diaries, Mary Jane Healy, May 9–[30?], 1883, May 13–September 8, 1884, aboard the cutter *Thomas Corwin.* Healy Papers, HM47578, Henry E. Huntington Library, San Marino, California.

25. Diary, Mary Jane Healy, May 3–December 22, 1890, aboard the cutter *Bear.* Healy Papers, HM47579.

26. Diary, Fred Healy, June 30–August 13, 1883, aboard the cutter *Thomas Corwin,* Healy Papers, HM47577.

27. Bockstoce, in *Whales, Ice, and Men,* notes that an estimated 150,000 walrus had been killed between 1869 and 1878 and more

than twice that many died in the process. Although a bowhead provided from one hundred to even three hundred barrels of oil, a walrus supplied only two-thirds to three-quarters of a barrel plus a pair of tusks, which sold for between $1.25 and 1.50 per pound. Commercial walrusing peaked between 1868 and 1883 and was finally outlawed in 1908, by which time reindeer herding, successful in Siberia, had been introduced into several villages to provide an alternative meat source.

28. Bob DeArmond, personal communication with the author, July 1995.

29. In a typed fragment of a biographical sketch dated July 10, 1902, Grace Nicholson speaks of cataloging a collection of Eskimo material that she later loaned the federal government for the Lewis and Clark Exposition, Portland, Oregon, where it won a silver medal (Grace Nicholson Papers, box 12. Henry E. Huntington Library, San Marino, California). The Nicholson ivories went to the Montclair Museum in Montclair, New Jersey.

30. Although the names used today for several Northwest Coast tribes are different from those used in Standley's day, I have chosen to maintain those he used and to place the current name in parentheses the first time a tribe is referenced. Because he never used the term *Nootka* (instead erroneously calling the Nootkan-speaking people of Vancouver Island by the name Bella Bella), for clarity's sake I have chosen to use Nuu-chah-nulth rather than Nootka. For further discussion see chapter 8 in this volume.

31. Mora was the white community located about one and a half miles from the mouth of the Quileute River. La Push was the Indian community, located at the river's mouth. In Standley's times the road coming from the north ended at Mora.

32. Basketry fragments recovered at the Hoko River site are at least two thousand years old. The hundreds of baskets, mats, and woven hats excavated from Ozette near Neah Bay are about five hundred years old. The Ozette material can be seen at the Makah Museum in Neah Bay.

33. Douglas Cole, *Captured Heritage: The Scramble for Northwest Coast Artifacts* (1995), xi.

Chapter Three. J. E. Standley and the Alaska-Yukon-Pacific Exposition

1. Standley's collection located at the Alaska Club is discussed in Curio Joe [J. E. Standley], "Relics of Alaska's Primative [*sic*] Natives," *Pacific Sportsman* 3 (5):160; "Alaska Curios in the Exhibit at the Alaska Club," *Seattle Post-Intelligencer,* September 29, 1907; and "An Exhibit of Alaskan Curios," *Westerner Magazine* 11 (3): 11.

2. *The Alaska Club Almanac* (1906), 57.

3. From 1904 to 1907 the Alaska Club was located on Second Avenue, after which it relocated to the Alaska Building and merged with the Arctic Club. Now called the Arctic Club, it remained at that address until 1916, when it moved to the corner of Third and Cherry Streets, into its new Arctic Building with signature walrus heads along the facade. Information on the Alaska and Arctic Clubs comes from the George F. Cotterill Papers and the William T. Perkins Papers; *Arctic Club, 1908–1958: Fiftieth Anniversary,* unpaginated; C. T. Conover, "Alaska Gold Rush Inspired Founding of Arctic Club," newspaper unidentified, October 23, 1950 (all Archives and Special Collections, University of Washington Libraries).

4. The Archives and Special Collections of the University of Washington Libraries in Seattle house the largest collection of primary information on the Alaska-Yukon-Pacific Exposition. The material includes private papers; official and commercial publications; scrapbooks of clippings from Seattle, Alaska, and national and international newspapers from June 1906 through October 1909; and many of local photographer F. H. Nowell's official exposition photographs; as well as periodicals such as the *Alaska-Yukon Magazine* that devoted numerous articles to the exposition. The Museum of History and Industry, Seattle; the Washington Historical Society, Tacoma; the Washington State Archives, Olympia; the Burke Museum of Natural History and Culture at the University of Washington; and the Seattle Public Library hold smaller collections.

5. "Pictures of Pioneer Days," in *King County State of Washington, 1909* (1909), 77, published for free distribution at the exposition; and *The Secretary's Report of the Alaska-Yukon-Pacific Exposition Held at Seattle, June 1st to October 16th, 1909* (Archives and Special Collections, University of Washington).

6. "The Alaska-Yukon-Pacific Exposition," *Daily Miner* (Ketchikan), August 26, 1908.

7. OTP #3, clipping file, December 1906–January 15, 1907.

8. After the exposition closed, the University of Washington commandeered three of its permanent and more than twenty of its temporary buildings. Information on the AYPE has come especially from *The Exposition Beautiful* (1909); I. A. Naduea, "The Alaska-Yukon-Pacific Exposition," *The Coast* 18 (3): 174–77, in a special edition on Alaska and the Greater Northwest; George A. Frykman, "The Alaska-Yukon-Pacific Exposition, 1909," *Pacific Northwest Quarterly* 52 (1): 89–99; and various articles in the *Alaska-Yukon Magazine,* especially "Alaska at the Fair," *Alaska-Yukon Magazine* 8 (4): 237–59.

9. For extensive critical analysis of the messages and meanings of world's fairs, see especially Robert Rydell, *All the World's a Fair: Visions of Empire at American International Expositions 1876–1916* (1984); Rydell, "The Culture of Imperial Abundance: World's Fairs in the Making of American Culture," in Simon J. Bronner, ed., *Consuming Visions: Accumulation and Display of Goods in America, 1880–1920* (1989), 191–216; Rydell and Nancy Gwinn,

eds., *Fair Representation: World's Fairs and the Modern World* (1994); and Burton Benedict, *The Anthropology of World's Fairs: San Francisco's Panama-Pacific International Exposition, 1915* (1983).

10. The Alaska Building's seven divisions were mines and minerals; fish and fisheries; furs, animals, and birds; agriculture, horticulture, and forestry; transportation; ethnology; and education, women's work, and art ("The Alaskan Exhibit," in *U.S. Government Participation in the Alaska-Yukon-Pacific Exposition,* Report of the U. S. Government Board of Managers, Alaska-Yukon-Pacific Exposition, Seattle, 1909 [1911], 75–84).

11. Letter, October 10, 1908, to J. E. Standley from commissioner J. C. McBride; letter, October 16, 1908, to Mr. J. C. McBride from J. E. Standley (Ye Olde Curiosity Shop Records).

12. Report to Honorable M. E. Hay, Lieutenant Governor, and Acting Governor Elmer E. Johnston, February 18, 1909, expressing anxiety about the Alaska Building exhibits. In a letter dated February 26, 1909, to Mr. H. W. Gilstrap of the Ferry Museum in Tacoma, W. A. Halteman, Executive Commissioner of the AYPE suggested: "The next time you come to Seattle . . . I would like to have you go with me to see the Olde Curiosity Shop here which is run by Mr. Stanley [*sic*], and from which it is probable that an attractive exhibit can be had" (Washington State Alaska-Yukon-Pacific Commission Papers 1908–10, Mss 030, Halteman folder, Washington State Library, Olympia).

13. Advertisement for Ye Olde Curiosity Shop in *The A.-Y.-P. Exposition Official Guide* (1909), 94.

14. My thanks to Kathleen Howard for alerting me to the Santa Fe Railway brochure, "Summer Excursion[s] to California and the North Pacific Coast, Alaska-Yukon-Pacific Exposition," 1909.

15. Letter from George T. Emmons to Josiah Collins, August 12, 1909 (Meany Papers, University of Washington Libraries).

16. Letter, Grace Nicholson to Miss Dorothy C. Miller, May 4, 1932, Montclair Art Museum. Nicholson's collection shown at the AYPE was sold to Henry Lang in 1911, and later made its way into the Montclair Art Museum, New Jersey.

17. Several Alaskans were contracted to collect for the Alaska Building. The Aleutian material sent by Alexander Shaisbnirkoff and George Kostromentinoff of Unalaska eventually went into the Washington State Museum at the University of Washington, as did a few pieces from J. J. Underwood of Nome and L. S. Robe of Fairbanks. Other exhibit contributors included Anna G. Lane of the Seward Peninsula; Hackman & Konig of Sherlock, Washington; and Rhodes & Co., a Seattle curio shop ("The Alaskan Exhibit," in *U.S. Government Participation in the Alaska-Yukon-Pacific Exposition,* Report of the U.S. Government Board of Managers, Alaska-Yukon-Pacific Exposition, Seattle, 1909 [1911], 82).

18. *The Exposition Beautiful,* 11.

19. A photograph of Alaskan women's auxiliary displays in the Alaska Building pictures cases of Athapaskan Indian beadwork. Although the labels on the cases themselves are not legible, nearby signage reads "O're the Trail, Valdez to Fairbanks" and "Cordova Auxiliary Woman's Work and Schools." The beadwork pictured is stylistically typical of the middle and upper Yukon River area (Fairbanks, Dawson, and the area of the Klondike gold rush) and Prince William Sound (University of Washington Libraries, Nowell X233A).

20. Athapaskan pillow and table covers required large pieces of laboriously tanned moosehide, so they could not be produced as cheaply or in as large quantities as Tlingit beaded wall pockets of fabric, hair seal, or gut, or Tlingit hair-seal moccasins. The latter were extensively wholesaled to Seattle and elsewhere, while Athapaskan beadwork was not.

21. Standley's exhibit at the AYPE was basically an expansion of that which had been on display at the Alaska and Arctic Clubs.

22. Curio Joe [J. E. Standley], "Relics of Alaska's Primative [*sic*] Natives," *Pacific Sportsman* 3 (5): 160.

23. U.S. Government Board of Managers, *Participation in the Alaska-Yukon-Pacific Exposition Message from the President of the United States, Transmitting the Report of the United States Government Board of Managers of the Government Participation in the Alaska-Yukon-Pacific Exposition* (1911), 20.

24. The Smithsonian-owned ethnological objects from the Northwest Coast and the Arctic that were exhibited at the AYPE included material similar to that in the Alaska Building, arranged in categories of use or technique and materials.

25. Recent Smithsonian-sponsored studies in the Southwest and California were the basis for Zuni and Hupa family groups, models of Mummy Cave Ruin (Tseiyakin) and the Hopi village of Walpi, and bird's-eye-view paintings of recently excavated Indian ruins at Casa Grande and Mesa Verde *(The Exhibits of the Smithsonian Institution and United States National Museum at the Alaska-Yukon-Pacific Exposition, Seattle, Washington, 1909* [1909]).

26. *The Canadian Display Makes Distinct Impression,* excerpt from *The Pacific Northwest Commerce,* ca. 1909, pp. 24–26.

27. *Exposition Beautiful,* 23.

28. In designing the figures for the totem poles at the south and Paystreak entrances, their creators relied heavily on the illustrations in Franz Boas, *The Social Organization and the Secret Societies of the Kwakiutl Indians,* 1897. They especially used the faces in plate 19, "Statue of a Chief Breaking a Copper;" plate 22, "Posts in House of Qoē'xsōt'ēnôx"; and figure 208, "Head Ring of Mē'ila [a frontlet that includes a pointed headdress]. Figure 21, "Heraldic Column from Xumta'spē," influenced body forms.

29. AYPE publications treated its better-known indigenous people with less ignorance and inflammatory rhetoric than those of "Uncle Sam's insular possessions." At least one publication saw the former as a model for the latter, noting that the Igorrotes were "Natives from the remotest islands of the Philippine Archipelago, brought here by the Government that we may observe their social, civic and domestic life, and that they, in turn, may absorb the atmosphere of enlightened civilization, [and] rub elbows with Indians of the many Alaskan tribes, whose racial and linguistic history, weird religious and superstitious traditions, are preserved intact" (*Exposition Beautiful*, 3).

30. The Paystreak also featured restaurants, pagoda-roofed souvenir stands, what was billed as the largest ferris wheel in the world, and such amusements and spectacles as the Battle of Gettysburg, a naval encounter between the *Monitor* and the *Merrimac* on a mechanically tossed sea, and, as Alaskans had feared, Gold Camps of Alaska and a Klondike Dance Hall.

31. Guest Book, p. 13.

32. Notes written in Stanley's Guest Book, pp. 15, 20, 59, 81, 83, 84, 96.

33. German-born Joseph Mayer went to the Klondike in 1895 and opened jewelry stores in Skagway and Dawson, specializing in jewelry incorporating gold nuggets. He moved to Seattle sometime near the turn of the century and established what became the largest jewelry manufacture west of the Mississippi ("Ties That Don't Bind: Ornament Made for Solid Style," *Seattle Times*, July 28, 1992). My thanks to Charles Cantrell of the Metal Arts Group for information and for sharing 1904 and 1907 Mayer & Bros. catalogs.

34. 1904 Catalog, Original Souvenir Spoons Solid Gold Souvenir Jewelry Presentation Jewels and Medals Fine Diamond Jewelry Etc. made by Mayer Bros. Seattle, Wa: Mayer & Bros., p. 14. The catalog erred in associating the Seattle Totem Pole with "Fort Wrangel." It had been taken from the Alaskan village of Tongass.

35. *The Secretary's Report of the Alaska-Yukon-Pacific Exposition Held at Seattle, June 1st to October 16, 1909* lists no curio shops operating on the Paystreak. However, the Alaska Fur Curio Company and Frost Arts and Crafts are listed under "Exhibit Earnings," indicating that they operated exhibit booths somewhere on the grounds. Mayer & Bros., who sold totem pole spoons and jewelry, is listed under "Souvenirs and Manufacturers."

36. Much of the history of Ravenna Park given here comes from "Ravenna Park" and "Cowen/Ravenna Parks" in Donald N. Sherwood, "Interpretive Essays of the History of Seattle's Parks and Playgrounds," (Archives, Museum of History and Industry, Seattle, n.d.). The Reverend William W. Beck purchased four hundred acres "around the bend in Lake Union" in 1888 and in 1989 added a ravine to the already named Ravenna Park, through which ran the stream connecting Green Lake and Lake Washington. He developed most of the land as plots for the town of Ravenna, but he withheld ten acres next to the park for his home, where for a short time he ran the Seattle Female College.

37. *Ravenna Park, Seattle* (1909), twenty-page photo booklet; brochure, *Ravenna or Big Tree Park* (1909).

38. Marius Barbeau's survey of Northwest Coast totem poles (*Totem Poles,* [1950–51]) pictures, among many others, the Kaigani Haida and Nuu-chah-nulth poles referenced in this discussion. The sharp intersection of underbrow and upper-cheek planes on the Ravenna Park poles and the small flat eyes with round pupils and painted whites are similar to those on Nuu-chah-nulth–carved posts photographed early in the twentieth century at Sarita, Barkley Sound, and unlike those on northern poles. On Nuu-chah-nulth poles the eyes are typically placed on the cheek plane, but the carvers of the Ravenna Park poles have positioned them on the underbrow plane to look down as they do on Tlingit and Haida poles.

39. Standley wrote about the Ravenna Park canoe twice in his Guest Book and on the back of a page cut from a second copy of *Ravenna Park, Seattle.* A note dated September 2, 1913, from Mrs. Beck to the University of Washington Museum described it as "a war canoe of the Clallam Indians of historic value. It is made of a huge cedar log—was captured & recaptured by smugglers—bryht back by the tribe & sold to us as a curio" (Burke Museum of Natural History and Culture, Ethnology Archives, Accession 619, 1913-132). He also described acquiring the canoe to his friend reporter H. E. Jamison in 1935 (H. E. Jamison, "Along the Waterfront," "Famous Old Canoe," *Seattle Star,* February 26, 1935).

40. For information on Henry Charles, see Wayne Suttles, *The Economic Life of the Coast Salish of Haro and Rosario Straits* (1974).

41. Burke Museum of Natural History and Culture, Ethnology Archives, Accession 619, 1913-132. The four poles remain in the museum's collection.

42. Burke Museum of Natural History and Culture, Ethnology Archives, Accession 619.

43. For later assessments of the impact of the AYPE, see, among others, Arthur J. Brown, "The Promotion of Emigration to Washington, 1854–1909," *Pacific Northwest Quarterly* 36 (1): 3–17; Dorothy O. Johanson and Charles M. Gates, *Empire of the Columbia* (1957); and George A. Frykman, "The Alaska-Yukon-Pacific Exposition, 1909," *Pacific Northwest Quarterly* 52 (1): 89–99.

44. The shop listing under "Guide to the City: What to See in and about Seattle" in *Seattle and the Pacific Northwest* (1909) read: "Ye Olde Curiosity Shop, on Colman Dock. Everything from a flea uniform to a whale jawbone."

45. Geological and natural history specimens, educational material from the Alaskan schools, pictures of Alaska, and a few Indian and Eskimo tools and baskets shown at the AYPE were accessioned at its close into what is now the Burke Museum of Natural History and Culture at the University of Washington.

46. Letter from George T. Emmons to Josiah Collins, August 12, 1909 (Meany Papers, University of Washington Libraries). Emmons describes his collection as "installed in nineteen double cases occupying considerable floorspace." In 1912 the university raised Emmons's asking price by appropriation and public subscription, and paid $14,500 for his collection of nineteen hundred Northwest Coast pieces (Cole, *Captured Heritage,* 221).

47. "An Exhibit of Alaskan Curios," *The Westerner* 11 (3): 11, advertised Standley's collection. Albert Cort Haddon saw it when he was in Seattle in mid-July to lecture at the exposition (AYPE clipping volume 9-SP, July 9–26, 1909, University of Washington Libraries).

48. The pamphlet *The Museum of Arts and Sciences of the Washington State Art Association, Seattle* (1910), published by the Washington State Art Association, reprinted endorsements for building a museum from local newspapers and noted individuals, discussed the association's planned program of activities, and listed and described the collections purchased or pledged for purchase. The new museum would be located centrally, include an auditorium, and cost between $250,000 and $300,000. See Anne H. Calhoun, *A Seattle Heritage: The Fine Arts Society* (1942) for the association's relationship to the Seattle Fine Arts Society, a rival organization, and information on the eventual merging of the two groups.

49. "Arts and Sciences Building Urged," *Seattle Post-Intelligencer,* January 9, 1910.

50. The January 9, 1904, article in the *Seattle Post-Intelligencer* laid the case for the Tozier collection needing a new home. It was described as "the largest and most complete collection either public or private of Northwestern curios in existence," three times as large as the collection of Northwest curios at the Smithsonian. Despite its having the potential of an international reputation, it was poorly exhibited in the Pierce County, Washington, courthouse. Several eastern museums were negotiating for it. Cole, *Captured Heritage,* discusses Tozier and collecting. I am grateful to Nancy S. Jackson for generously sharing research and a study she made on Tozier for the Burke Museum in 1984.

51. "Tozier Curios Purchased for Local Museum," *Seattle Post-Intelligencer,* October 9, 1909; "Tacomans Try to Block Moving of Indian Collection," *Seattle Post-Intelligencer,* October 11, 1909.

52. Guest Book, p. 41.

53. Washington State Art Association, *Museum of Arts and Sciences of the Washington State Art Association, Seattle* (1910). See also "Indian Art and History," *Museum-Auditorium Monthly* 1 (2): 2–3.

54. Recorded dates for activities of the Washington State Art Association and the addresses of its galleries have assisted in the dating of the Curiosity Shop catalogs in which Standley mentions the purchase of his collection. In 1906 the association's gallery was located in the new Carnegie Public Library at Fourth Avenue and Madison Street. In 1912 the location was on Fifth Avenue between University and Seneca Street. In November 1914 new galleries were opened at 423 University Street.

55. Nancy Jackson, "Captain Dorr F. Tozier," study of Accession 3768, Burke Museum of Natural History and Culture, p. 7.

56. In 1917, the year after George G. Heye bought Standley's collection, he also purchased much of Tozier's Northwest Coast material. The Burke Museum at the University of Washington acquired other Tozier material through a local curio shop, the Hudson Bay Fur Company.

Chapter Four. "Just What a First Class Museum Should Have": Museum Collecting

1. Account ledger, Ye Olde Curiosity Shop.

2. J. Alden Mason, "George G. Heye, 1874–1956" *Leaflet No. 6,* Museum of the American Indian, Heye Foundation, 1958, 11. Information on Heye and the Heye Foundation also comes from: Kevin Wallace, "Slim-Shin's Monument," *New Yorker Magazine,* November 16, 1960, 104–46; "The History of the Museum," *Indian Notes and Monographs, Miscellaneous Series,* No. 55, Museum of the American Indian Heye Foundation, 1964; Vincent Wilcox, "The Museum of the American Indian, Heye Foundation," *American Indian Art Magazine* 3 (2): 40–49, 78–81; Claudia Sue Kidwell, "Every Last Dishcloth: The Prodigious Collecting of George Gustav Heye," in Shepard Krech III and Barbara A. Hail, eds., *Collecting Native America* (1999), 232–58. I am grateful to Duane King for sharing his files on Heye with me.

3. George G. Heye financed G. B. Gordon of the Free Museum of Science and Art at the University of Pennsylvania (later the University Museum) to gather duplicate artifacts for him while Gordon was collecting on the Kuskokwim River in 1907. Susan A. Kaplan and Kristin Barsness, *Raven's Journey: The World of Alaska's Native People* (1986), outlines the relationship between Heye and Gordon and the museum at the University of Pennsylvania.

4. Heye's catalog number is written to the left of each entry on the typed list that Ye Olde Curiosity Shop provided (Archives, National Museum of the American Indian, Smithsonian Institution, box OC142, folder 25).

5. See James G. R. Smith's catalog *Arctic Art: Eskimo Ivory* (1980) for examples of carved graveyards; also see Dorothy Jean Ray's *Eskimo Art: Tradition and Innovation in North Alaska* (1977) and her later publications for a schema of Alaskan Inupiat engraving styles.

6. List dated November 7, 1916, in Standley's hand, of seventy objects sent on approval; thirty-six items are marked with a "K" for "kept" (Archives, National Museum of the American Indian, Smithsonian Institution, box OC142, folder 25).

7. The Museum of the American Indian's journal lists several gifts from Standley: a "goat horn spoon. Haida" *(Indian Notes* 1 [2]: 99, April 1924); "dentalium shell beads; thin shell disc beads; triangular haliotis shell pendant, Nez Perce reservation, Lapwai" *(Indian Notes* 2 [1]: 80, January 1925); and a "fish-net of sinew with wooden floats and antler sinker attached. Eskimo, Kotzebue Sound, Alaska," (*Indian Notes* 3 [4]: 296, October 1926).

8. Ye Olde Curiosity Shop invoice, September 15, 1922, to George Heye (Archives, National Museum of the American Indian, Smithsonian Institution, box OC285, folder 10).

9. The Makah Museum and the National Museum of the American Indian (formerly George Heye's Museum of the American Indian) are working to clarify the relationship between the original Young Doctor ensemble that went to the museum and the 1920s copy of it that was in Standley's shop until it was shipped to Neah Bay in 1990. The combination of the serpent supported by two figures is one that Young Doctor carved several times. Photographs taken of Captain Dorr F. Tozier's collection while it was located in the Tacoma Ferry Museum picture two such sets, as well as a large model canoe with figures that also appears to be the work of Young Doctor (Washington State Historical Society Special Collections, Ferry Museum, box 1 #16). Information on Young Doctor is found in the exhibition brochure by the Makah Cultural and Research Center, "Riding in His Canoe: The Continuing Legacy of Young Doctor" (1998); James G. McCurdy, *Indian Days at Neah Bay* (1961); Frances Densmore, *Nootka and Quileute Music* (1939; reprint, 1972); and various writings of James G. Swan. See also Carolyn Marr, J. Lloyd Colfax, and Robert D. Monroe, *Portrait in Time: Photographs of the Makah by Samuel G. Morse, 1896–1903* (1987).

10. In association with research for this book, letters were sent to more than one hundred museums in the United States and Canada that had been referenced in Ye Olde Curiosity Shop records or whose location or collection content suggested that they might hold material that had been procured from the shop. Several European museums mentioned in the shop records were also contacted.

11. "600 Elephants Seattle-Bound as 'Olde' Shop Stirs Again," *Seattle Star,* October 1946.

12. Standley's "List of Museums That Bought from Us" in the address book labeled "Address of Where to Buy" includes the Royal Ontario Museum, Toronto, Canada; the Museum of the American Indian, New York; the Riverside Museum, California; the Museum of Wrangle, Alaska; the Hadden Hall Museum, London; the Mission Inn, Riverside, California; the H. J. Palmers Chiropractic Institute, Davenport, Iowa; the Smithsonian Institution, Washington, D.C.; BuckHorn Sanatoria; and the National Museum, Stockholm, Sweden. The earlier address book, on which Standley wrote "See Where to Buy in Safe," appears to have been used over a number of years. The penmanship varies and entries appear under the proper letter, or are written in remaining space near the bottom of nearby pages. For instance, basket suppliers appear on the B pages but also on adjacent C and D pages. The order within categories and many of the entries in the later "Address of Where to Buy" follow that of the earlier book in which they have been crossed out.

Standley wrote "See Where to Buy Book in Safe" on a sticker he pasted on the older book. It is torn, however, leaving only a remnant of further written instruction: "Use this por . . . re scrap p." This may explain why the fronts and backs of all but three of the last nineteen pages of "See Where to Buy in Safe," starting in the Ts, are filled with miscellaneous business cards, news clippings, notes about suppliers and collectors, and such. Some of these items are dated ranging between 1921 and the early 1930s. Standley appears to have decided to recopy the alphabetized list into the new book "Address of Where to Buy" and use the remainder of the old book for scrap paper on which to corral related miscellany.

Standley would celebrate his seventy-fifth birthday in 1929, and organizing information necessary for running the shop had become a concern. Also in the late 1920s he began to write down anecdotes on scrap paper and in his Guest Book with plans to write a book. He never got to it.

13. Douglas Cole's *Captured Heritage: The Scramble for Northwest Coast Artifacts* (1985; reprint, 1995) provides an exhaustive history of competitive museum collecting of Northwest Coast artifacts in the decades surrounding 1900.

14. Currelly's clerical career was short. Turned out of the church after his brief missionary experience because of both the type of theological training he had received and his personal bent toward a scientific explanation of scripture, Currelly went to England in 1902 to pursue a doctoral degree. His entertaining autobiography, *I Brought the Ages Home* (1956), anecdotally narrates his adventures and triumphs of collecting during his years of archaeological work in Egypt and elsewhere, and through dealers and other collectors.

15. Currelly's friend William H. Holmes of the Smithsonian Institution made the comparison (Currelly, *I Brought the Ages Home,* 233).

16. Currelly *(I Brought the Ages Home,* 89) argued that "the things that are wanted by one group of people, and for which, therefore, the people of the time look, may not be the things that are interesting to the people of a later period, and of course the only thing to do is to go back to the original object for the information."

17. Currelly, *I Brought the Ages Home,* 184.

18. After a 1912 legislative mandate for a museum in Toronto, the trustees established five museums to work in concert. The Royal Ontario Museum of Archaeology, with Currelly as its director, was founded alongside the Royal Ontario Museums of Paleontology, Natural History (soon changed to Zoology), Geology, and Mineralogy.

19. After purchasing Pueblo ceramics in Santa Fe with the help of Edgar L. Hewett, who was running a school for the study of Southwestern archaeology there, Currelly visited in San Diego then traveled north. In Victoria, British Columbia, he met with medical doctor and naturalist C. F. Newcombe, who had collected totem poles for a number of natural history museums. Newcombe helped Currelly acquire a Haida crest pole by carver Matthew Williams and a Kwakiutl housepost from Owikeno village on Rivers Inlet. (Currelly, *I Brought the Ages Home,* 205; letter to author from Ken Lister, Royal Ontario Museum, September 4, 1997; Cole, *Captured Heritage,* 238–39).

20. The correspondence in the Registration Archives of the Royal Ontario Museum between the museum and Ye Olde Curiosity Shop is extensive. Unusually complete, although not entirely, the correspondence conveys a great deal about the personalities and strategies of both Standley and Currelly, as well as the effect of the larger economic health of the times on transactions and how they took place.

21. Currelly, *I Brought the Ages Home,* 206.

22. Royal Ontario Museum (ROM) correspondence with Ye Olde Curiosity Shop. Registration Archives, File 912.42.1 ROM correspondence April 26, 1912–May 12, 1913.

23. This first shipment, of April 26, 1912, included three boxes and one crate that contained 129 articles, which with the 35 percent discount came to $450.30.

24. Letter April 26, 1912, J.E.S to ROM.

25. Letter July 8, 1912, J.E.S to Dear Friend Currelly.

26. Letter May 12, 1913, J.E.S to Friend Currelly.

27. See John Bockstoce, *Whales, Ice, and Men: The History of Whaling in the Western Arctic* (1986), for a comprehensive study of western Arctic whaling.

28. ROM Registration Archives, File 917.11 (correspondence June 2–October 24, 1917) concerns the tusk. Its purchase was funded by Sir Edmund Osler.

29. Letters J.E.S. to ROM, June 2 and 26, 1917.

30. See "A Carved Mammoth Tusk from Alaska," in *1962 Annual Report, Art and Archaeology Division, Royal Ontario Museum* (1963), where James VanStone describes each vignette pictured on the tusk. He does not cite Ye Olde Curiosity Shop as the source, but does include the Happy Jack attribution that Standley provided in correspondence to the museum. Dorothy Jean Ray's explanation of her attribution to Joe Kakarook is found in *Eskimo Art: Tradition and Innovation in North Alaska* (1977), fig. 258.

31. Letter J.E.S. to Currelly, June 16, 1917.

32. ROM Registration Archives, File HC2841–HC2842 (correspondence October 20, 1928–April 11, 1929), concerns the stone stove and cooking pot. Anderson, who had spent four years on eastern Victoria Land and Coronation Gulf, collected material between the Coppermine River and King William Land. In 1921, when living in Seattle, he offered his collection to several museums, among them the Newark Museum, which purchased a portion of it (correspondence files, Newark Museum). The large and very heavy stone stove and kettle were still left in 1928, and Anderson approached Standley about selling them for him. Standley's shop carried other Coronation Gulf material, but whether it came from Anderson is not known.

33. Over the years Standley notified local newspapers when something of interest came into the shop. The short news clip "Relic of Primitive Eskimo Comes to Seattle from Civilization's Outpost," *Seattle Daily Times,* October 19, 1928, was such a case. Until he could sell the stove and "kettle," Standley kept them in a back room. When showing them to a local reporter, he identified them as from "the blond Eskimo in Banks Land" and explained that the lamp was used by igniting oil poured into it to provide light in their igloos (Typescript of memorial tribute given by H. E. Jamison, radio announcer of Arm Chair cruises, October 25, 1940, the day of Standley's death). Sir John Franklin, the first explorer to enter the Coronation Gulf region, and others who followed reported seeing people with European-like features, gray or blue eyes, and red or brown hair. Vilhjálmur Stefánsson's suggestion that these "Blond Eskimo" were descended in part from the Norsemen who had settled on the south and west coasts of Greenland about 1000 A.D., caused bitter debate and made spectacular newspaper copy. It is curious, however, that Standley did not identify the stove and kettle other than by location when he offered them to the ROM. He certainly would have taken note of such intriguing information in the newspaper and may well have seen Stefánsson's 1928 article "The Blond Eskimos," *Harpers Magazine* 156: 191–98.

34. Letter November 8, 1928, Clark Wissler to J.E.S. (American Museum of Natural History, Department of Anthropology, Alph. files 1927–1939). Other museums Standley queried about the size of similar stoves were the Museum of the American Indian, Heye Foundation, New York; the U.S. National Smithsonian Museum; and the Field Museum, Chicago.

35. ROM Registration Archives, File HC2841–HC2842 (correspondence October 20, 1928–April 11, 1929).

36. ROM Registration Archives, File 929.20.1-.11, 1929 (correspondence March 8–18, 1929) details this transaction.

37. ROM Registration Archives, File HC2841–HC2842.

38. ROM Registration Archives, File 929.74.1-, 1929 (correspondence April 23–July 18, 1929) concerns this shipment.

39. ROM Registration Archives, File 929.74.1-, 1929 (correspondence April 23–July 18, 1929).

40. Currelly, *I Brought the Ages Home,* 207–8, 292.

41. Letter to the author from Ken Lister, curator, Department of Anthropology, ROM, May 12, 1998.

42. ROM Registration Archives, 1930 Files HC3115–HC3139, HC3144, HN1156 (correspondence January 8–October 15, 1930).

43. ROM Registration Archives, 1931 Files HC3230–HC3242 (correspondence March 17–June 16, 1931).

44. ROM Registration Archives, File 936.33.1- (correspondence June 20, 1935–March 12, 1936) concerns the sled with ivory runners.

45. John Cotton Dana published his ideas, sometimes repeating them, in several small books—*The New Museum* (1917*), A Plan for a New Museum: The Kind of Museum It Will Profit a City to Maintain* (1920), and *Should Museums Be Useful? Possibilities in Museum Development* (1927)—all published by the Elm Tree Press in Woodstock, Vermont. He also frequently wrote about his ideals in *Library Journal.*

46. Material in the Newark Museum's permanent collection was often duplicated in the lending collection (later named the Educational Loan Collection). By 1926, although still a part of the museum, the lending department had begun to function independently, with its own staff handling loans of more than twelve thousand objects each year and a museum truck making regular deliveries to city schools. Its former supervisor, Ruth Hessler, noted in 1979 that the museum's lending collection had become an inspiration for museums in many communities, but its approach was unique. Rather than sending out objects permanently fixed into rigidly themed "suitcase exhibits," the museum loaned out individual objects so that students might handle them and teachers use them as they wished. The museum's Educational Loan Collection still loans out individual objects (Ruth Hessler, "The Lending Collection," special issue, "The Dana Influence: The Newark Museum Collections," *Newark Museum Quarterly* 30 [4]: 7–10).

47. It appears that there were fourteen to sixteen catalogs in all. Ten catalogs plus two brochures have been located to date. Of these, only the shop's fortieth anniversary catalog, from 1939, is dated.

48. Dana wrote about the trip in the work by Dana, Mary W. Plummer, and Theresa Hitchler, *The Far Northwest* (1906).

49. The Newark Museum's records pertaining to Ye Olde Curiosity Shop include several letters and lists regarding a transaction in summer 1919 (June–July) and another in spring 1921 (March–May), as well as the catalog records of all pieces accessioned (Newark Museum Archives).

50. Dana, *The New Museum,* 32–33.

51. The Newark Museum also collected from other curio shops, especially in the American Southwest.

52. I am indebted to University of Washington graduate student Sylvia Ferrari for research and analysis of information linking the Newark Museum and Ye Olde Curiosity Shop.

53. Letter from Mrs. Osborne Selmer, Skagway, to Eric Weiss, Librarian, Portland Art Museum, undated. Other information on Rasmussen's life comes from the typescript "Brief Biography of Axel Rasmussen, by his sister Mrs. Jennie Fell, Oxford, Indiana, 3/12/55" (both in Rasmussen Document File, Portland Art Museum). Both documents are also the main sources for biographical information in Erna Gunther, *Art in the Life of the Northwest Coast Indians* (1966). Axel Rasmussen is not to be confused with explorer and ethnographer Knud Rasmussen, who led the sixth and seventh Thule Expeditions of the early 1930s to Greenland and for decades studied Greenland's Polar Eskimos.

54. The Axel Rasmussen Collection was purchased by the Portland Art Museum in 1948, by way of Earl H. Stendahl Gallery, Hollywood, California. The Northwest Coast portion of the collection was published in Gunther, *Art in the Life of the Northwest Coast Indians.*

55. Sometimes Rasmussen devoted a day to looking for artifacts in Seattle, where he usually purchased from Ye Olde Curiosity Shop, the Hudson Bay Fur Company, and Mrs. Ferguson's Curio Shop. His careful records show that transactions with the Curiosity Shop occurred on January 1, 1930; March 3, 1931; August 12, 1932; and January 31, 1944.

56. In 1993 curator James VanStone found no records referencing Ye Olde Curiosity Shop in the Field Museum's Department of Anthropology but believed there might be shop tags on some of its baskets. These may have been gifts to the museum, purchased at Standley's shop.

57. Correspondence between Standley and the Smithsonian is located in the Smithsonian Archives, Record Unit 192, United States National Museum, 1877–1975. The museum dealt courteously and systematically with correspondence, whatever its source, and kept everything associated with each transaction: incoming and outgoing letters, internal memos, shipping records, and in Standley's case, the postcards and Seattle booster cards he sent. In those days the Smithsonian staff was small, and his letters were answered by the assistant secretary in charge of the National Museum, an R. Rathburn.

58. Standley, "A Word from Curio Joe," *Pacific Sportsman* 3 (2): 58.

59. Letter, March 29, 1994, from Jane Walsh, Department of Anthropology, Smithsonian Institution.

60. This warm sense of personal ownership still maintains, as was clear when I worked in the Public Information Office of the Smithsonian's Museum of Natural History for a period in 1979.

People called or wrote with scores of questions and each was thoughtfully answered, whether the request was for the identification of a rock found in the backyard, for suggestions of Indian names for a cabin or boat, or to know what the ancient Sumerian language sounded like.

61. Letter, October 20, 1928, J.E.S. to the Museum of Natural History New York, Archives, Department of Anthropology, American Museum of Natural History.

62. Correspondence between Standley and G. T. Emmons, Clark Wissler, and N. C. Nelson (1928–32) is housed in the Archives, Department of Anthropology, American Museum of Natural History.

63. H. E. Jamison, "Along the Waterfront," *Seattle Star,* February 24, 1936. The Seattle Art Museum has no record of Standley's projected gift, however.

64. In 1964, with a major financial bequest from the wife of pioneer Judge Thomas Burke, the Washington State Museum became the Burke Memorial Washington State Museum. "The First Hundred Years: A Century of Natural History at the Burke Museum," *Landmarks: Magazine of Northwest History and Preservation* 4 (1985) outlines the history of the Burke Museum in a special centennial issue. Bill Holm, "The Northwest Coast Collections in the Burke Museum," in *Spirit and Ancestor: A Century of Northwest Coast Indian Art at the Burke Museum* (1987), 11–22, considers the ethnological collections.

65. A letter of March 29, 1937, from Ye Olde Curiosity Shop to Meany asked for his help in finding out what early ships came into the Seattle harbor and when, in hopes of identifying "a very fine cannon of Spanish or India origin which was found near Seattle a number of years ago." Meany replied: "Off hand, I do not know of a ship that would account for the cannon" (Meany Papers, University of Washington Libraries).

66. "Seattle State Museum Urged," *Seattle Post-Intelligencer,* January 2, 1923.

67. Letter, March 5, 1908, Thomas F. Kane, president, University of Washington to Henry A. McLean, chairman AYPE State Commission (Washington State Library MSS 030, MacLean folder).

68. One instance of Washington State Museum personnel arranging for museum collections occurred in 1924, when F. S. Hall, at the time director of the museum, acted as an agent for the Kent Scientific Museum in Grand Rapids, Michigan, to purchase a collection of 112 tools and clothing from the "Alaska Eskimo and Coronation Gulf Blond Eskimo from The Alaska Curio Shop in Seattle" (Public Museum of Grand Rapids, Accession Record 3065). Although mail for Ye Olde Curiosity Shop occasionally arrived addressed to the Alaska Curio Shop, it is more likely that Hall's purchase was from Mrs. H. B. Ferguson, one of Standley's smaller competitors. In 1904 Ferguson began listing herself as a source for Alaska curios, under "Curios," in the *Seattle City Directory.* Beginning in 1920 she registered her business as the Alaska Curio Shop and continued through 1935. The Kent Scientific Museum collection now belongs to the Public Museum of Grand Rapids, Michigan.

69. The Alaska-Yukon-Pacific Exposition closed on October 16, 1909, and Standley offered the University of Washington the whale bones almost immediately. Later in the month he inquired again, more urgently: "I want to haul them before the Wreckers tear up the [Eskimo Village] Building" (letter, J.E.S. to Professor Meany, October 31, 1909). By December the whale bones had not been installed and Standley sent a postcard to Meany: "I was out there last week but failed to see them." Meany passed it on to the recently appointed assistant curator, F. S. Hall, with a note: "Please get answer sent to this 3rd call and return." Letter to Professor Meany from J.E.S., October 16, 1909 (Burke Museum, Accession Files, no. 1909–27); postcard to Professor Meany from J.E.S., December 2, 1909 (Meany Papers, University of Washington Libraries).

70. Letter, June 19, 1929, from J.E. Standley to University of Washington. Standley seems to be referring to the M. H. deYoung Museum in San Francisco's Golden Gate Park (Burke Museum, Accession Files, no. 2313, 1929–39).

71. Letter, September 10, 1929, J.E.S. to State Museum; letter, October 3, 1929, J.E.S. to Mrs. Spier, director of the State Museum (Burke Museum, Accession Files, no. 2313, 1929–39).

72. The *St. Paul* was operated on the coast by Pacific Packing and Navigation from 1901 until 1924. The ship opened to the public as a museum in June 1934 and closed in 1940. It was the last wooden full-rigged ship in the Northwest.

73. On a clipping about the Foss purchase ("From the Crow's Nest," *Seattle Sunday Times,* April 4, 1937), Standley wrote: "Get Jameson [*sic*] to write up and ask help from citizens Donations to the Ships Marine Museum and Acquarium." His friend, journalist H. E. Jamison, who wrote the column "Along the Waterfront" for the *Seattle Star,* enjoyed Standley, and over the years wrote about him warmly.

74. Letter, September 24, 1935 to J. E. Standley from F. W. Schmoe, Director, Puget Sound Academy of Science (Ye Olde Curiosity Shop records).

75. Letter, October 8, 1927, W. I. Bonney, Washington State Historical Society, to J.E.S.

76. Museums with one or more documented pieces from the shop include the Alaska State Museum, Juneau; the Joslyn Art Museum, Omaha, Nebraska; the Mississippi Historical Society, Jackson; the Mitchell Indian Museum, Kendall College, Evanston, Illinois; the Phoebe Hearst Museum, Berkeley, California;

the Sheldon Jackson Museum, Sitka, Alaska; and the Museum of Natural History, University of Florida, Gainesville. The Riverside Mission Inn in California purchased bells and possibly other items from the shop.

77. A notation in the Guest Book (p. 44) regarding the British Museum (or *a* British museum) has remained elusive. In it Standley wrote that a Mr. Geddes, his wife, and daughter from London "Bot store Relics Phalics for Brittish Museum 1915 he was here to establish Steam ship Offices; his line We sent Curios via it."

78. Georgina Russell and others, "The Wellcome Non-Medical Material," *Museums Journal,* Supplement 86 (1986), discusses the dispersals by the Wellcome Trust of Sir Henry Wellcome's non-medical collections.

79. During the Depression and afterward, as the country moved toward then entered World War II, museum budgets were tight. When Standley's competitor, Seattle's Hudson Bay Fur Company, attempted to sell off its curio inventory in the early 1940s after it lost its lease, the company had great difficulty finding buyers, even at bargain prices (Hudson Bay Fur Company file, Maxwell Museum, University of New Mexico).

Chapter Five. Uncommon Treasures for Attractions and Amusements

1. B. J. Palmer's own signature appears twice in Standley's Guest Book, once where he signed it himself and once where Standley cut out the signature from a letter and pasted it in. Standley also noted Palmer's visits at four other places in the Guest Book, and near the end of his life, he erased previous signatures on page one and wrote over them a paragraph of memories about Palmer. A February 27, 1924, entry notes, "Dr. B. J. Palmer, wife & son of Davenport Iowa. Bolos, Borongs, Kreis, Spears, Knives, Totems for his Institute. Big old Totem Pole Bot by Chiropractic Club Presented to the Dr."

2. Palmer's filing system seems to have primarily entailed sticking current papers, no matter the topic, into file boxes, systematically filling one box after another. This extensive and seemingly nonselective system was not simple sloppiness or laziness; rather, it can be seen as integral to Palmer's lifelong commitment to a profession that he believed eventually would come to be accepted. Retaining a record of every aspect of his life and of the early years of chiropractic, and saving this history in its every detail for future analysis, could eventually help legitimize the field.

3. Palmer was particularly stressed by a major controversy within the profession over the neurocalometer, a device that revolutionized one aspect of chiropractic. A diagnostic instrument that measured localized body heat more accurately than the practitioner's hands, the neurocalometer was given to him by a friend who had invented the instrument. When Palmer insisted on renting the devices for a hefty monthly fee rather than selling them outright to his colleagues, they were enraged. This and other philosophical differences created deep antagonisms that were harbored for decades and in effect split the profession. Palmer's stress was overcome in part through travel and collecting and also through the therapeutic benefit of physically building the fantasy attraction he named "A Little Bit O' Heaven."

4. The Palmer Mansion, Palmer's "museum," was closed after the deaths of Mabel Palmer in 1949 and Palmer himself in 1961. What remained of A Little Bit O' Heaven was dismantled in 1981. The College began restoration of the Palmer Mansion to house a museum of the history of chiropractic in 1996, projecting to open in 2003. Too little of A Little Bit O' Heaven was left to allow reconstruction, although some of its components, especially the sculptures, will be displayed in the forthcoming museum.

5. The lively, often opinionated narrative of *'Round the World with B. J.* (1926) is based on letters Palmer sent home weekly to be broadcast on Tuesday and Friday nights over his radiophone station WOC. They were then published in his personal house organ, "The Fountain News," which was mailed to "all in his Chiropractic professional family." His son, David, then fourteen years old, took the photographs for the book. Other family publications include Palmer, *The Bigness of the Fellow Within* (1949); David D. Palmer, *The Palmers: Memoirs of David D. Palmer* (1977); and Mabel Palmer, *Stepping Stones* (1942). Wes and Dorothy Sheader, *The Palmer Mansion: A Pictorial Tour* (1995), discusses many of the most important or unusual pieces in Palmer's collection and includes small photographs of A Little Bit O' Heaven.

6. The Palmer archives include complete records of transactions with the suppliers of novelties sold at the kiosk.

7. Palmer College of Chiropractic, *A Little Bit O' Heaven Tour Guide,* 55th ed. (n.d.), 9, quoted in Lisa Stone and Jim Zanzi, *Sacred Spaces and Other Places: A Guide to Grottos and Sculptural Environments in the Upper Midwest* (1993).

8. Between its opening day on July 1, 1924, and January 1, 1953, 1,680,259 people visited A Little Bit O' Heaven *(A Guide Book, A Little Bit O' Heaven & The Wishing Buddha,* unpaginated, n.d.). By the time the attraction closed in 1981, visitors had numbered more than three million (Sheader and Sheader, *The Palmer Mansion,* 10).

9. Palmer's son, David D., talks about his alligator and other responsibilities in *The Palmers: Memoirs of David D. Palmer* (1977).

10. The WOC Radio–sponsored tour, advertised as "On to Alaska and Return: A Romantic Tour to the Land of the Midnight Sun," brought a bit of income to the college while allowing Palmer to visit a place he had never been.

11. Typescript "West of Where the West Begins," Palmer College Archives, Elevator Shaft 13272–13275. On longer trips, Palmer typed up daily reports such as this one, which he mailed home to his typesetter to prepare for publication.

12. Replica poles, large and small, have almost all been at least loosely based on historic poles made in Northwest Coast Native communities but with some juxtapositions and changes. Compared with the Seattle Totem Pole, near the top of the tall pole given to Palmer, the woman with her frog child is missing, at the bottom of the pole the mink and whale are juxtaposed and the raven between them has been replaced with a humanoid face. Also at the bottom a large crescent referencing the moon that Raven's grandfather kept in a box before Raven gifted it to mankind replaces a figure of Grandfather.

13. The four Palmer College totem poles are in very poor condition, with the wood badly cracked and the surfaces peeling layers of paint from standing outside for many years. At least two poles relate in carving style to other poles in Ye Olde Curiosity Shop photographs, poles made by local, probably Nuu-chah-nulth, carvers. In the 1920s Standley's shop was the most likely place to find large poles. A notation in Standley's Guest Book dated February 27, 1924, includes "Totems for his Institute" and "Big old Totem Poles Bot by Chiropractic Club Presented to the Dr." Further information about these poles may someday be found in the college's "elevator shaft" archives.

14. Palmer, *The Bigness of the Fellow Within,* 370.

15. The snuff boxes are ivory cylinders set into wooden bases. Their rounded ivory lids pierced in the center might be interpreted as phallic.

16. One phallus-shaped maul in the shop's collection and pictured in an old photo is labeled in Standley's hand: "Sex-Worship Phalic Relic, dug out of a well on the Columbia River, Wash." Prehistoric stone tools from the Columbia and Fraser Rivers are a major focus of Wilson Duff, *Images Stone B.C.: Thirty Centuries of Northwest Coast Stone Sculpture* (1975).

17. The Native American objects in the Palmer collection include the stone maul, two miniature and four large totem poles, all of which are still in the Palmer Mansion, and other pieces now in the Putnam Museum of History and Natural Science, in Davenport. The Putnam collection now includes four Navajo rugs, several Woodlands beaded pieces, and a group of Eskimo artifacts, primarily clothing and ivories, given to Palmer by Julius Warmbath after he traveled with Admiral Robert Peary to the Arctic. (It was taxidermist Warmbath who earlier had been instructed to stuff the Palmer's St. Bernard.) The Plains material falls into two categories: a headdress, peace pipe, bow and arrow, war clubs and pouches acquired, perhaps as gifts, after a man described as the grandson of South Dakota Blackfeet Chief Blackhawk made Palmer an honorary chief; and the Indian outfit he purchased from an Indian store after having received the title. David Palmer may have disposed of some objects before they went to the Putnam Museum.

18. Palmer, *The Bigness of the Fellow Within,* 369.

19. Charles Trick Currelly, *I Brought the Ages Home* (1956).

20. Information on Robert L. Ripley comes primarily from undated articles and news releases supplied by Ripley Entertainment, Inc., *Current Biography,* July 1945, and from discussions with Edward Meyer, curator of the Ripley collections.

21. Standley's grandson Joe James recalls that Ripley would call ahead to notify the shop that he would be coming. He believes that Ripley came in several times in the 1930s and remembers two of these visits, especially the midnight visit in 1936 when Ripley purchased the clamshell and the forty-foot totem pole. During Ripley's time in the Northwest and Alaska, he bought four large totems poles, all still in the Ripley collections, and several smaller ones.

22. At another time a Ripley cartoon featured a four-tusked walrus head that belonged to Mack's Totem Shop in Seattle.

23. The article "Ripley Buys Totem Pole Here," announcing the purchase, appeared in Seattle's *Financial District Weekly Review,* on January 8, 1937, the day that the move from Colman Dock began. Ripley's purchases were also discussed in an Ernie Pyle column titled "Whale Louse," in *Citizen* (syndicated), February 1, 1942.

24. The Potlatch Man that Ripley bought, visible in the left corner of the store in the 1934 Webster & Stevens photograph of Ye Olde Curiosity Shop (see fig. 1.15), is discussed in "Down the Hatch," *Seattle Post-Intelligencer,* November 18, 1936.

25. There is little doubt that Standley, with the help of Williams, wrote the description of the Potlatch Man for the guidebook used at Ripley's 1939 world's fair exhibition: "This totem pole is a replica of the Indian Doctor or Medicine Man of the Haidah Tribe of Alaska Indians known as the 'Shaman.' The two human figures upon the knee represent twins, as all the ancestors for past hundred years bore twins. The frog coming out of his mouth represents the casting out of the evil spirits. The eagle covers his breast, the fearless Thunder Bird, Rampant. His protectors under the feet are two heads of Black Whale Killers, represents the Doctor is in charge of the fish food of the sea. The eagles upon his arms denote the fighting protectors, ready for the fray. The figure is 10 feet in height, 3 feet in width. It's the only one ever seen in the United States."

26. Welcome speech for the Potlatch Man, from its carver Sam Williams, recorded in 1958 by Joe James.

27. Ripley's Believe It or Not!® museums were also opened in the following tourist areas: Gatlinburg, Tennessee; Estes Park, Colorado; Myrtle Beach, South Carolina; Lake Ozark, Missouri;

Santa Rosa, California; San Antonio, Texas; New Orleans; Newport, Oregon; Hollywood, California; and Surfer's Paradise, Australia. Some locations were short-lived, others still exist today.

28. Information on the Charbneau miniature collection and connection with Ye Olde Curiosity Shop comes from Standley family members and news clippings. "Little Things Mean a Lot in This Miniature Museum," *Seattle Times,* July 15, 1962, talks of the collection going to the Wenatchee Museum. "Cricket Fight Items May Go to California," *Wenatchee Daily World,* April 24, 1969, describes the Chinese sport of cricket fighting as well as the cricket cages, pottery arena, dishes, ticklers, and caskets involved. See also "World's Largest Exhibit of Smallest Curiosities Collected by Jules Charbneau," (People's Outfitting Co., February 1935) and "Jules' Tiny S. F. Exhibition May Be World's Fair Gem" (referring to the 1958 Brussels World's Fair), *San Francisco (?) Call-Bulletin,* April 24, 1958; "Little Things Mean a Lot in this Miniature Museum," *Seattle Times,* July 15, 1962. A plan in the early 1960s for the Charbneau collection to come to a museum in Wenatchee, Washington, where Charbneau's daughter Isabella Charbneau lived, did not work out and the collection was sold in 1969. Some of it returned to Ye Olde Curiosity Shop; some went to the Ripley's Believe It or Not! museums and elsewhere.

29. A catalog of a Charbneau display titled "World's Largest Exhibit of Smallest Curiosities" (People's Outfitting Co., 1935) lists 493 miniatures.

30. In the early 1960s there were plans for the Charbneau Miniature Collection to go to the North Central Washington Museum of Art in Wenatchee, Washington, where the Warrens lived. After these failed, in 1969 it was put up for sale.

31. Guest Book, pp. 40, 74, 76, 81. In many cases the addresses given in the Guest Book are sufficient to allow a reference to be researched. Friends in Alameda, California, discovered that the Simon J. Gray family added an "Alaska room" to its twenty-one-room mansion to display the souvenirs from their Alaska trip, and daughter Estelle, a concert violinist, brought not one (as Standley noted) but eight huskies from Alaska ("So We're Told," *Berkeley Gazette,* October 28, 1952).

32. A Guest Book entry, dated April 8, 1927, p. 81, includes the card of Father Paul M. Dobberstein at work on his grotto in West Bend, Iowa. Standley's corner note "he died 1929" is incorrect, for Dobberstein died in 1954, at which time work on the grotto was taken over by Father Louis H. Grieving, who was succeeded in 1994 by Deacon Gerald Streit. Publications by the soon named Grotto of the Redemption outline its history: *An Explanation of the Grotto of the Redemption* (n.d.); Duane Hutchinson, *Grotto Father: Artist-Priest of the West Bend Grotto* (1989), and Louis H. Grieving, *A Pictorial Story of the Grotto of the Redemption* (1993). Palmer and Dobberstein's grottoes are discussed in the context of other grottoes in the region in Lisa Stone and Jim Zanzi, *Sacred Spaces and Other Places: A Guide to Grottos and Sculptural Environments in the Upper Midwest* (1993).

Chapter Six. Curiosities and Charisma: Exotica and Daddy Standley

1. Ernie Pyle, "Whale Louse," a nationally syndicated column, January 1, 1942. Pyle's column was syndicated nationally and appears to have been titled differently in different newspapers.

2. Ye Olde Curiosity Shop's collections have nourished a public fascination with the miniature and the gigantic. Susan Stewart probes its complexity in *On Longing: Narratives of the Miniature, the Gigantic, the Souvenir, the Collection* (1984).

3. "Great Thoughts, Good News, on Head of Pin," caption on photograph of a visitor looking at the Lord's Prayer on a pinhead, *Seattle Star,* July 16, 1927. *World's Largest Exhibit of Smallest Curios,* a booklet published by People's Outfitting Company to accompany a February 1935 exhibit of miniatures from the collection of Jules Charbneau, Standley's son-in-law, attributes the "Original Lord's Prayer Pin" to A. Shiller. The artifact was exhibited at the Chicago World's Fair in 1893, stolen, eventually returned, and was included in Charbneau's 1935 exhibit. Standley (Guest Book, p. 7) credited Godfrey Lundberg as the first to originate a stamping die that could transfer the entire Lord's Prayer onto the head of a pin. Lundberg passed away in 1932.

4. "World's Smallest Carving in City," *Seattle Star,* March 1935; typescript of tribute presented on the radio on October 25, 1940, the day of Standley's death, by Standley's friend H. E. Jamison, the radio announcer of Arm Chair cruises.

5. "Puget Sound Mermaids Go on Wild Spree," *Seattle Post-Intelligencer,* August 28, 1923; L. W. Pedrose, "Seattle," *Western Gift, Art, and Novelty Shop* (Los Angeles), October 1923; Frank Lynch, "Everything's Real at Olde Curiosity Shop except Greatest Attraction, but Anyone Should Know There're No Mermaids," *Seattle Post-Intelligencer,* February 7, 1949.

6. "Mermaid-Hunting a Sport of Sea-Sheiks: Puget Sound Nimrods Nab Nimble Nymph," *Seattle Post-Intelligencer,* August 24, 1923.

7. Byron Fish, "Unplanned Mummyhood, Gloria Comes Here to Live; Still Young at 500 or 1,000," *Seattle Times,* November 12, 1948; Joe James, personal communication with the author. The shop's mummies Gloria and Sylvester were featured in a special program titled "Mummies Frozen in Time," broadcast on the Learning Channel, August 17, 1999.

8. Information on Sylvester's history comes primarily from Doug Welch, "Mystery of Sylvester the Mummy," *Seattle Post-Intelligencer,* October 12, 1955; Merle Sevey, "Northwest Wonderland: Washington State," *National Geographic* 117 (4): 505; and Susan Mahnke, "The Toughest, Oldest (and Driest) Cowboy

of Them All," in *Old Farmer's 1979 Almanac* (1979), 158. In Jeanne Godden's column, "Is Mummy a Fake? Say It's Not So" *(Seattle Times,* July 6, 1998), Joe James noted "we get all kinds of crazy stories," in response to a claim by Jeff Smith that associated Sylvester with Smith's great-grandfather Soapy Smith. James purchased Sylvester in 1955 from Mrs. B. C. Childs of Los Angeles.

9. Joe James, interview with the author, June 24, 1994.

10. "Head Hunter Trophy Is in Seattle Now: Jo-Jo, Example of Polistic Art of Shrinking, Is in Standley Collection," unidentified Seattle newspaper, mid-1930s.

11. Among overviews on the Jivaro and head shrinking, see M. W. Stirling, "Historical and Ethnographic Material on the Jivaro Indians," *Bureau of American Ethnology Bulletin* 117 (1938): 76–78; and Rafael Karsten, *The Head-Hunters of the Western Amazons: The Life and Culture of the Jivaro Indians of Eastern Ecuador and Peru* (Helisingfors, 1973). For their use in relationship to the avenging soul, see Michael J. Harner, "Jivaro Souls," *American Anthropologist* 64 (2): 258–72. Among the more useful sources on fraudulent *tsantsas* is G. E. S. Turner, "Counterfeit 'Tsantsas' in the Pitt Rivers Museum," *Man* 44 (53–70): 57–58. See also Marshall H. Saville, "Bibliographic Notes on the Shrinking of Human Heads in South America," *Museum Notes* 6 (1): 56–74, published by the Heye Foundation. I thank graduate student Cricket Appel for research on the topic of shrunken heads and Nancy Rosoff, formerly of the National Museum of the American Indian, for further information.

12. The process of head shrinking involved removing the skull, then shrinking the flesh by boiling it and filling it with hot pebbles, then sand, over a period of several days. The skin was then blackened and the lips were sewn shut to keep the spirit from escaping. Counterfeit shrunken heads tend to lack certain cuts used in extracting the skull and ways of sewing that are characteristic of real *tsantsas.* On authentic shrunken heads, facial hair has been removed and both the eyes and lips are sewn or pinned shut. Monkey and especially sloth heads were shrunk by Shaur and Achuar warriors/elders in authentic headshrinking ceremonies as a way of teaching chants and techniques to novices. Whether any of them were sold to collectors is not known.

13. In 1999 the National Museum of the American Indian (formerly the Museum of the American Indian, Heye Foundation) repatriated its authentic shrunken heads to the Federacion Interprovincial de Centros, Shuar-Achuar, in Ecuador.

14. Standley kept the addresses of Texan suppliers of armadillo baskets in his address book, "Address of Where to Buy." In addition to Charles Apelt, of Apelt Armadillo Farm in Comfort, Standley listed G. F. Bryan of Morales, J. D. Johns of Boerne, Volney Striegler of Cain (who wholesaled smaller shells for $9 a dozen in the late 1920s), N. Nowotny Supply Co. of San Antonio, and R. Ortega and Co. of El Paso (who also wholesaled the Mexican featherwork that the shop carried for a while). Standley's "See Where to Buy in Safe" also notes C. R. Boles of Morales, Texas, who bought out a Mr. Ball, and offered "baby armos" for seventy-five cents each.

15. O. C. Lightner, "Publisher of Hobbies Magazine Visits Country's Best Curio Store," *Hobbies* 36 (8): 14–16, with a photograph of Standley standing at the back of his shop with totem poles.

16. *Seattle Star,* December 12, 1933.

17. Doug Welch, "'Daddy' Standley Dies after Short Illness," *Seattle Post-Intelligencer,* October 26, 1940.

18. "Daddy Standley, Venerable Curio Dealer, Dies at 86," *Seattle Daily Times,* October 25, 1940.

19. Beulah Hurst, "Interesting Citizens You Meet in Admiral District," *Admiral District Tribune,* December 23, 1930.

20. "Daddy Standley, Venerable Curio Dealer, Dies at 86," *Seattle Daily Times,* October 25, 1940.

21. "Our Tourist Guides Pass Chamber Quiz," *Seattle Post-Intelligencer,* May 5, 1939.

22. The article "Beauty Spots and Rides in and around Seattle," *Seattle Post-Intelligencer,* July 16, 1912, notes "The Post-Intelligencer . . . is indebted for these outlines to J.E. Standley of Ye Olde Curiosity Shop."

23. Standley's notes on scraps of paper.

24. Seattle Chamber of Commerce brochure, sent by Standley in correspondence to the Smithsonian Institution, 1920 (Smithsonian Archives, Record Unit 192, USNM).

25. The shop's other Seattle booster cards included "Seattle Points of Interest," "Seattle Bids You Welcome," "Camp Lewis at American Lake," and "Visit the 42-Story Smith Tower (Day or Night)."

26. In 1932, in a statement of good citizenship, Standley urged the electorate to vote by placing a wooden figure of a man in the window of a Third Avenue restaurant with the sign "Don't be a Wooden Head. Go and Register." Standley, "Friends," *Seattle Daily Times,* January 14, 1932.

27. Note written by Standley on clipping, "Frozen Fish are Piled up Like Cordwood," *Seattle Star,* October 4, 1923; note written by Standley on clipping, "From the Crow's Nest," *Seattle Sunday Times,* April 4, 1937.

28. For example, a photograph of the Alaska exhibit at the National Mining Exhibition of the American Mining Congress i n October 1921 pictures two of Standley's totem poles and his Chilkat blanket at the entrance.

29. Standley's handwritten notes in his copy of Franz Boas's *The Social Organization and the Secret Societies of the Kwakiutl Indians* (1897) and elsewhere record the book's importance to the planning for Seattle's AYPE ("They coppied figures for the several

floats etc.") and later civic celebrations ("Herb Schonefeld used this book to get ideas for Seattle's Potlatch Carnival. Indian Paraphernalia was a big hit."). The book was well used, for when Schonefeld returned it to Standley two years later in 1913, it had been newly rebound, compliments of the Seattle Carnival Association.

30. Guest Book, p. 84; undated, unidentified clipping, "Blue Wing Indians Are Well Equipped," notes that the shop also loaned "Doukabattle, the god of consultation," and such valuable pieces as a ceremonial blanket (a Chilkat blanket).

31. Guest Book, p. 96.

32. In the 1920s the Olympic Hotel displayed the shop's large blue semiporcelain Fou dog in a Chinese art and industrial exhibit, and the Frederick & Nelson Department Store borrowed a ship etched on an ostrich egg, ships in bottles, and a small ivory replica of the revenue cutter *Bear* for a maritime exhibit held in its auditorium. The shop's large Fou dog on exhibit at the Olympic Hotel is pictured in a news photo, *Seattle Post-Intelligencer,* January 2, 1925. The article, "History of Sea Displayed, Ship's Models on Exhibit" *(Seattle Daily Times,* September 28, 1926), notes that for its maritime exhibit, Frederick & Nelson also borrowed nautical instruments and pictures from the Peabody Museum in Salem, Massachusetts.

33. "Lummi Indians to Take Part in Filming of Picture in the San Juan Islands," *Bellingham Herald,* July 19, 1927.

34. Guest Book, p. 38.

35. Details of Queen Marie's trip are found in Henry Gray, *The Famous Ride of Queen Marie* (1967), and "Official Itinerary, Tour of Her Majesty Marie, Queen of Rumania through the United States and Canada" (1926). Marie, the wife of King Ferdinand of Rumania, was the daughter of Queen Victoria's son, the Duke of Edinburgh, and his wife, the Grand Duchess Marie, daughter of Czar Alexander II of Russia.

36. Despite many of Queen Marie's possessions coming to the Maryhill Museum in Goldendale, Washington, after her death, there is no record of the basket and totem pole mentioned in Standley's notes. They probably went back to Rumania as mementos. Most objects in the Maryhill Museum collection that belonged to the queen actually came from her friend, the sugar heiress Alma Spreckels. When the queen found herself in financial straits, Spreckels bought furniture and other items from her and donated them to the museum. Information on Queen Marie's visit to Ye Olde Curiosity Shop comes from Guest Book (1926), p. 79; a letter dated August 11, 1926, to J. E. Standley from Robert Papworth, Secretary "Aboard the Special Train conveying Her Majesty the Queen of Roumania"; and "Standley Adds Milestone at Old Curiosity Shop," *Seattle Daily Times,* February 24, 1931. The spellings Rumania, Romania, and Roumania were all used at the time discussed.

37. H. E. Jamison, "Congratulations to Daddy Standley" in the column "Along the Waterfront," *Seattle Star,* February 24, 1939.

38. The Standleys completed raising their family in the home at 1750 Palm Way, at the intersection of California Avenue and Palm. After his wife Isabelle's death in 1920, Standley lived there with his daughter Ruby James, her husband Russell, and their children Emabelle and Joe James. Standley's son Edward and daughter-in-law Edna Standley lived next door and shared the side yard.

39. Descriptions of Totem Place come from family memory and "Seattle Man, One of West's Oldest Advertisers, Who Collects Curios," *Philatelic West* (1919); H. Geithmann, "He Made His Hobby His Life Work," column titled "The Haversack," unidentified magazine, January 26, 1926; Buelah Hurst, "Interesting Citizens You Meet in Admiral District," *Admiral District Tribune,* December 23, 1930; "Making the Rounds—Curio," *Town Crier,* January 21, 1931; H. E. Jamison, "Along the Waterfront," *Seattle Star,* February 24, 1936; Virginia Yancey, "'Daddy' Standley's Home Resembles Curio Shop," newspaper unknown, October, 1935; H. E. Jamison, "Congratulations to Daddy Standley," *Seattle Star,* February 25, 1939 (core of article based in Jamison's February 24, 1936 *Seattle Star* article); "'Daddy' Standley, 86 Today, Refuses Flatly to Look Back," *Seattle Daily Times,* February 24, 1940; "Little Things Mean a Lot in This Miniature Museum," *Seattle Times,* July 15, 1962.

40. Joe James remembers that the Totem Place yard won the "best home play yard" contest every year until "finally they told us, look, you've got the best one but if you win it again this year everybody is going to lose interest, so you guys come in second." The family decided it best not to enter the contest any more.

41. "Seattle Man, One of West's Oldest Advertisers, Who Collects Curios," *The Philatelic West,* 1919.

42. In 1992 "Ye Olde Curiosity House" was a feature in the Fourth Annual Tour of Homes sponsored by the Southwest Seattle Historical Society ("Homes with History, Site #3: Ye Olde Curiosity House," Wednesday, April 29, 1992, 6).

Chapter Seven. Totem Poles, Ye Olde Curiosity Shop, and Seattle

1. The card "History of the Indian Carved Totem Pole," distributed circa 1916, included an engraving of the Seattle Totem Pole and Alaskan writer L. L. Bales's explanation of it. The card offered facsimiles "made by Tlinket Tribe" in twelve-, eighteen-, twenty-five-, thirty-, and forty-two-inch lengths.

2. The Tongass Raven Pole was in the family of Mary Ebbetts, a Tlingit woman from Tongass. When she married Robert Hunt, the Hudson's Bay Company factor at Fort Rupert, Tlingit and Kwakwa̱ka̱'wakw privileges were joined. After Ebbetts's move to Fort Rupert, Kwakwa̱ka̱'wakw artist Charlie James

carved a copy of the original pole, which was raised in Fort Rupert in 1905 in conjunction with a large potlatch. Marius Barbeau, *Totem Poles,* vol. 2, Anthropological Series 30, National Museum of Canada Bulletin 119 (1950), plate 399, pictures both the Tongass pole taken to Seattle and the copy at Fort Rupert. Both poles include the same figures, but the Tongass pole is carved in Tlingit style, while the Fort Rupert one is in Kwakwa̲ka̲'wakw style.

3. For the history and meaning of the Seattle Totem Pole, see Viola Garfield, *The Seattle Totem Pole* (1940; revised and expanded, 1980). It is unclear from Garfield's discussion of the meaning whether she knew the article that John R. Swanton of the Bureau of American Ethnology had published just a few years after the pole had been erected in Seattle (Swanton, "Explanation of the Seattle Totem Pole," *Journal of American Folk-Lore* 2 [1905]: 108–11, and frontispiece). In this article Swanton compared the details of the stories on the pole as told to Edmond Meany by David E. Kininnook, a Tlingit Indian from Ketchikan, with those that George Hunt provided Franz Boas at about the same time, as well as versions of the stories that Swanton had gathered during interviewing at Wrangell. See also Aldona Jonaitis, "Northwest Coast Totem Poles," in Ruth B. Phillips and Christopher B. Steiner, eds., *Unpacking Culture: Art and Commodity in Colonial and Postcolonial Worlds* (1999), 104–21; Paul Dorpat, "Seattle's Stolen Totem," in *Seattle Then and Now,* vol. 2 (1988), 32–35; and Marius Barbeau, *Totem Poles,* 2 vols., Anthropological Series 30, National Museum of Canada Bulletin 119 (1950), 656–57.

4. *Seattle Post-Intelligencer,* November 19, 1898.

5. Ye Olde Curiosity Shop sold large "Totem History" cards for decades, in at least two versions. The earlier one included an engraving of the Seattle pole, the later a drawing. The imaginative explanation of the pole's meaning is the same on both cards, although the introductory paragraphs vary. Both incorrectly cite 1897 as the date the pole arrived in Seattle and say it was carved from a cedar log, although it was actually of hemlock.

6. Sometime before L. L. Bales died in late 1929, Standley purchased the copyright to Bales's article "Totem Poles," first published in *Outdoor Life* (May 1908): 423–41. Although Standley does not appear to have ever republished the article, several years after Bales's death, parts of the article were included in "The Indians Won't Tell," published in two parts in the October and November 1938 issues of *Alaska Sportsman,* with Bales listed as the author. On discovering the latter article, Standley contacted the magazine asking to be given credit for owning the original. Both articles consider the meanings and uses of totem poles, but neither discusses the Seattle pole specifically; both are problematic and filled with misinformation.

7. Edmond Meany, "Story Told by the Totem Pole," *Seattle Post-Intelligencer,* September 4, 1904.

8. Standley sent one of his "Totem History" cards to the *Seattle Post-Intelligencer,* which published a slightly edited version of it on November 1, 1938, as "Our Totem Pole," thereby further circulating Bales's misinformation. Even respected local photographer Asahel Curtis wrote a letter to the editor of the *Seattle Post-Intelligencer,* paying tribute to "Daddy" Standley, who was able to tell the history of the pole ("Daddy Standley," *Seattle Post-Intelligencer,* November 11, 1938).

9. Garfield, *Seattle Totem Pole* (1940; revised and expanded, 1980).

10. "Firebug Ends Life of Noted Totem Pole," *Seattle Post-Intelligencer,* October 23, 1938.

11. I am indebted to Seattle historian Paul Dorpat for sharing with me a scrapbook made by Delia Whittelsey of *Seattle Post-Intelligencer* newspaper clippings about totem poles and Seattle, dating October 1938–March 1941. Many of the clippings concern the Seattle Totem Pole.

12. "Woman Denies Totem Village Was Deserted," *Seattle Post-Intelligencer,* November 24, 1938; "Skipper Knows, He Paddled Away on Seattle Totem Pole," *Seattle Post-Intelligencer,* December 25, 1938.

13. Rachel Van Devanter, "The Story of the Totem," *Seattle Post-Intelligencer,* November 7, 1938.

14. *National Geographic* 63 (February 1933): plate x.

15. A. J. Goddard, historian for the Alaska-Yukon Pioneers, proposed a statue of a prospector ("Fireman Climbs High to Fight Totem Fire," *Seattle Post-Intelligencer,* October 24, 1938). A letter to the editor from Sigrid M. Carlson recommended the statue "The Sourdough" by Alonzo Victor Lewis *(Seattle Post-Intelligencer,* November 2, 1938).

16. Letters to the editor, *Seattle Post-Intelligencer:* "Concrete Pole," November 12, 1938; "The Totem Pole," November 17, 1938.

17. [Daddy] J. E. Standley, "Expert on Totem Poles," *Seattle Post-Intelligencer,* October 28, 1938.

18. "Famed Totem Pole Moved From Square," *Seattle Post-Intelligencer,* April 12, 1939; "Totem Pole Repair Bids Received," *Seattle Post-Intelligencer,* May 26, 1939; "Cedar Spar Needed To Replace Famous Totem Pole," *Seattle Post-Intelligencer,* July 20, 1939.

19. "Queets Men Make Bid for Totem Work," *Seattle Post-Intelligencer,* November 11, 1938; "Indians Seek Seattle Job," *Seattle Post-Intelligencer,* November 8, 1938.

20. "'Pale Faces Would Carve Totem Pole," *Seattle Post-Intelligencer,* November 4, 1938.

21. Doug Welch, "Carving of Seattle's Totem Pole Goes to 'Non-Sculpting' Indians," *Seattle Post-Intelligencer,* August 5, 1939; "Totem Pole May Be Carved by White Man," *Seattle Post-Intelligencer,* August 12, 1939.

22. "Forester Would Get Totem Pole for City," *Seattle Post-Intelligencer,* October 19, 1939; "At Long Last Indians to Get Famed Totem," *Seattle Post-Intelligencer,* December 9, 1939.

23. Viola Garfield, *The Seattle Totem Pole* (1980), 3–4. For the replica pole a seventy-foot red cedar log donated by Haida artist James Peele was cut to fifty-six feet, with a six-foot diameter base.

24. "The Rains Come—but Not the Dedication," *Seattle Post-Intelligencer,* July 27, 1940 (here the newspaper again repeated the incorrect Bales-Standley identifications of the figures on the pole); "Big Potlatch Doings All Set for Today," *Seattle Post-Intelligencer,* July 27, 1940. In 1973 the 1939 Seattle Totem Pole was taken down again, repaired, and repainted in colors closer to the original by Tsimshian carver Jack Hudson, then reinstalled with steel supports.

25. Erika Doss, *Spirit Poles and Flying Pigs: Public Art and Cultural Democracy in American Communities* (1995) examines a selection of recent and controversial public art projects. The discussion of the Cincinnati Gateway project is particularly interesting when thinking about the Seattle Totem Pole. The winged pigs the gateway incorporated in reference to Cincinnati's pork-processing history became an emblem of reintegrated community and civic pride, but only after emotional and divisive public debate.

26. Lloyd J. Averill and Daphne K. Morris, *Northwest Coast Native and Native-Style Art: A Guidebook to Western Washington* (1995), locates and describes these and scores of other totem poles in western Washington.

27. Among others, the National Furriers Association chose the Seattle Totem Pole as its emblem (letter to the editor, J. E. Standley, "Expert on Totem Poles," *Seattle Post-Intelligencer,* October 28, 1938).

28. Catalog A, "Price List of 1001 Curious Things, Copyright, Compliments of J. E. Standley, Proprietor Ye Olde Curiosity Shop, Colman Dock, Seattle, U. S. A." (1910).

29. Darwinism was explicitly mentioned in the "Guide to Ketchikan, presented by Berthelsen & Pruell Curios Jewelery," n.d. "The natives are Darwinians to the very letter. Their belief in the origin of man from animals is expressed not only in their verbal legends, but also on their totem poles."

30. L. L. Bales, "Totem Poles," *Outdoor Life* 31 (5): 423–41, and Reverend J. P. D. Llwyd, *The Message of an Indian Relic* (1909), are two of the longer discussions on totem poles that were published in the popular literature early in the twentieth century. Llwyd's essay focuses in part on the Seattle Totem Pole.

31. Small cards titled "Alaska Indian Totem Poles" or "History of Indian Totem Poles," and a section of a larger card titled "History of the Indian Carved Totem Pole in Alaska," include variations on the explanation of Standley's earliest card.

32. The term *grotesque* originally referred to a style of art that interwove fanciful or fantastic human and animal forms with foliage in a way that distorted the natural into absurdity, ugliness, or caricature *(Oxford English Dictionary,* 2d ed. [Oxford: Clarendon Press, 1989]).

33. Information card, "Alaska Indian Totem Poles," Ye Olde Curiosity Shop; undated brochure "Visit Seattle Show Place, Seattle's Hudson Bay Fur Company" (Seattle Public Library, Northwest Collection, uncatalogued, box 35); booster card from Bear Totem Store, acquired in 1930 in Alaska by B. J. Palmer (Palmer College Archives, Elevator Shaft box 186, file 16,619-3).

34. "Preserving a 'Westminster Abbey' of Canadian Indians," *Illustrated London News,* May 21, 1927; Lloyd W. MacDowell, *The Totem Poles of Alaska and Indian Mythology* (1895), unpaginated.

35. L. L. Bales, "Totem Poles," *Outdoor Life* 31 (5): 429.

36. Undated brochure, "Visit Seattle Show Place, Seattle's Hudson Bay Fur Company" (Seattle Public Library, Northwest Collection, uncatalogued, box 35); booster card from Bear Totem Store, acquired in 1930 in Alaska by B. J. Palmer (Palmer College Archives, Elevator Shaft box 186, file 16,619-3).

37. The discussion of totemism in recent work by Nora Marks Dauenhauer and Richard Dauenhauer makes clear concepts that have been misunderstood, at least in part, by both scholars and the general public. A shorter explanation, by Nora Marks Dauenhauer, is found in "Tlingit *At.oów:* Traditions and Concepts," in Steven C. Brown, *The Spirit Within: Northwest Coast Native Art from the John H. Hauberg Collection* (1995). These ideas are dealt with in greater detail in Dauenhauer, *Haa Shuká, Our Ancestors: Tlingit Oral Narratives* (1987), *Haa Tuwunáagu Yís: For Healing our Spirit: Tlingit Oratory* (1990), and *Haa Kusteeyí, Our Culture: Tlingit Life Stories* (1994).

38. Lloyd W. MacDowell, *The Totem Poles of Alaska and Indian Mythology* (1895), unpaginated.

39. "Washington Hotel Opens: Views of Splendid Interior of Seattle's New Hostelry," *Seattle Daily Times,* October 21, 1908. The New Washington Hotel, at Second Avenue and Virginia Street, succeeded the original Washington Hotel, which stood for only three years in turreted splendor overlooking the city from atop Denny Hill. This earlier building, Seattle's first really grand hotel, was begun as the Denny Hotel soon after the great fire of 1889. The Depression of 1893 slowed construction, and the hotel changed hands before it finally opened in May 1903 under a new name, the Washington Hotel. Many mourned the loss of this impressive destination when the old Washington Hotel was taken down barely three years later in May 1906 in conjunction with the sluicing of Denny Hill into Elliott Bay to provide a more level downtown. Its successor, the New Washington Hotel, was located on essentially the same site on the new Denny Regrade as the original Washington Hotel had been, but signi-

ficantly lower; the new hotel's fourteenth floor stood at the ground-floor level of the old hotel.

40. As it became increasingly difficult for Rookwood Pottery to compete with manufacturers of machine-made terracottas and tiles, its architectural department waned and eventually disappeared. Rookwood struggled through the Great Depression making art pottery, went into bankruptcy in 1941, reopened after a few years, then suspended operations entirely in 1967.

41. Herbert Peck, *The Book of Rookwood Pottery* (1968), discusses the company's architectural department. It lists other Seattle customers for Rookwood as the Sorrento Hotel and the Seattle Theater (the specific work is unnamed). Like the New Washington Hotel, the Sorrento opened in 1908 with a pottery fireplace, but a far less extravagant one. It is still a part of the hotel. The Seattle Theater opened in 1892, before Rookwood's architectural department was under way, so it must have ordered the faience work later. The building was demolished in 1915 to make way for the Arctic Building. The Oregon Hotel in Portland also commissioned work from Rockwood.

42. The model poles on which the Rookwood poles were based are pictured in three shop catalogs. In Catalog B the Seattle-type pole and the Shakes-type pole are numbers 2 and 7 among eleven poles in a single grouped photograph. Versions of these same poles are numbers 10 and 11 in Catalogs C and D.

43. Comparing the left-hand Rookwood version of the Seattle Totem Pole, with its counterpart in the photograph in Catalog B (1915) and the postcard ("Totem Poles in Ye Olde Curiosity Shop Seattle," 367) not illustrated here, one sees that the Rookwood designer has copied but shortened the wings of the raven at the bottom, and interpreted the blow hole of the whale as a separate face perched on an awkward head configuration identical to that in the postcard. Both the constricted raven above the whale and the legs of the bear next above are also rendered as in the photographs. The three upper figures of Standley's original pole are missing and the upper raven's head repeats the head at the pole's bottom. The constricted raven (note the wings) is also repeated on the mantel supports.

Again, beginning at the bottom, the Rookwood version of the Chief Shakes Pole at the right of the fireplace replicates the lower human figure holding a staff. It then deviates with a constricted bird head with an open mouth and bulbous tongue, and above that a whale, figures inspired by a yet unidentified pole. The faience pole then returns to the figures on Standley's Chief Shakes Pole, with a raven, a crouched man sheltered within the wings of another raven whose head emerges from a round aura, and above that a carved box topped with the upper raven's head minus the body and the potlatch-ringed hat. The beak at the top suggests that the artist was looking at a photograph which had been taken from below, as is the case with the postcard.

44. I am grateful to University of Washington student Amy Loelle Adams for generously sharing her research on the history of the New Washington Hotel.

45. "City Gets Two Totem Poles," *Seattle Post-Intelligencer*, July 21, 1939. Purchased with pennies contributed by state schoolchildren (a program sponsored by the Snohomish County Parent Teacher Association), this last Chief Shelton pole was presented to symbolize "the cordial relations between the Indians and the whites since the treaty signed at Nisqually."

46. "State Totem Pole Will Be Dedicated," *Seattle Post-Intelligencer*, April 24, 1940; and "Chief Shelton Totem Pole Gift to State," *Seattle Post-Intelligencer*, May 12, 1940, outlined the dedication ceremonies.

47. "Pole Presented by J. E. Standley," *Seattle Post-Intelligencer*, October 2, 1939. Other news articles discussing and picturing the original West Seattle pole include "Real Totem Pole Given West Side," *West Seattle Herald*, September 7, 1939; and "View from New Totem Pole Draws Praise," *Seattle Star*, October 2, 1939. The original pole was pictured on the 1956 cover of the *Seattle Telephone Directory* as well as the May 1959 cover of *Sunset: The Magazine of Western Living*, where it was discussed on page 87.

48. The literature on the Heiltsuk (Bella Bella) is limited. For Heiltsuk art, see Martha Black, *Bella Bella: A Season of Heiltsuk Art* (1997). See also Suzanne F. Hilton, "Haishais, Bella Bella, and Oowekeene," in Wayne Suttles, ed., *Northwest Coast*, vol. 7, *Handbook of North American Indians* (1990), 312–22.

49. Standley did not apply names and tribal affiliations indiscriminately. He called Salish speakers Siwash—a term that is now considered derogatory but was commonly used and considered more neutral in the early twentieth century—and Neah Bay people Makah. For reasons not understood Standley never used Nootka, the name widely used at the time for the Nootkan speakers of Vancouver Island (now called the Nuu-chah-nulth). Instead, he called them Bella Bella, whether they were living on Vancouver Island or in Seattle. In one case he placed quotations around Bella Bella, indicating that he knew it was an assigned name.

50. "Face-Lifting for Totem," *Seattle Times*, September 7, 1955.

51. "New Totem Pole to be Dedicated," newspaper unknown, August 1966. The carvers of the new pole, Michael Morgan and Robert Fleischman, were assisted by their wives: Mrs. Morgan painted the pole and Mrs. Fleischman provided sandwiches and "spiritual assistance."

52. Standley's supplier book "See Where to Buy in Safe" records the name of Thomas Deasy, the Indian agent in Masset (later in Victoria), as a supplier for black jadeite totem poles, pipes, and plaques (perhaps platters).

53. When assigning the title *captain,* Standley seems to have confused Charles Edenshaw with Captain James Edenso (Edenshaw), originally from Masset, a man well known for his navigation skills. Captain Jim was not a carver. When rewriting the supplier book in the later 1920s, Standley was surely remembering from earlier days carver Charles Edenshaw, who died in 1920.

54. I am indebted to several people for assistance with information on Sam Williams and his family: to Ida Williams, the wife of Sam's son, Ray, and Barbara Williams, Ray's daughter, for information on the Williams family; to Nuu-chah-nulth artist Art Thompson (related to the Williamses) for discussing the Nuu-chah-nulth carvers in Seattle with me; to University of Washington graduate student Katie Bunn-Marcuse for sharing research on Sam Williams's poles that has been essential to this chapter; and to Carmen McKillop, who knew Sam Williams when he carved for Mack's Totem Shop.

55. Letter, George Hunt to Franz Boas, June 22, 1904, quoted in Douglas Cole, *Captured Heritage: The Scramble for Northwest Coast Artifacts* (1995), 296, xi.

56. Captain Jack's poles at Friendly Cove were erected after he married a Muchalat woman in the late 1870s. The poles combine his and his wife's crests.

57. The similarities and differences in Sam Williams's and Wilson Williams's carving styles are evident when comparing two large poles, one carved by each, that are now located at the Makah Cultural and Research Center at Neah Bay.

58. "Totem Will Be According to Indian Hoyle," *Seattle Post-Intelligencer,* August 11, 1939.

59. Among other carvers who have sold to Ye Olde Curiosity Shop are John Hudson; Danny, Baptist, "Bob," and Francis James; and Joe, George, and Hyacinth David.

60. It is not clear from whom Standley obtained his earlier Japanese carved items. The address given for Takenoya Brothers & Company in his supplier book "Address of Where to Buy" is 13, Hongo, I-Chome, Honho-Ku, Tokyo. It also lists S. Nakamura & Company, Tokyo Central, P.O. Box 303, Tokyo.

61. The Takenoya Company totem pole pendants replicated the Raven Flood, Chief Shakes, Chief Johnson, Kahlteen, Alert Bay, and Kian totem poles.

62. The Takenoya family now operates a gift shop, Takenoya Arts, Incorporated, in the Halekulani Hotel in Honolulu.

63. Ye Olde Curiosity Shop records also include an intriguing photograph of a full-sized version of the Kahlteen totem pole carved in the 1920s at Kanda Art Studio, Fuzisawa Station, perhaps as a challenge.

64. I thank Charles Cantrell, president of the Metal Arts Group, for providing information on the company and making available the Mayer Bros. catalog in his collection. After Metal Arts Group was purchased in 1999 by J. H. Recognition Company of Portland, Oregon, most of the Mayer Bros. dies were destroyed.

65. Victoria Wyatt, *Images from the Inside Passage: An Alaskan Portrait by Winter & Pond* (1988), provides information on the photographers and reproduces more than a hundred of their photographs.

Chapter Eight. "1001 Curious Things": Merchandizing Native American Goods

1. For ease of discussion I have assigned each catalog an identifying letter. The brochures and catalogs are as follows (see the appendix for full descriptions): Brochure, 1907; Catalog A, 1910–13; Catalog B, 1915; Catalog C, 1916, with separate "Supplement Price List"; Catalog D, ca. 1920; Brochure, 1923; Catalog E, mid-1920s; Catalog F, late 1920s; Catalog G, early 1930s; Catalog H, 1939; Catalog I, 1940; and postdating Standley, Catalog J, early 1950s.

2. The 1915 "1001 list" includes teeth, tusks, and bones from Alaskan beavers, seals, walruses, and whales; natural oddities such as an alligator egg from the Amazon, two-inch fish scales, and several assortments of "School Collections" of sea specimens and marine animals.

3. See Jonathan Batkin and Patricia Fogelman Lange, "Human Figurines of Cochiti and Tesuque Pueblos, 1870–1920: Inspirations, Markets, and Consumers," in Jonathan Batkin, ed., *Clay People* (1999), 41–63, for information on Tesuque "rain gods" and the regional myths about Aztec and Montezuma that were used to sell Pueblo pottery in the decades around the turn of the century.

4. Like Standley, Southwestern suppliers Benham Indian Trading Company in Phoenix and J. S. Candelario in Santa Fe advertised starters for Indian corners (Jonathan Batkin, "Tourism Is Overrated: Pueblo Pottery and the Early Curio Trade, 1810–1910," in Ruth B. Phillips and Christopher B. Steiner, *Unpacking Culture: Art and Commodity in Colonial and Postcolonial Worlds* [1999], 293).

5. Many of the objects made of agate, abalone, and mother-of-pearl probably came from Denver wholesale supplier H. H. Tammen. They included brooches, cuff links, scarf pins, and manicure sets with abalone inlay; amber, coral, and pearl necklaces; agate watch fobs, charms, and writing accessories; and mother-of-pearl jewel boxes, clocks, and dresser accessories. The Japanese elephant-ivory carvings of the late 1920s were primarily cigarette holders, miniature animal figures, and jewelry.

6. Items collected between 1900 and 1912 by William W. Sale and Neeta Tobey Sale, and donated in 1998 to the Alaska State Museum, Juneau, parallel and in some cases duplicate those in Ye Olde Curiosity Shop's 1915 and 1916 catalogs. For illustrations and discussion of the Sale collection and its history, see John W.

Krug and Caryl Sale Krug, *One Dog Short: The Odyssey and Collection of a Family in Alaska during the Gold Rush Years* (1998).

7. Standley's supplier books record Frank P. Williams of St. Michael, Alaska, as a source for ivory, and Tom Powers of Unalakleet for Eskimo relics.

8. Dorothy Jean Ray discusses the history of the billiken in the greatest detail in *Artists of the Tundra and the Sea* (1961; reprint 1980), 122–24, and "The Billiken," *Alaska Journal* 4 (1): 25–31. At Ye Olde Curiosity Shop there was a more earthy explanation of the billiken—the figure was considered an artistic rendition of a small child sitting on a pot and "Billy can."

9. Joe James remembers Lemke and his work. Lael Morgan, *Art and Eskimo Power: The Life and Times of Alaskan Howard Rock* (1988), discusses Rock's intermittent art career and his relationship with commercial manufacturers of Alaska curios in Seattle.

10. See Dorothy Jean Ray, *A Legacy of Arctic Art* (1996), for a discussion of the Federal Trade Commission suit and the work of Eskimo men who were employed by some of the accused companies.

11. George Pettitt, *The Quileute of La Push, 1775–1945* (1950; reprint, 1976), discusses baskets in the early 1940s. Although several Quileute women knew how to make the old types of utilitarian baskets, by this time most weavers made only "tourist baskets" as objets d'art and souvenirs. Canoes with paddlers, whales, ducks, wolf masks, geometrics, whorls, and pinwheels dominated the designs on them. Double-handled shopping baskets, bowl baskets with looped edges, and yarn baskets were the other most common types.

12. My thanks to John Putnam and Rebecca Andrews for sharing information in their unpublished study of the Makah baskets from Neah Bay in the collections at the Burke Museum of Natural History and Culture.

13. According to Peter Corey of the Sheldon Jackson Museum in Sitka, Alaska, there are a number of Makah-type trinket baskets in Alaskan private collections that were made in the early twentieth century. They were purchased in Alaska as Alaskan baskets.

14. See James G. Swan, *The Indians of Cape Flattery, at the Entrance to the Strait of Juan de Fuca, Washington Territory* (1870), 11; for photographs of the Samuel Morse collection, see Carolyn Marr, J. Lloyd Colfax, and Robert D. Monroe, *Portrait in Time: Photographs of the Makah by Samuel G. Morse, 1896–1903* (1987).

15. H. E. Jamison, "Along the Waterfront," *Seattle Star,* February 24, 1936.

16. Standley's supplier books also list Makah basket maker Mrs. Charley Swan and Quileute basket makers Mrs. Tom Brown and Mrs. R. M. Black from Mora. Other names, not identified by tribe, from whom Standley bought baskets were Mrs. Francis Cleveland and Mrs. William Tyler of Port Angeles and Mary Tate of Portage, Washington. Johanie H. Sailto brought in baskets from Hoh, Washington, and James Slowman provided baskets from Tofino, British Columbia.

17. Miriam Curtis, widow of Wilbur Washburn, whose family ran the store at Neah Bay from 1934 to 1963, remembers that Washburn's Store supplied Makah baskets to shops across the country. Although she knew Standley, Curtis does not believe Ye Olde Curiosity Shop was ever a customer. I am grateful to University of Washington graduate student Dawn Glinsman for sharing her 1997 interviews with Curtis and basket makers at Neah Bay.

18. For analysis of the early tourist trade in Alaska, see Frank Norris, *Gawking at the Midnight Sun: The Tourist in Early Alaska* (1985); and Norris, "Showing off Alaska: The Northern Tourist Trade, 1878–1941," *Alaska History* 2 (2):1–17.

19. See Frances Paul, *Spruce Root Basketry of the Alaska Tlingit* (1944), for techniques and motif names; also George T. Emmons, "The Basketry of the Tlingit," *American Museum of Natural History Memoirs* 3 (2): 229–77; and Emmons, "Basketry," in Frederica de Laguna, ed., *The Tlingit Indians* (1991), 213–22.

20. Joe James, interview with the author, July 12, 1994.

21. See Kate Duncan, *Northern Athapaskan Art: A Beadwork Tradition* (1989), 185, for discussion of Tlingit moccasins. Tlingit moccasins in museum collections are more commonly made of moosehide, at least in part because those of hair seal were less sturdy than those with moosehide soles and easily wore out or became damaged. The quality of hair-seal moccasins varied, and to the serious collector they were of less interest than the blunt or pointed-toe Tlingit skin moccasins beaded with the colorful foliate-scroll patterning also used on ceremonial clothing.

22. Standley's supplier books list other sources for hair-seal moccasins, including Sally Walters of Yakutat (for hair-seal moccasins and bags); George Davis of Angoon; Mrs. C. R. Bell of Kake ("her goods are fine & cheap"); Paul Nannauck of Kake ("wants to make any kind of hair seal moccasins. Hair seal dolls. hair seal bags beaded small. Hair seal Heart hangers marked Alaska"); Mr. J. Coyle, Alaskan address not given; The Nugget Shop in Juneau; and Berthelsen & Pruell Curios, Jewelry of Ketchikan. E. Abercrombie of Ketchikan is listed elsewhere for moccasins ("prices large $12 a dozen, small $6 a dozen, both less 40%").

23. Standley's "Address of Where to Buy" supplier book lists sources for Eskimo moccasins as Ira Rank of Nome; Mrs. Fransen, an Eskimo woman living in Seattle; Mary Gordon, an Eskimo woman who also made beadwork dolls with parkas, no address; and Thos. Wheeler of South Tacoma Avenue ("Moccasins in a pinch, hair seals, mens 6–9 $21, ladies 3–6 $18.00"). Wheeler's prices were likely higher than Standley wished to pay unless absolutely necessary.

24. Joe James, interview with the author, July 12, 1994.

25. Ye Olde Curiosity Shop stopped carrying koa seed articles in the 1950s after the health department determined that they were poisonous and a danger to children.

26. The 1929 catalog, "Genuine Indian Bead Work and Art Goods," from the Mohonk Lodge offered several types of "Tulip bags." Another such bag is included in the undated brochure "Genuine Indian Beadwork and Curios" from the Rocky Boy Mission. Jonathan Batkin suspects that both enterprises purchased the tulip bags from a manufacturer elsewhere.

27. A short history of Skookum Dolls can be found in Wendy Lavitt, "Strong Spirits of the Doll World," *Dolls: The Collector's Magazine* (December–January 1992): 149–51. In 1916 George Borgfeldt and Co. registered the Skookum trademark, "Skookum (Bully good) Indian USA," and manufactured dolls that were distributed on the East Coast by the Arrow Novelty Company. The H. H. Tammen Company of Denver later wholesaled them in the West. Although Lavitt repeats a common assertion that Tammen also had the dolls made in a sort of cottage industry, research by Batkin questions this.

28. Indian leather dolls and a forty-inch Indian Chief doll and matching thirty-eight-inch Indian Squaw. These two dolls were probably the shop's large display Skookum Dolls, included in the last "1001 Curious Things" list, in Catalog G.

29. The Chilkat blanket the shop sold at auction in 1976 was first purchased from a private collection in the 1960s.

30. In addition to appearing in the "1001 Curious Things" lists, Navajo rugs are advertised in Catalogs E, F (see fig. 8.13), and G (with the instruction "write for prices").

31. Except for A. E. Taylor of Peach Springs, Arizona, and the Indian Oasis Trading Co. at Sells, Arizona, Standley's suppliers of Navajo goods (blankets or jewelry) were located in New Mexico: the Kirk Brothers of Gallup, Mike Kirk of Manuelito, Walter Beck of Fruitland, Julius Ganz [Gans] of Santa Fe, and Gallup Mercantile (acquired by the Ilfield Company in 1924).

32. Jonathan Batkin has noted that in the early twentieth century, it was common for mail-order curio dealers to borrow text and illustrations from each other's catalogs. For information on the Southwestern curio trade, see Batkin, "Some Early Curio Dealers of New Mexico," *American Indian Art Magazine* 23 (3): 68–81; and Batkin, "Tourism Is Overrated: Pueblo Pottery and the Early Curio Trade, 1880–1910," in Ruth B. Phillips and Christopher B. Steiner, *Unpacking Culture: Art and Commodity in Colonial and Postcolonial Worlds* (1999), 282–97. This chapter has benefited from extended discussion and valuable observations about curio shops and curio catalogs with Batkin.

33. Mexican Zerapes were advertised in Catalogs D through G, and the text in each catalog is slightly different; the quotation comes from Catalog F. Henry Beach of El Paso is listed as a supplier in the 1920s and Pablo Lopez of Aguacalientes, Mexico, during both the 1920s and 1930s.

34. Standley's "Address of Where to Buy" lists Juan de Aguero of Santa Cruz, New Mexico, as a supplier for "Chemayo" blankets and tops.

35. The sources listed for Navajo jewelry in Standley's supplier book are Mike Kirk, Manuelito, New Mexico; Andrew Prude, Mescalero, New Mexico; Mr. Manuel Mares's The "Wig Wam" Curio Shop, Raton, New Mexico; and A. E. Taylor, Peach Spring [*sic*] Trading Co., Peach Springs, Arizona. In later years the shop ordered from Maisels, in Albuquerque, New Mexico.

36. Allie BraMe's 1928 journal reported that she and her husband purchased "a wonderful lot of old Alaskan carved boxes and carved ivory, totem poles and old shields" from Seattle curio shops. On July 17, after returning from a trip to Vancouver, they "went to Ye Old Curiosity Shop and bought arrow points from the boys there." My thanks to Allie Walling BraMe's heirs and Diana Pardue of the Heard Museum for sharing BraMe's journal entries.

37. Thomas Wilson, "The Swastika, the Earliest Known Symbol, and Its Migrations; with Observations on the Migration of Certain Industries in Prehistoric Times," *Report of the U.S. National Museum for the Year Ending June 30 (1894)*, 757–1,101.

38. Marsha Bol discusses the merchandising of Lakota tourist art in, "Defining Lakota Tourist Art," in Ruth B. Phillips and Christopher B. Steiner, eds., *Unpacking Culture: Art and Commodity in Colonial and Postcolonial Worlds* (1999), 214–28.

39. J. H. Austin began selling Plains paraphernalia by mail order in 1891. Standley saved a price list from Austin and lists him in both supplier books; James Irving's name does not appear in the Curiosity Shop records. The Irving catalog is interesting for other reasons as well. It includes the same small drawing of a tepee that appeared on the cover of the shop's Catalog A. Irving also supplied Sioux moccasins and pipe bags of the type that Standley offered in the mid-1920s (Catalog E).

40. John C. Ewers, *Plains Indian Sculpture: A Traditional Art from America's Heartland* (1986), includes an extensive discussion of catlinite pipes.

41. Frank Russell, *The Pima Indian* (1980), pictures a Pima-made cinch braided from horsehair.

42. The supplier books, especially "Address of Where to Buy," list seven sources for horsehair weaving, all in prison communities.

43. See Roland Barthes, "The Rhetoric of the Image," in Stephen Heath, trans., *Image Music, Text* (1977), 32–51, for discussion of the denotative and connotative messages in news photographs.

Chapter Nine. Ye Olde Curiosity Shop since 1940

1. "Curiosity Shop Keeper, 83, but He Has Modern Ideas," *Seattle Daily Times,* February 22, 1937.

2. "Owns Most Curious Store in the West," *The Grit,* October 15, 1925.

3. "'Olde Curiosity Shop's' Owner Celebrates Natal Day by Seeing Sights," *Seattle Star,* February 25, 1935. The accompanying photograph of Standley in his yard is headlined: "'Dad' Is 81 but Still Spry."

4. H. E. Jamison, "Along the Waterfront," *Seattle Star,* February 24, 1936.

5. "Waterfront Back to Normal: 'Daddy' Standley is on the Job," *Seattle Daily Times,* November 24, 1937. The tusks that were being reinstalled suffered damage and eventually were discarded. One was hit by a truck sometime during the war years and broken beyond repair but the other remained outside. It was placed outside again at the Pier 51 shop until it disintegrated.

6. "'Daddy' Standley, 84, Waits on Trade," newspaper unknown, February 24, 1938; "'Daddy' Standley Prunes Shrubbery on His Eighty-Fourth Birthday," *Seattle Star,* February 25, 1938.

7. "'Daddy' Standley Cuts the Cake," *Seattle Post-Intelligencer,* February 25, 1939; H. E. Jamison, "Along the Waterfront: Congratulations to Daddy Standley," *Seattle Star,* February 25, 1939.

8. "'Daddy' Standley, 86 Today, Refuses Flatly to Look Back," *Seattle Daily Times,* February 24, 1940.

9. Doug Welch, "'Daddy' Standley Dies after Short Illness," *Seattle Post-Intelligencer,* October 26, 1940. See also "'Daddy' Standley Ill, Receives Transfusion," *Seattle Post-Intelligencer,* October 25, 1940; and "Daddy Standley, Venerable Curio Dealer, Dies at 86," *Seattle Daily Times,* October 25, 1940; the story was also published on October 25 in a different edition, under the title "Death Takes Daddy Standley, Long a Figure on Waterfront."

10. Typescript of memorial tribute given for Standley by H. E. Jamison, radio announcer, Arm Chair cruises, October 25, 1940 (core of text taken from Jamison column "Along the Waterfront," *Seattle Star,* February 24, 1936).

11. The shipment of ebony elephants is discussed in "Marine News: Six-Hundred Elephants Seattle-Bound as 'Olde' Shop Stirs Again," *Seattle Times,* October, 1946; and "The Stroller," *Seattle Times,* February 8, 1947. The elephants were said to be roughed out on wood blocks by children, after which a series of hands successively more skillful worked on them until the finishing touches were added by master carvers. The elephants were considered to bring good luck.

12. B. W. I. Willock in St. Johns, Antigua, British West Indies, supplied koa seed bags and black-eyed susan mats and bags. Black-eyed susan items were eventually forbidden by law because the seeds could be toxic to children.

13. Rod Sauvageau of Tradewinds Auction Gallery, Inc., Vancouver, Washington, managed the three auctions in which the shop collections were sold. The first—held November 26–28, 1976, at the Holiday Inn in Cleveland, Ohio—was solely of shop material and included 760 items. The second auction, also solely of shop material, took place in Seattle at the Seattle Hyatt House at Sea-Tac Airport on May 20–22, 1977, and included 751 items. The third auction took place on March 22–23, 1980, at the Seattle Airport Hilton Hotel. It combined "the Joseph R. James Family Collection" of Ye Olde Curiosity Shop material with the "Alaska Jim Williams Collection" made by "an old 'Sourdough' who spent a good share of his life with the Eskimos." Together there were 650 pieces.

14. Joe James especially regrets having been talked into auctioning the gold medal that his grandfather had received for his exhibit at the Alaska-Yukon-Pacific Exposition in 1909. J. E. Standley's name was engraved on it.

15. "Seattle Waterfront," *Holiday* 18, no. 10 (July 1950): 99; *National Geographic* 17 (4): 506.

16. "A Shop for the Curious," *Mature Outlook,* February 1997; Robin Honig, "Collection of Curiosities," *Profiles: The Magazine of Continental Airlines,* July 1995, 26. Paul Dorpat's *Seattle Times* column, "Now and Then," featured the shop on November 16, 1994, subtitled "Collector of Curiosities."

17. Jean Godden, "Sell UW? Here's How It Might Go," *Seattle Times,* October 27, 1996.

18. The Bonham's Tribal Art Sale, December 9, 1996, included "#288 A Blackfoot Bears' claw and bead necklace," described as twenty inches long, strung with twenty claws spaced with blue faceted beads.

19. "Odyssey at the Pier," *Seattle Times,* June 27, 1998.

20. Robert L. Jamieson Jr., "Curiosities Galore Keep Luring People to Waterfront Shop," *Seattle Post-Intelligencer,* October 7, 1999, pp. A1, A17.

21. "Funk 'n' Junk, Seattle, Ye Olde Curiosity Shop," *Sunset Magazine,* May 1959, 87.

BIBLIOGRAPHY

Alaska Club
1906 *The Alaska Club Almanac.* Seattle: Alaska Club.

Alaska Steamship Company
1906 *Trip to Wonderful Alaska.* Seattle: Alaska Steamship Company.
1917 *Alaska Steamship Company, Copper River & Northwestern Ry* [Railway]. Seattle: Alaska Steamship Company.

Alaska-Yukon-Pacific Exposition Publishing Co.
1909 *A.-Y.-P. Exposition Official Guide.* Seattle: Alaska-Yukon-Pacific Exposition Publishing Co.
1909 The Secretary's Report of the Alaska-Yukon-Pacific Exposition Held at Seattle, June 1st to October 16, 1909. Seattle.

Amundsen, Roald
1927 *My Life as an Explorer.* New York: Doubleday, Page & Company.

Anderson, N. K.
1995 "The Kiss of Enterprise": The Western Landscape as Symbol and Resource. In W. H. Truettner, ed., *The West as America.* Washington, D.C.: Smithsonian Institution Press.

Anderson, William T., ed.
1992 *Mermaids, Mummys, and Mastodons: The Emergence of the American Museum.* Washington, D.C.: American Museums Association.

Appadurai, Arjun
1986 *The Social Life of Things: Commodities in Cultural Perspective.* New York: Cambridge University Press.

Arctic Club
1958 *Arctic Club, 1908–1958: Fiftieth Anniversary.* Seattle: Arctic Club.

Averill, Lloyd J., and Daphne K. Morris
1995 *Northwest Coast Native and Native-Style Art: A Guidebook for Western Washington.* Seattle: University of Washington Press.

Bales, L. L.
1904 From the Northland—L. L. Bales Alaska Guide and Mail Carrier. *Pacific Sportsman* 1 (2): 32.
1905 A Tale of the Tundra. *Pacific Sportsman* 2 (3): 148–49.
1908 Totem Poles. *Outdoor Life* 11 (5): 423–41.
1938 The Indians Won't Tell. *Alaska Sportsman* 4, no. 10 (October): 16–18.

Baltimore and Ohio Railroad
1926 Official Itinerary, Tour of Her Majesty Marie, Queen of Rumania through the United States and Canada. B & O Railroad.

Barbeau, Marius
[1950–51] *Totem Poles.* 2 vols. Anthropological Series 30, National Museum of Canada Bulletin 119.

Barthes, Roland
1977 The Rhetoric of the Image. In Roland Barthes, *Image, Music, Text.* Trans. Stephen Heath. Pp. 32–51. New York: Hill and Wang.

Batkin, Jonathan
1998 Some Early Curio Dealers of New Mexico. *American Indian Art Magazine* 23 (3): 68–81.
1999 Tourism Is Overrated: Pueblo Pottery and the Early Curio Trade, 1880–1910. In Ruth B. Phillips and Christopher B. Steiner, eds., *Unpacking Culture: Art and Commodity in Colonial and Postcolonial Worlds.* Pp. 282–97. Berkeley: University of California Press.

Batkin, Jonathan, ed.
1999 *Clay People.* Santa Fe: Wheelwright Museum.

Batkin, Jonathan, and Patricia Fogelman Lange
1999 Human Figurines of Cochiti and Tesuque Pueblos, 1870–1920: Inspirations, Markets, and Consumers. In Jonathan Batkin, ed., *Clay People.* Pp. 41–63. Santa Fe: Wheelwright Museum.

Beauties of Washington State
1916 *Beauties of Washington State.* N.p.

Bellamy, Partridge
1929 *Amundsen the Splendid Norseman.* New York: Frederick A. Stokes, Co.

Benedict, Burton
1983 *The Anthropology of World's Fairs: San Francisco's Panama-Pacific International Exposition, 1915.* Berkeley, Calif.: Scolar Press.

Benson, Keith R.

1985 Exploration in a Pioneer Land: The Young Naturalists' Society and the Birth of the Museum Idea in the Washington Territory. *Landmarks: Magazine of Northwest History and Preservation* 4 (1): unpaginated.

1986 The Young Naturalists' Society: From Chess to Natural History Collections. *Pacific Northwest Quarterly* 77 (3): 82–93.

Berner, Richard C.

1991 *Seattle 1900–1920: From Boomtown, Urban Turbulence, to Restoration.* Seattle: Charles Press.

1992 *Seattle 1921–1940: From Boom to Bust.* Seattle: Charles Press.

Black, Martha

1997 *Bella Bella: A Season of Heiltsuk Art.* Seattle: University of Washington Press.

Blackman, Margaret

1989 *Sadie Brower Neakok: An Inupiaq Woman.* Seattle: University of Washington Press.

Boas, Franz

1897 *The Social Organization and the Secret Societies of the Kwakiutl Indians.* Annual Report of the U.S. National Museum for 1895. Pp. 311–738. Washington, D.C.: Government Printing Office.

Bockstoce, John

1977 *Steam Whaling in the Western Arctic.* New Bedford, Mass.: Old Dartmouth Historical Society.

1986 *Whales, Ice, and Men: The History of Whaling in the Western Arctic.* Seattle: University of Washington Press.

Bol, Marsha

1999 Defining Lakota Tourist Art. In Ruth B. Phillips and Christopher B. Steiner, eds., *Unpacking Culture: Art and Commodity in Colonial and Postcolonial Worlds.* Pp. 214–28. Berkeley: University of California Press.

Bronner, Simon

1989 *Consuming Visions: Accumulation and Display of Goods in America, 1880–1920.* New York: W. W. Norton.

Brown, Arthur J.

1945 The Promotion of Emigration to Washington, 1854–1909. *Pacific Northwest Quarterly* 36 (1): 3–17.

Calhoun, Anne H.

1942 *A Seattle Heritage: The Fine Arts Society.* Seattle: Lowman & Hanford Co.

Canadian Display

1909 *The Canadian Display Makes Distinct Impression,* excerpt from *The Pacific Northwest Commerce.* N.p.

Chicago Milwaukee & St. Paul Ry.

ca. 1910 *The Wonder Mountain.*Chicago Milwaukee & St. Paul. Ry.

Clifford, James

1988 *The Predicament of Culture: Twentieth-Century Ethnography, Literature, and Art.* Cambridge: Harvard University Press.

1997 *Routes: Travel and Translation in the Late Twentieth Century.* Cambridge: Harvard University Press.

Cohodas, Marvin

1997 *Basket Weavers for the California Curio Trade: Elizabeth and Louise Hickox.* Tucson: University of Arizona Press.

Cole, Douglas

1995 [1985] *Captured Heritage: The Scramble for Northwest Coast Artifacts.* Reprint with new preface. Norman: University of Oklahoma Press. First edition, Seattle: University of Washington Press.

Csikszentmihalyi, Mihalyi, and Eugene Rochberg-Halton

1981 *The Meaning of Things: Domestic Symbols and the Self.* Cambridge: Cambridge University Press.

Currelly, C. T.

1956 *I Brought the Ages Home.* Toronto: Royal Ontario Museum.

Damas, David, ed.

1984 *Arctic.* Vol. 5 of William C. Sturtevant, ed., *Handbook of North American Indians.* Washington, D.C.: Smithsonian Institution Press.

Dana, John Cotton

1917 *The New Museum.* Woodstock, Vt.: Elm Tree Press.

1920 *A Plan for a New Museum: The Kind of Museum It Will Profit a City to Maintain.* Woodstock, Vt.: Elm Tree Press.

1927 *Should Museums Be Useful? Possibilities in Museum Development.* Woodstock, Vt.: Elm Tree Press.

Dana, John Cotton, Mary W. Plummer, and Theresa Hitchler

1906 *The Far Northwest.* Newark, N. J.: N.p.

Dauenhauer, Nora Marks

1987 *Haa Shuká, Our Ancestors: Tlingit Oral Narratives.* Juneau, Alaska: Sealaska Heritage Foundation; Seattle: University of Washington Press.

1988, 1990 *Haa Tuwunáagu Yis: For Healing Our Spirit: Tlingit Oratory.* Juneau, Alaska: Sealaska Heritage Foundation; Seattle: University of Washington Press.

1995 Tlingit *At.oów*: Traditions and Concepts. In Steven C. Brown, ed., *The Spirit Within: Northwest Coast Native Art from the John H. Hauberg Collection.* Pp. 21–29. New York, N.Y.: Rizzoli; Seattle: University of Washington Press.

Densmore, Frances
1972 [1939] *Nootka and Quileute Music.* Bureau of American Ethnology Bulletin 124. Washington D.C.: Government Printing Office. Reprint, New York: DaCapo Press.
Dickens, Charles
1841 *The Old Curiosity Shop.* London.
Dickson, Lovat
1986 *The Museum Makers: The Story of the Royal Ontario Museum.* Toronto: Royal Ontario Museum.
Dominguez, Virginia R.
1986 Marketing Heritage. *American Ethnologist* 23 (3): 546–55.
Dorpat, Paul
1984 *Seattle Now & Then.* Vol. 1. Seattle: Tartu Publications.
1988 *Seattle Now & Then.* Vol. 2. Seattle: Tartu Publications.
1994 *Seattle Now & Then.* Vol. 3. Seattle: Tartu Publications.
Doss, Erika
1995 *Spirit Poles and Flying Pigs: Public Art and Cultural Democracy in American Communities.* Washington, D.C.: Smithsonian Institution Press.
Duff, Wilson
1975 *Images Stone B.C.: Thirty Centuries of Northwest Coast Stone Sculpture.* Seattle: University of Washington Press.
Duncan, Kate C.
1989 *Northern Athapaskan Art: A Beadwork Tradition.* Seattle: University of Washington Press.
Emmons, George T.
1903 The Basketry of the Tlingit. *American Museum of Natural History Memoirs* 3 (2): 229–77.
1991 Basketry. In Frederica de Laguna, ed., *The Tlingit Indians.* Pp. 213–22. Seattle: University of Washington Press.
Everett Daily Herald
1905 *Snohomish County Washington: The Richest of Puget Sound.* Everett: Everett Daily Herald.
Ewers, John C.
1986 *Plains Indian Sculpture: A Traditional Art from America's Heartland.* Washington, D.C.: Smithsonian Institution Press.
Frykman, George A.
1961 The Alaska-Yukon-Pacific Exposition, 1909. *Pacific Northwest Quarterly* 52 (1): 89–99.
Garfield, Viola
1980 [1940] *The Seattle Totem Pole.* Rev. and exp. ed. Seattle: University of Washington Press.
Gillingham, D. W.
1955 *Umiak!* London: Museum Press Limited.
Goetzmann, William H., and Kay Sloan
1983 *Looking Far North: The Harriman Expedition to Alaska, 1899.* Princeton, N.J.: Princeton University Press.
Gordon, Beverly
1986 The Souvenir: Messenger of the Extraordinary. *Journal of Popular Culture* 20 (3): 135–47.
1988 *American Indian Art: The Collecting Experience.* Madison, Wis.: Elvehjem Museum.
Graburn, Nelson
1976 *Ethnic and Tourist Arts: Cultural Expressions from the Fourth World.* Berkeley: University of California.
Graburn, Nelson H. H., Molly Lee, Jean-Loup Rousselot, with Robin K. Wright and Kate C. Duncan
1996 *Catalogue Raisonné of the Alaska Commercial Company Collection, Phoebe Apperson Hearst Museum of Anthropology.* Berkeley: University of California Press.
Gray, Henry
1967 *The Famous Ride of Queen Marie.* N.p.
Grieving, Louis H.
1993 *A Pictorial Story of the Grotto of the Redemption.* West Bend, Iowa: Grotto of the Redemption.
Grotto of the Redemption
n.d. *An Explanation of the Grotto of the Redemption.* Multiple reprints. West Bend, Iowa: Grotto of the Redemption.
Gunther, Erna
1966 *Art in the Life of the Northwest Coast Indians.* Portland, Oreg.: Portland Art Museum.
Haeberlin, H. H., James A. Teit, and Helen H. Roberts
1927 *Coiled Basketry in British Columbia and Surrounding Regions.* Bureau of American Ethnology Annual Report for 1919–1924. Pp. 119–484. Washington, D.C.: Government Printing Office.
Harner, Michael J.
1962 Jivaro Souls. *American Anthropologist* 64 (2): 258–72.
Harrison, E. S.
1909 Alaska at the Fair. *Alaska-Yukon Magazine* 8 (4): 237–59.
Himmelheber, Hans
1993 *Eskimo Artists: Fieldwork in Alaska, June 1936 until April 1937.* Fairbanks: University of Alaska Press. English ed. with introduction by Anne Fienup-Riordan.
Hinkley, Ted
1965 The Inside Passage: A Popular Gilded Age Tour. *Pacific Northwest Quarterly* 56 (April): 67–74.
Hinsley, Curtis
1992 Collecting Cultures and the Cultures of Collecting: The Lure of the American Southwest. *Museum Anthropology* 16 (1): 12–20.
Hobsbawm, Eric, and Terence Ranger, eds.
1983 *The Invention of Tradition.* Cambridge: Cambridge University Press.

Hoffman, Walter James
1897 *The Graphic Art of the Eskimos: Based upon the Collections in the National Museum.* Annual Report of the U.S. National Museum, 1895. Pp. 739–968. Washington, D.C.: Government Printing Office.

Holm, Bill
1987 The Northwest Coast Collections in the Burke Museum. In Holm, *Spirit and Ancestor: A Century of Northwest Coast Indian Art at the Burke Museum.* Pp. 11–22. Seattle: University of Washington Press.

Holt, Emmabelle and Richard
1994 Interview with the author. July 26, Seattle.

Howard, Kathleen, and Diana Pardue
1996 *Inventing the Southwest: The Fred Harvey Company and Native American Art.* Flagstaff, Ariz.: Northland Publishing Company.

Hunt, William R.
1986 *Stef: A Biography of Vilhjálmur Stefánsson, Canadian Arctic Explorer.* Vancouver: University of British Columbia Press.

Hutchinson, Duane
1989 *Grotto Father: Artist-Priest of the West Bend Grotto.* West Bend, Iowa: Grotto of the Redemption.

Jackson, Nancy
1984 Captain Dorr F. Tozier. Unpublished study of Accession 3768, Burke Museum of Natural History and Culture, Seattle, Washington.

James, George Wharton
1903 *Indian Basketry and How to Make Indian and Other Baskets.* New York: Henry Walkan.

James, Joe
1993 Interview with the author. August 3, Seattle.
1994 Interview with the author. June 27, Seattle.
1994 Interview with the author. July 12, Seattle.

Johanson, Dorothy O., and Charles M. Gates
1957 *Empire of the Columbia.* New York: Harper.

Jonaitis, Aldona
1999 Northwest Coast Totem Poles. In Ruth B. Phillips and Christopher B. Steiner, eds., *Unpacking Culture: Art and Commodity in Colonial and Postcolonial Worlds.* Pp. 104–21, 362. Berkeley: University of California Press.

Jules-Rosette, Bennetta
1984 *The Messages of Tourist Art: An African Semiotic System in Comparative Perspective.* New York: Plenum Press.

Kaplan, Susan A., and Kristin Barsness
1986 *Raven's Journey: The World of Alaska's Native People.* Philadelphia, Pa.: University Museum.

Karp, Ivan, and Steven D. Levine, eds.
1991 *Exhibiting Cultures: The Poetics and Politics of Museum Display.* Washington, D.C.: Smithsonian Institution Press.

Karsten, Rafael
1935 *The Head-Hunters of Western Amazonas: The Life and Culture of the Jivaro Indians of Eastern Ecuador and Peru.* Societas Scientiarum Fennica. Commentationes Humanarum Litterarum 7 (1) Helsingfors.

Keithan, Edward
1963 *Monuments in Cedar.* Seattle: Superior Publishing Company.

Kilian, Bernhard
1983 *The Voyage of the Schooner Polar Bear: Whaling and Trading in the North Pacific and Arctic, 1913–1914.* John Bockstoce, ed. New Bedford, Mass.: New Bedford Whaling Museum.

King County, Washington
1909 *King County, State of Washington 1909.* Published for free distribution at the Alaska-Yukon-Pacific Exposition. Seattle.

Krech, Shepard III, and Barbara A. Hail, eds.
1999 *Collecting Native America: 1870–1960.* Washington, D.C.: Smithsonian Institution Press.

Krug, John W., and Caryl Sale Krug
1998 *One Dog Short: The Odyssey and Collection of a Family in Alaska during the Gold Rush Years.* Juneau: Alaska Department of Education.

Lavitt, Wendy
1992 Strong Spirits of the Doll World. *Dolls: The Collector's Magazine.* December–January, 149–51.

Lee, Molly
1991 Appropriating the Primitive: Turn of the Century Collection and Display of Alaskan Native Art. *Arctic Anthropology* 28 (1): 6–15.
1998 *Baleen Basketry of the North Alaskan Eskimo.* Seattle: University of Washington Press.
1998 Tourism and Taste Cultures: Collecting Native Art in Alaska at the Turn of the Twentieth Century. In Ruth B. Phillips and Christopher B. Steiner, eds., *Unpacking Culture: Art and Commodity in Colonial and Postcolonial Worlds.* Pp. 267–81, 366. Berkeley: University of California Press.

Lipton, Barbara, ed.
1979 John Cotton Dana and the Newark Museum. *Newark Museum Quarterly* 30 (3): 3–58.

Llwyd, J. P. D.

1909 *The Message of an Indian Relic.* Seattle: Lowman and Hanford Co.

London County Council

1912 *Guide for the Use of Visitors to the Horniman Museum.* 2d ed. London: London County Council.

Lowman & Hanford Stationery & Printing Co.

n.d. *Dictionary of the Chinook Jargon as Spoken on Puget Sound and the Northwest.* Seattle: Lowman & Hanford Stationery & Printing Co.

MacCannell, Dean

1976 *The Tourist: A New Theory of the Leisure Class.* New York: Schocken Books.

1984 Reconstructed Identity: Tourism and Cultural Identity in Third World Communities. *Annals of Tourism Research* 11: 375–91.

McCracken, Grant

1988 *Culture and Consumption: New Approaches to the Symbolic Character of Consumer Goods and Activities.* Bloomington: University of Indiana.

McCurdy, James G.

1961 *Indian Days at Neah Bay.* Seattle: Superior Publishing Company.

MacDowell, Lloyd W.

1895 *The Totem Poles of Alaska and Indian Mythology.* Cover title *Alaska Totem Poles.* Seattle: Alaska Steamship Company.

McKillop, Carmen

1997 Interview with the author. August. Winslow, Wash.

Makah Cultural and Research Center

1998 *Riding in His Canoe: The Continuing Legacy of Young Doctor.* Brochure. Neah Bay, Wash.: Makah Cultural and Research Center.

Marr, Carolyn, J. Lloyd Colfax, and Robert D. Monroe

1987 *Portrait in Time: Photographs of the Makah by Samuel G. Morse, 1896–1903.* Neah Bay, Wash.: Makah Cultural Research Center in cooperation with the Washington State Historical Society.

Mason, J. Alden

1927 Eskimo Pictorial Art. *Museum Journal* 18 (3): 248–83.

1958 George G. Heye, 1874–1956. *Leaflet No. 6.* Museum of the American Indian, Heye Foundation.

Mohonk Lodge

1929 *Genuine Indian Bead Work and Art Goods.* Catalog. Clinton, Okla.: Mohonk Lodge.

Moorehead, Warren K.

1917 *Stone Ornaments Used by Indians in the United States and Canada; Being a Description of Certain Charm Stones, Gorgets, Tubes, Bird Stones and Problematical Forms.* Andover, Mass.: Andover Press.

Morgan, Lael

1988 *Art and Eskimo Power: The Life and Times of Alaskan Howard Rock.* Fairbanks, Alaska: Epicenter Press.

Morgan, Murray

1962 *Skid Road: An Informal Portrait of Seattle.* Rev. ed. New York: Viking Press.

Muensterberger, Werner

1995 *Collecting, An Unruly Passion: Psychological Perspectives.* San Diego, Calif.: Harcourt Brace.

Murdoch, John

1988 [1892] *Ethnological Results of the Point Barrow Expedition.* Ninth Annual Report of the Bureau of American Ethnology. Pp. 19–441. Reprint, Washington, D.C.: Smithsonian Institution.

Museum of the American Indian, Heye Foundation

1964 *The History of the Museum. Indian Notes and Monographs.* Miscellaneous Series, No. 55. New York: Museum of the American Indian, Heye Foundation.

Naduea, I. A.

1909 The Alaska-Yukon-Pacific Exposition. *The Coast* 18 (3): 174–77.

Nelson, Edward William

1984 [1899] *The Eskimo About Bering Strait.* Eighteenth Annual Report of the Bureau of American Ethnology, 1896–1897. Pp. 3–518. Washington, D.C.: Government Printing Office; reprint, Washington, D.C.: Smithsonian Institution Press.

Nelson, Gerald B.

1977 *Seattle: The Life and Times of an American City.* New York: Alfred A. Knopf.

Newark Museum

1979 The Dana Influence: The Newark Museum Collections. *Newark Museum Quarterly* 30 (4): 1–52.

Newell, Gordon, and Don Sherwood

1956 *Totem Tales of Old Seattle.* Seattle: Superior Publishing Company.

Noble, Dennis, comp.

1990 *Historical Register U.S. Revenue Cutter Service Officers, 1790–1914.* Washington, D.C.: U.S. Coast Guard Historian's Office.

Norris, Frank

1985 *Gawking at the Midnight Sun: The Tourist in Early Alaska.* Anchorage: Alaska Historical Commission.

1987 Showing off Alaska: The Northern Tourist Trade, 1878–1941. *Alaska History* 2 (2): 1–17.

Oregon-Washington Railway and Navigation Company
n.d. *The Land That Lures: Summer in the Pacific Northwest.* Oregon-Washington Railway and Navigation Company.

Palmer, B. J.
1926 *'Round the World with B. J.* Davenport, Iowa: Palmer College of Chiropractic.
1993 [1949] *The Bigness of the Fellow Within.* Davenport, Iowa: Palmer College of Chiropractic.

Palmer, David D.
1977 *The Palmers: Memoirs of David D. Palmer.* Davenport, Iowa: Palmer College of Chiropractic.

Palmer, Mabel
1942 *Stepping Stones.* Davenport, Iowa: Palmer College of Chiropractic.

Palmer College of Chiropractic
n.d. *A Little Bit O' Heaven Tour Guide.* 55th ed. Davenport, Iowa: Palmer College of Chiropractic.
n.d. *A Guide Book: A Little Bit O' Heaven and the Wishing Buddha.* Davenport, Iowa: Palmer College of Chiropractic.

Paul, Frances
1944 *Spruce Root Basketry of the Alaska Tlingit.* Lawrence, Kans.: Haskell Institute.

Peck, Herbert
1968 *The Book of Rookwood Pottery.* New York: Crown.

Pedersen, C. T.
n.d. My Arctic Adventures. Typescript. Archives and Manuscripts Department, Library, University of Alaska, Anchorage.

People's Outfitting Company
1935 World's Largest Exhibit of Smallest Curios. February.

Pettitt, George A.
1950 *The Quileute of La Push, 1775–1945.* University of California Anthropological Records 14 (1). Berkeley: University of California Press; reprint, Millwood, N.Y.: Kraus Reprints, 1976.

Phillips, Ruth
1998 *Trading Identities: The Souvenir in Native North American Art from the Northeast, 1700–1900.* Seattle: University of Washington Press.

Phillips, Ruth B., and Christopher B. Steiner, eds.
1999 *Unpacking Culture: Art and Commodity in Colonial and Postcolonial Worlds.* Berkeley: University of California Press.

Powell, Jay, and Vickie Jensen
1976 *Quileute of La Push.* Seattle: University of Washington Press.

Quiggin, A. Hingston
1942 *Haddon, the Head Hunter: A Short Sketch of the Life of A. C. Haddon.* Cambridge: Cambridge University Press.

R. L. Polk and Company
1889–1928 *Seattle City Directories.* Seattle: R. L. Polk and Company.

Rainier National Park
ca. 1920 *Rainier National Park: Summer Fun amid Snow and Flowers.* N.p.

Ravenna Park, Seattle
1908–9 *Ravenna Park, Seattle.* Twenty-page booklet of photographs. Seattle.

Ray, Dorothy Jean
1969 *Graphic Arts of the Alaskan Eskimo.* Native American Arts 2. U.S. Department of the Interior. Washington, D.C.: Indian Arts and Crafts Board.
1974 The Billiken . . . The Story of This Strange Creation That Has Become Identified with Alaska. *Alaska Journal* 4 (1): 25–31.
1977 *Eskimo Art: Tradition and Innovation in North Alaska.* Seattle: University of Washington Press.
1980 [1961] *Artists of the Tundra and the Sea.* Rev. ed. Seattle: University of Washington Press.
1981 *Aleut and Eskimo Art: Tradition and Innovation in South Alaska.* Seattle: University of Washington Press.
1996 *A Legacy of Arctic Art.* Seattle: University of Washington Press.
1996 [1975] *The Eskimos of Bering Strait, 1650–1898.* Seattle: University of Washington Press.

Rocky Boy Mission
n.d. *Genuine Indian Beadwork and Curios.* Catalog. Rocky Boy, Mont.: Rocky Boy Mission.

Russell, Frank
1980 *The Pima Indian.* Tucson: University of Arizona Press.

Russell, Georgina, et al.
1986 The Wellcome Non-Medical Material. *Museums Journal* 86, Supplement.

Russell, Janet N., and Jack W. Berryman
1979 Parks, Boulevards, and Outdoor Recreation: The Promotion of Seattle as an Ideal Residential City and Summer Resort, 1890–1910. *Journal of the West* (January): 5–17.

Rydell, Robert
1984 *All the World's a Fair: Visions of Empire at American International Expositions, 1876–1916.* Chicago: University of Chicago Press.

1989 The Culture of Imperial Abundance: World's Fairs in the Making of American Culture. In Simon J. Bronner, ed., *Consuming Visions: Accumulation and Display of Goods in America, 1880–1920.* Pp. 191–216. New York: W. W. Norton.

Rydell, Robert, and Nancy Gwinn

1994 *Fair Representation: World's Fairs and the Modern World.* Amsterdam: VU Press.

Sale, Roger

1994 [1976] *Seattle: Past to Present.* Seattle: University of Washington Press.

Santa Fe Railway

1909 *Summer Excursions: California and the North Pacific Coast—Alaska Yukon Pacific Exposition.* Brochure. Santa Fe Railway.

Saville, Marshall

1929 Bibliographic Notes on the Shrinking of Human Heads in South America. *Museum Notes* 6 (1): 56–74.

Seattle Publishing Company

1909 *The Exposition Beautiful.* Seattle: Seattle Publishing Company.

1909 *Seattle and the Pacific Northwest.* Seattle: Seattle Publishing Company.

Sheader, Wes, and Dorothy Sheader

1995 *The Palmer Mansion: A Pictorial Tour.* Davenport, Iowa: Palmer College of Chiropractic.

Sherwood, Donald N.

n.d. Interpretive Essays of the History of Seattle's Parks and Playgrounds. Unpublished typescript. Museum of History and Industry, Seattle.

Smith, James G.

1980 *Arctic Art: Eskimo Ivory.* New York: Museum of the American Indian.

Smithsonian Institution

1909 *The Exhibits of the Smithsonian Institution and U.S. National Museum at the Alaska-Yukon-Pacific Exposition, Seattle, Washington, 1909.* Washington, D.C.: Smithsonian Institution Press, of Judd & Detweiler, Inc.

Speidel, William C.

1967 *Sons of the Profits, or There's No Business Like Grow Business! The Seattle Story, 1851–1901.* Seattle: Nettle Creek Publishing Company.

Spencer, Robert F.

1959 *The North Alaskan Eskimo: A Study in Ecology and Society.* Bureau of American Ethnology Bulletin 171. Washington, D.C.: Smithsonian Institution Press.

Standley, J. E.

1905 [J. E. S.] From the Northland. *Pacific Sportsman* 1 (2): 78–79.

1905 ["Curio Joe"] Among the Quilayutes. *Pacific Sportsman* 2 (3): 149–50.

1905 ["Curio Joe"] An Eskimo's Saratoga Trunk. *Pacific Sportsman* 2 (11): 453.

1906 ["A Word from Curio Joe"], *Pacific Sportsman* 3 (2): 58.

1906 ["Curio Joe"] Relics of Alaska's Primative [*sic*] Natives. *Pacific Sportsman* 3 (5): 160.

1906 ["Curio Joe"] Habits of a Dam Builder. *Pacific Sportsman* 3 (6): 202.

1906 ["Curio Joe"] A Budget of Observations. *Pacific Sportsman* 3 (11): 384.

1907 An Alaska Fishing Rig. *Pacific Sportsman* 4 (9): 305.

Stefánsson, Vilhjálmur

1912 *My Life with the Eskimo.* New York: Harper and Brothers.

1964 *Discovery: The Autobiography of Vilhjálmur Stefánsson.* New York: McGraw-Hill.

Steiner, Christopher

1999 Authenticity, Repetition, and the Aesthetics of Seriality: The Work of Tourist Art in the Age of Mechanical Reproduction. In Ruth B. Phillips and Christopher B. Steiner, eds., *Unpacking Culture: Art and Commodity in Colonial and Postcolonial Worlds.* Pp. 87–103. Berkeley: University of California Press.

Stewart, Susan

1984 *On Longing: Narratives of the Miniature, the Gigantic, the Souvenir, the Collection.* Baltimore, Md.: Johns Hopkins University Press.

Stirling, Matthew W.

1938 Historical and Ethnographic Material on the Jivaro Indians. *Bureau of American Ethnology Bulletin* 117: 76–78.

Stone, Lisa, and Jim Zanzi

1993 *Sacred Spaces and Other Places: A Guide to Grottos and Sculptural Environments in the Upper Midwest.* Chicago: School of the Art Institute of Chicago Press.

Suttles, Wayne, ed.

1990 *Northwest Coast.* Vol. 7 of William Sturtevant, ed., *Handbook of North American Indians.* Washington, D.C.: Smithsonian Institution Press.

1974 *The Economic Life of the Coast Salish of Haro and Rosario Straits.* New York: Garland Publishing.

Swan, James G.

1870 *The Indians of Cape Flattery, at the Entrance to the Strait of Juan de Fuca, Washington Territory.* Smithsonian Contributions to Knowledge 16. Washington, D.C.: Smithsonian Institution Press.

Swanton, John R.

1905 Explanation of the Seattle Totem Pole. *Journal of American Folk-Lore* 11: 108–10, and frontispiece.

Swenson, Olaf

1844 *Northwest of the World: Forty Years Trading and Hunting in Northern Siberia.* New York: Dodd, Mead & Co.

Turner, G. E. S.

1944 Counterfeit 'Tsantsas' in the Pitt Rivers Museum. *Man* 44: 53–70.

U.S. Government Board of Managers

1911 *Participation in the Alaska-Yukon-Pacific Exposition, Message from the President of the United States, Transmitting the Report of the United States Government Board of Managers of the Government Participation in the Alaska-Yukon-Pacific Exposition.* Washington, D.C.: Government Printing Office.

VanStone, James

1963 *A Carved Mammoth Tusk from Alaska.* 1962 Annual Report, Art and Archaeology Division, Royal Ontario Museum. Toronto: University of Toronto Press.

Vulcan Iron Works

1909 *General History, Alaska-Yukon-Pacific Exposition.* N.p.

Wade, Edwin L.

1985 The Ethnic Art Market in the American Southwest, 1880–1980. In George Stocking Jr., ed., *Objects and Others: Essays on Museums and Material Culture.* Madison: University of Wisconsin.

Wallace, Kevin

1960 Slim-Shin's Monument. *New Yorker Magazine,* November 16, 104–46.

Warren, James R.

1981 *King County and Its Queen City: Seattle.* Woodland Hills, Calif.: Windsor Publications, Inc.

Washington State Art Association

1910 *The Museum of Arts and Sciences of the Washington State Art Association, Seattle.* Seattle: Washington State Art Association.

Waterfront Awareness Publishers

1982 *Historic Colman Dock Exhibit.* Seattle: Waterfront Awareness Publishers.

Weigle, Marta, and Barbara Babcock

1996 *The Great Southwest of the Fred Harvey Company and the Santa Fe Railway.* Tucson: University of Arizona Press.

Weschler, Lawrence

1995 *Mr. Wilson's Cabinet of Wonder: Pronged Ants, Horned Humans, Mice on Toast and Other Marvels of Jurassic Technology.* New York: Vintage Books.

Westerner Magazine

1909 An Exhibit of Alaskan Curios. *Westerner Magazine* 11 (3): 11.

White, Richard

1998 *Remembering Ahanagran: History and Storytelling in a Family's Past.* New York: Hill and Wang.

Wickersham, James

1927 *A Bibliography of Alaskan Literature.* Fairbanks: Alaska Agricultural College and School of Mines, Miscellaneous Publications, Vol. 1, No. 1.

Wilcox, Vincent

1978 The Museum of the American Indian, Heye Foundation. *American Indian Art Magazine* 3 (2): 40–49, 78–81.

Wright, Robin K., ed.

1991 *A Time of Gathering: Native Heritage in Washington State.* Seattle: University of Washington Press.

Wyatt, Victoria

1984 *Shapes of Their Thoughts.* Norman: University of Oklahoma Press.

1988 *Images from the Inside Passage: An Alaskan Portrait by Winter & Pond.* Seattle: University of Washington Press.

Ziontz, Lenore

1985 The State Museum Comes of Age. In a special section celebrating The First Hundred Years: A Century of Natural History at the Burke Museum. *Landmarks: Magazine of Northwest History and Preservation* 4 (1): unpaginated.

Newspapers and Magazines

Admiral District Tribune, West Seattle

Alaska-Yukon Magazine

The Alaskan, Sitka

The Coast

The Daily Miner, Ketchikan

Fairbanks Daily News Miner

Hobbies

Holiday

National Geographic

Outdoor Life

Pacific Northwest Quarterly

Pacific Sportsman

Philatelic West

Seattle Daily Times (Seattle Times)
Seattle Magazine
Seattle Post-Intelligencer
Seattle Star
Sunset Magazine
Wenatchee Daily World
Westerner Magazine

Unpublished Sources

Delia Whittelsey. Scrapbook of newspaper clippings about totem poles, primarily from *Seattle Post-Intelligencer* but also from the *Seattle Times.* October 1938–March 1941. Paul Dorpat Collection, Seattle.

Records, Ye Old Curiosity Shop, Seattle

Auction catalogs: 1976, 1977, 1980
Catalogs, catalog supplements, brochures (see appendix for titles)
Guest Book 1899–1940
Newspaper clippings
Objects still in shop and in James family private collections
Other record books: "Address of Friends, Jan-1-1928," "Where, What"
Photographs 1900 to present
Postcards, other memorabilia, 1899–1940
Scraps of paper with miscellaneous notes written by J. E. Standley
Supplier books: "Address of Where to Buy," "See Where to Buy in Safe"

Archival Material and Museum Records

Alaska State Archives, Juneau
Alaska State Library, Juneau
American Museum of Natural History, New York
British Museum, London
Burke Museum of Natural History and Culture, University of Washington, Seattle
Davenport Public Museum, Iowa
Horniman Museum, London, England
Huntington Library, San Marino, Calif.
Maxwell Museum, University of New Mexico, Albuquerque
Museum of History and Industry, Seattle
National Museum of the American Indian, Smithsonian Institution, Washington, D.C.
National Museum of Natural History, Smithsonian Institution, Washington, D.C.
Newark Museum, New Jersey
Palmer Chiropractic College, Davenport, Iowa
Phoebe Apperson Hearst Museum, Berkeley, Calif.
Portland Art Museum, Oregon
Public Museum of Grand Rapids, Mich.
Ripley Entertainment, Inc., Orlando, Fla.
Royal Ontario Museum, Toronto
Seattle Public Library
Smithsonian Institution, Washington, D.C.
University of Alaska, Anchorage
University of Alaska, Fairbanks
University of Washington Libraries, Manuscripts, Special Collections and University Archives Division
Washington Historical Society, Tacoma
Washington State Archives, Olympia

INDEX

Page numbers in boldface type indicate illustrations or sidebars.

YOCS is an abbreviation for Ye Olde Curiosity Shop.